Sachi's MONSTROUS Appetite

5

Chomoran

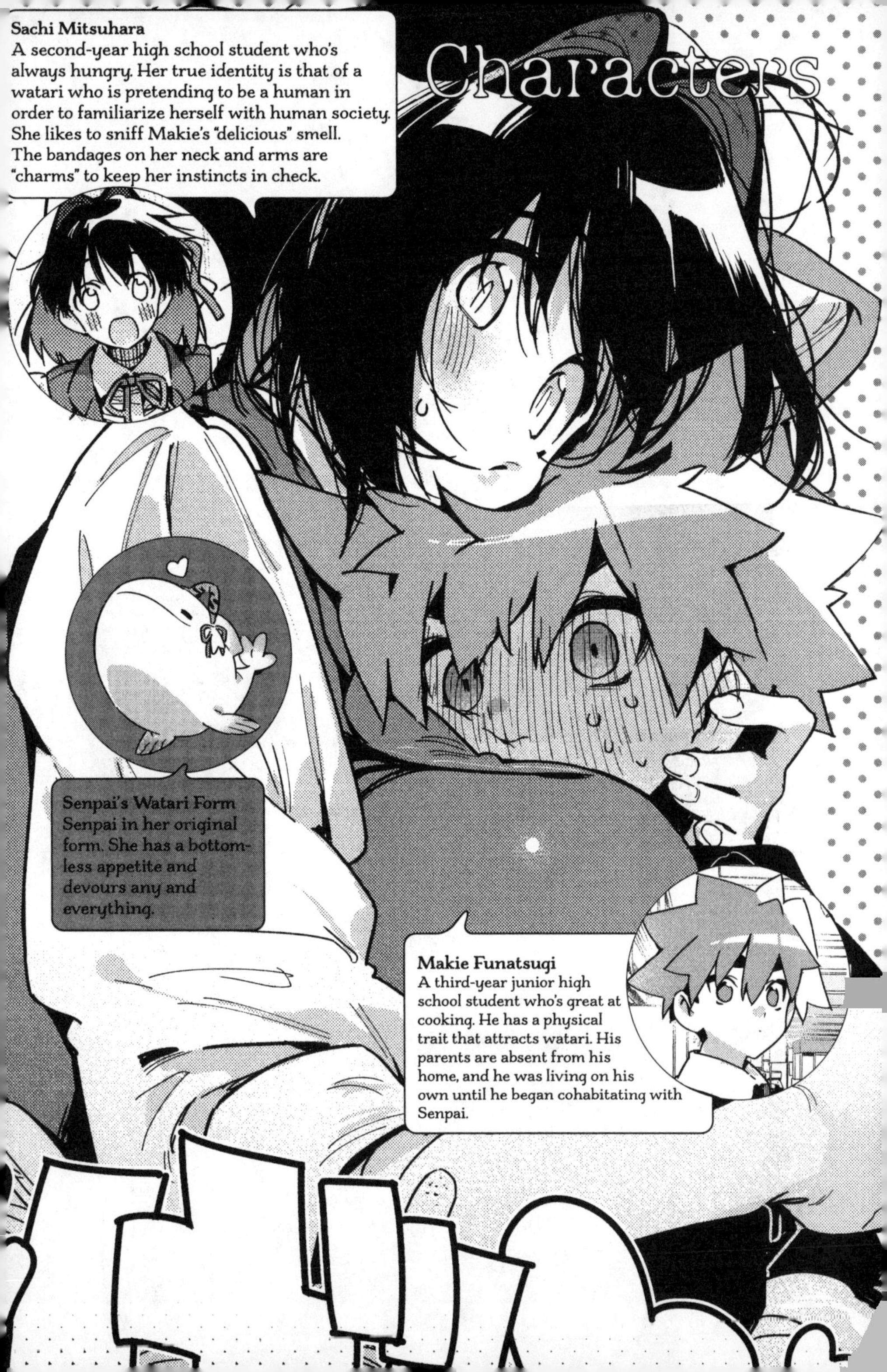
Characters
Sachi Mitsuhara
A second-year high school student who's always hungry. Her true identity is that of a watari who is pretending to be a human in order to familiarize herself with human society. She likes to sniff Makie's "delicious" smell. The bandages on her neck and arms are "charms" to keep her instincts in check.
Senpai's Watari Form
Senpai in her original form. She has a bottomless appetite and devours any and everything.
Makie Funatsugi
A third-year junior high school student who's great at cooking. He has a physical trait that attracts watari. His parents are absent from his home, and he was living on his own until he began cohabitating with Senpai.

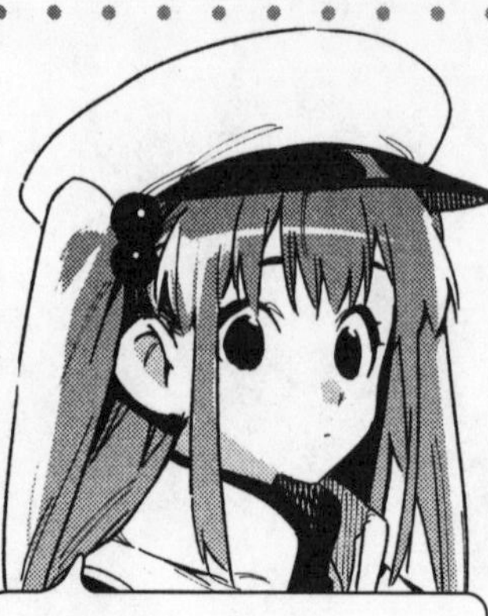

Izumi Izumi
A watari that mimics humans as well as other creatures and blends in by planting false memories in those around it. It has decided to continue living in the form of a girl who lives next door to the Funatsugi household.

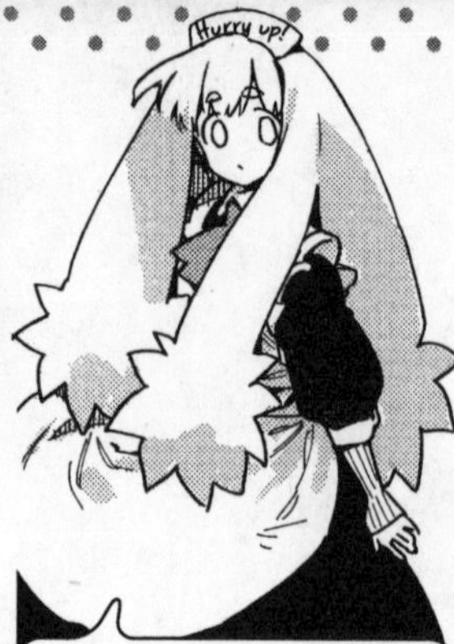
Hurry up!

Miss Maid
The Manager's maid. Keep an eye on her headband.

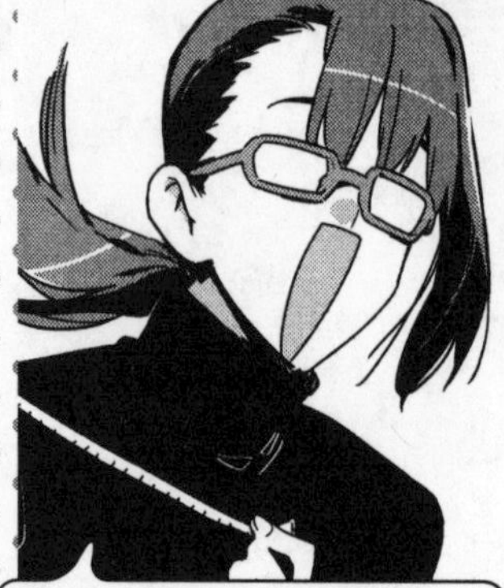

Miss Manager
She manages the watari for the town that Makie lives in. She has tasked Senpai with the job of protecting the town from dangerous watari.

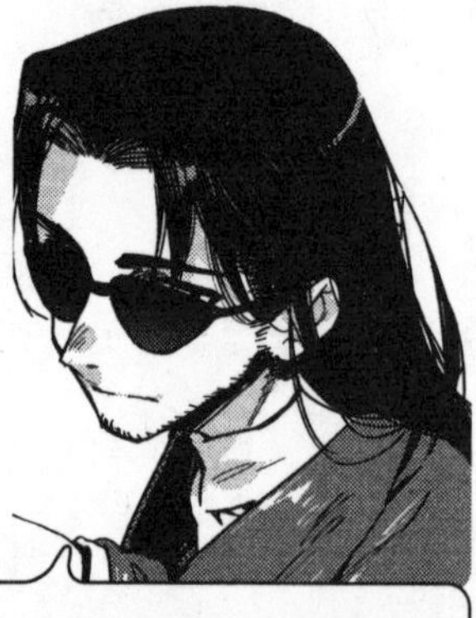

Tatemochi
A man of few words who is actually a watari. He works (part-time) under Musashino.

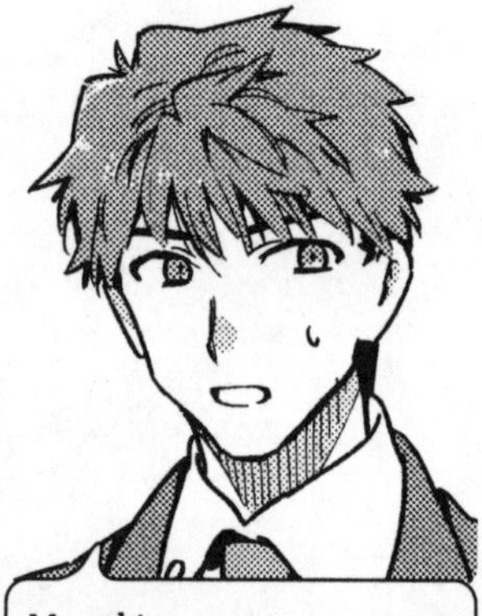

Musashino
Handles watari-related problems within the metropolitan area. He gave Makie a warning about his unique physical trait.

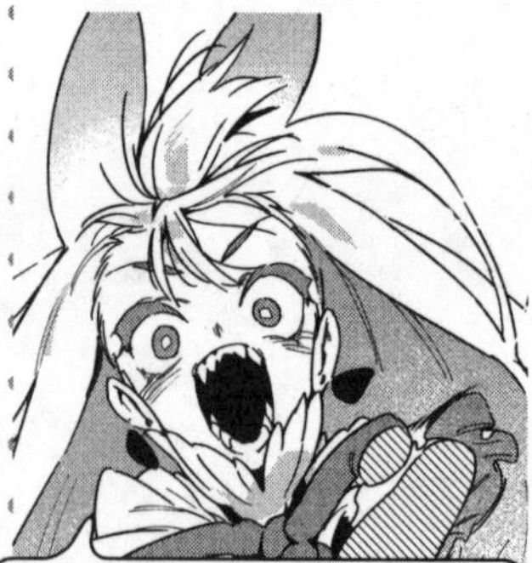

Hakuja
A watari who resides in Izumo. She suddenly attacked Makie and the others after they arrived in Izumo. She seems like a formidable opponent.

Story

Makie and Mitsuhara-senpai managed to drive off the giant "kanetsuki" watari that threatened their town, but the battle has severely depleted Senpai's energy, leaving her unable to maintain her human form. Her instability now causes her to shrink and grow at random. To help her get out of this predicament, Makie followed Miss Manager's recommendation to go to Izumo, Senpai's hometown. Upon arriving, they are joined by Tatemochi and Izumi. They begin their journey to get to the bottom of Senpai's roots, but before they can get too far, they're suddenly attacked by a mysterious watari who goes by the name "Hakuja"!

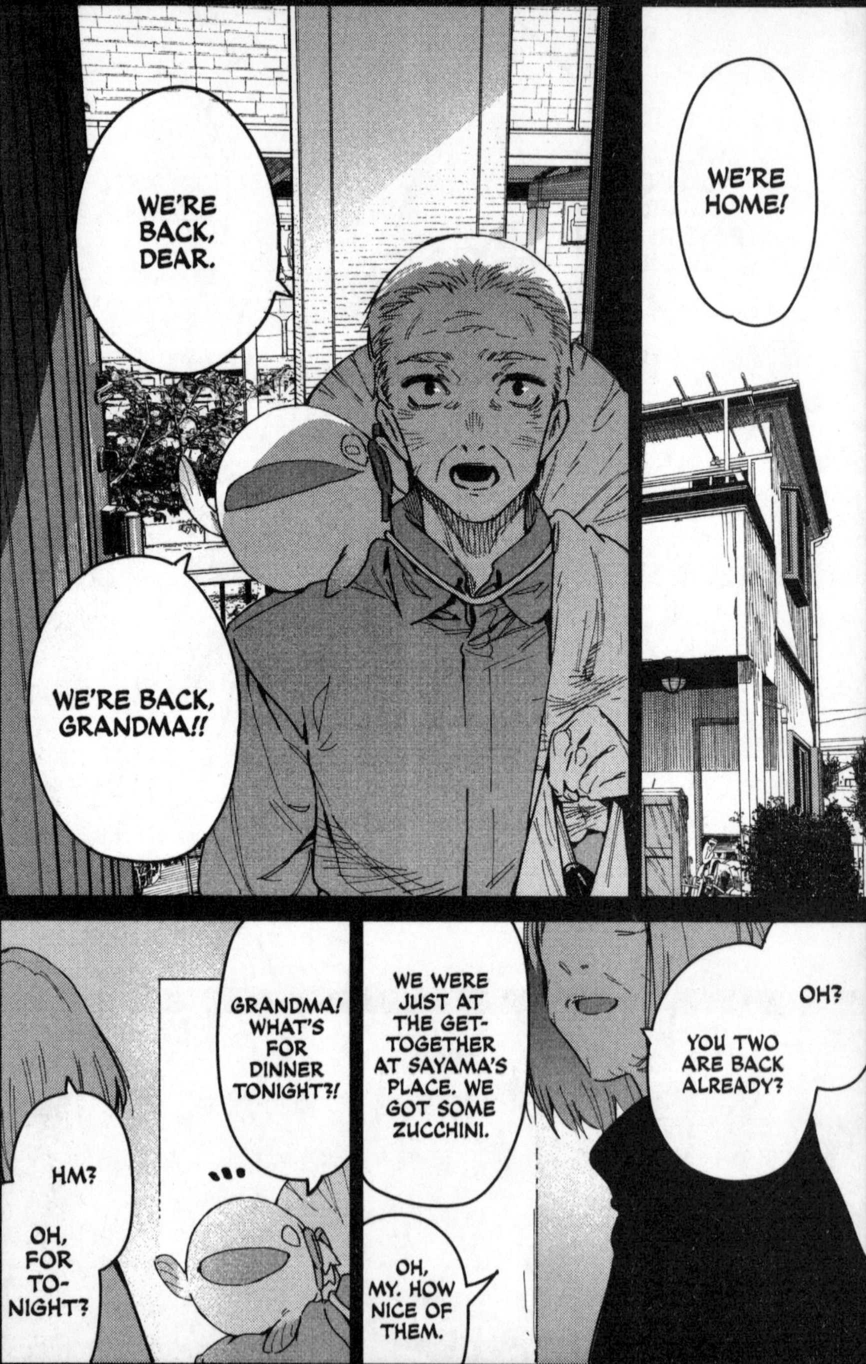
WE'RE HOME!
WE'RE BACK, DEAR.
WE'RE BACK, GRANDMA!!
OH?
YOU TWO ARE BACK ALREADY?
WE WERE JUST AT THE GET-TOGETHER AT SAYAMA'S PLACE. WE GOT SOME ZUCCHINI.
OH, MY. HOW NICE OF THEM.
GRANDMA! WHAT'S FOR DINNER TONIGHT?!
...
HM?
OH, FOR TO-NIGHT?

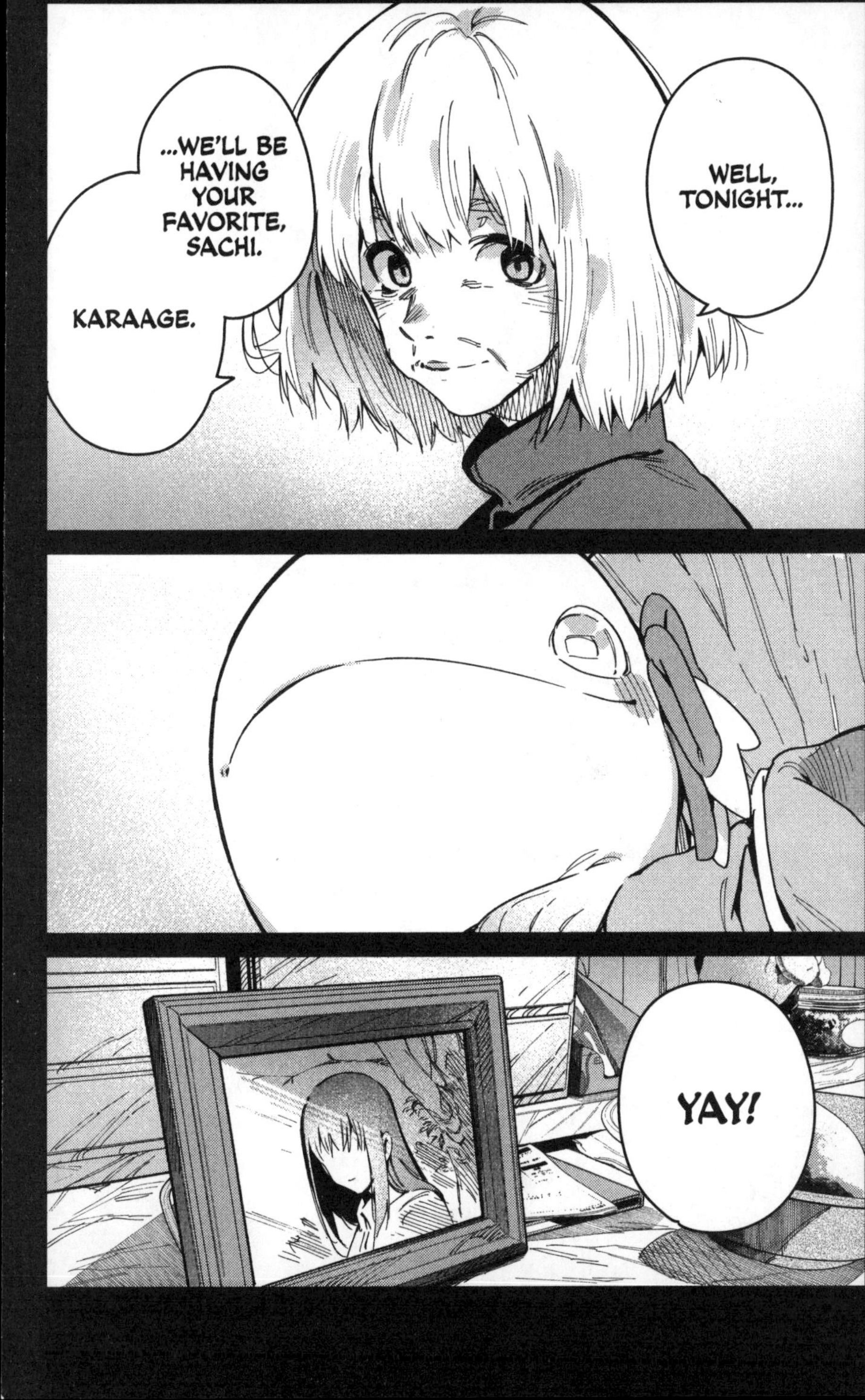
WELL, TONIGHT...
...WE'LL BE HAVING YOUR FAVORITE, SACHI.
KARAAGE.
YAY!

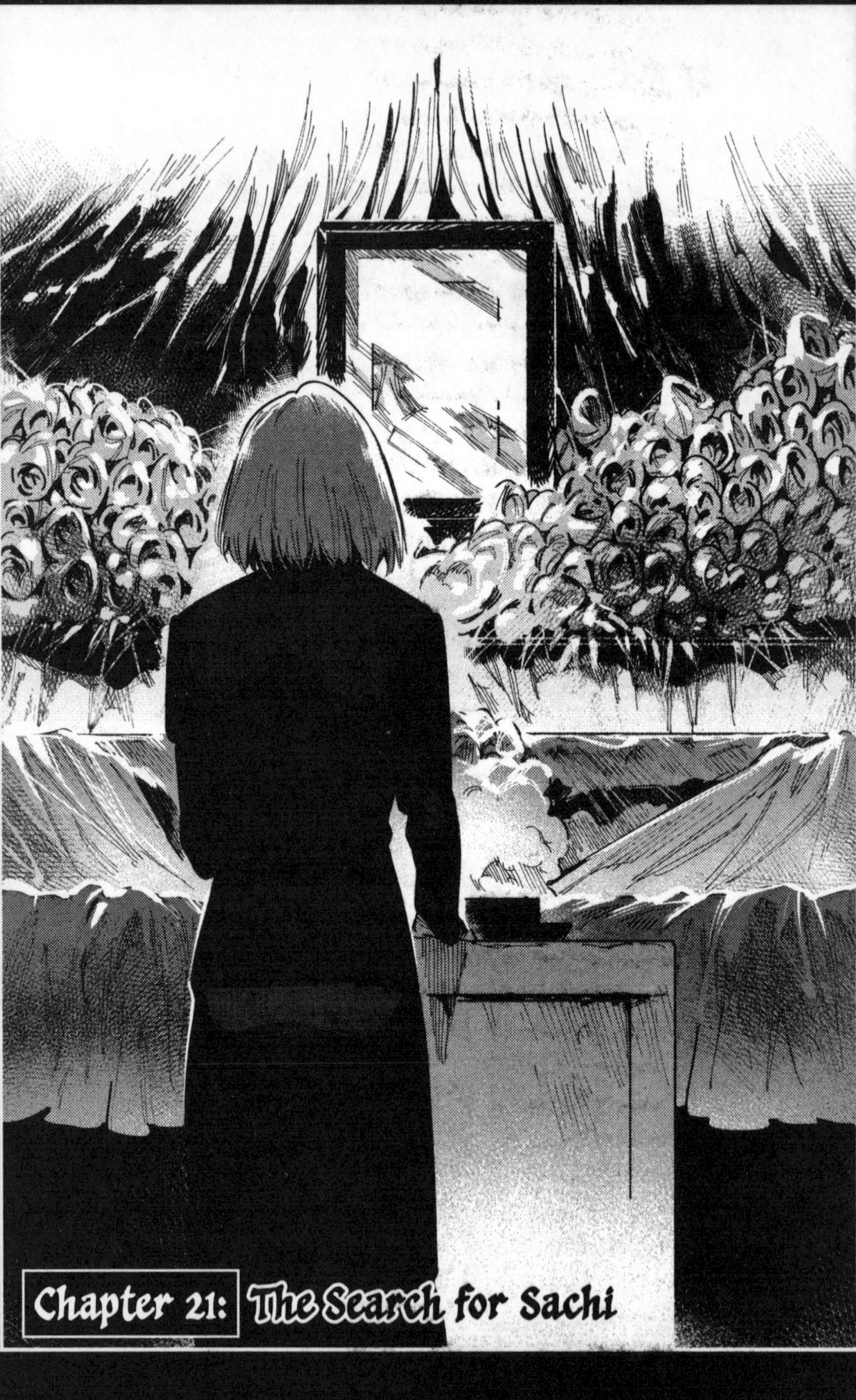
Chapter 21: The Search for Sachi

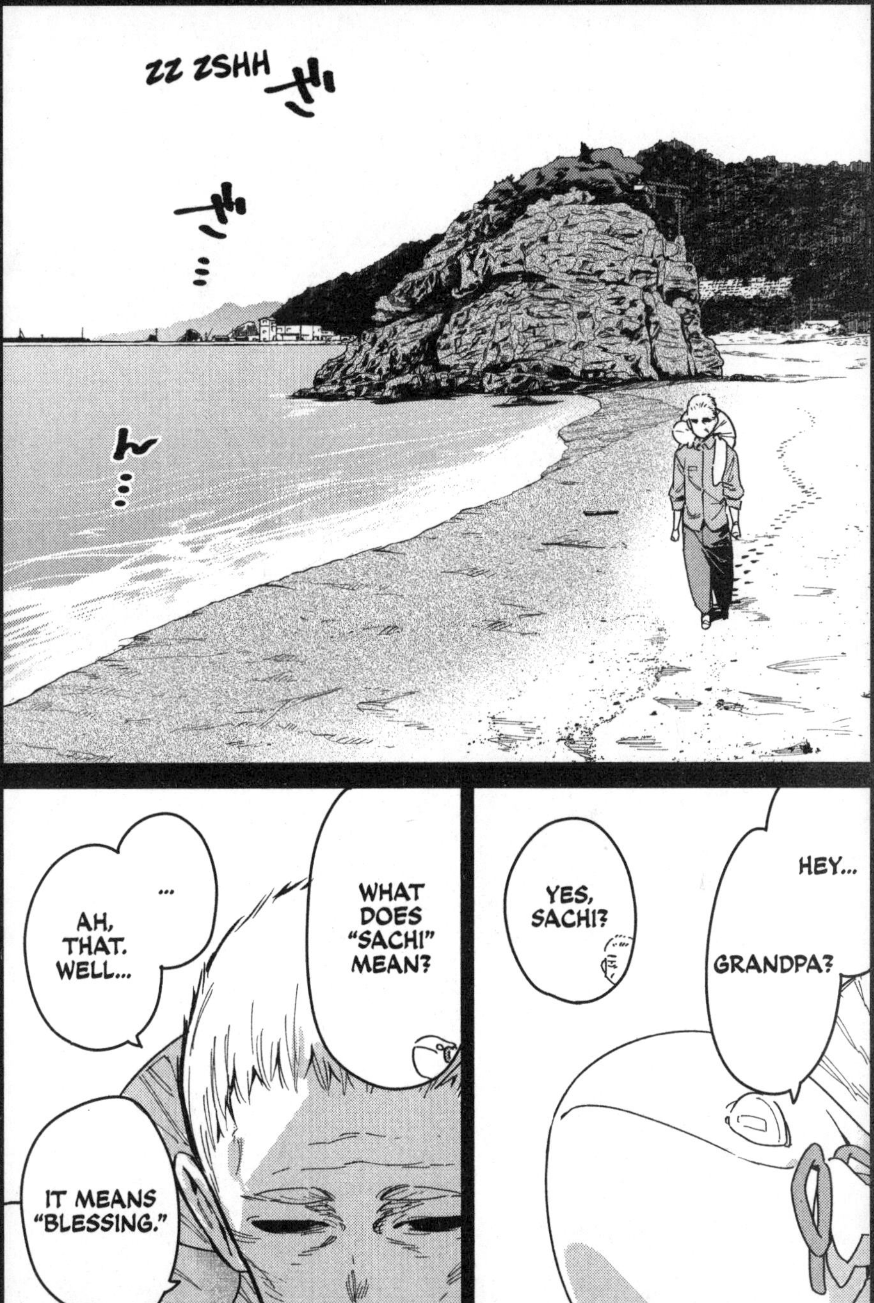
HEY...
GRANDPA?
YES, SACHI?
WHAT DOES "SACHI" MEAN?
... AH, THAT. WELL...
IT MEANS "BLESSING."

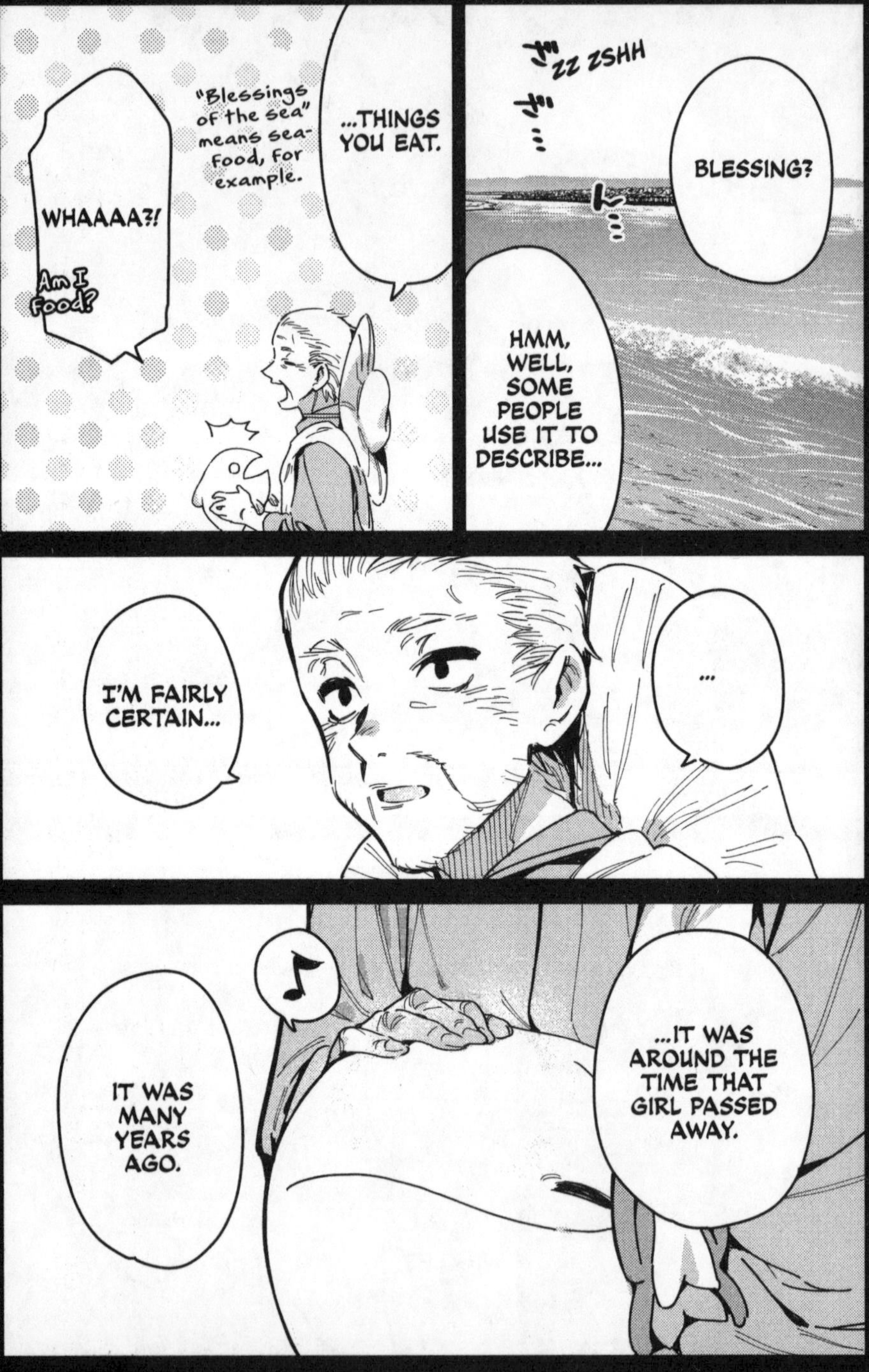
ZZ ZSHH
BLESSING?
HMM, WELL, SOME PEOPLE USE IT TO DESCRIBE...
...THINGS YOU EAT.
"Blessings of the sea" means seafood, for example.
WHAAAA?!
Am I Food?
...
I'M FAIRLY CERTAIN...
...IT WAS AROUND THE TIME THAT GIRL PASSED AWAY.
IT WAS MANY YEARS AGO.

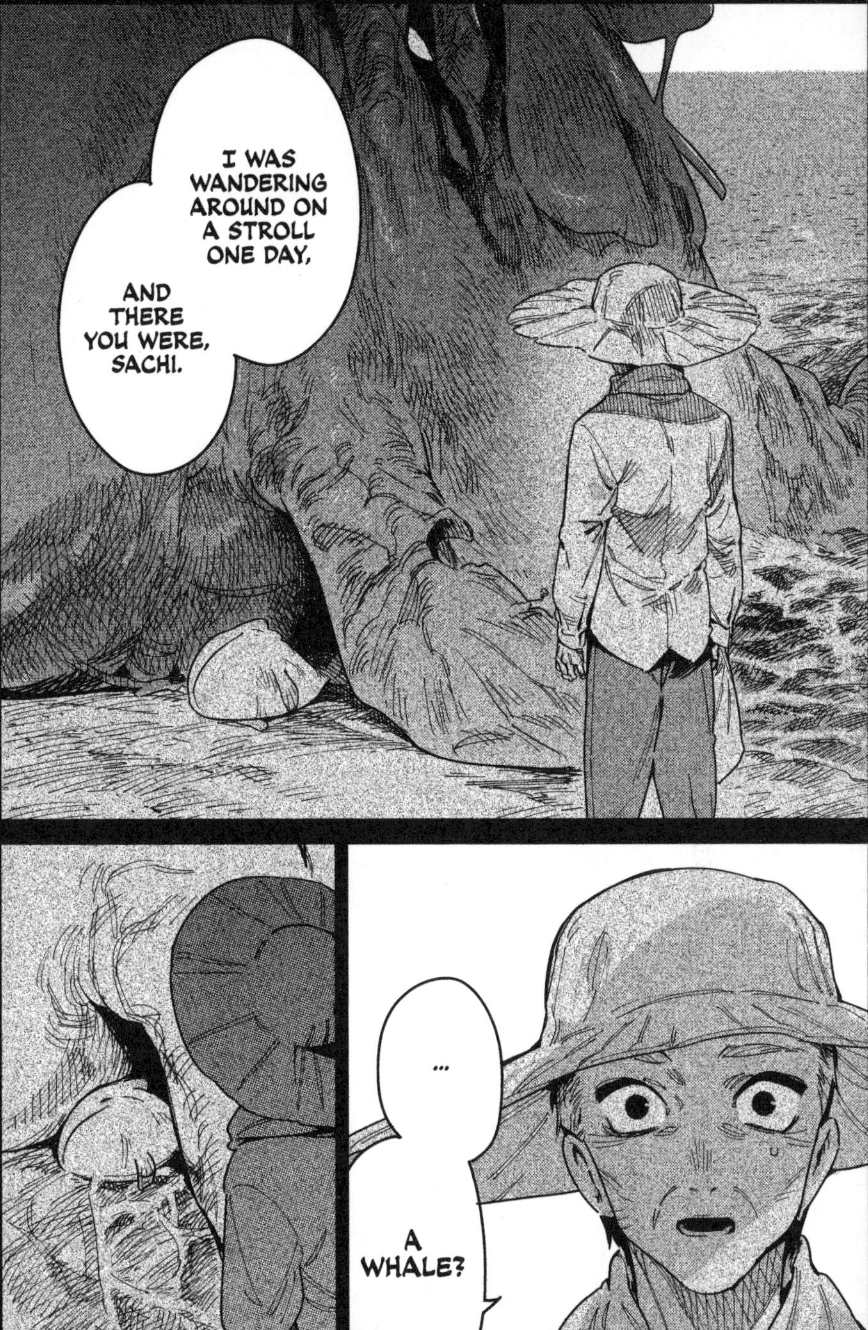
I WAS WANDERING AROUND ON A STROLL ONE DAY,
AND THERE YOU WERE, SACHI.
...
A WHALE?

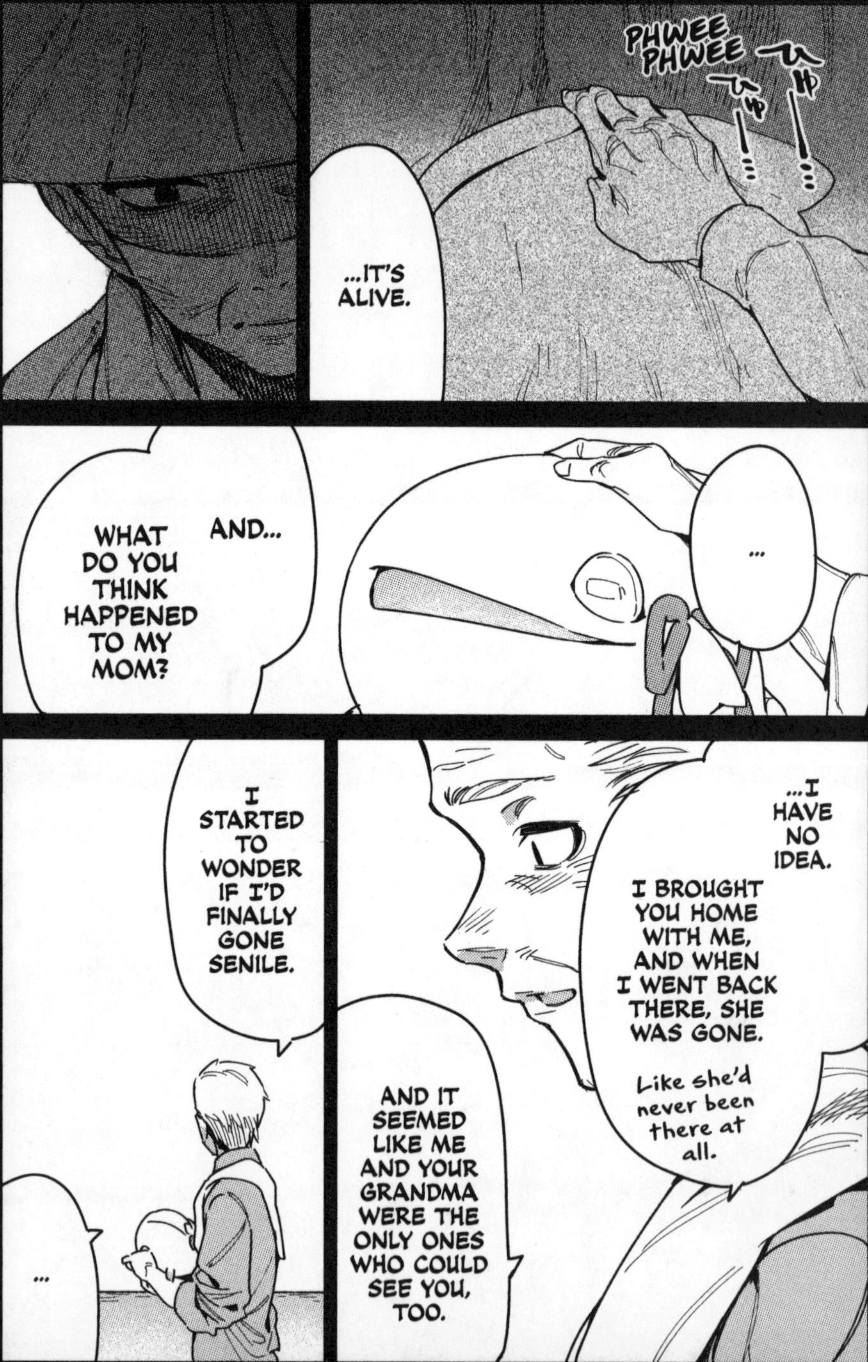
PHWEE PHWEE
...IT'S ALIVE.
...
AND...
WHAT DO YOU THINK HAPPENED TO MY MOM?
...I HAVE NO IDEA.
I BROUGHT YOU HOME WITH ME, AND WHEN I WENT BACK THERE, SHE WAS GONE.
Like she'd never been there at all.
AND IT SEEMED LIKE ME AND YOUR GRANDMA WERE THE ONLY ONES WHO COULD SEE YOU, TOO.
I STARTED TO WONDER IF I'D FINALLY GONE SENILE.
...

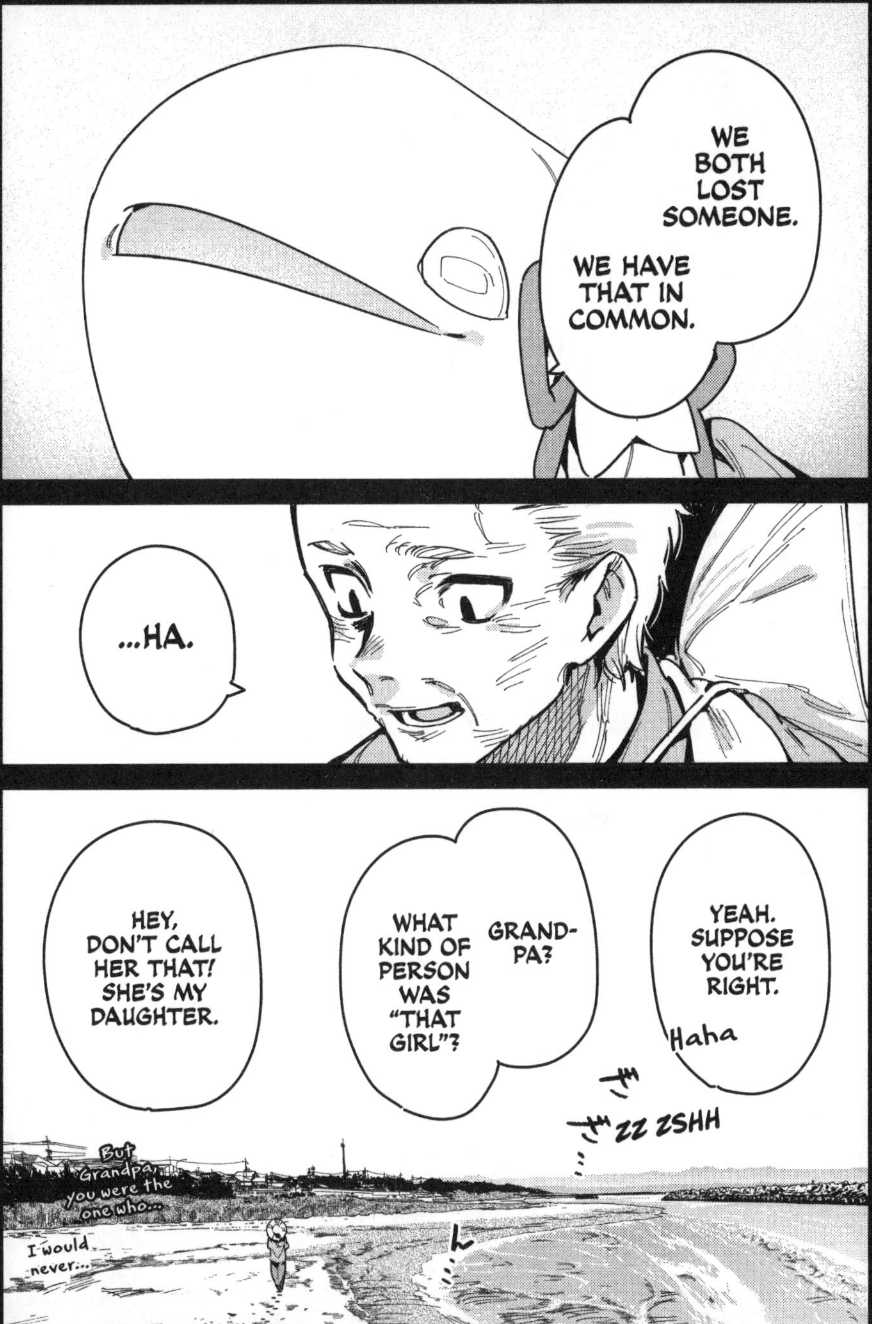
WE BOTH LOST SOMEONE.
WE HAVE THAT IN COMMON.
...HA.
YEAH. SUPPOSE YOU'RE RIGHT.
Haha
GRANDPA?
WHAT KIND OF PERSON WAS "THAT GIRL"?
HEY, DON'T CALL HER THAT! SHE'S MY DAUGHTER.
ZZ ZSHH
But Grandpa, you were the one who...
I would never...

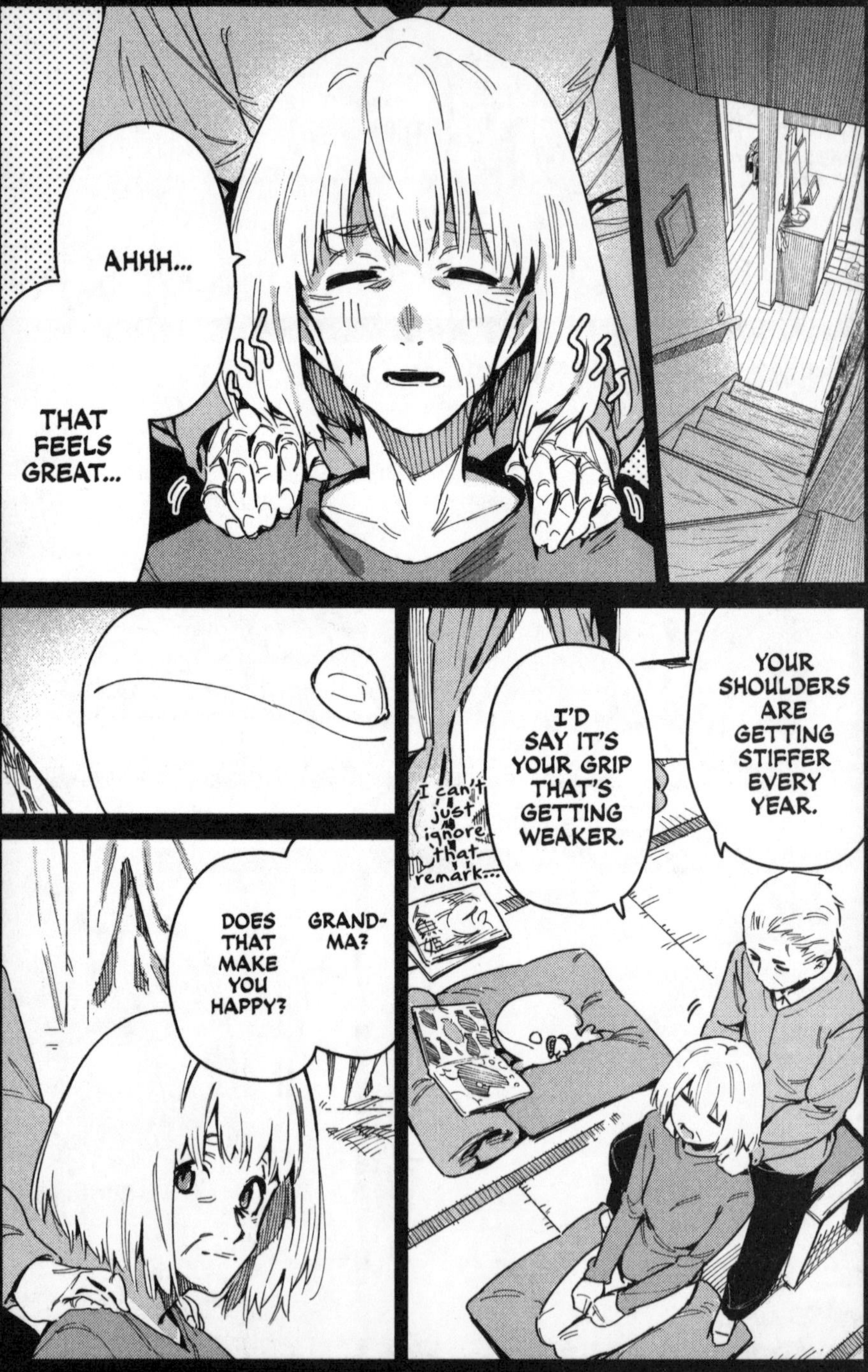
AHHH...
THAT FEELS GREAT...
YOUR SHOULDERS ARE GETTING STIFFER EVERY YEAR.
I'D SAY IT'S YOUR GRIP THAT'S GETTING WEAKER.
I can't just ignore that remark...
GRAND-MA?
DOES THAT MAKE YOU HAPPY?

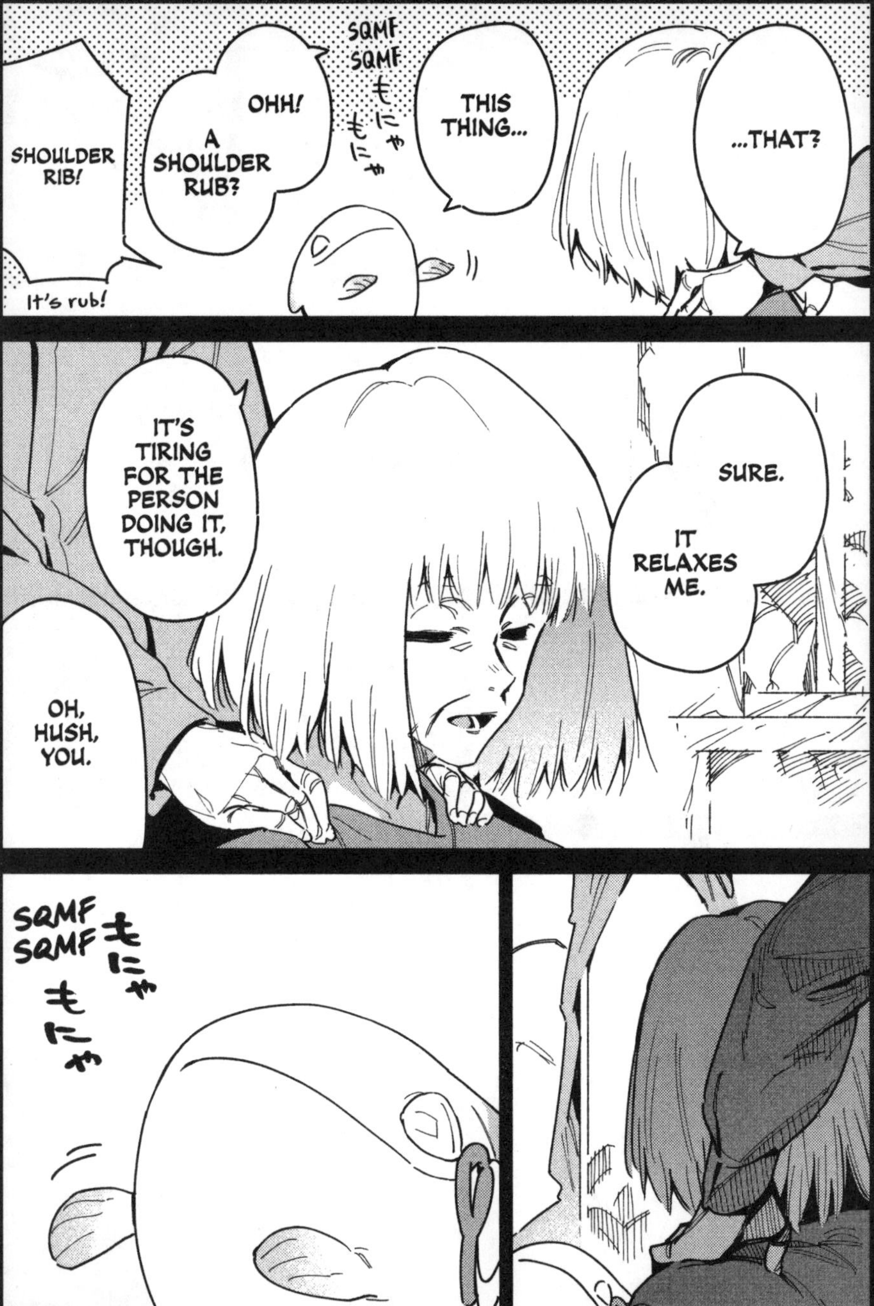
...THAT?
THIS THING...
SQMF SQMF
もにゃもにゃ
OHH! A SHOULDER RUB?
SHOULDER RIB!
It's rub!
SURE. IT RELAXES ME.
IT'S TIRING FOR THE PERSON DOING IT, THOUGH.
OH, HUSH, YOU.
SQMF SQMF
もにゃもにゃ

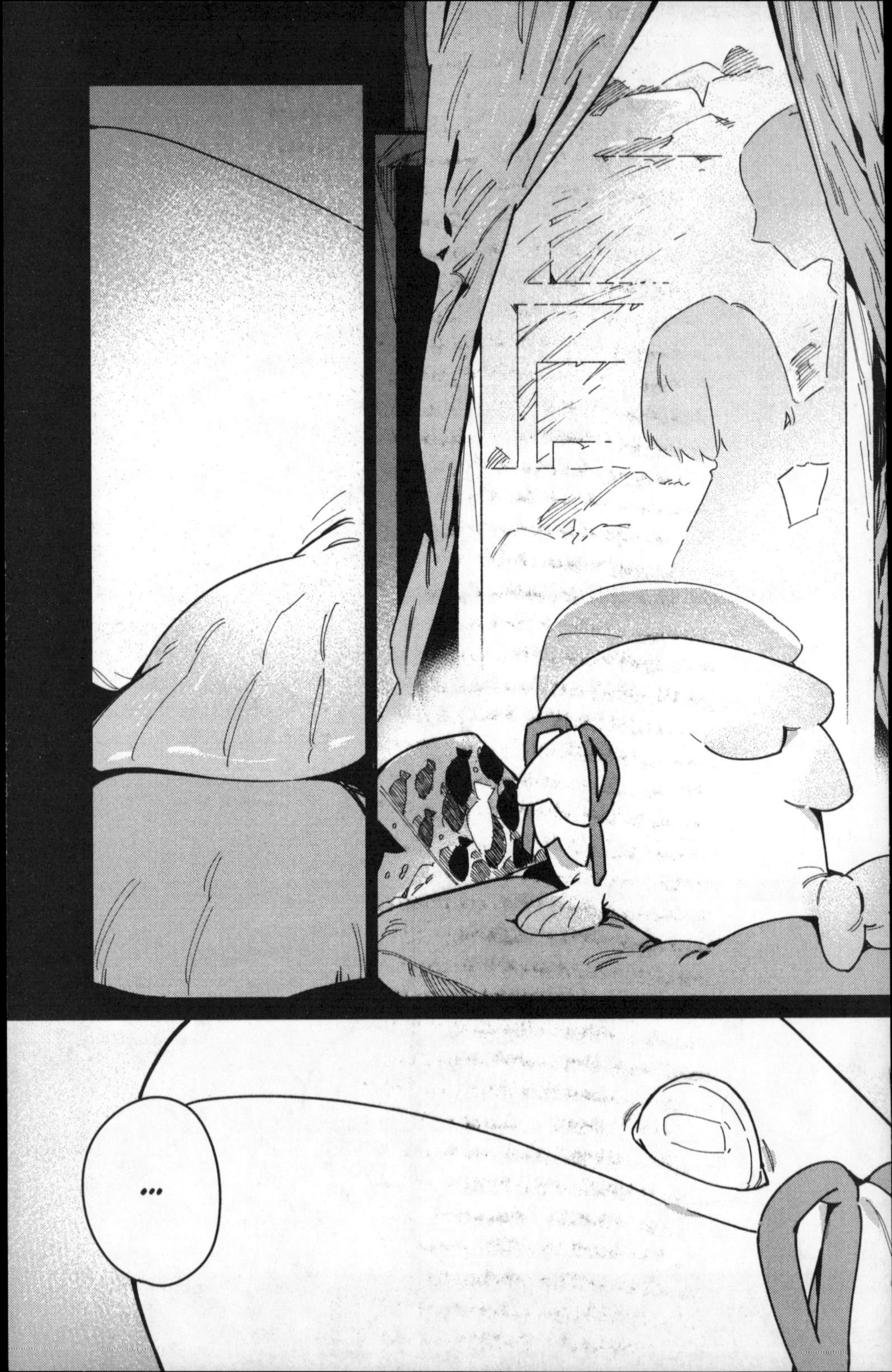
...

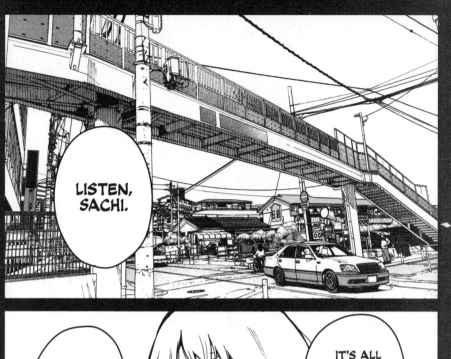

LISTEN, SACHI.
IT'S ALL RIGHT FOR YOU TO STAY JUST AS YOU ARE NOW.
THERE'S NO NEED FOR YOU TO BECOME HUMAN.
...BUT WHAT ABOUT SHOULDER RIBS...?
GRANDPA GIVES THOSE TO ME.
BEING YOUR USUAL HEALTHY AND HAPPY SELF IS MORE THAN ENOUGH, SACHI.
GRAND-MA...
Get down from there. It's dangerous.

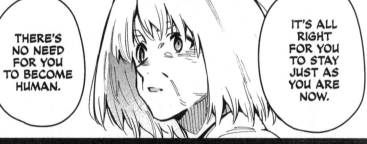

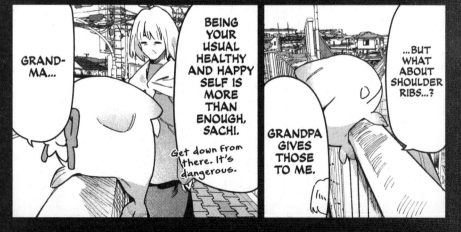

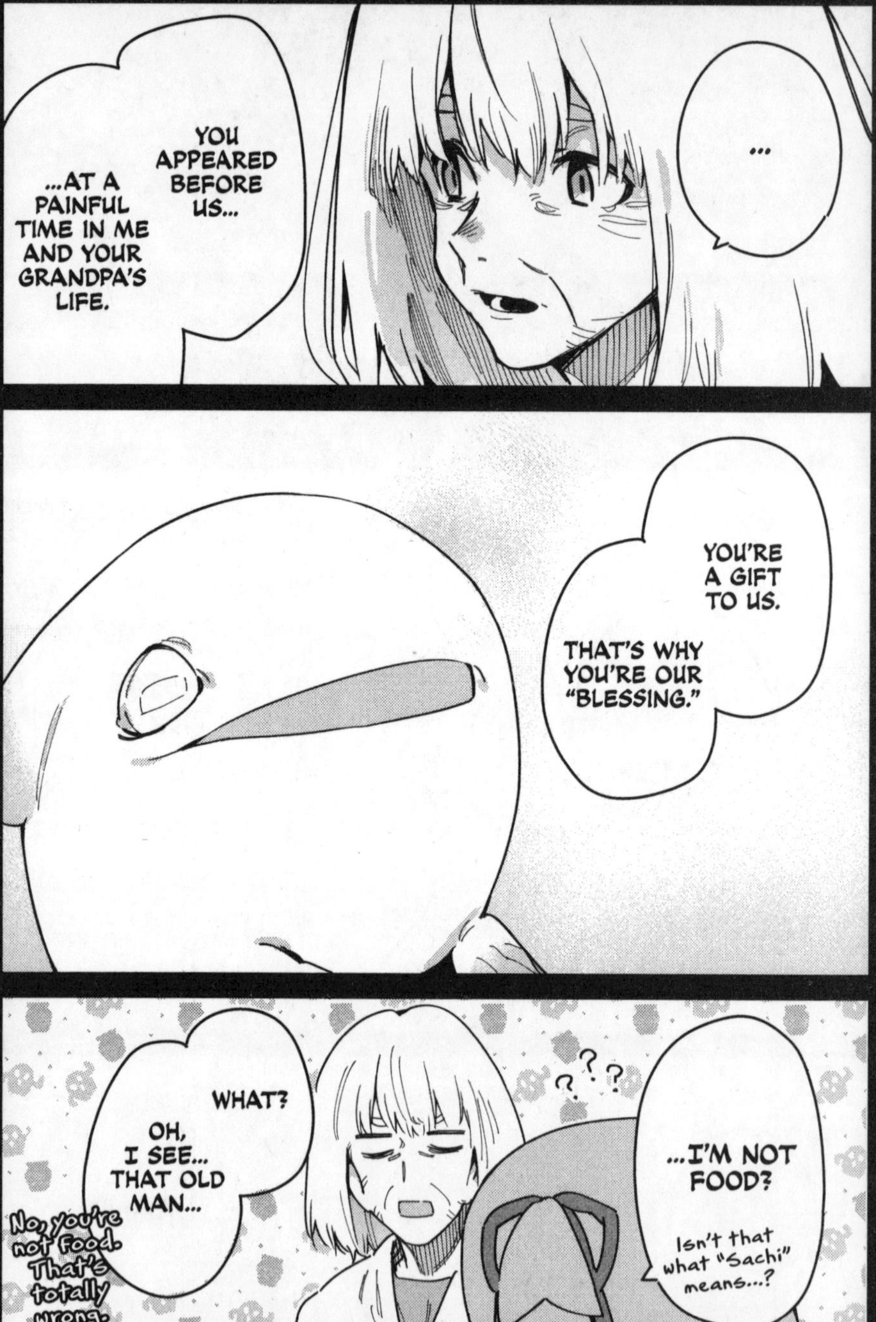
...
YOU APPEARED BEFORE US...
...AT A PAINFUL TIME IN ME AND YOUR GRANDPA'S LIFE.
YOU'RE A GIFT TO US.
THAT'S WHY YOU'RE OUR "BLESSING."
...I'M NOT FOOD?
Isn't that what "Sachi" means...?
??
WHAT?
OH, I SEE... THAT OLD MAN...
No, you're not food. That's totally wrong.

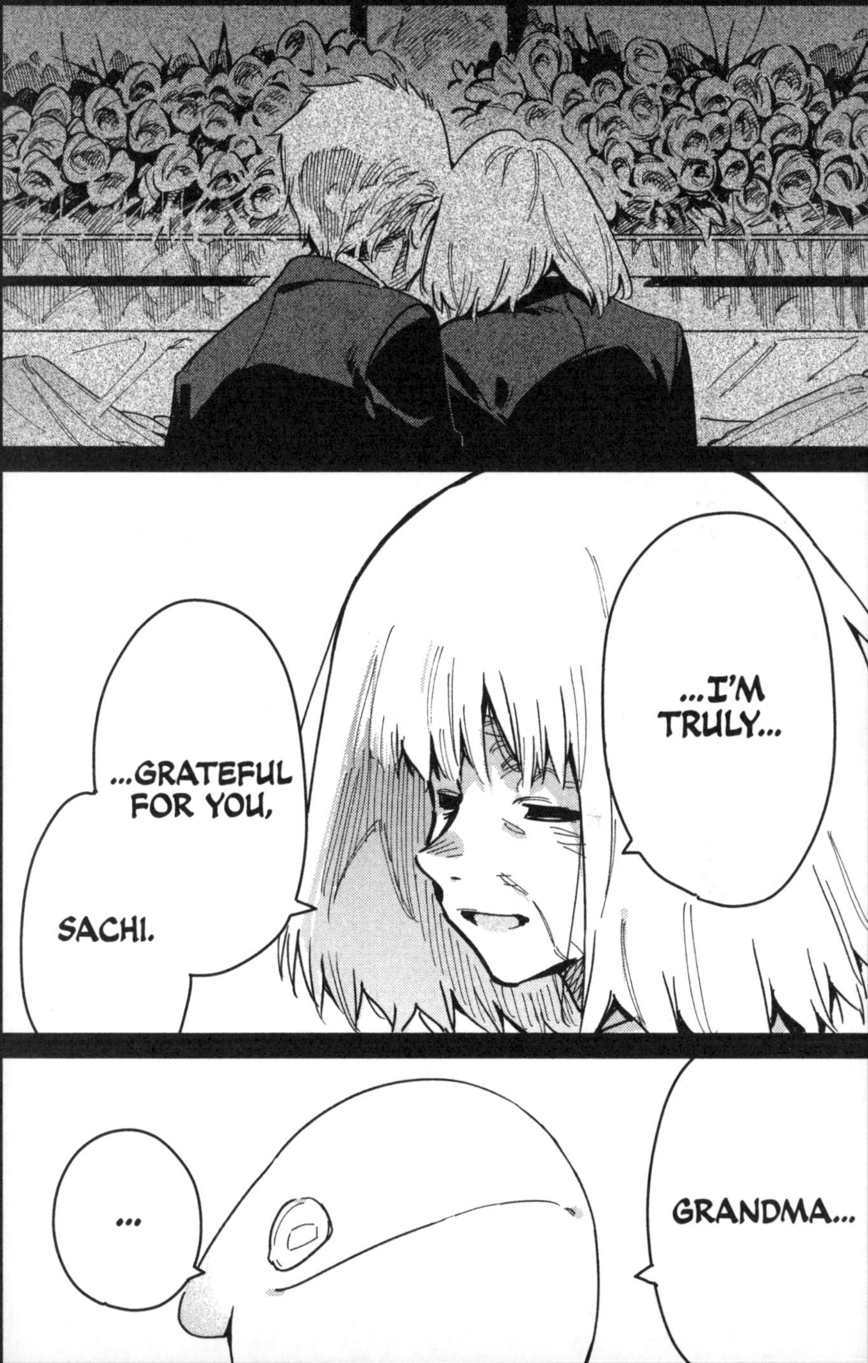
...I'M TRULY...
...GRATEFUL FOR YOU,
SACHI.
GRANDMA...
...

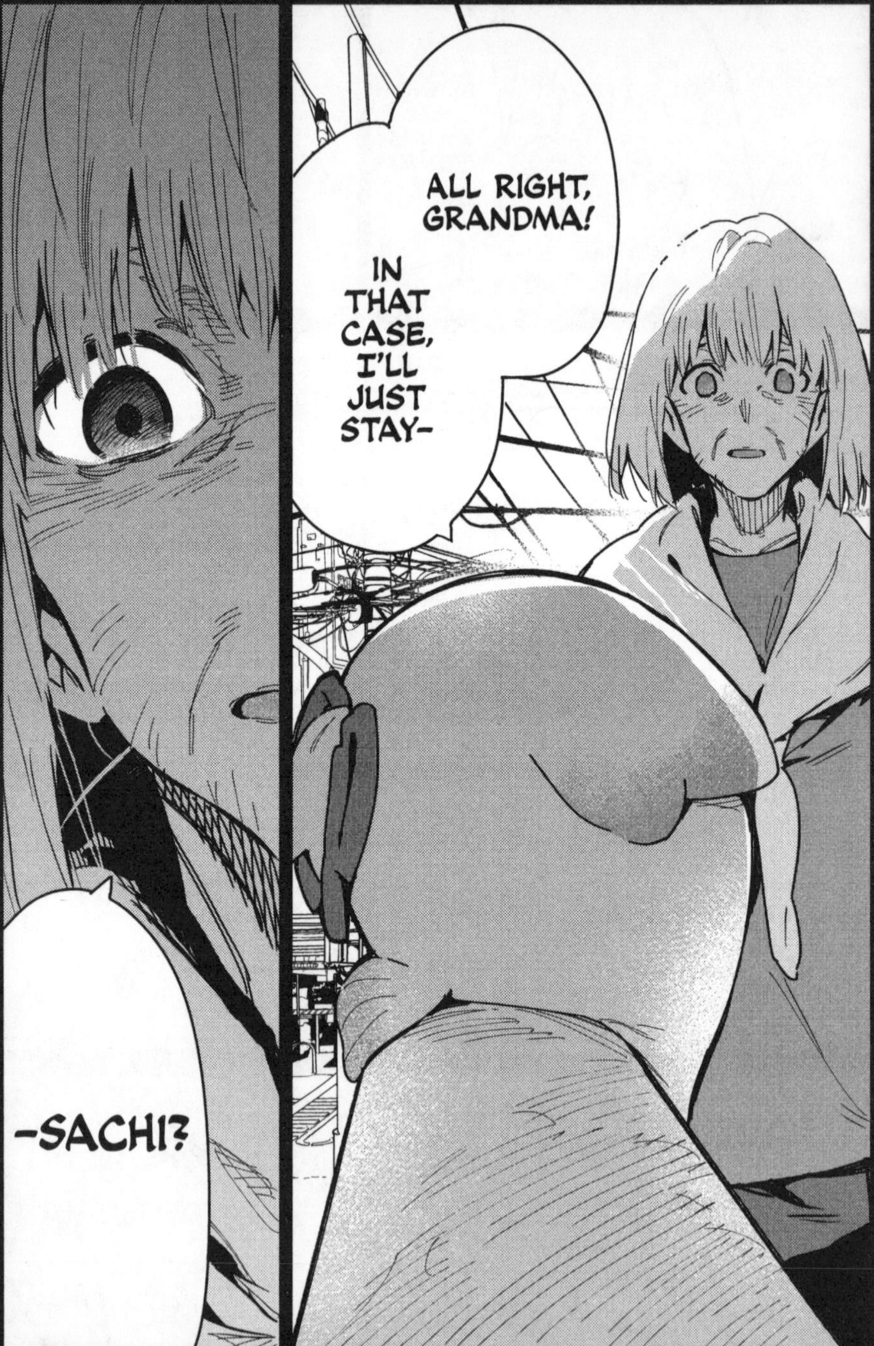
ALL RIGHT, GRANDMA!
IN THAT CASE, I'LL JUST STAY-
-SACHI?

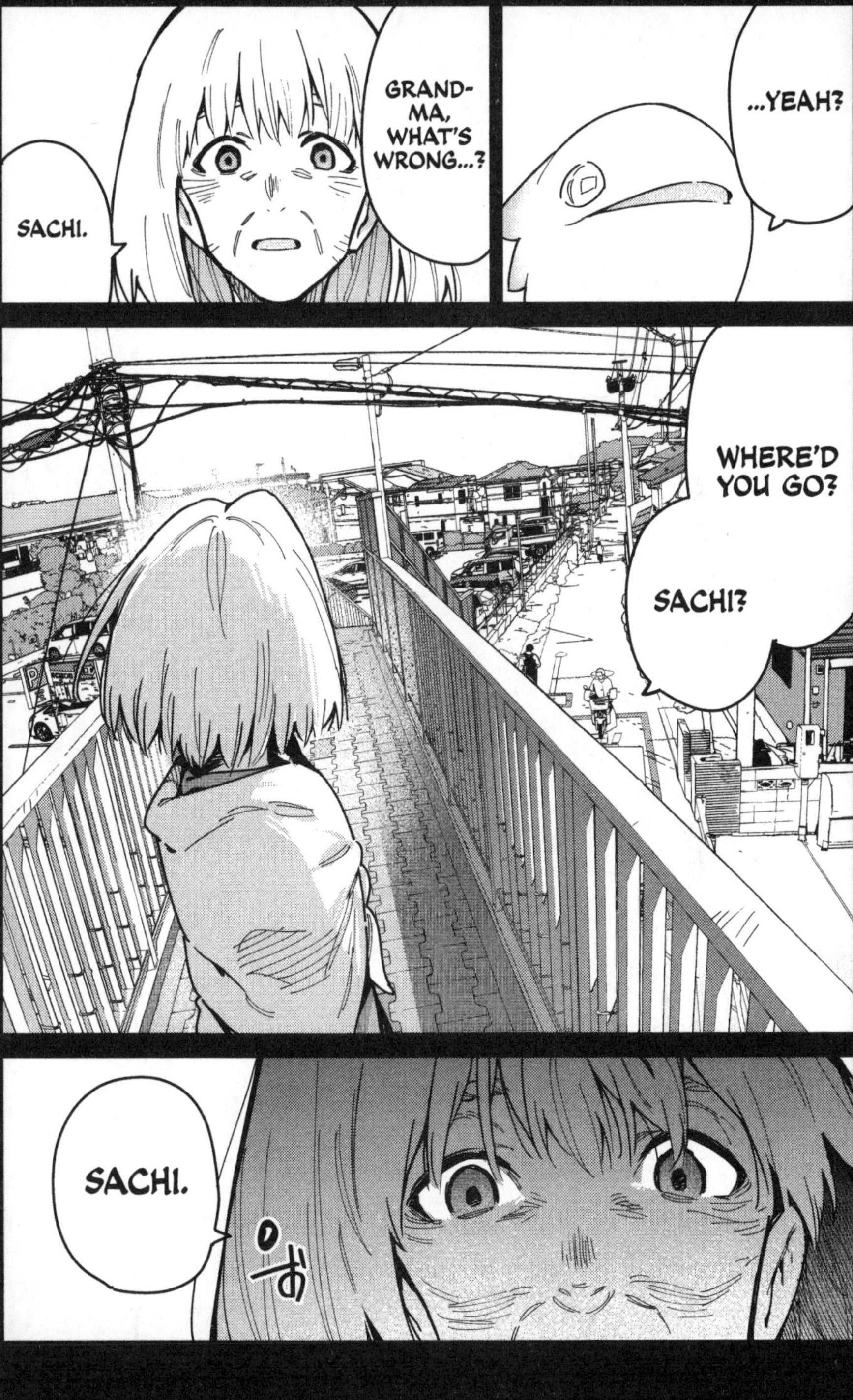
...YEAH?
GRAND-MA, WHAT'S WRONG...?
SACHI.
WHERE'D YOU GO?
SACHI?
SACHI.
お

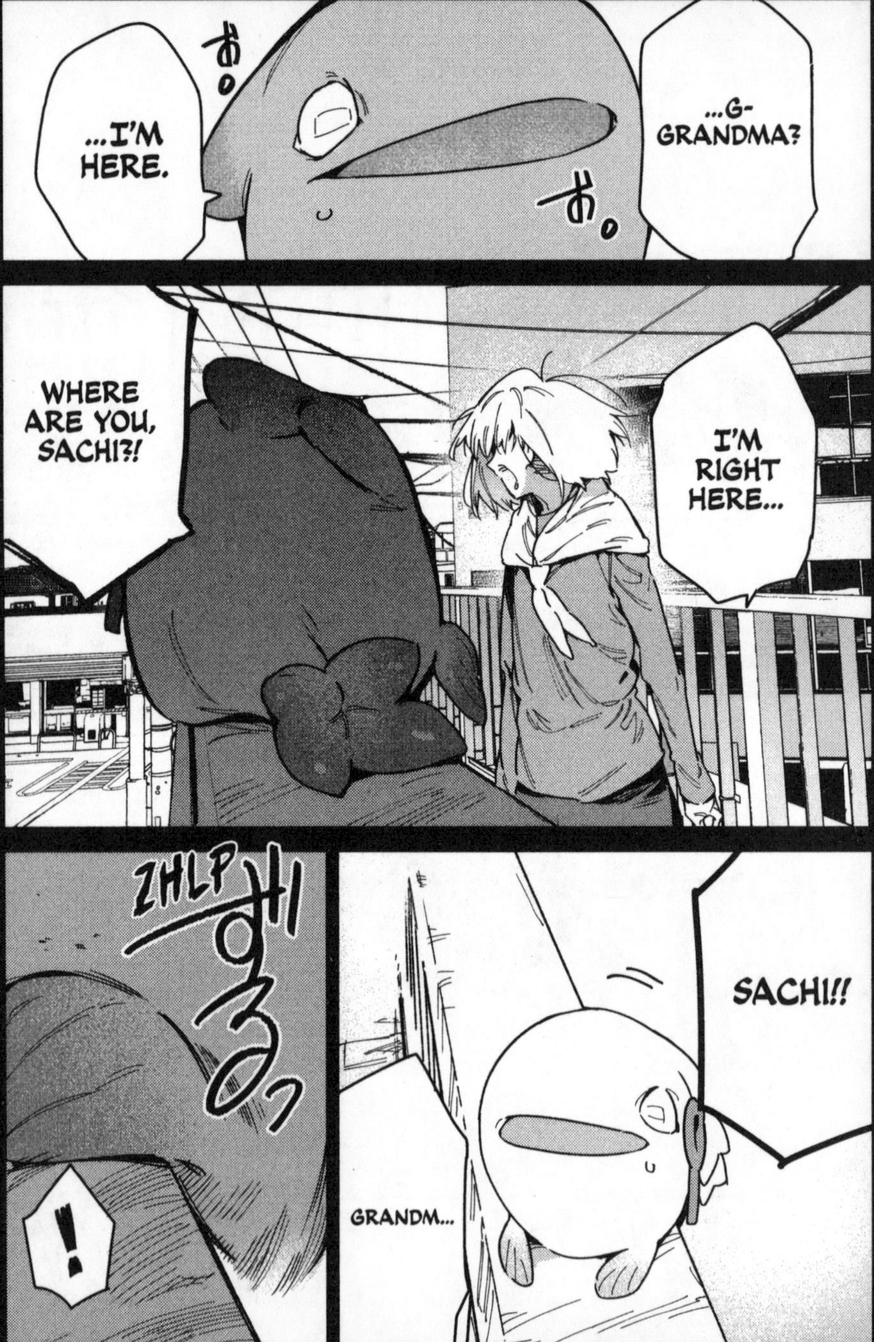
...G- GRANDMA?
...I'M HERE.
I'M RIGHT HERE...
WHERE ARE YOU, SACHI?!
SACHI!!
GRANDM...
ZHLP
!

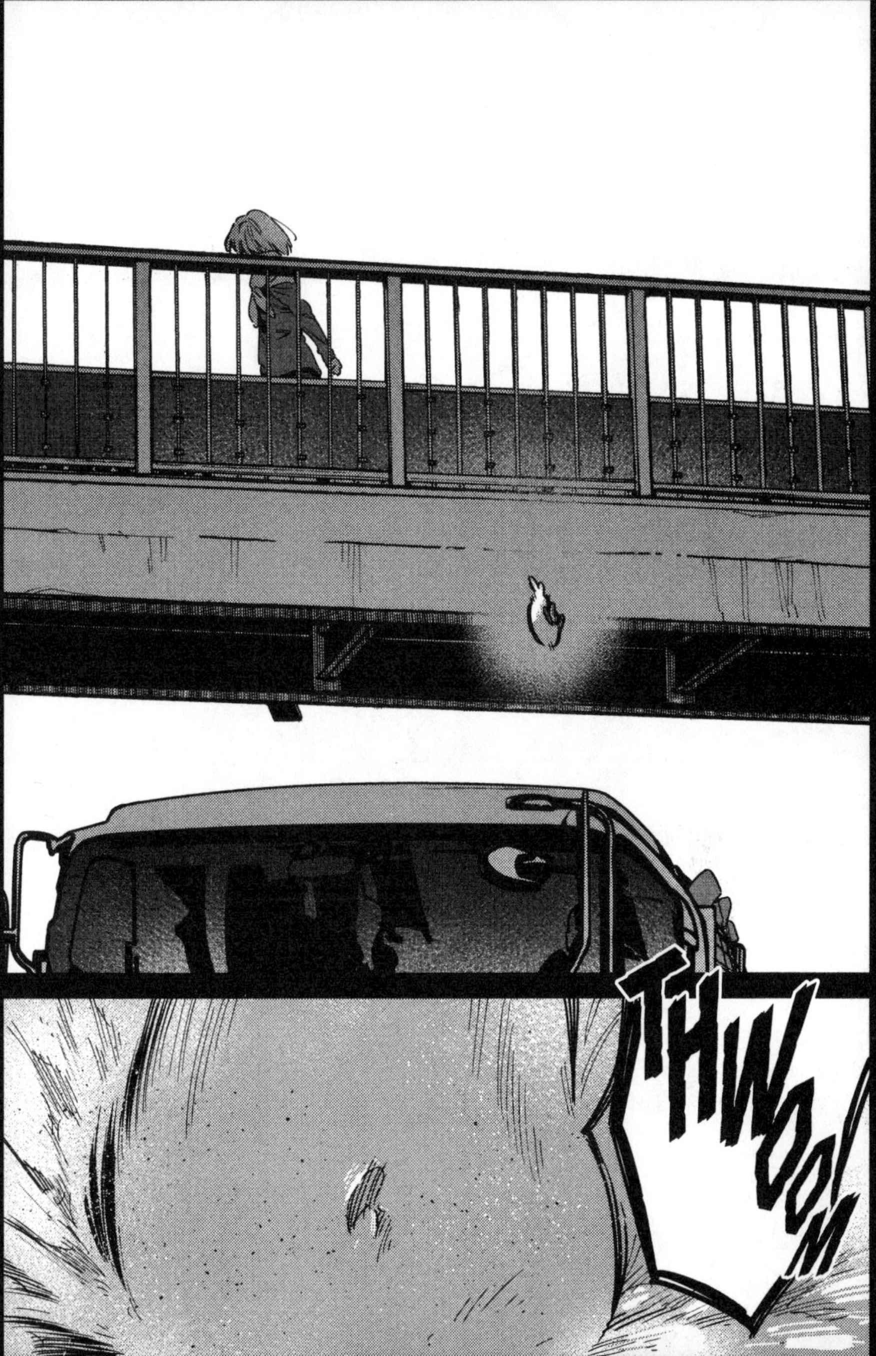
THWOOM

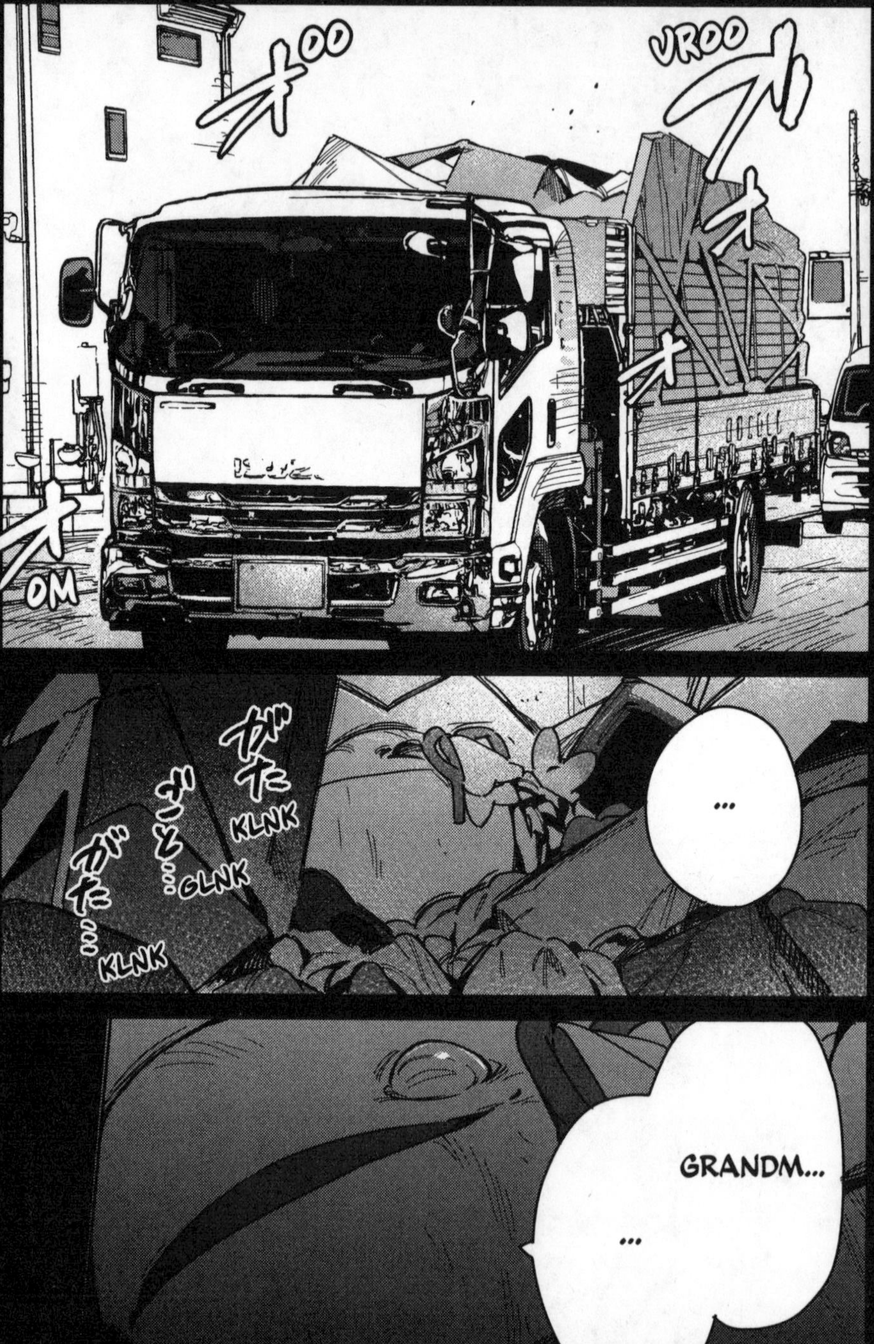

VROO
OO
OM
...
KLNK
GLNK
KLNK
GRANDM...
...

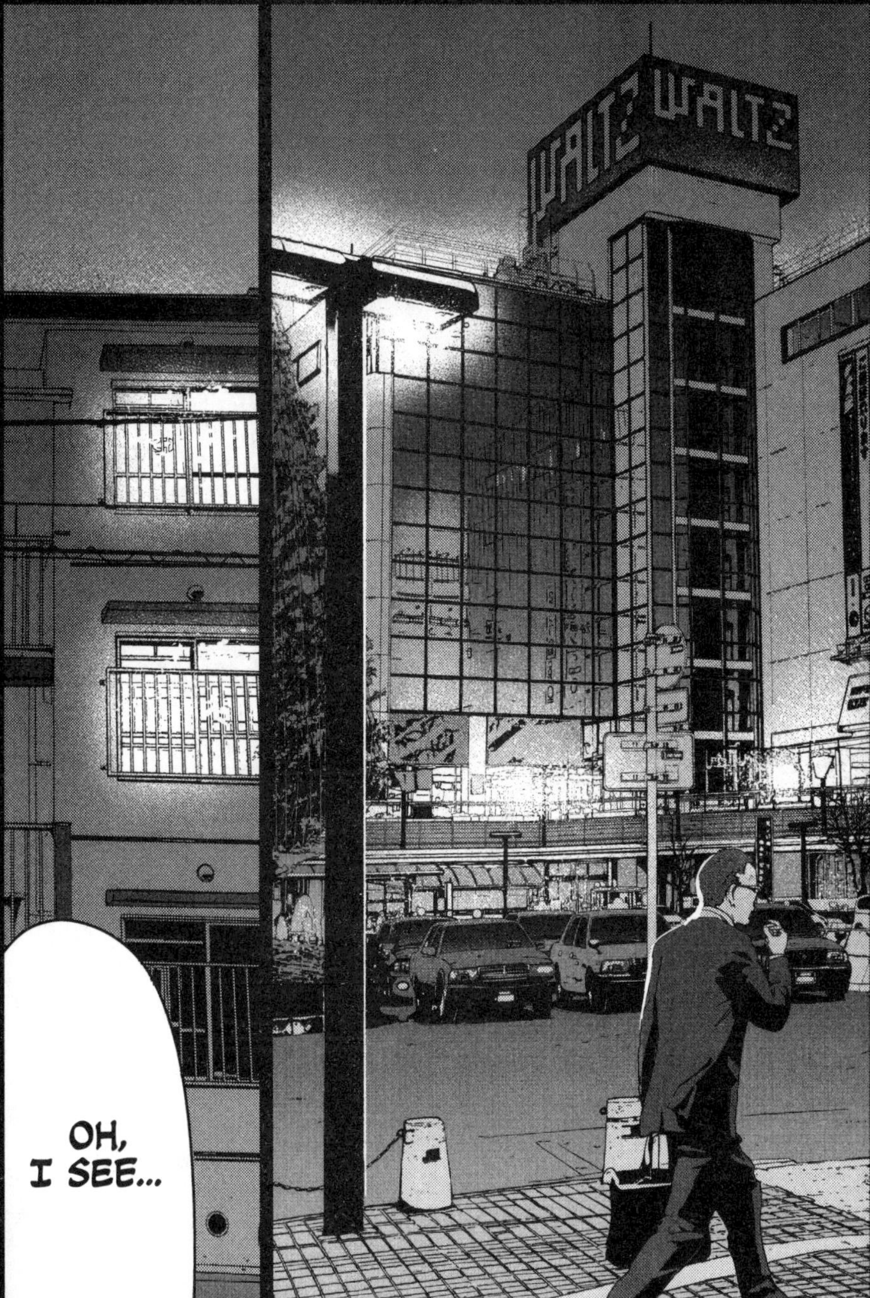
OH, I SEE...

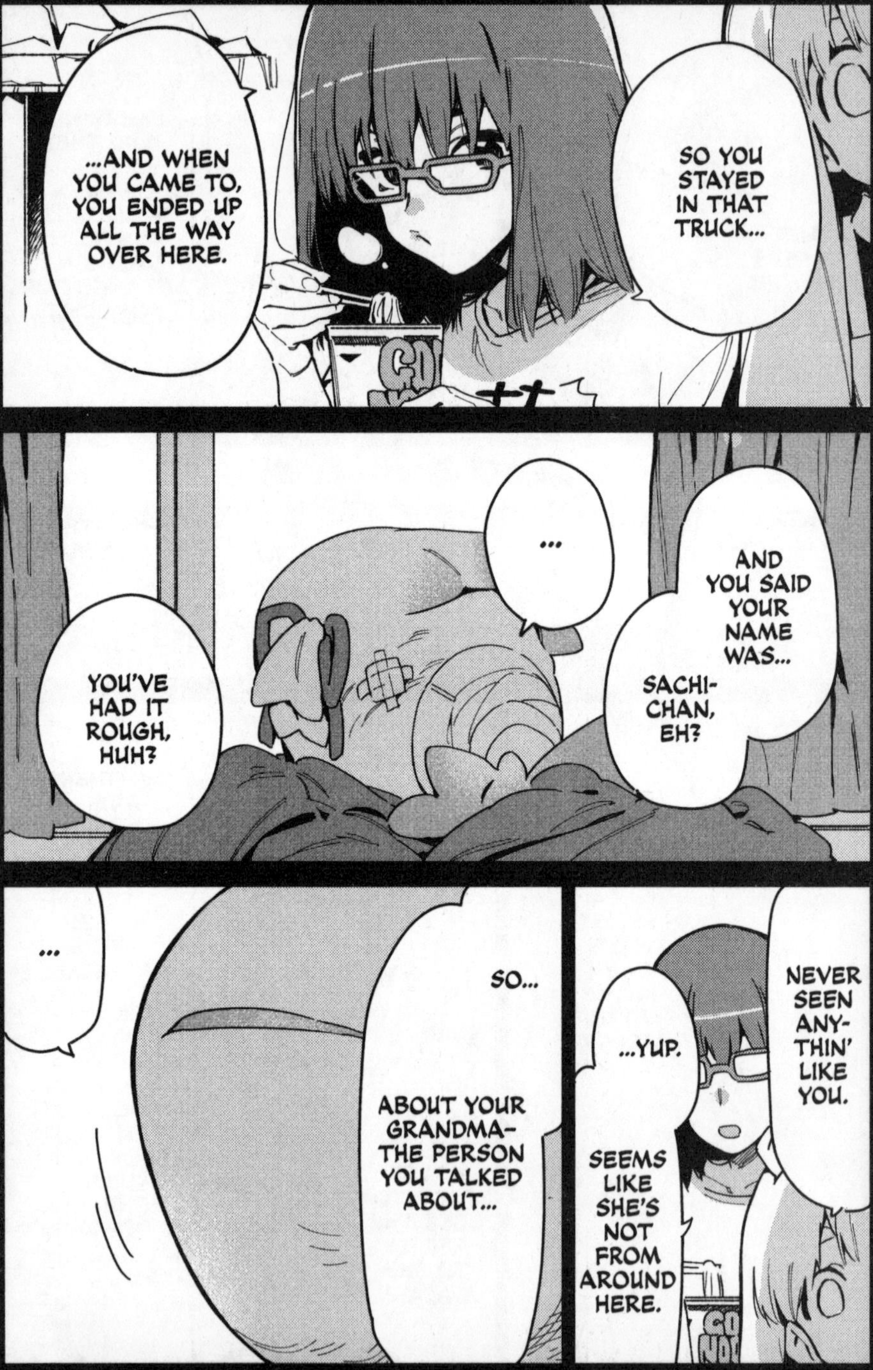
SO YOU STAYED IN THAT TRUCK...
...AND WHEN YOU CAME TO, YOU ENDED UP ALL THE WAY OVER HERE.
AND YOU SAID YOUR NAME WAS...
SACHI-CHAN, EH?
...
YOU'VE HAD IT ROUGH, HUH?
NEVER SEEN ANYTHIN' LIKE YOU.
...YUP.
SEEMS LIKE SHE'S NOT FROM AROUND HERE.
SO...
ABOUT YOUR GRANDMA–THE PERSON YOU TALKED ABOUT...
...

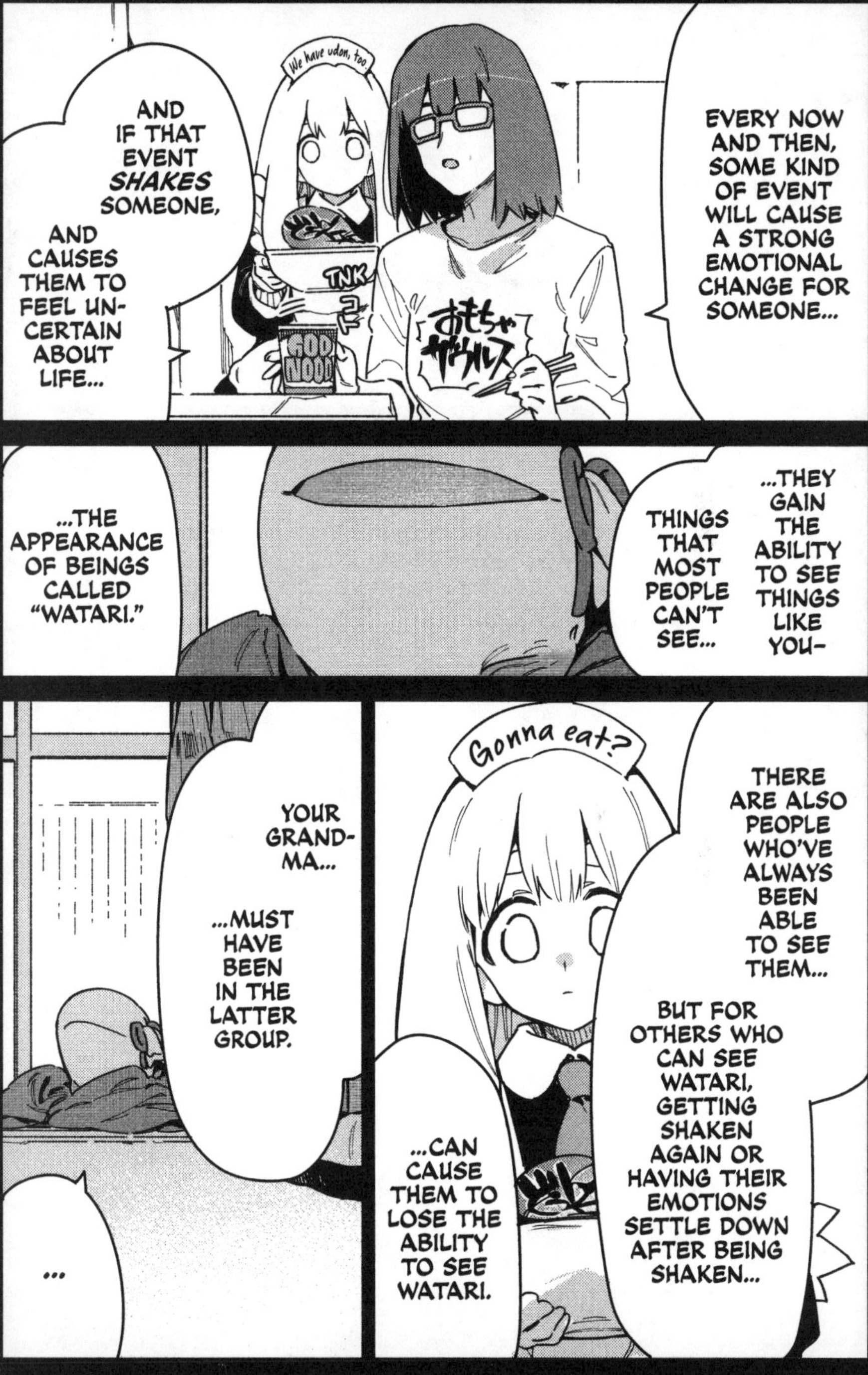
We have udon, too.
EVERY NOW AND THEN, SOME KIND OF EVENT WILL CAUSE A STRONG EMOTIONAL CHANGE FOR SOMEONE...
AND IF THAT EVENT *SHAKES* SOMEONE,
AND CAUSES THEM TO FEEL UN-CERTAIN ABOUT LIFE...
...THEY GAIN THE ABILITY TO SEE THINGS LIKE YOU-
THINGS THAT MOST PEOPLE CAN'T SEE...
...THE APPEARANCE OF BEINGS CALLED "WATARI."
Gonna eat?
THERE ARE ALSO PEOPLE WHO'VE ALWAYS BEEN ABLE TO SEE THEM...
BUT FOR OTHERS WHO CAN SEE WATARI, GETTING SHAKEN AGAIN OR HAVING THEIR EMOTIONS SETTLE DOWN AFTER BEING SHAKEN...
...CAN CAUSE THEM TO LOSE THE ABILITY TO SEE WATARI.
YOUR GRAND-MA...
...MUST HAVE BEEN IN THE LATTER GROUP.
...

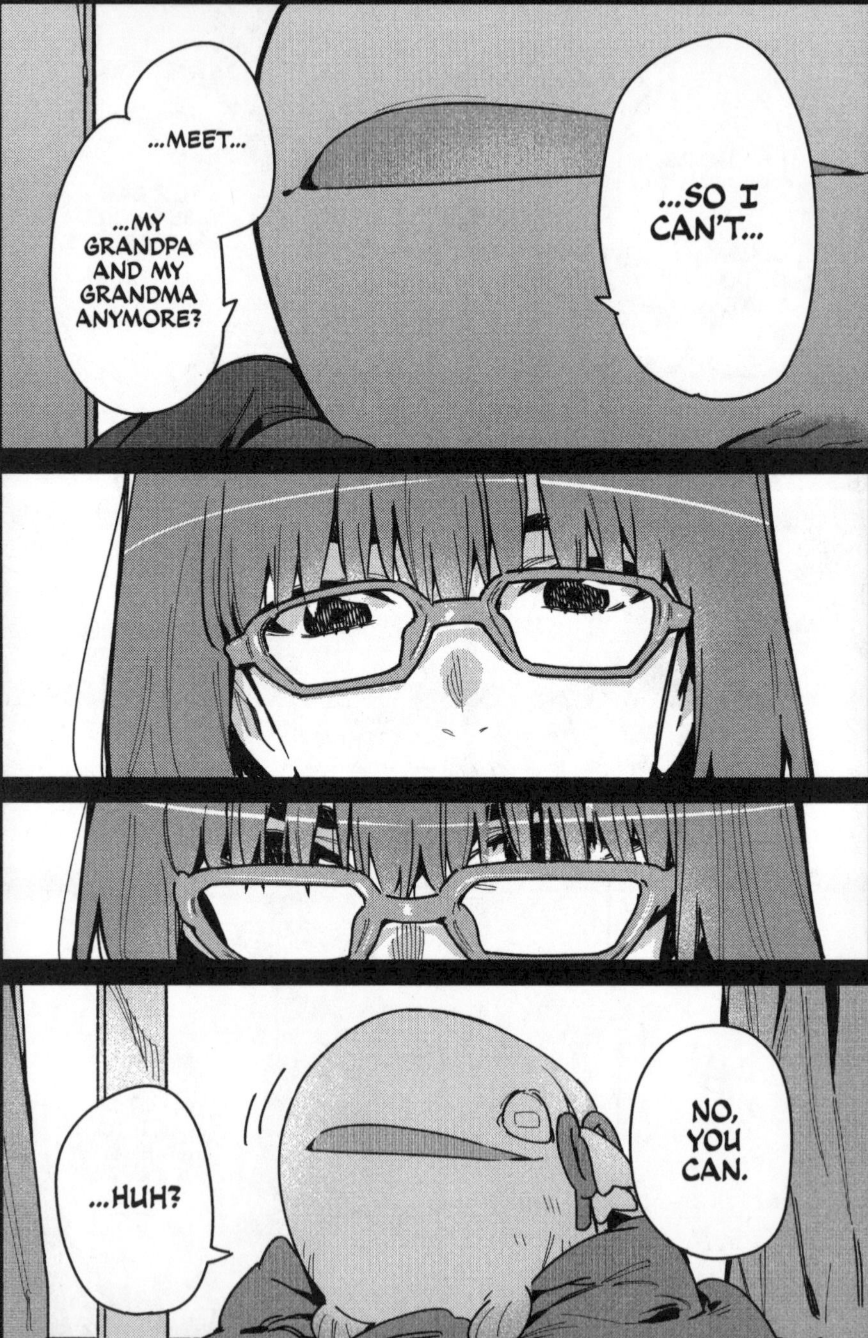
...SO I CAN'T...
...MEET...
...MY GRANDPA AND MY GRANDMA ANYMORE?
NO, YOU CAN.
...HUH?

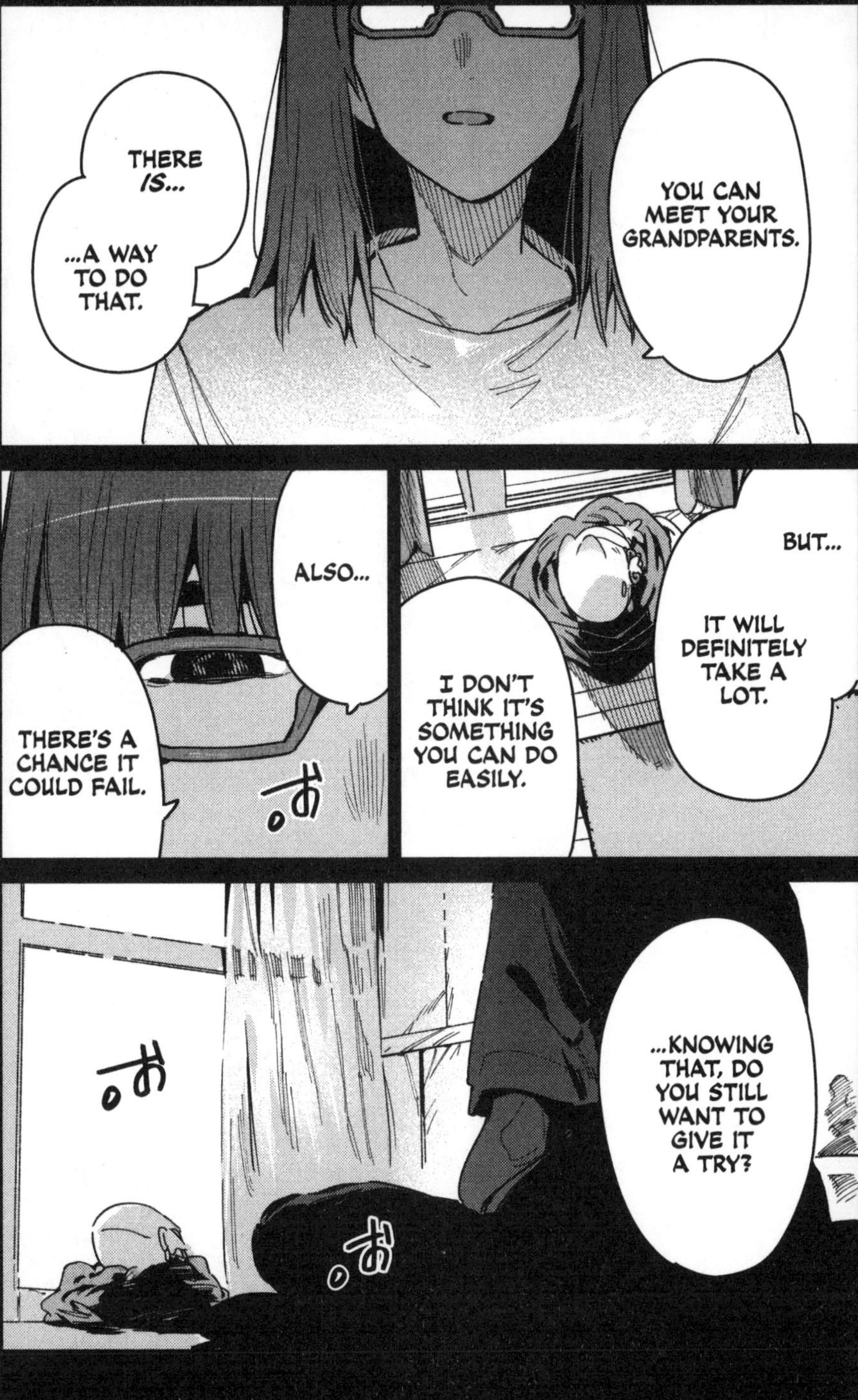
YOU CAN MEET YOUR GRANDPARENTS.
THERE *IS*...
...A WAY TO DO THAT.
BUT...
IT WILL DEFINITELY TAKE A LOT.
I DON'T THINK IT'S SOMETHING YOU CAN DO EASILY.
ALSO...
THERE'S A CHANCE IT COULD FAIL.
お。
お。
...KNOWING THAT, DO YOU STILL WANT TO GIVE IT A TRY?
お。

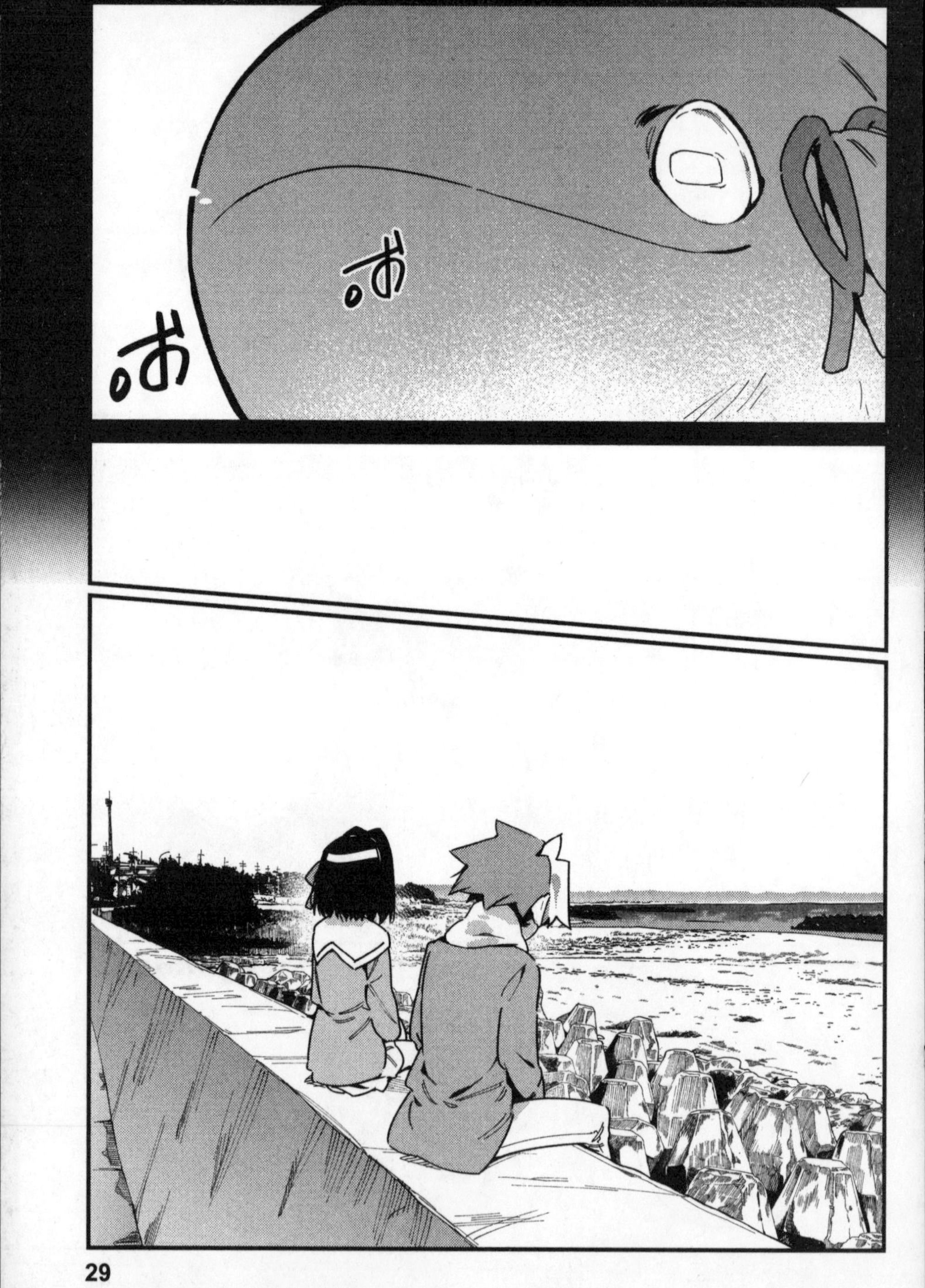
ぉお
ぉお

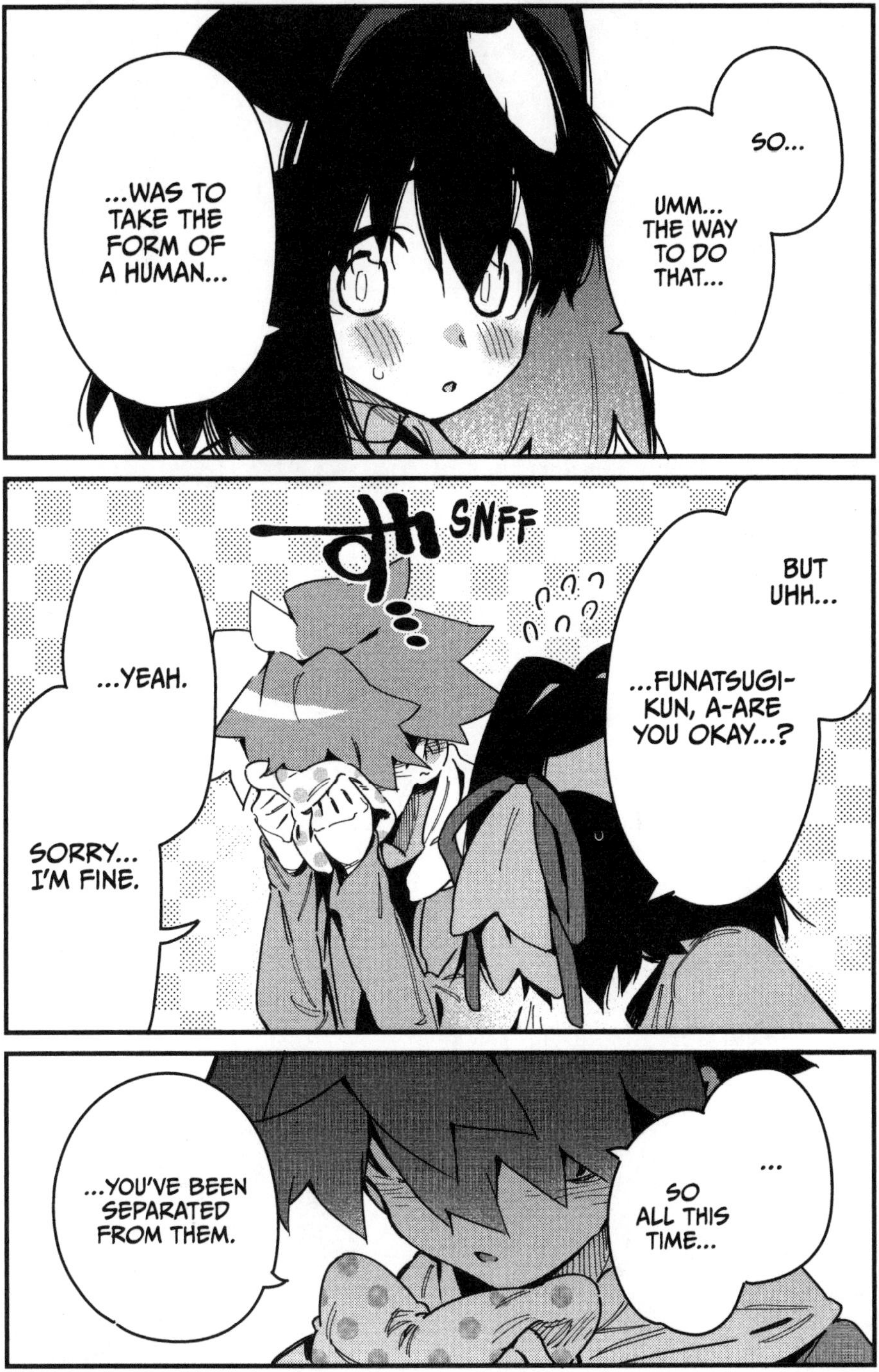
SO...
UMM... THE WAY TO DO THAT...
...WAS TO TAKE THE FORM OF A HUMAN...
BUT UHH...
...FUNATSUGI-KUN, A-ARE YOU OKAY...?
SNFF
...YEAH.
SORRY... I'M FINE.
...
SO ALL THIS TIME...
...YOU'VE BEEN SEPARATED FROM THEM.

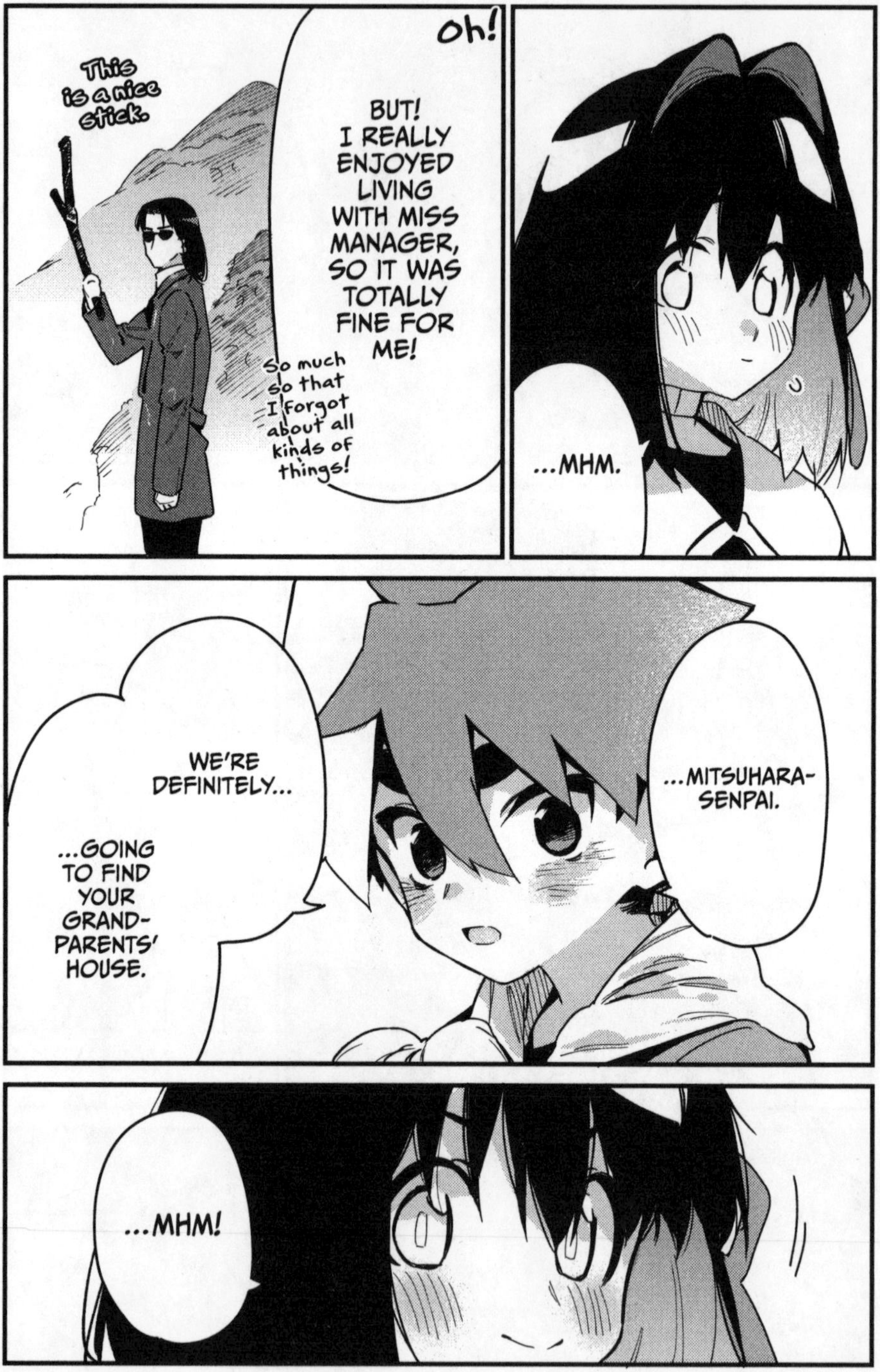
...MHM.
Oh!
BUT! I REALLY ENJOYED LIVING WITH MISS MANAGER, SO IT WAS TOTALLY FINE FOR ME!
So much so that I forgot about all kinds of things!
This is a nice stick.
...MITSUHARA-SENPAI.
WE'RE DEFINITELY...
...GOING TO FIND YOUR GRAND-PARENTS' HOUSE.
...MHM!

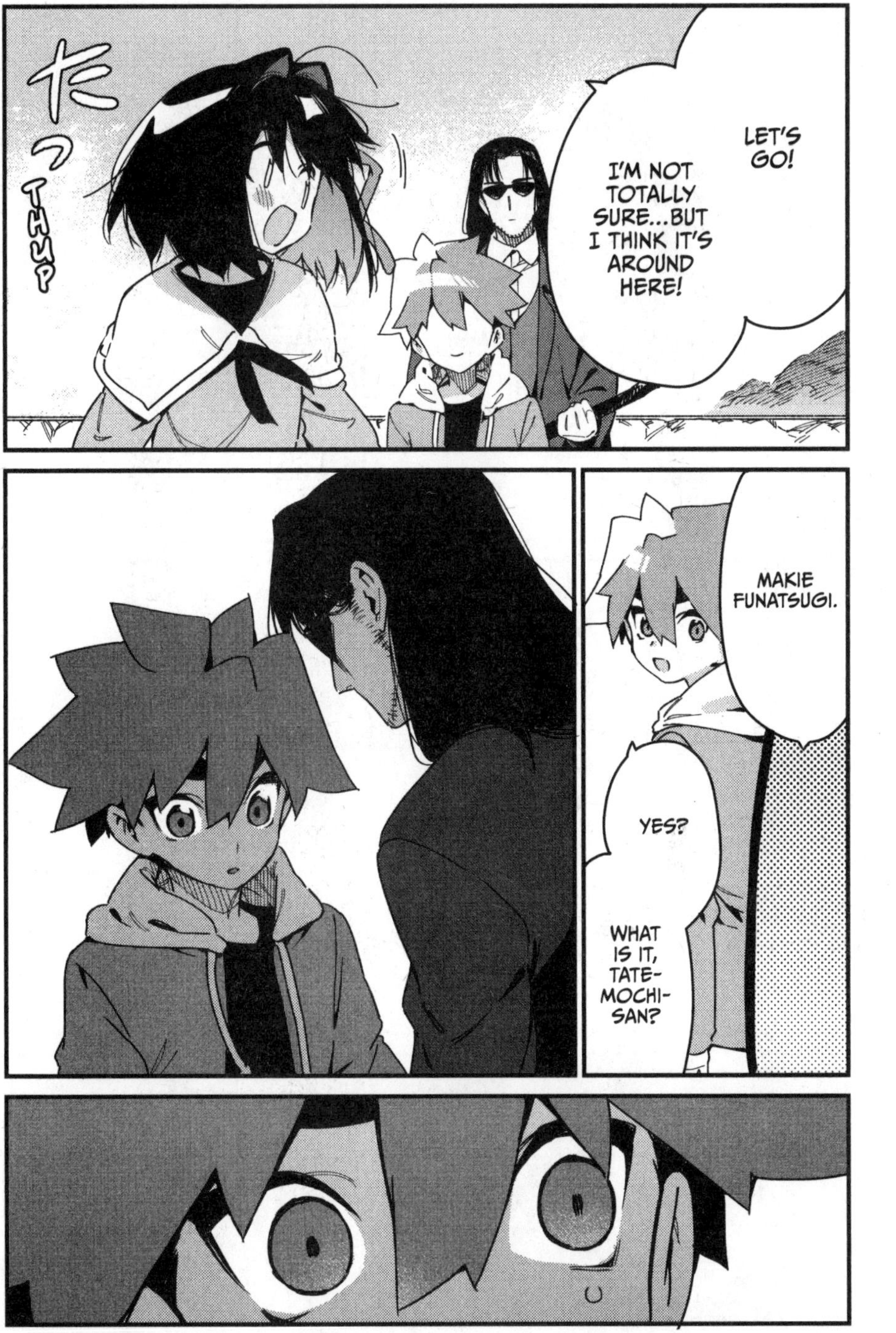
LET'S GO!
I'M NOT TOTALLY SURE...BUT I THINK IT'S AROUND HERE!
たっ
THUP
MAKIE FUNATSUGI.
YES?
WHAT IS IT, TATE-MOCHI-SAN?

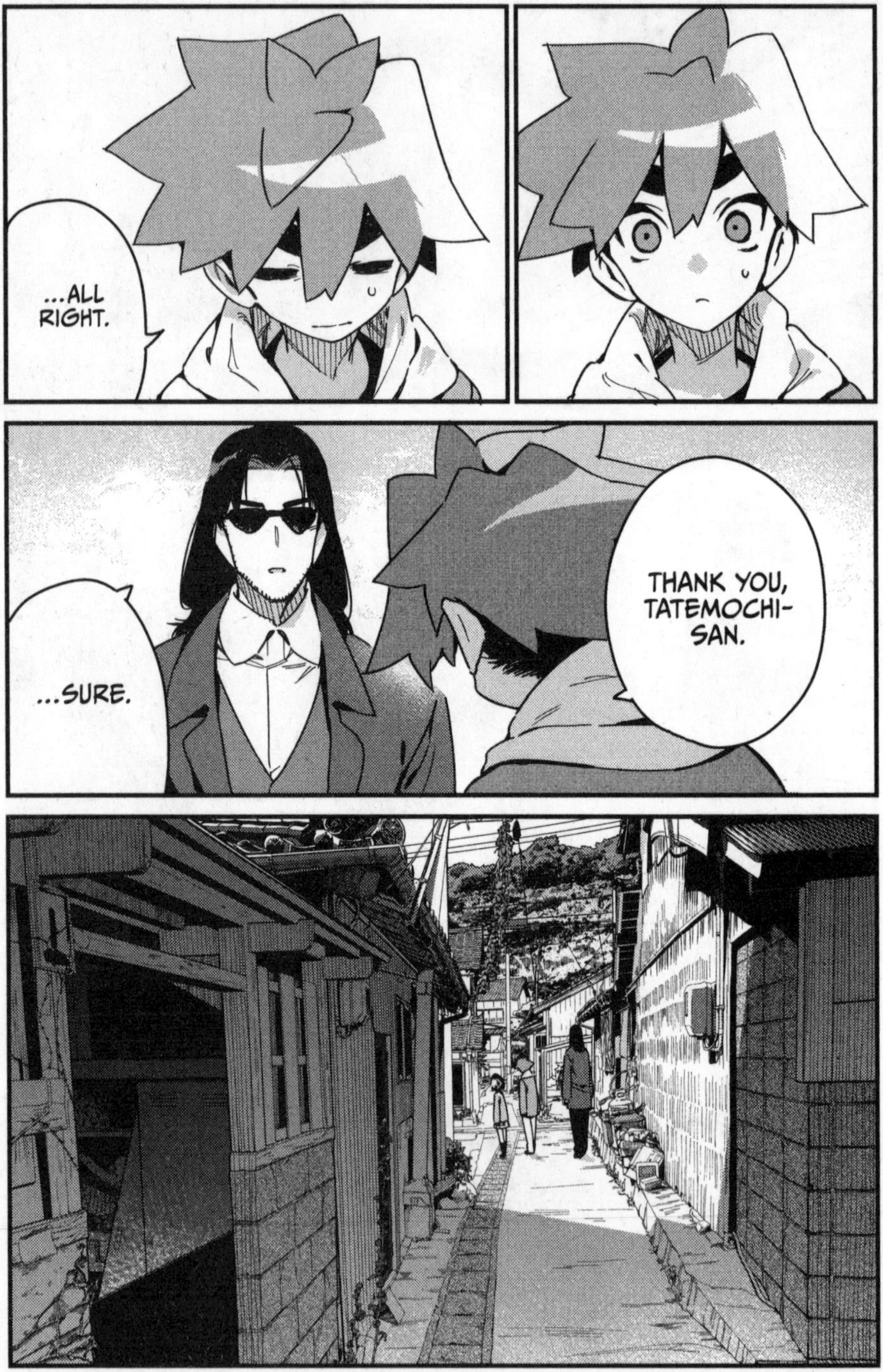
...ALL RIGHT.
THANK YOU, TATEMOCHI-SAN.
...SURE.

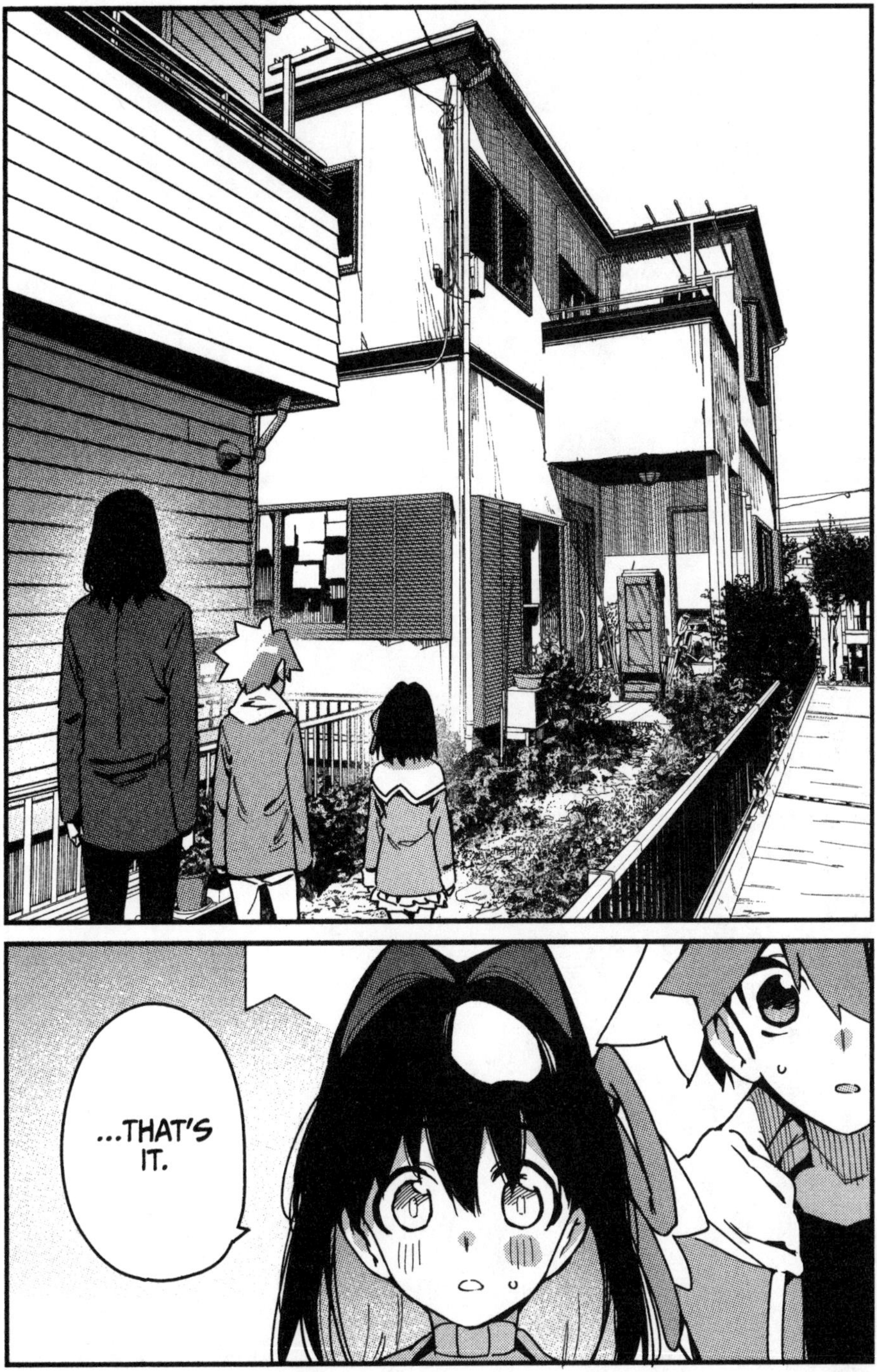
...THAT'S IT.

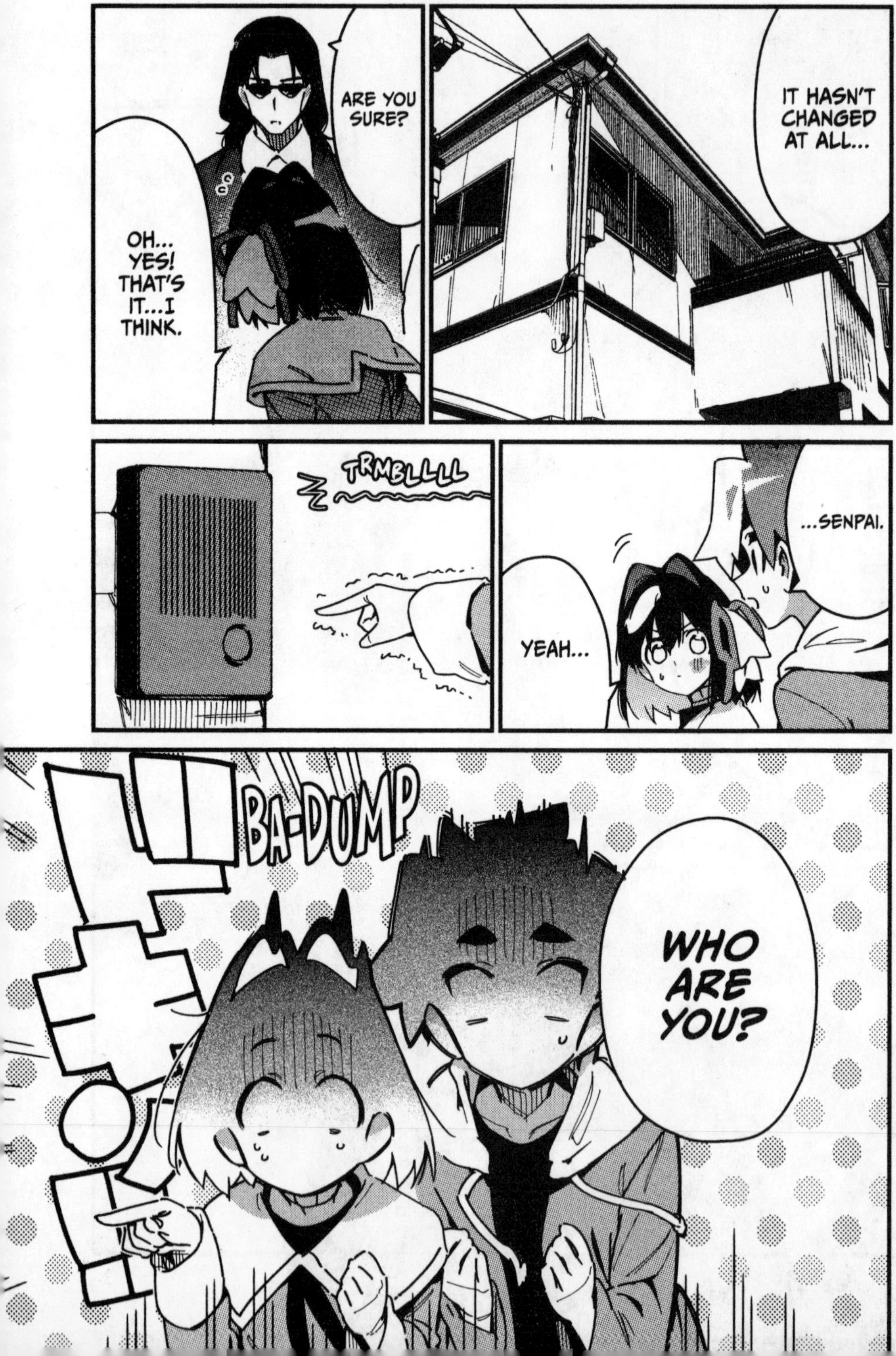
IT HASN'T CHANGED AT ALL...
ARE YOU SURE?
OH... YES! THAT'S IT...I THINK.
...SENPAI.
YEAH...
TRMBLLLL
WHO ARE YOU?
BA-DUMP

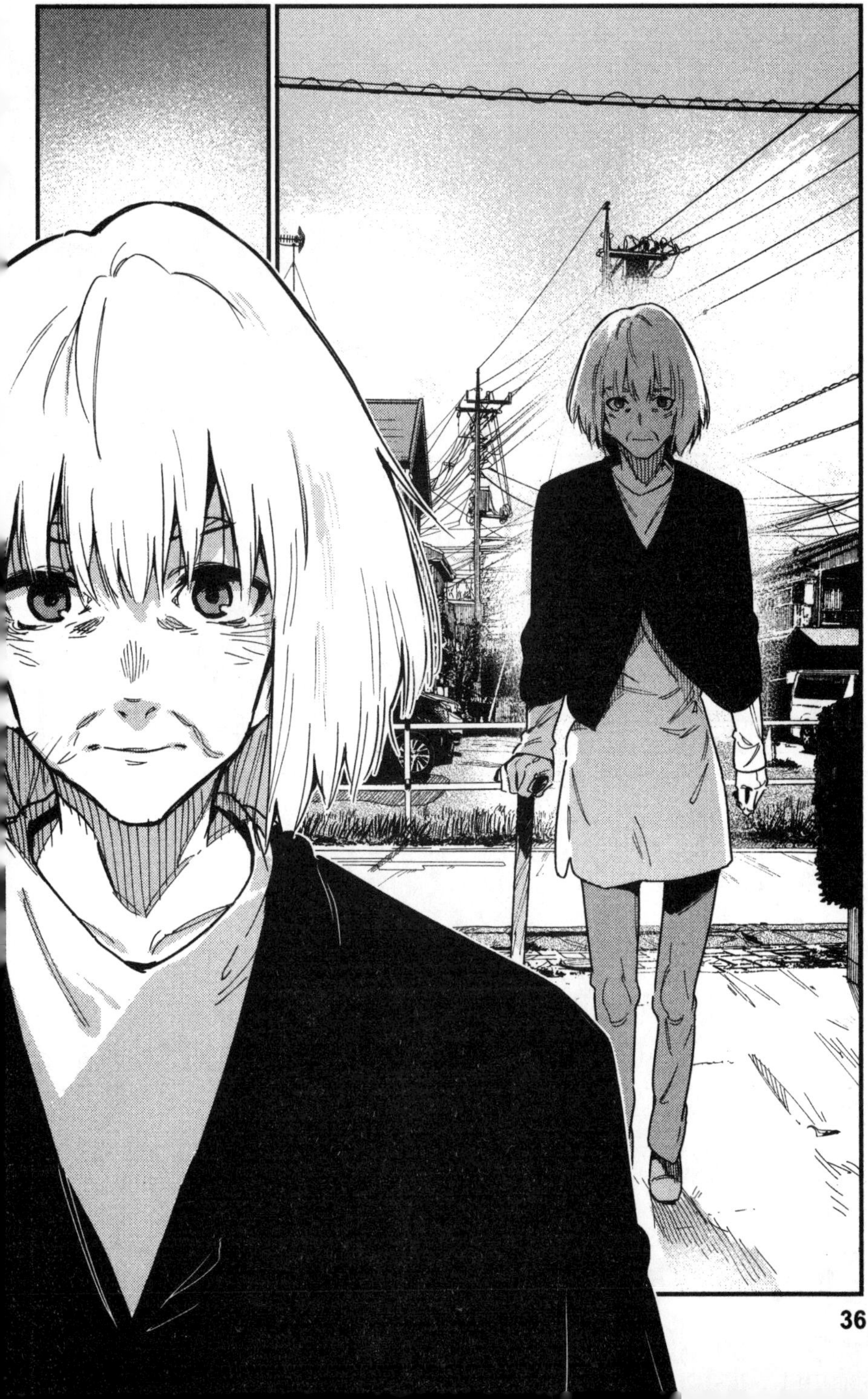

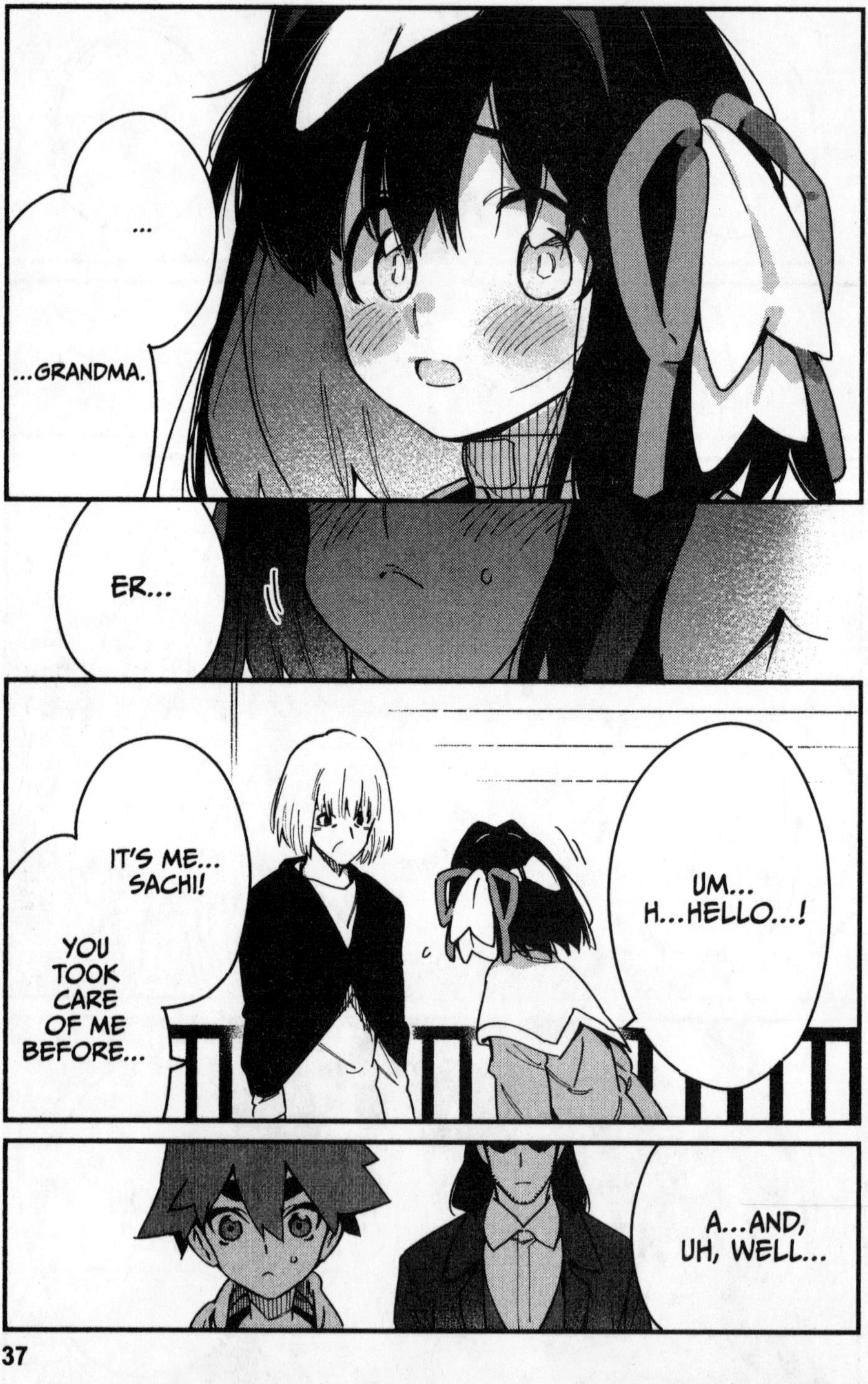
...
...GRANDMA.
ER...
UM... H...HELLO...!
IT'S ME... SACHI!
YOU TOOK CARE OF ME BEFORE...
A...AND, UH, WELL...

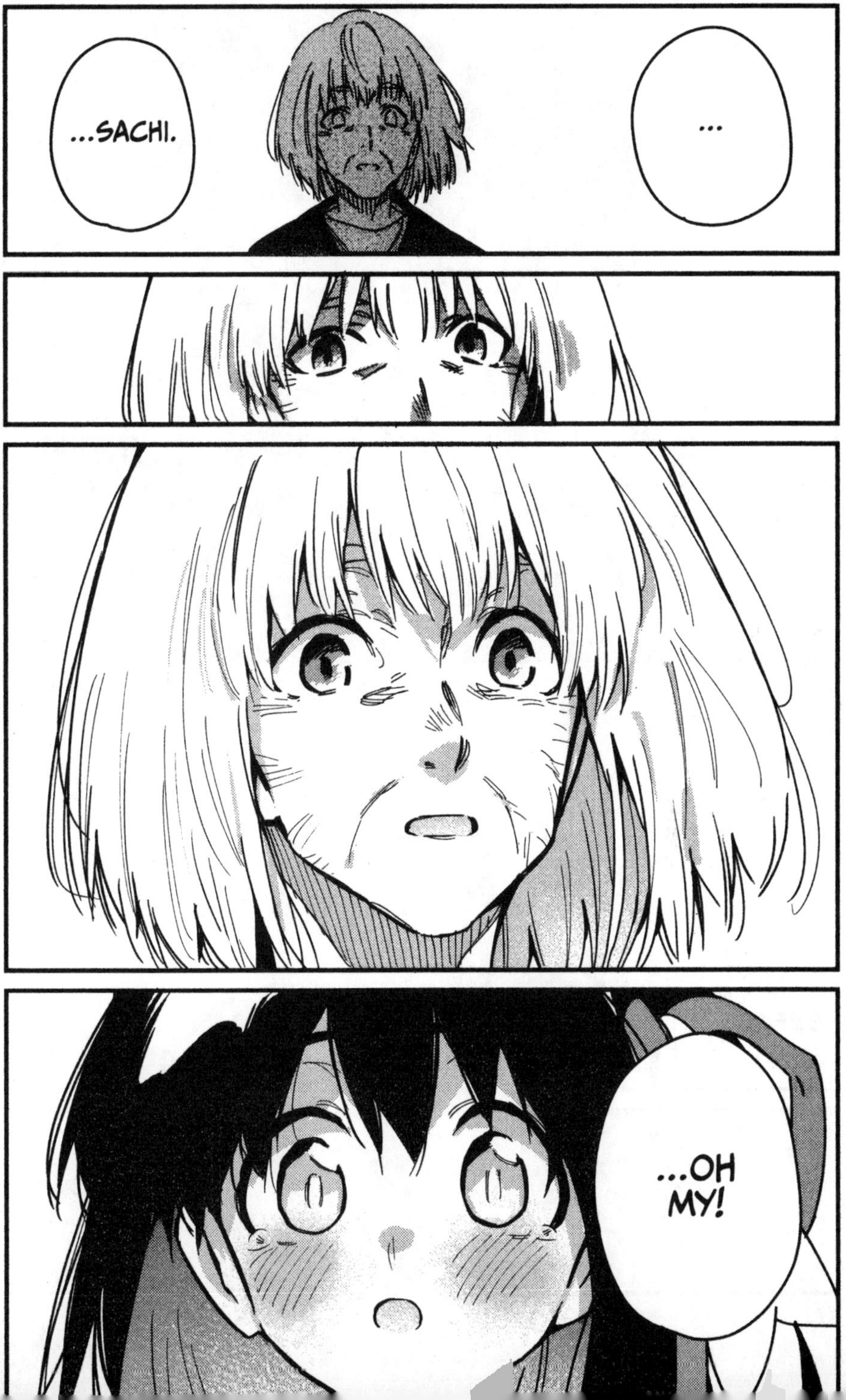
...
...SACHI.
...OH MY!

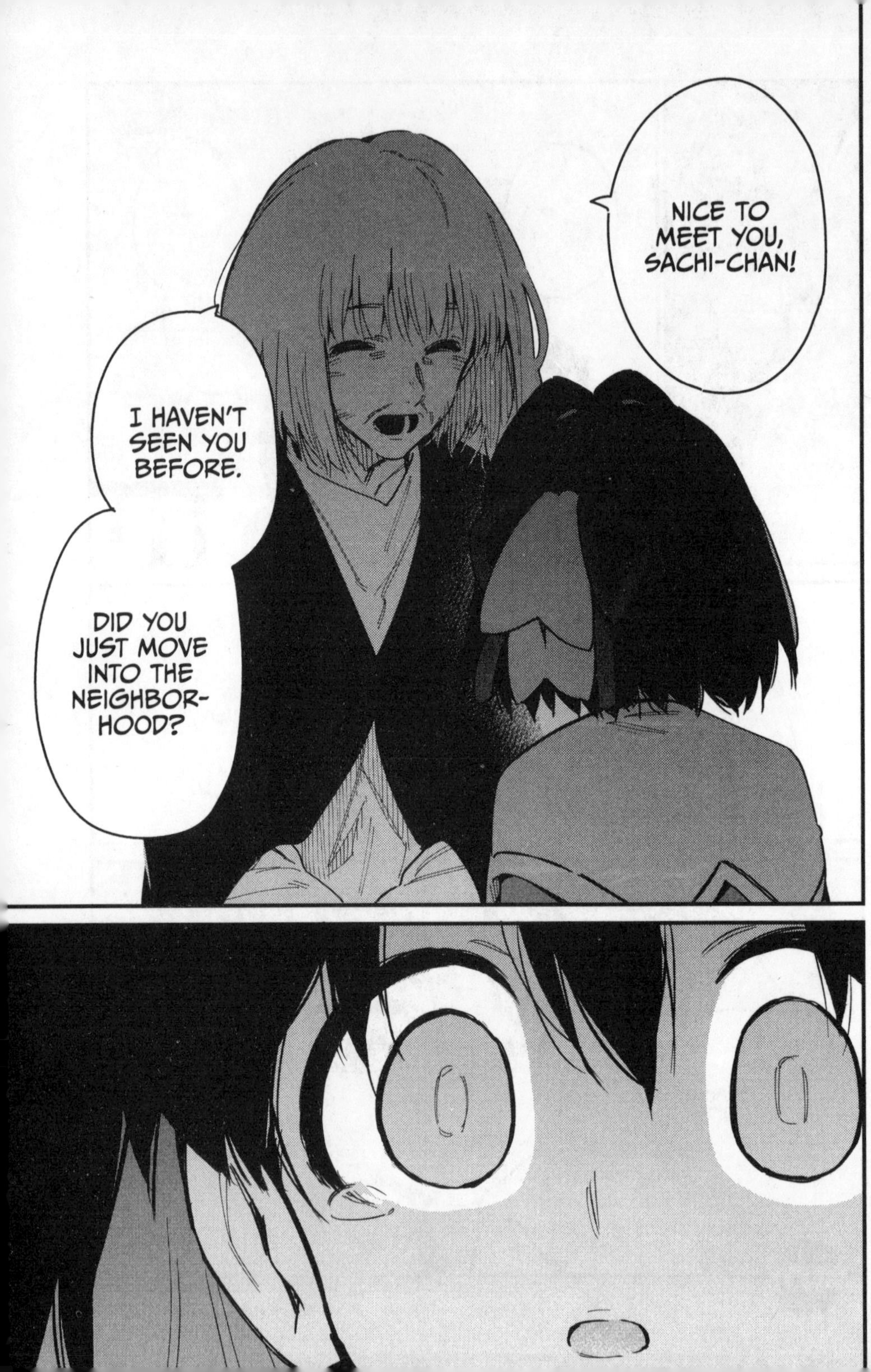
NICE TO MEET YOU, SACHI-CHAN!
I HAVEN'T SEEN YOU BEFORE.
DID YOU JUST MOVE INTO THE NEIGHBOR-HOOD?

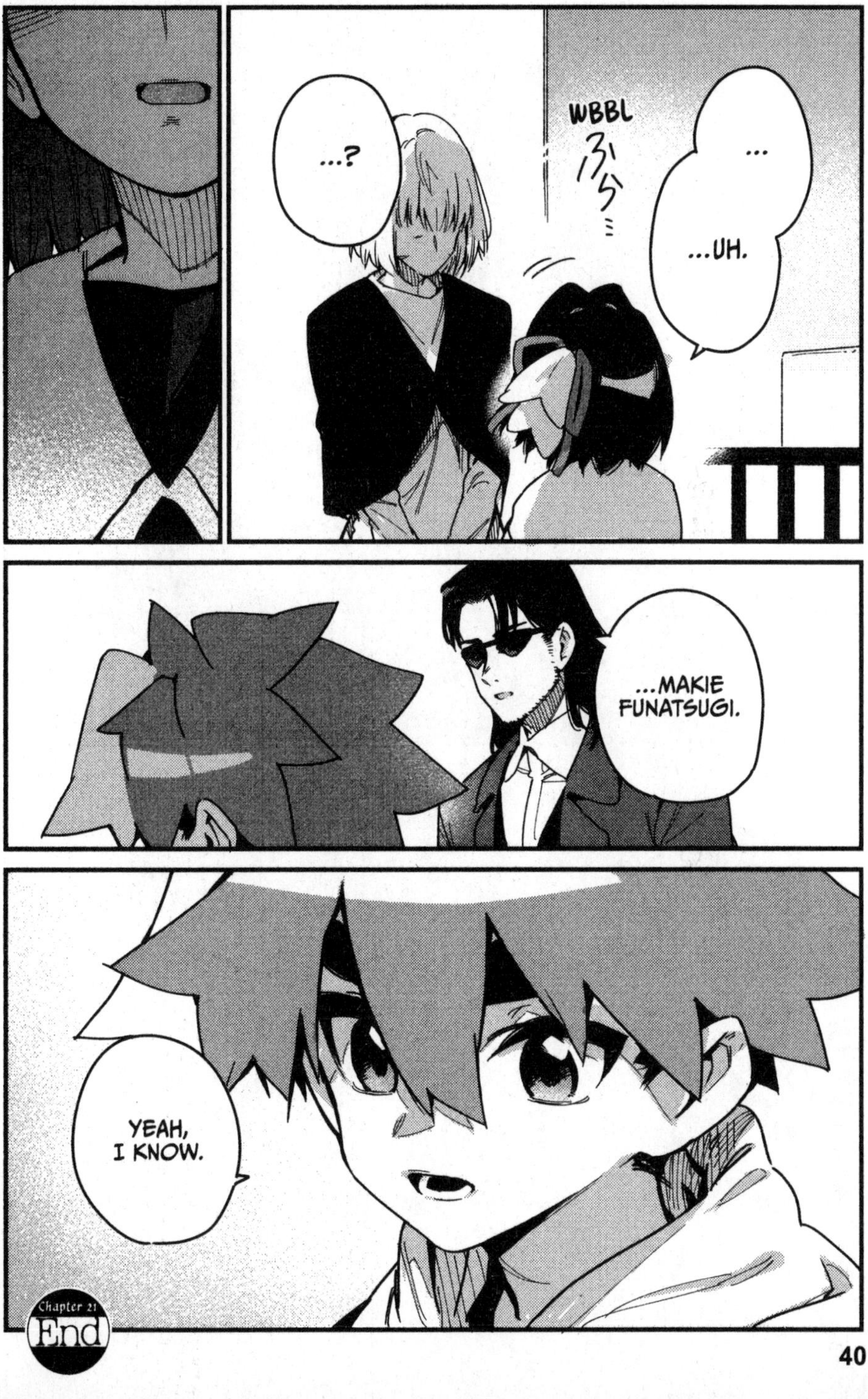
...
...UH.
WBBL
...?
...MAKIE FUNATSUGI.
YEAH, I KNOW.

Chapter 21 End

Sachi's MONSTROUS Appetite

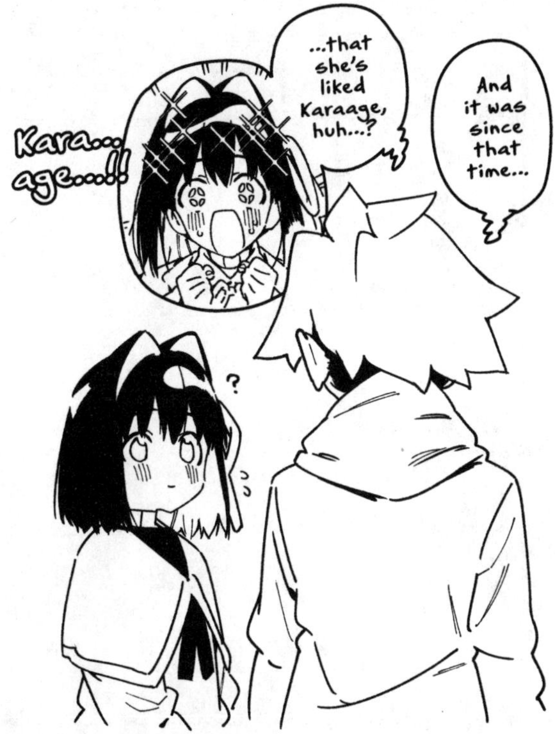
And it was since that time...
...that she's liked Karaage, huh...?
Kara... age...!!
?

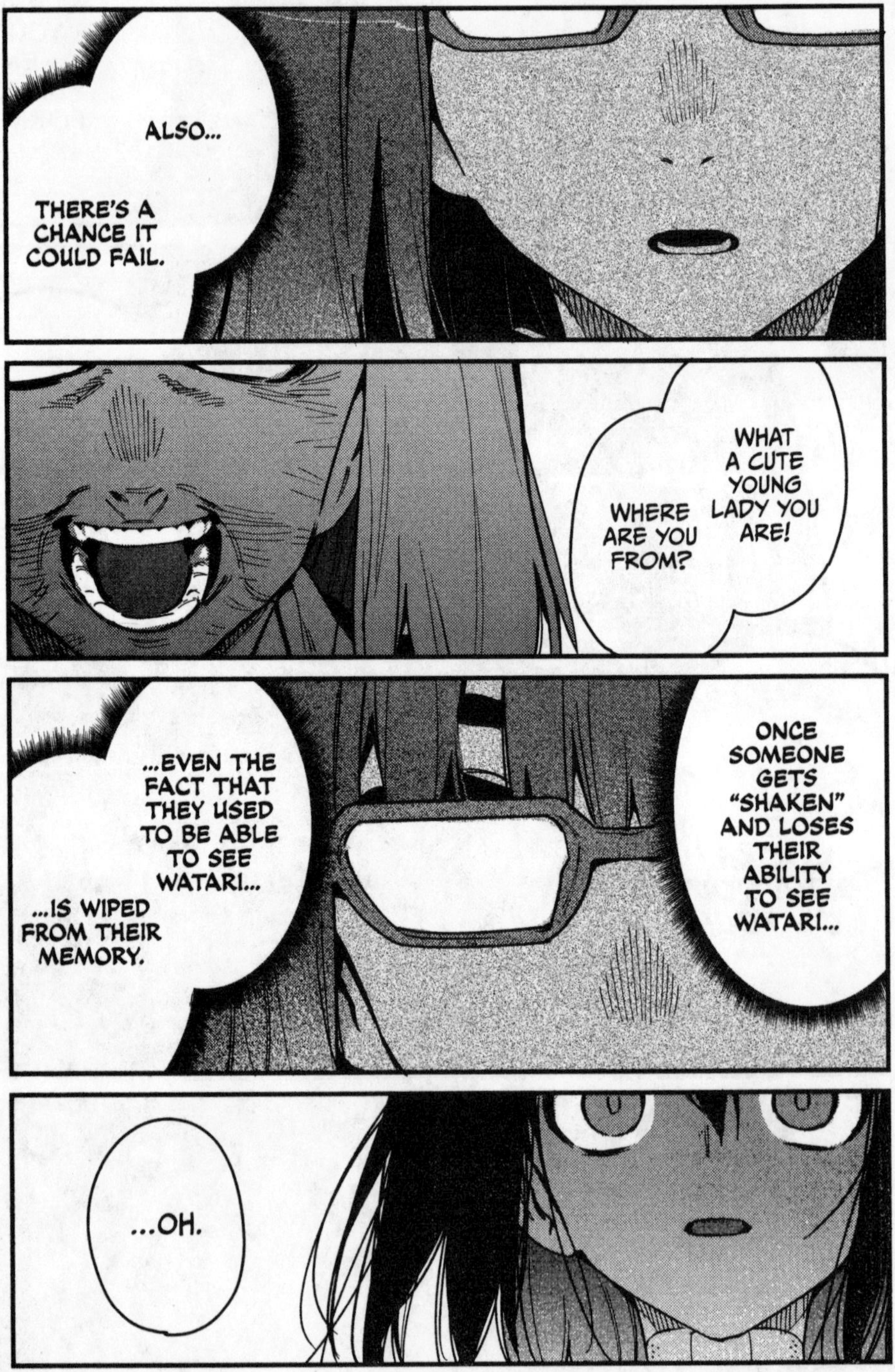
ALSO...
THERE'S A CHANCE IT COULD FAIL.
WHAT A CUTE YOUNG LADY YOU ARE!
WHERE ARE YOU FROM?
ONCE SOMEONE GETS "SHAKEN" AND LOSES THEIR ABILITY TO SEE WATARI...
...EVEN THE FACT THAT THEY USED TO BE ABLE TO SEE WATARI...
...IS WIPED FROM THEIR MEMORY.
...OH.

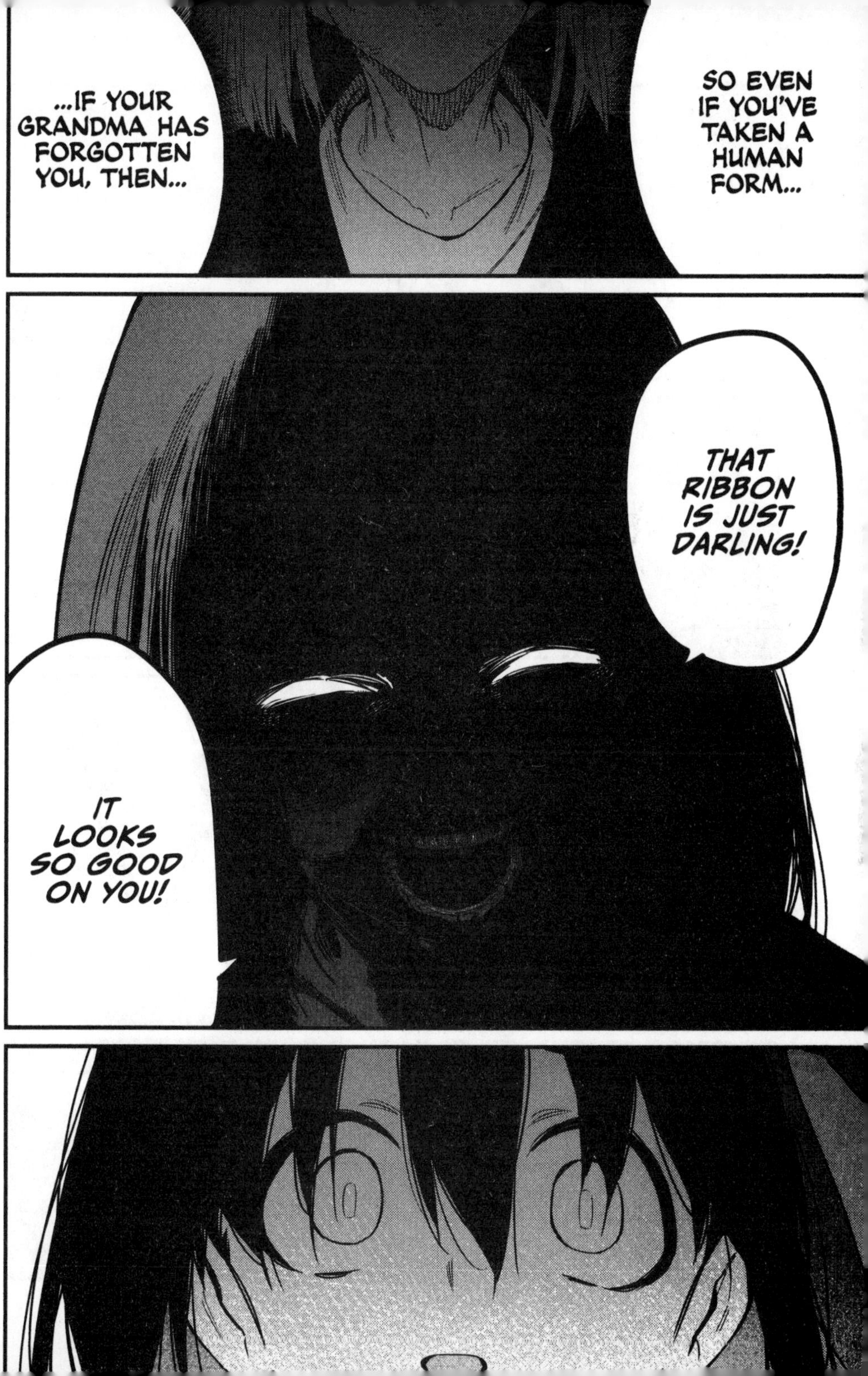
SO EVEN IF YOU'VE TAKEN A HUMAN FORM...
...IF YOUR GRANDMA HAS FORGOTTEN YOU, THEN...
THAT RIBBON IS JUST DARLING!
IT LOOKS SO GOOD ON YOU!

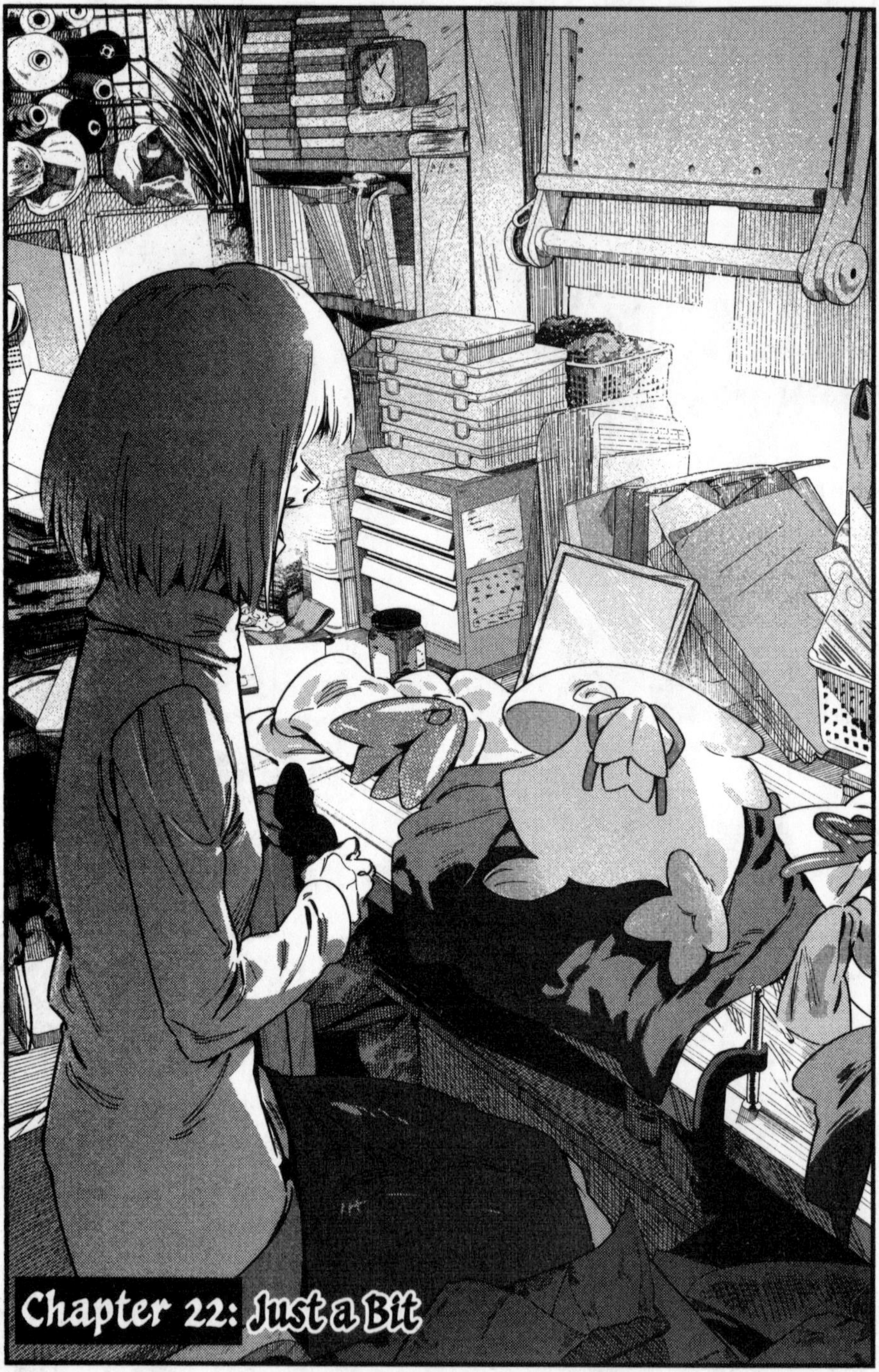
Chapter 22: Just a Bit

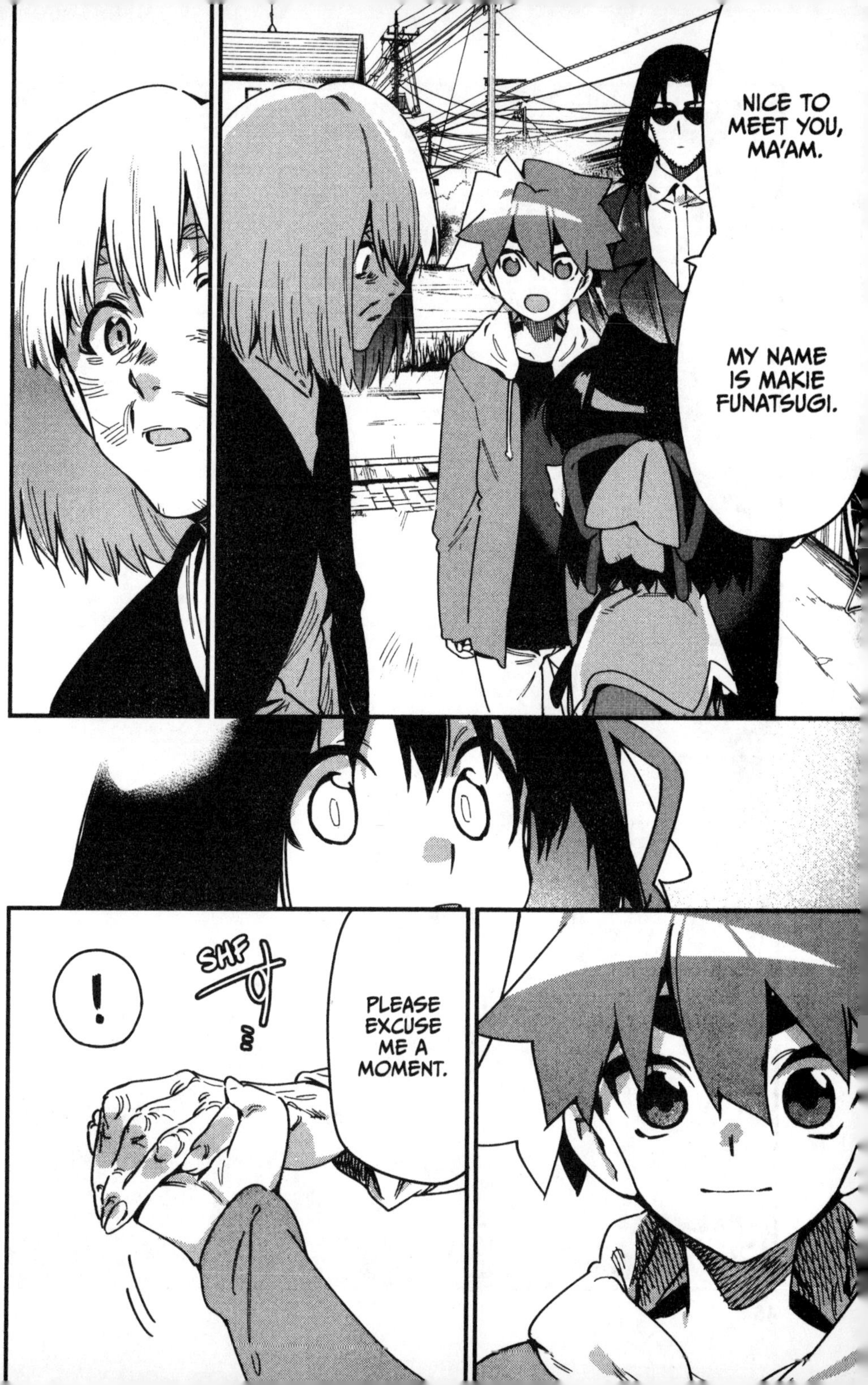
NICE TO MEET YOU, MA'AM.
MY NAME IS MAKIE FUNATSUGI.
PLEASE EXCUSE ME A MOMENT.
SHF
!

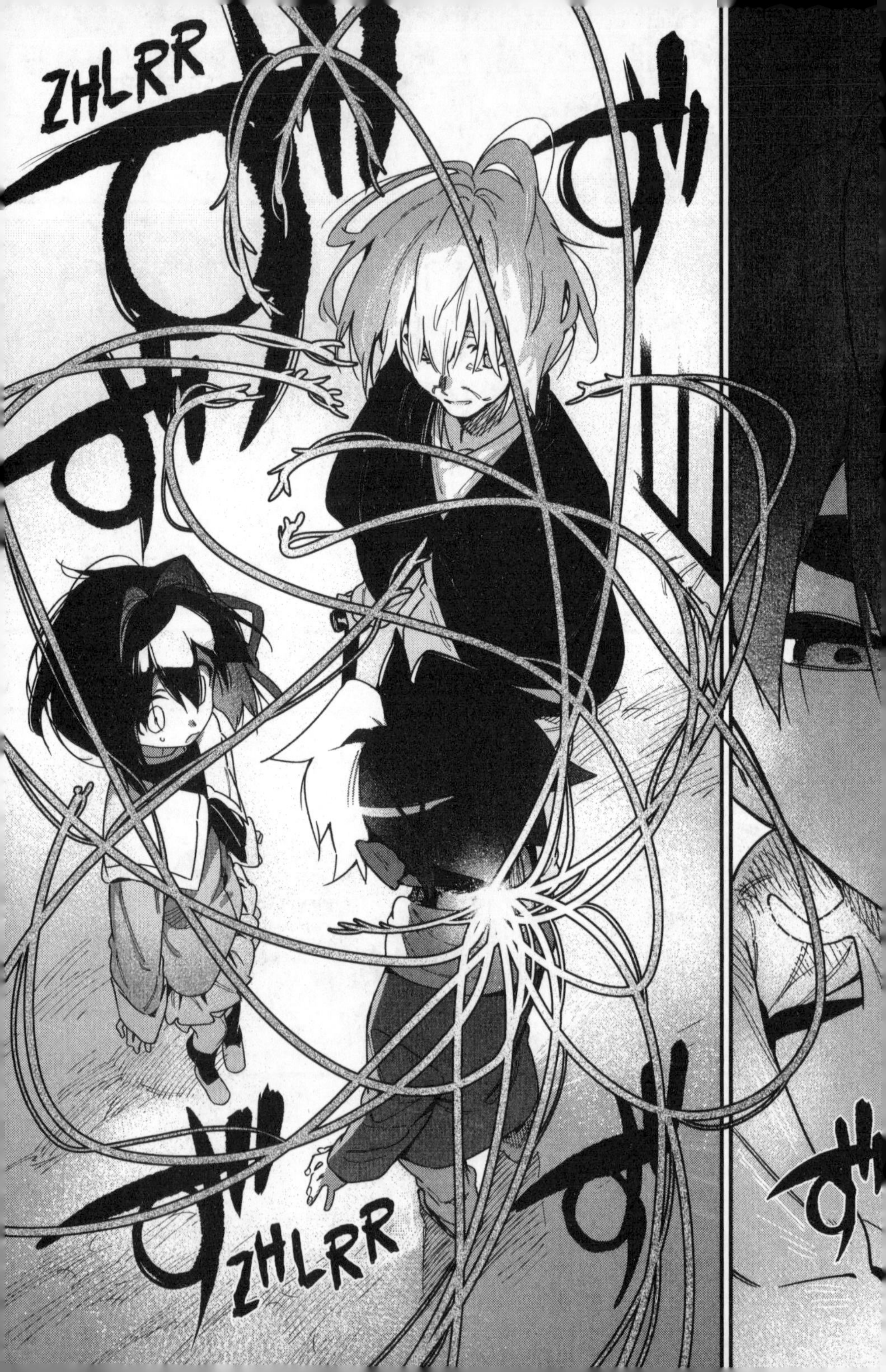
ZHLRR
ZHLRR

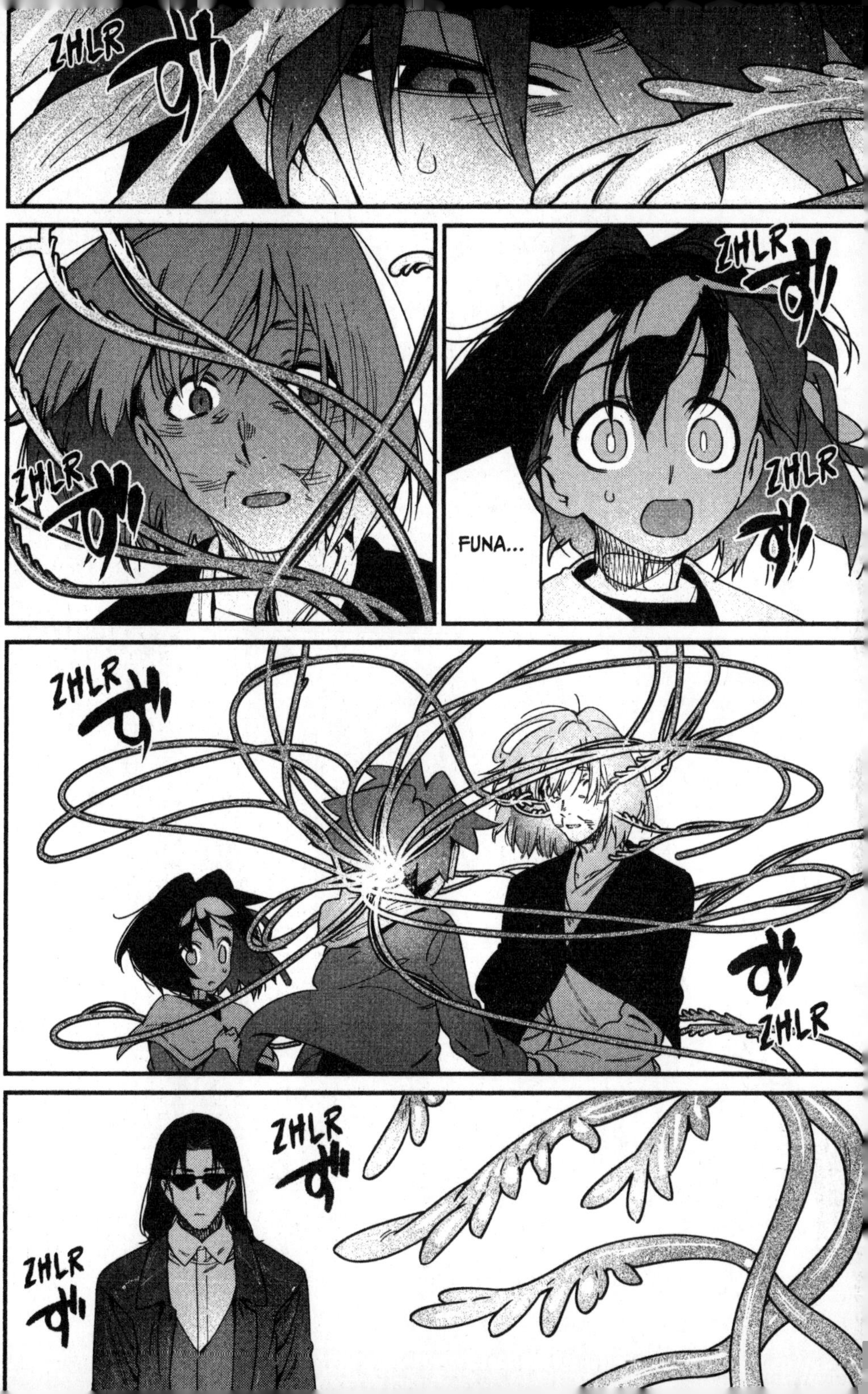
ZHLR
ZHLR
ZHLR
FUNA...
ZHLR
ZHLR
ZHLR
ZHLR
ZHLR

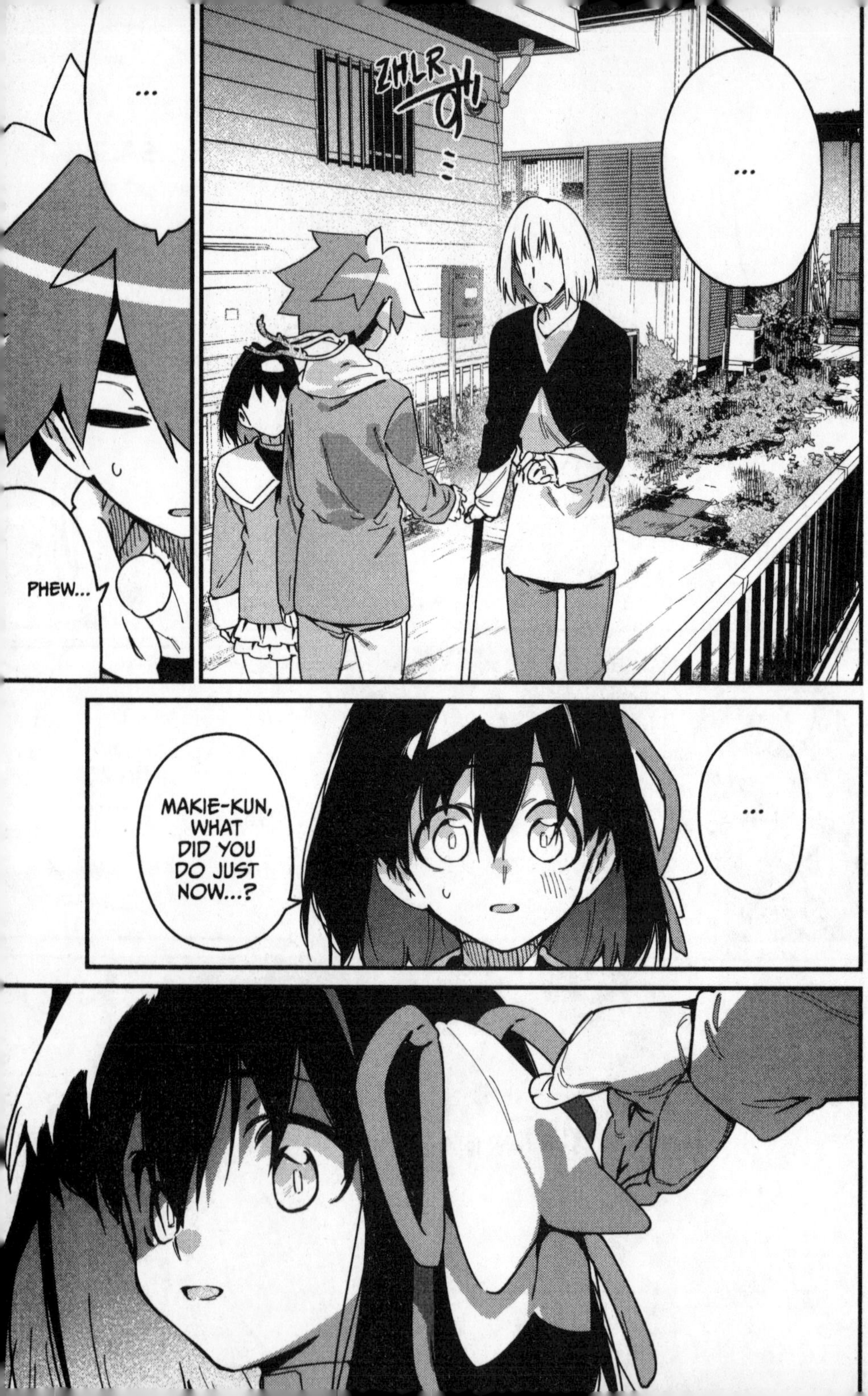
...
ZHLR
...
PHEW...
...
MAKIE-KUN, WHAT DID YOU DO JUST NOW...?

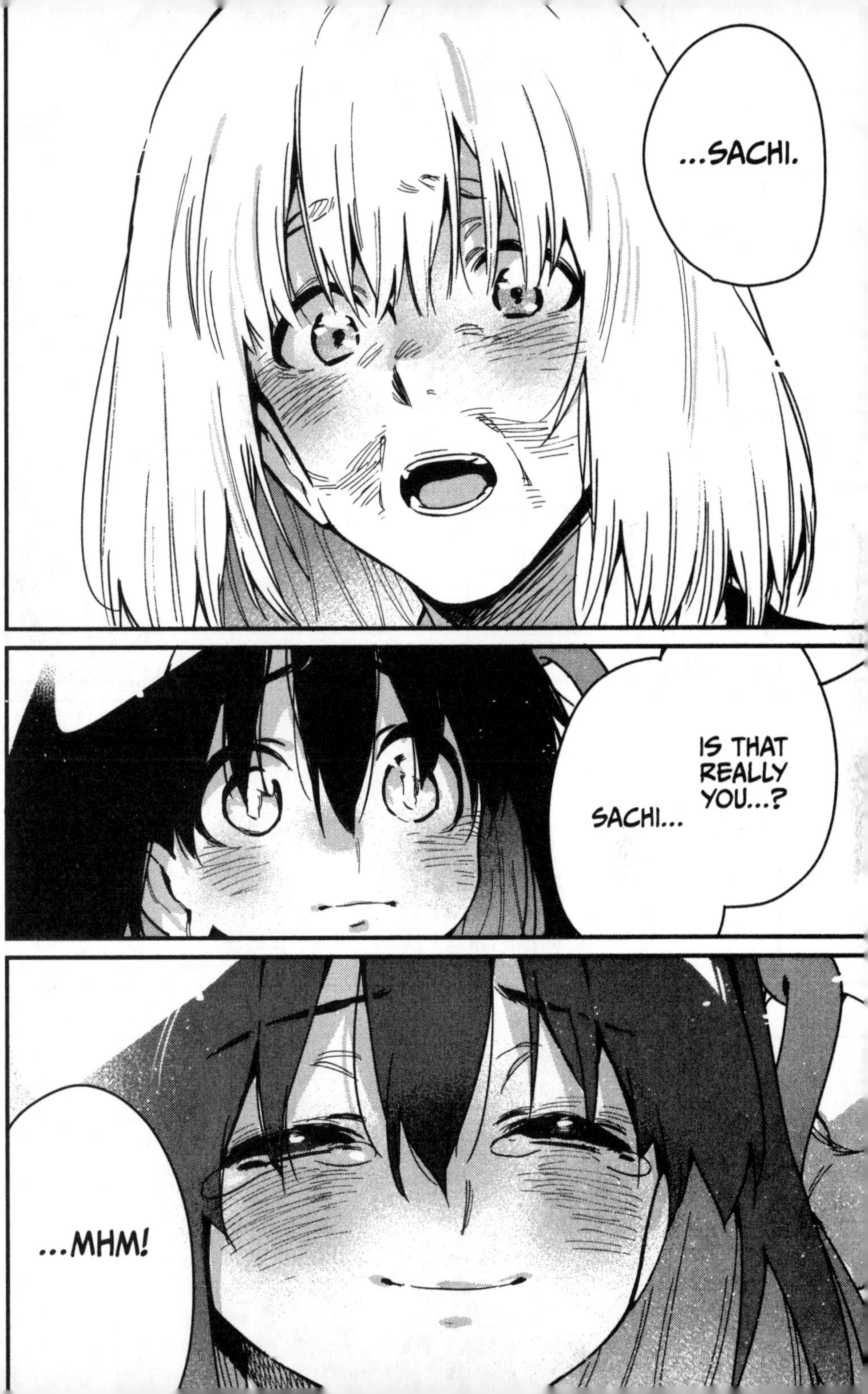
...SACHI.
SACHI... IS THAT REALLY YOU...?
...MHM!

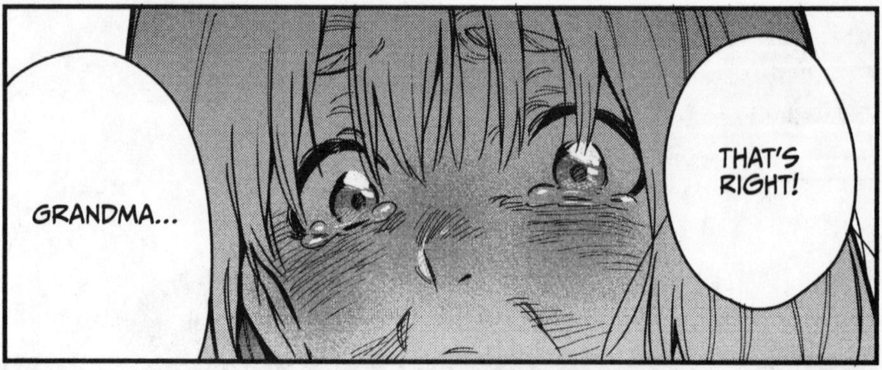
THAT'S RIGHT!
GRANDMA...
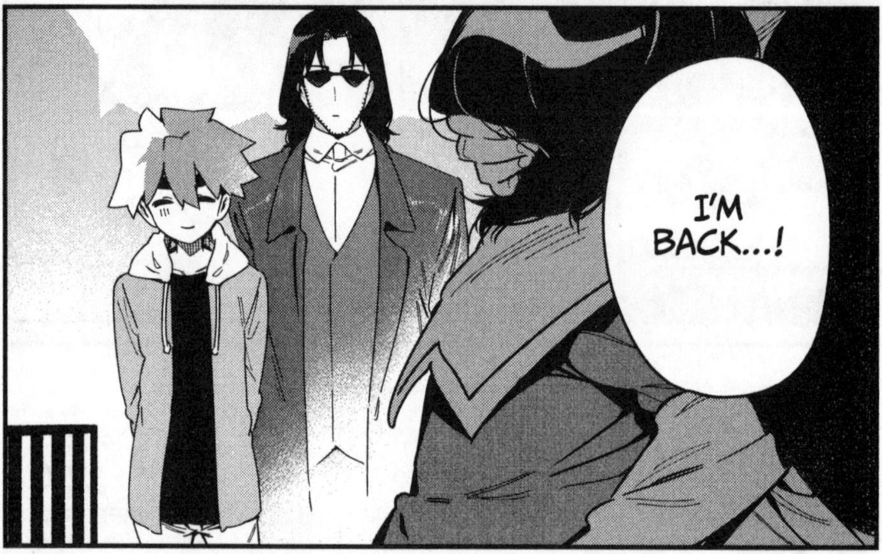
I'M BACK...!
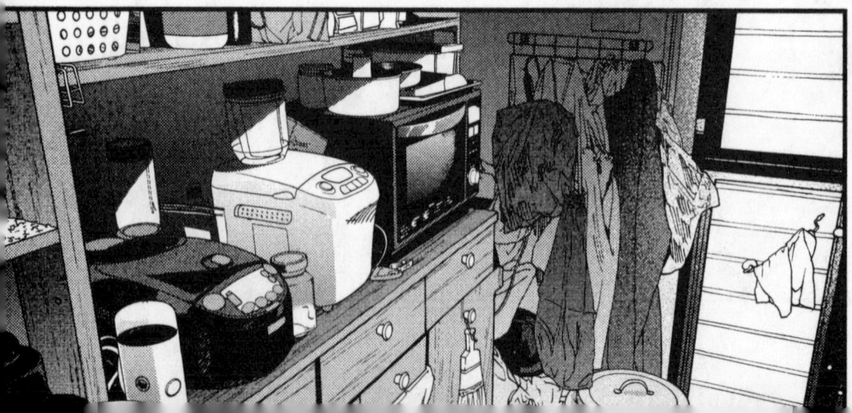

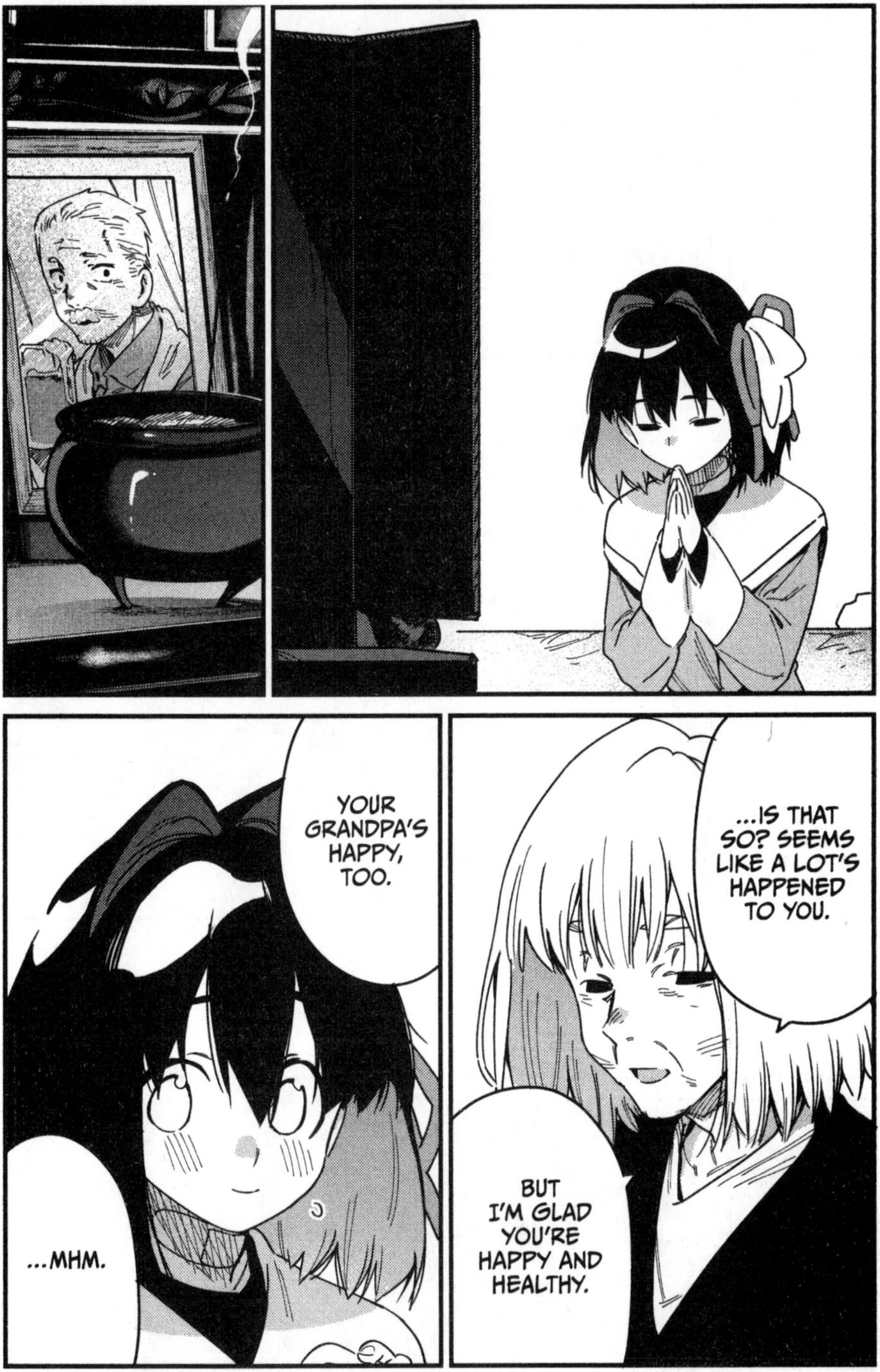
...IS THAT SO? SEEMS LIKE A LOT'S HAPPENED TO YOU.
BUT I'M GLAD YOU'RE HAPPY AND HEALTHY.
YOUR GRANDPA'S HAPPY, TOO.
...MHM.

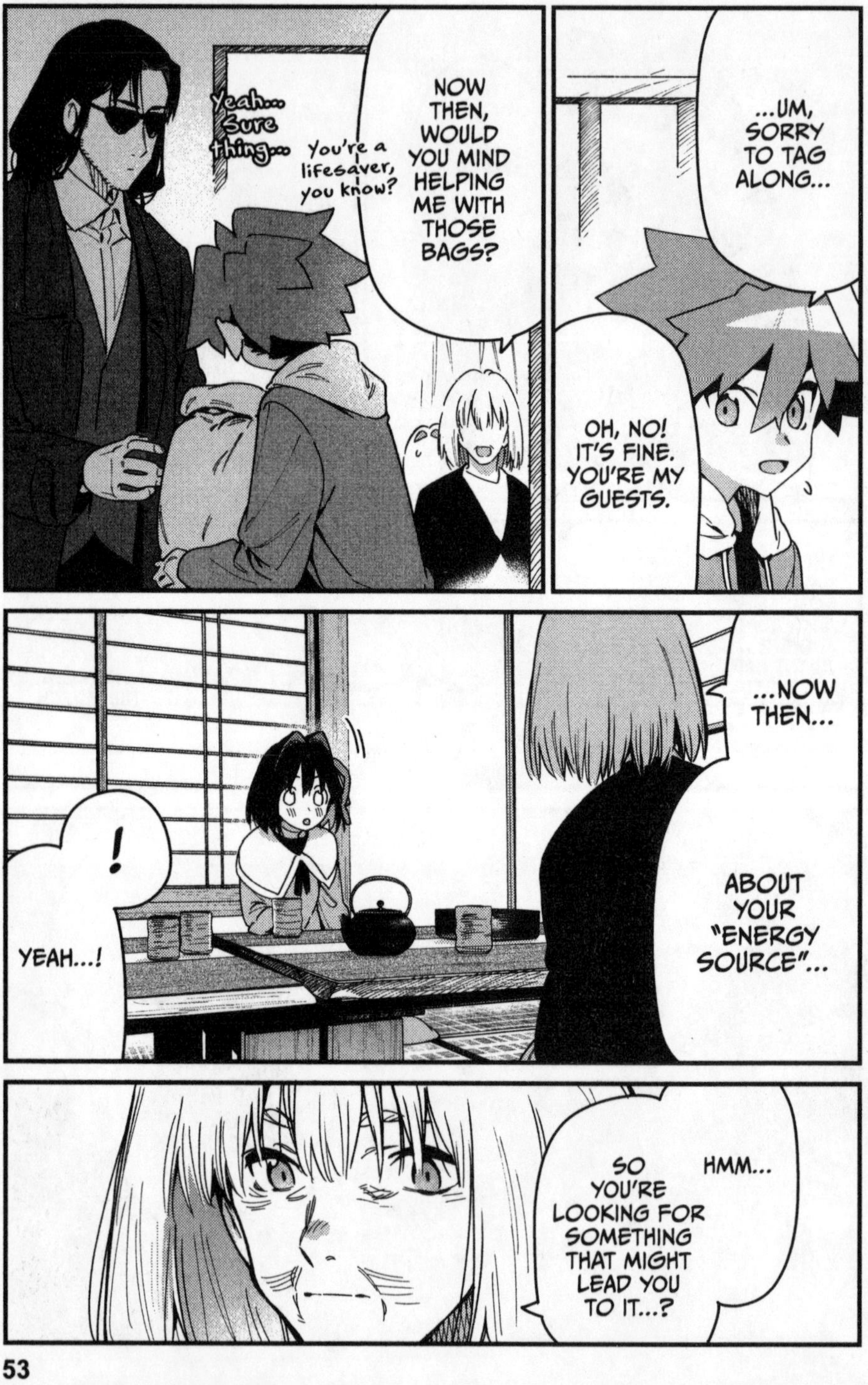
...UM, SORRY TO TAG ALONG...
OH, NO! IT'S FINE. YOU'RE MY GUESTS.
NOW THEN, WOULD YOU MIND HELPING ME WITH THOSE BAGS?
You're a lifesaver, you know?
Yeah... Sure thing...
...NOW THEN...
ABOUT YOUR "ENERGY SOURCE"...
!
YEAH...!
HMM...
SO YOU'RE LOOKING FOR SOMETHING THAT MIGHT LEAD YOU TO IT...?

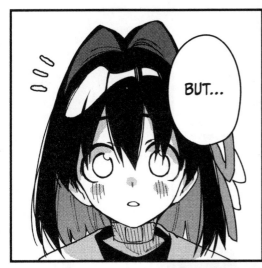

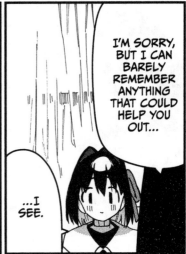

I'M SORRY, BUT I CAN BARELY REMEMBER ANYTHING THAT COULD HELP YOU OUT...
...I SEE.
BUT...
WHEN YOUR GRANDPA PICKED YOU UP FROM THE BEACH,
HE TOLD ME THAT...
HE WENT BACK TO THE BEACH IMMEDIATELY AFTER HE BROUGHT YOU HOME.
THERE MAY HAVE BEEN SOMETHING LIKE THAT THERE, BUT IT HAD COMPLETELY VANISHED BY THE TIME HE RETURNED.
INSTEAD...
ALL HE FOUND WAS EVIDENCE THAT SOMETHING HUMONGOUS HAD BEEN DRAGGED OFF SOMEWHERE.

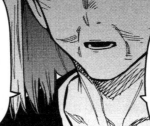

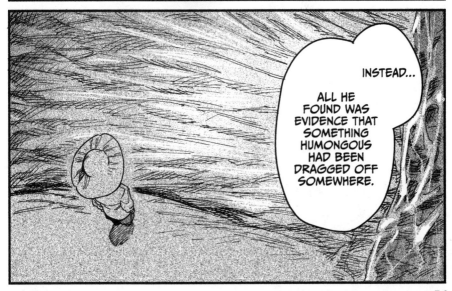

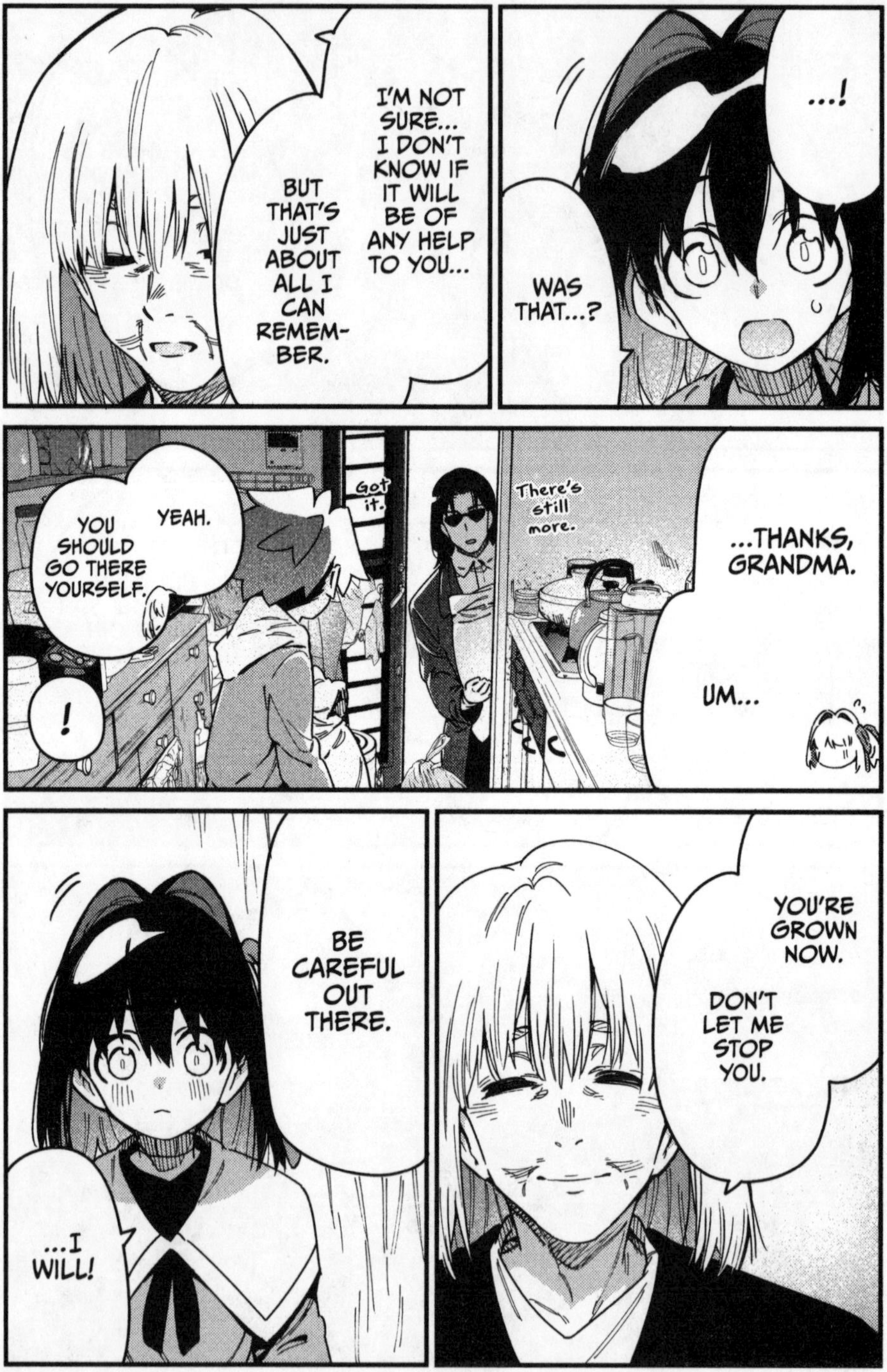
...!
WAS THAT...?
I'M NOT SURE... I DON'T KNOW IF IT WILL BE OF ANY HELP TO YOU...
BUT THAT'S JUST ABOUT ALL I CAN REMEMBER.
...THANKS, GRANDMA.
UM...
There's still more.
Got it.
YEAH.
YOU SHOULD GO THERE YOURSELF.
!
YOU'RE GROWN NOW.
DON'T LET ME STOP YOU.
BE CAREFUL OUT THERE.
...I WILL!

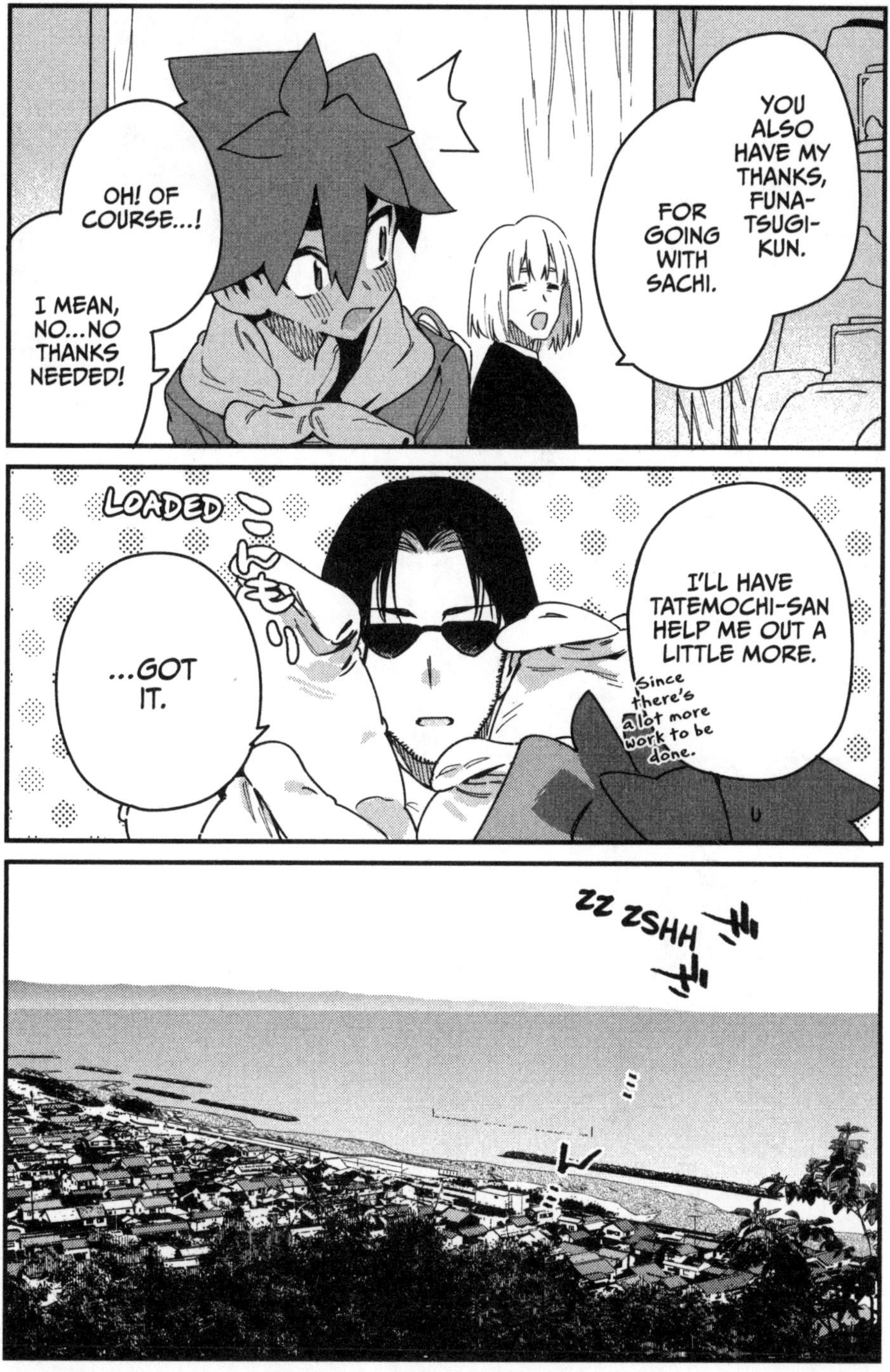
YOU ALSO HAVE MY THANKS, FUNA-TSUGI-KUN.
FOR GOING WITH SACHI.
OH! OF COURSE...!
I MEAN, NO...NO THANKS NEEDED!
I'LL HAVE TATEMOCHI-SAN HELP ME OUT A LITTLE MORE.
Since there's a lot more work to be done.
LOADED
...GOT IT.
HHSZ ZZ

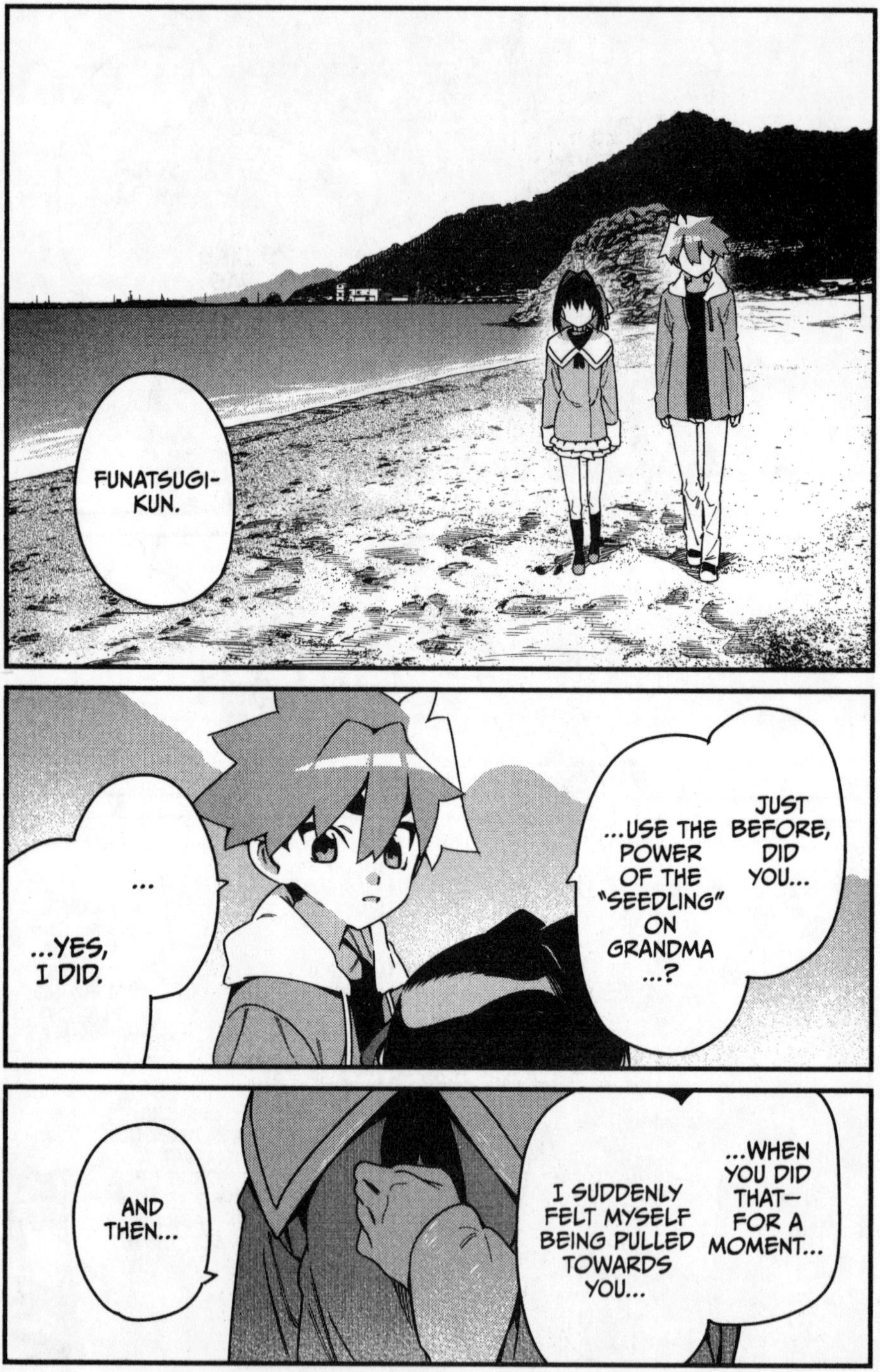
FUNATSUGI-KUN.
JUST BEFORE, DID YOU...
...USE THE POWER OF THE "SEEDLING" ON GRANDMA ...?
...
...YES, I DID.
...WHEN YOU DID THAT— FOR A MOMENT...
I SUDDENLY FELT MYSELF BEING PULLED TOWARDS YOU...
AND THEN...

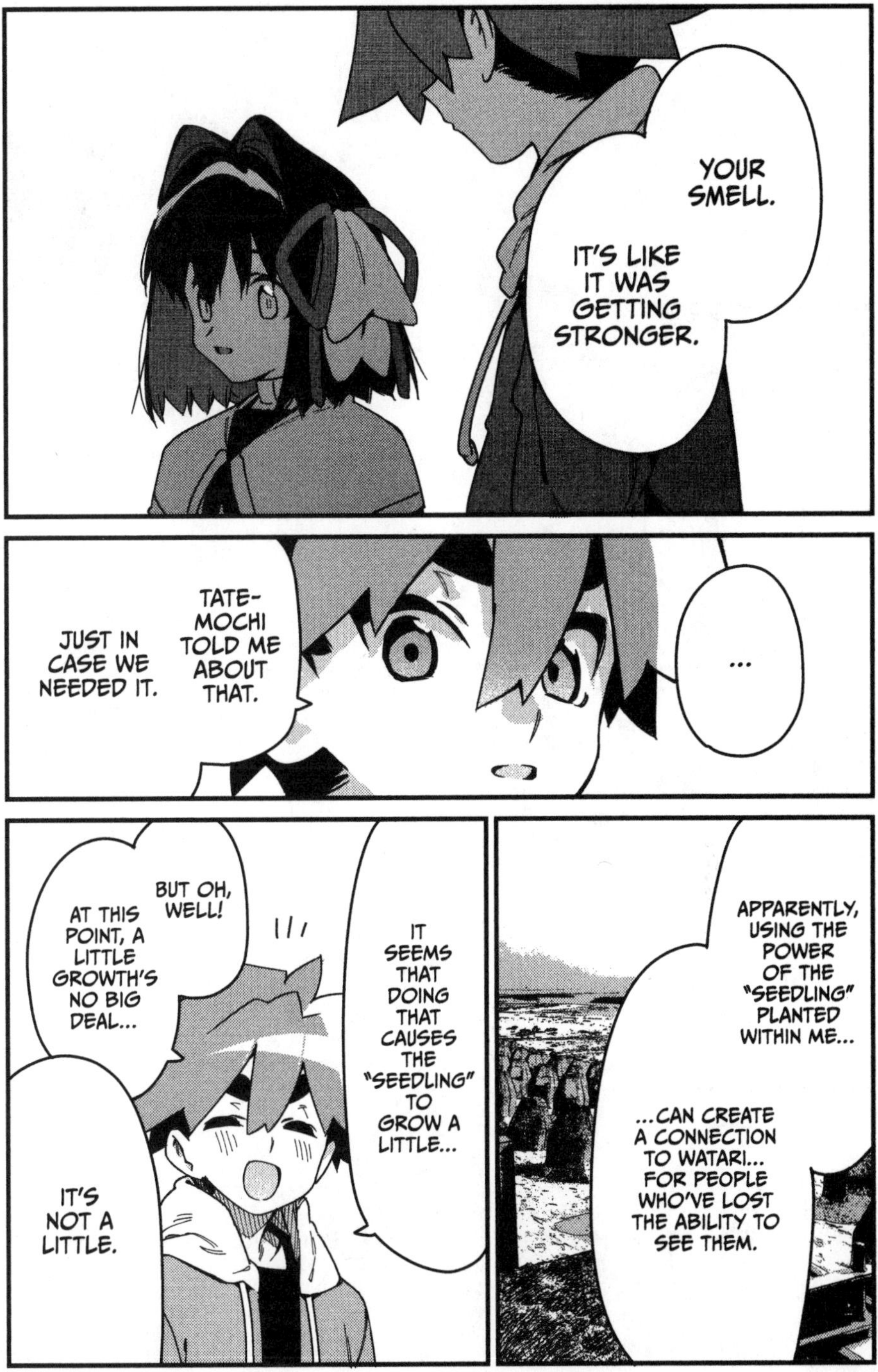
YOUR SMELL.
IT'S LIKE IT WAS GETTING STRONGER.
...
TATE-MOCHI TOLD ME ABOUT THAT.
JUST IN CASE WE NEEDED IT.
APPARENTLY, USING THE POWER OF THE "SEEDLING" PLANTED WITHIN ME...
...CAN CREATE A CONNECTION TO WATARI... FOR PEOPLE WHO'VE LOST THE ABILITY TO SEE THEM.
IT SEEMS THAT DOING THAT CAUSES THE "SEEDLING" TO GROW A LITTLE...
BUT OH, WELL!
AT THIS POINT, A LITTLE GROWTH'S NO BIG DEAL...
IT'S NOT A LITTLE.

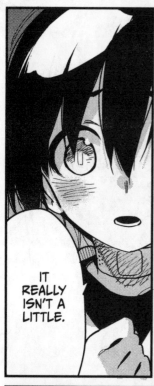

IT REALLY ISN'T A LITTLE.

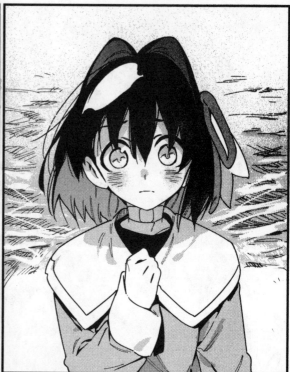

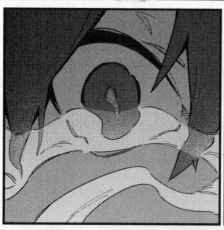

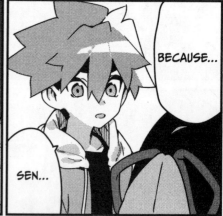

BECAUSE...

SEN...

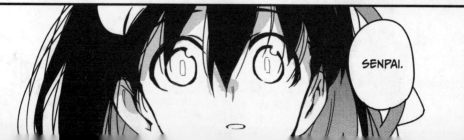

SENPAI.

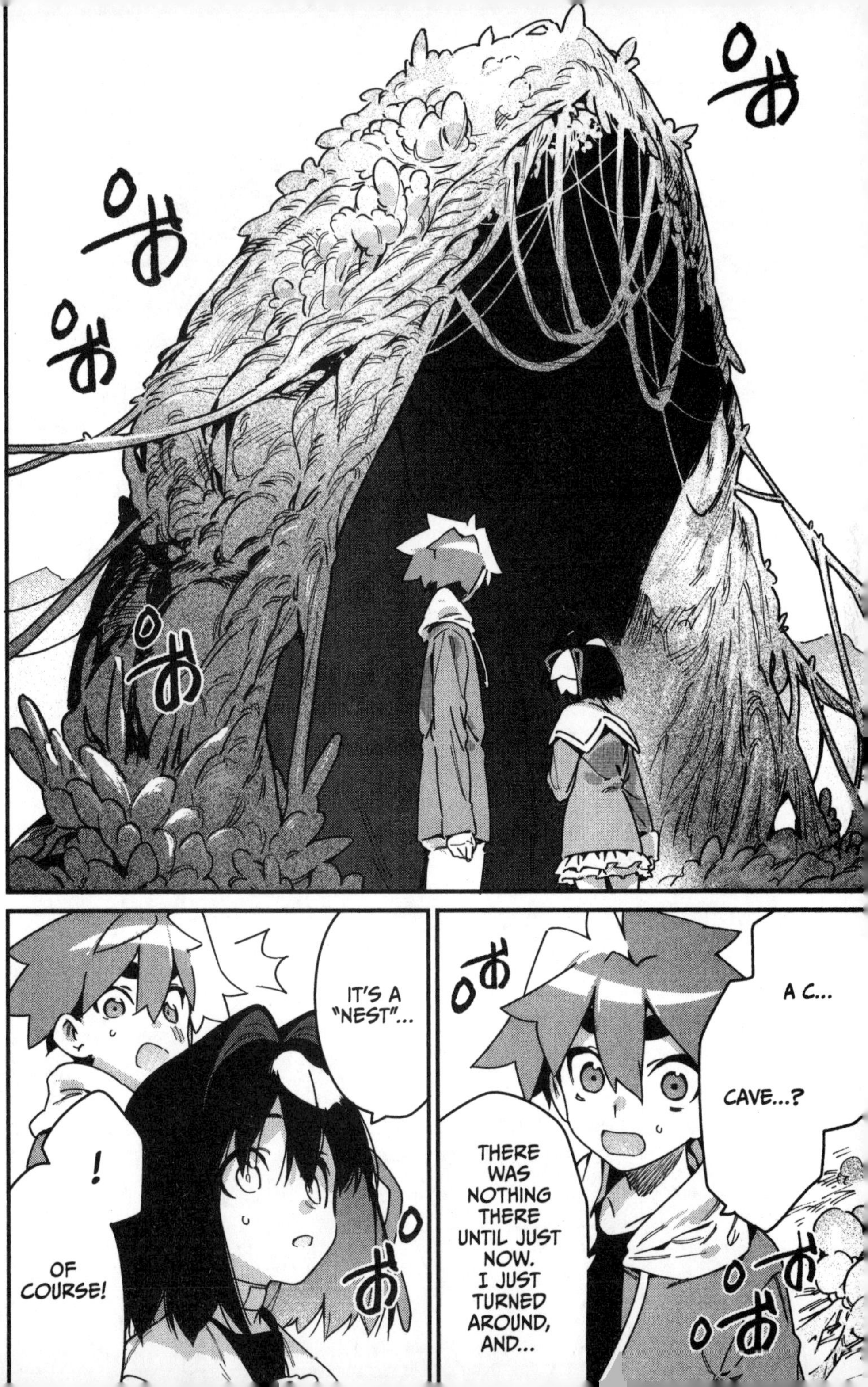
お
お
お
お
お
A C...
CAVE...?
THERE WAS NOTHING THERE UNTIL JUST NOW. I JUST TURNED AROUND, AND...
お
お
IT'S A "NEST"...
!
OF COURSE!
お

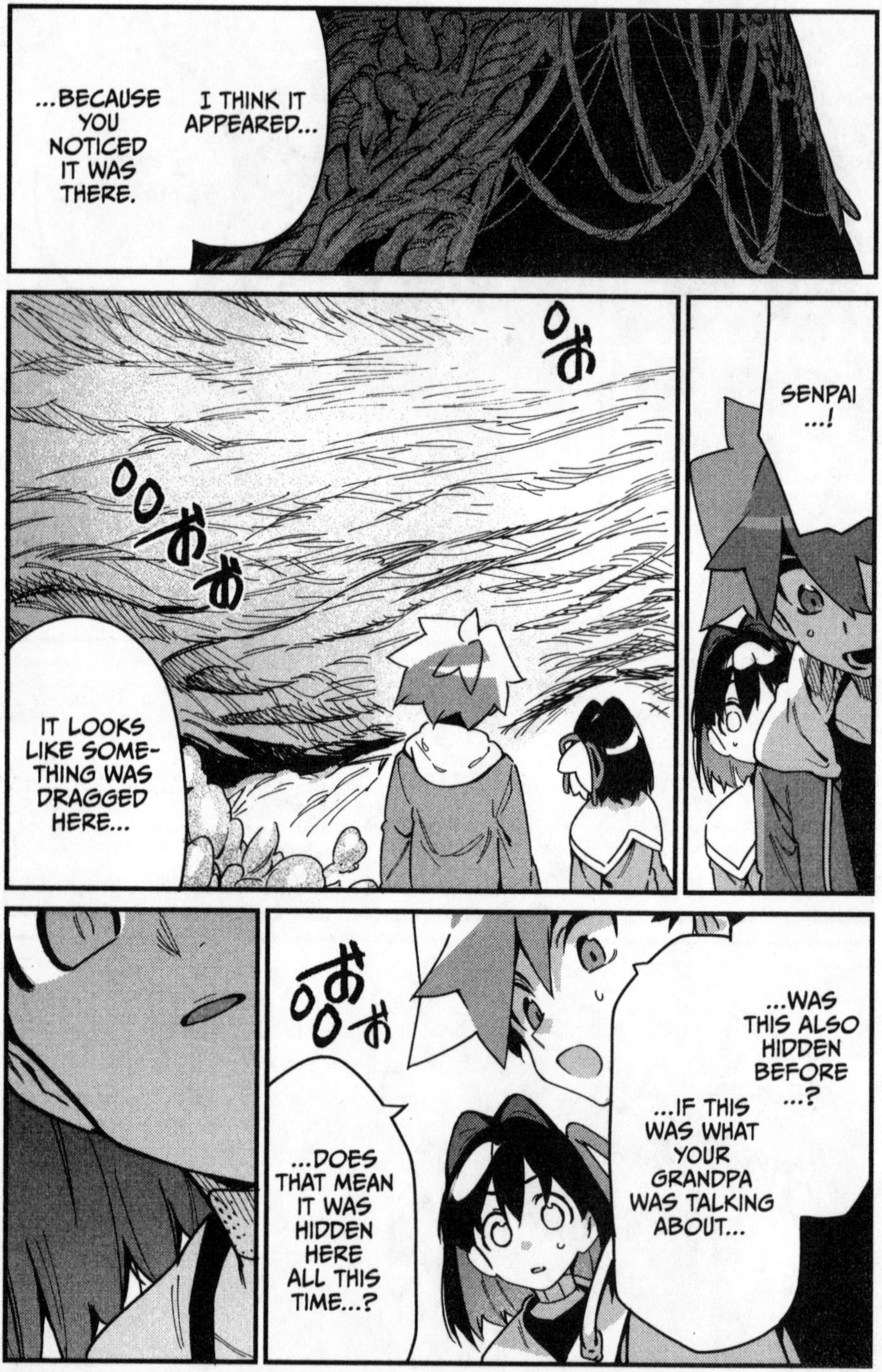
I THINK IT APPEARED...
...BECAUSE YOU NOTICED IT WAS THERE.
SENPAI ...!
oお
ooおぉ
IT LOOKS LIKE SOME-THING WAS DRAGGED HERE...
...WAS THIS ALSO HIDDEN BEFORE ...?
...IF THIS WAS WHAT YOUR GRANDPA WAS TALKING ABOUT...
oおぉ
...DOES THAT MEAN IT WAS HIDDEN HERE ALL THIS TIME...?

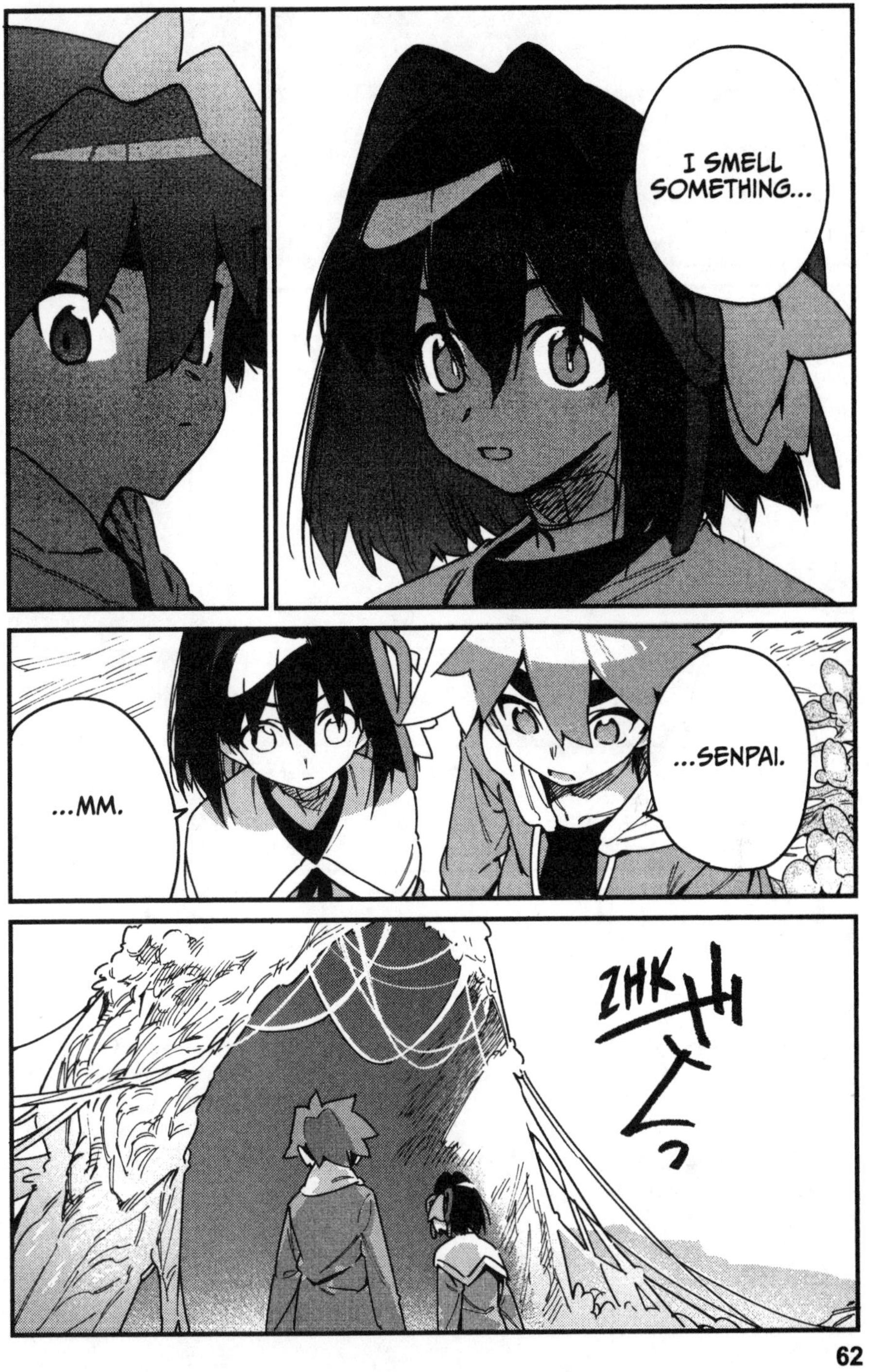
I SMELL SOMETHING...
...SENPAI.
...MM.
ZHK
ざくっ

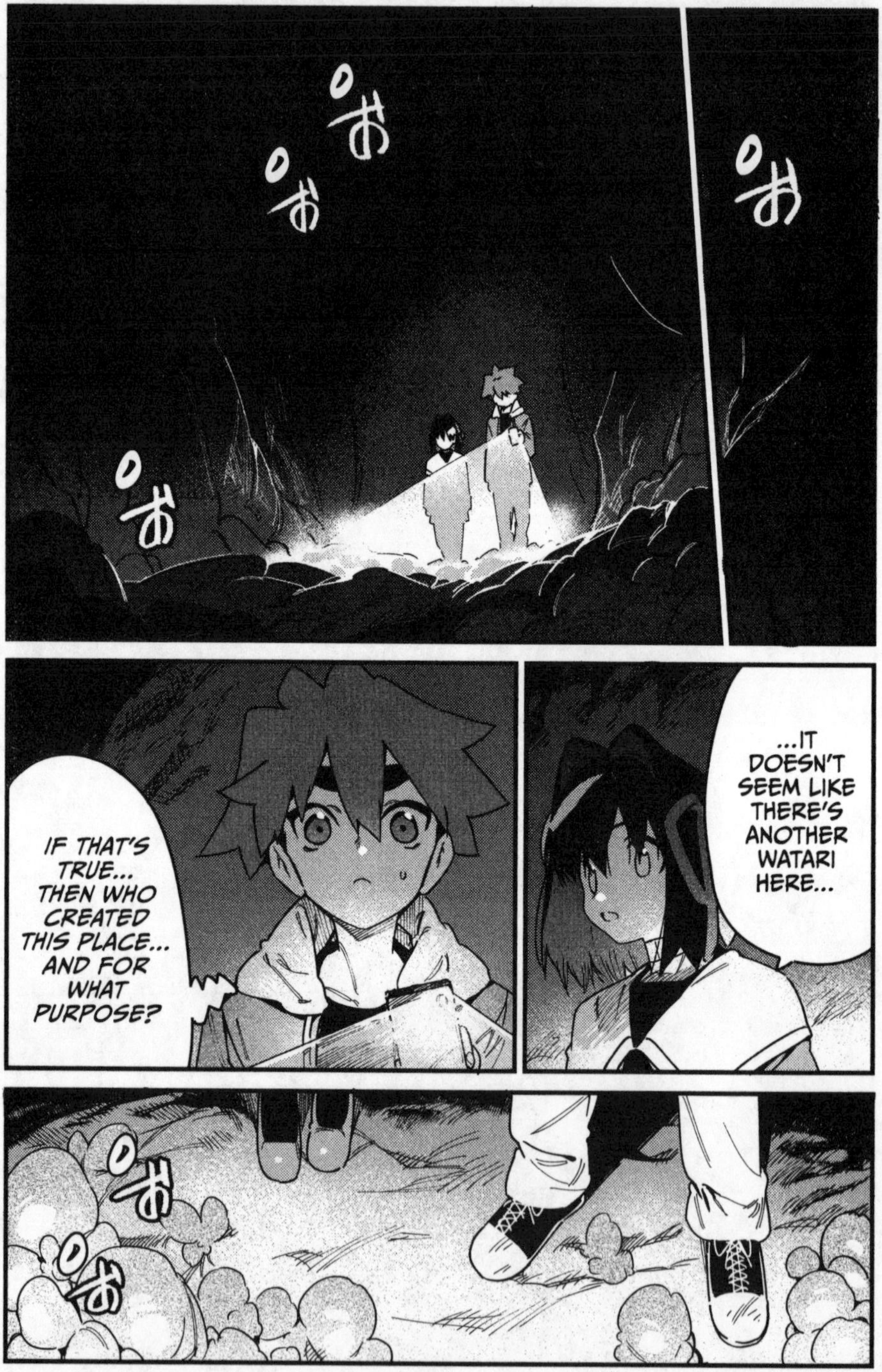
...IT DOESN'T SEEM LIKE THERE'S ANOTHER WATARI HERE...
IF THAT'S TRUE... THEN WHO CREATED THIS PLACE... AND FOR WHAT PURPOSE?

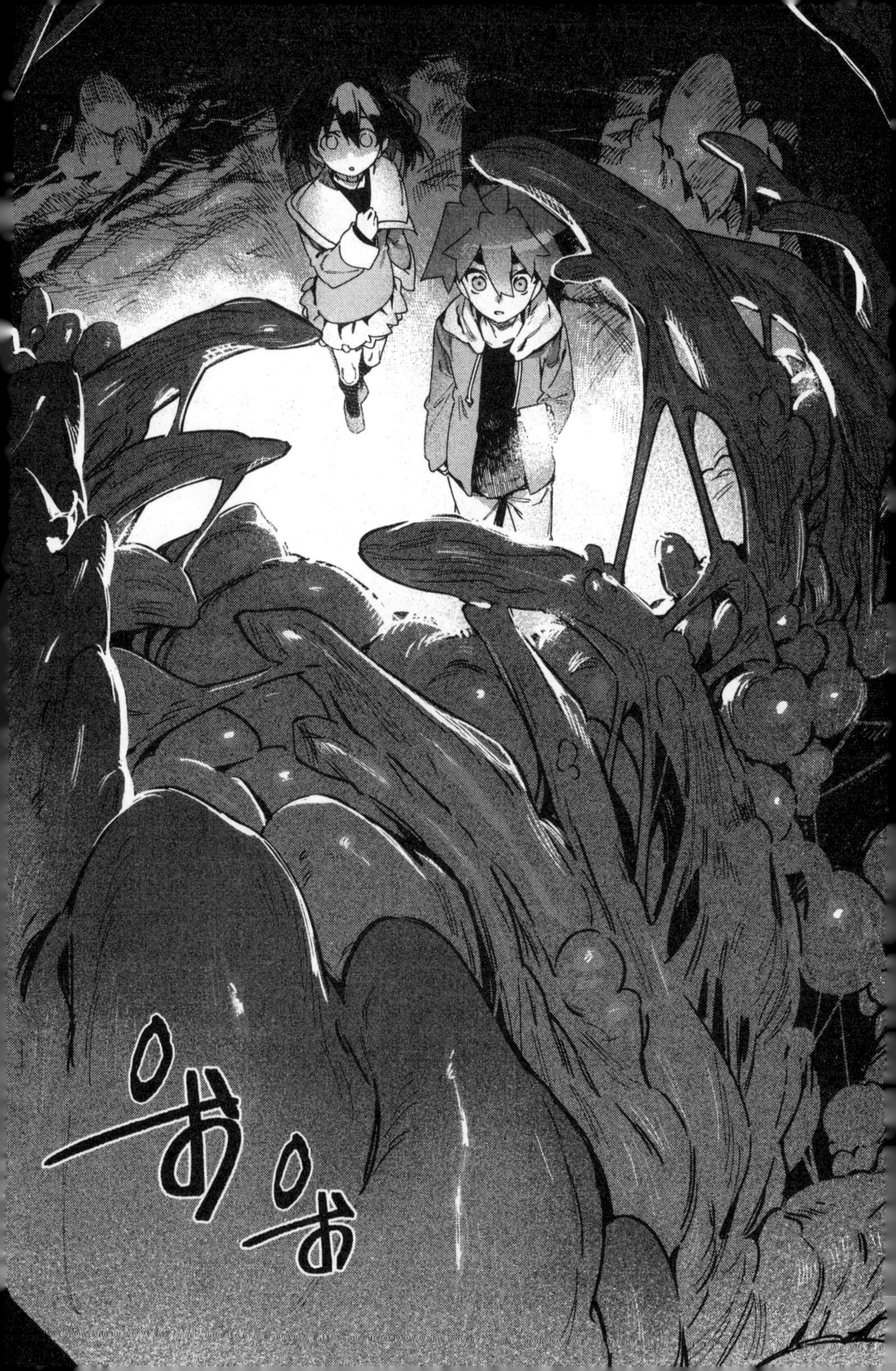
おぉ

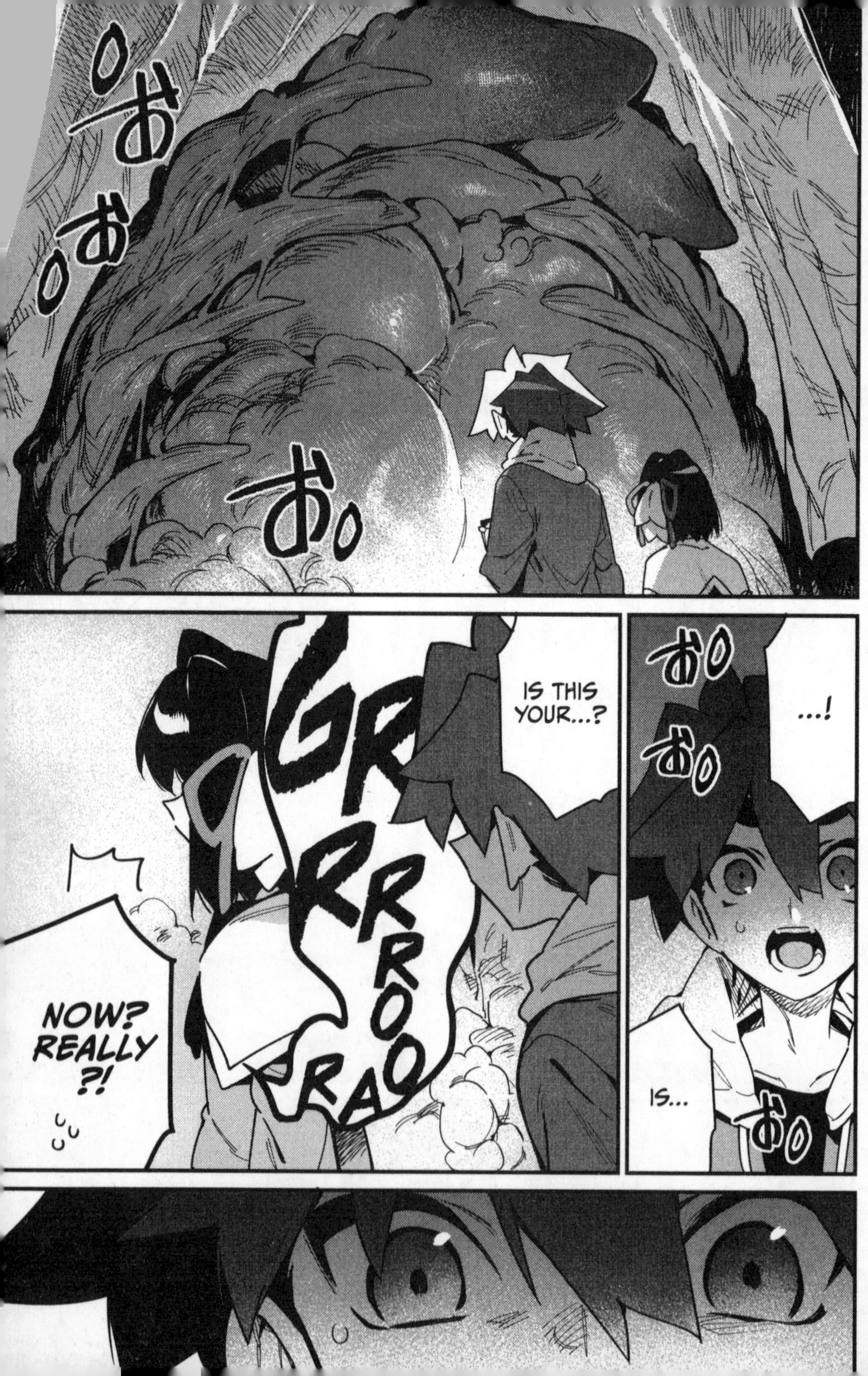
おぉ
おぉ
おぉ
おぉ
...!
おぉ
IS...
おぉ
IS THIS YOUR...?
GRRRROOOAR
NOW? REALLY ?!

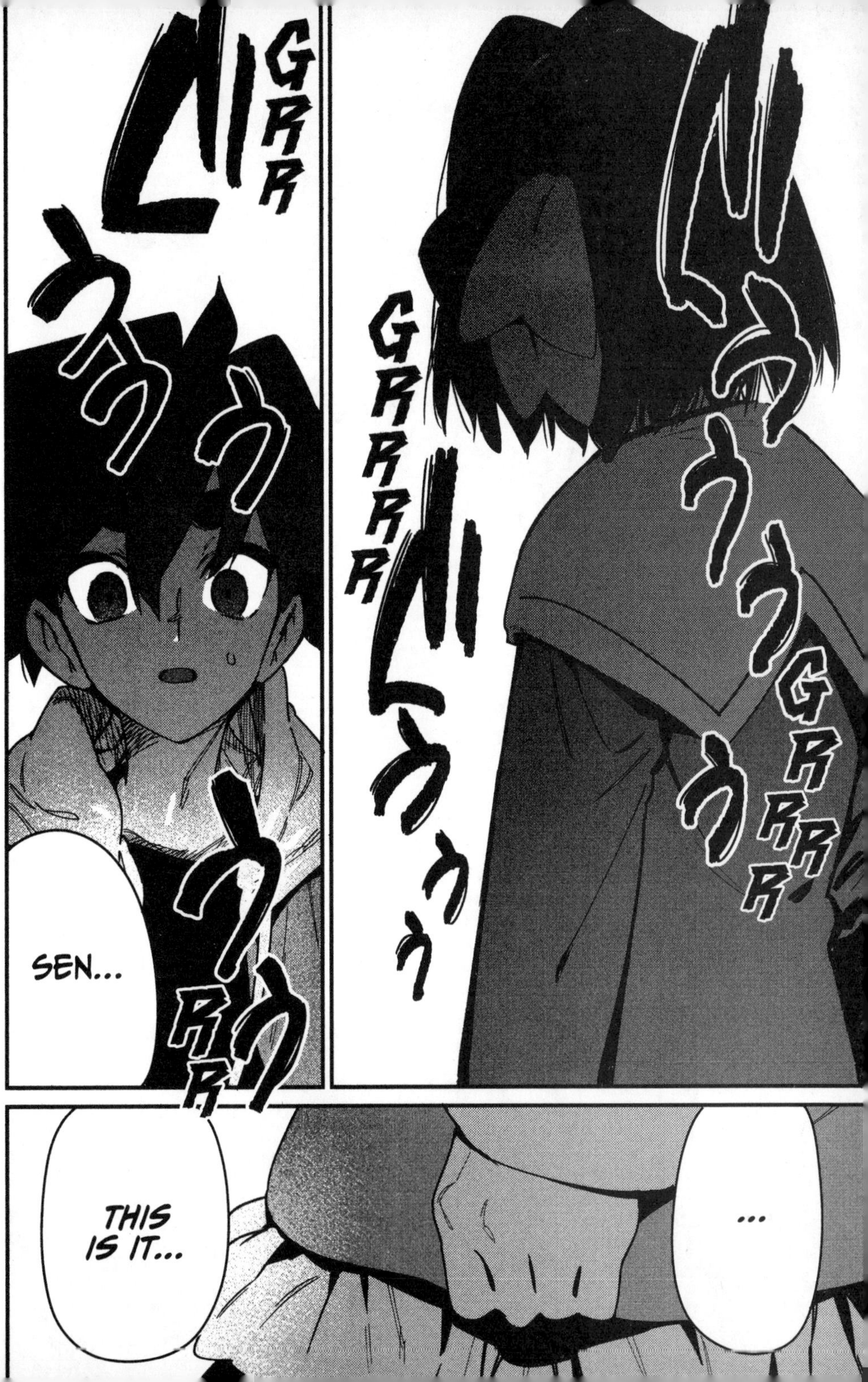
GRRRRRR
GRRRR
GRR
SEN...
RRR
...
THIS IS IT...

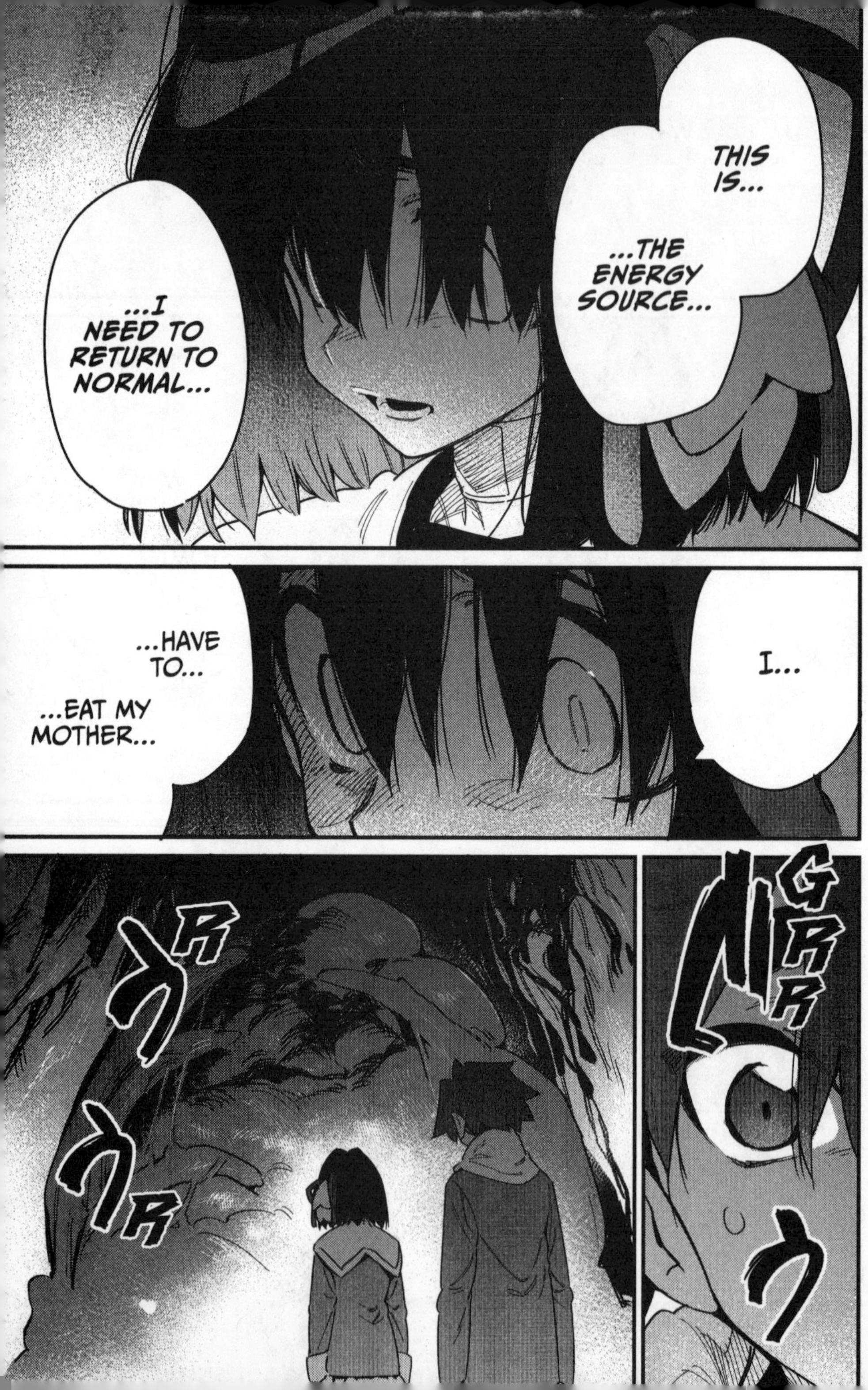
THIS IS...
...THE ENERGY SOURCE...
...I NEED TO RETURN TO NORMAL...
I...
...HAVE TO...
...EAT MY MOTHER...
GRR
R
R

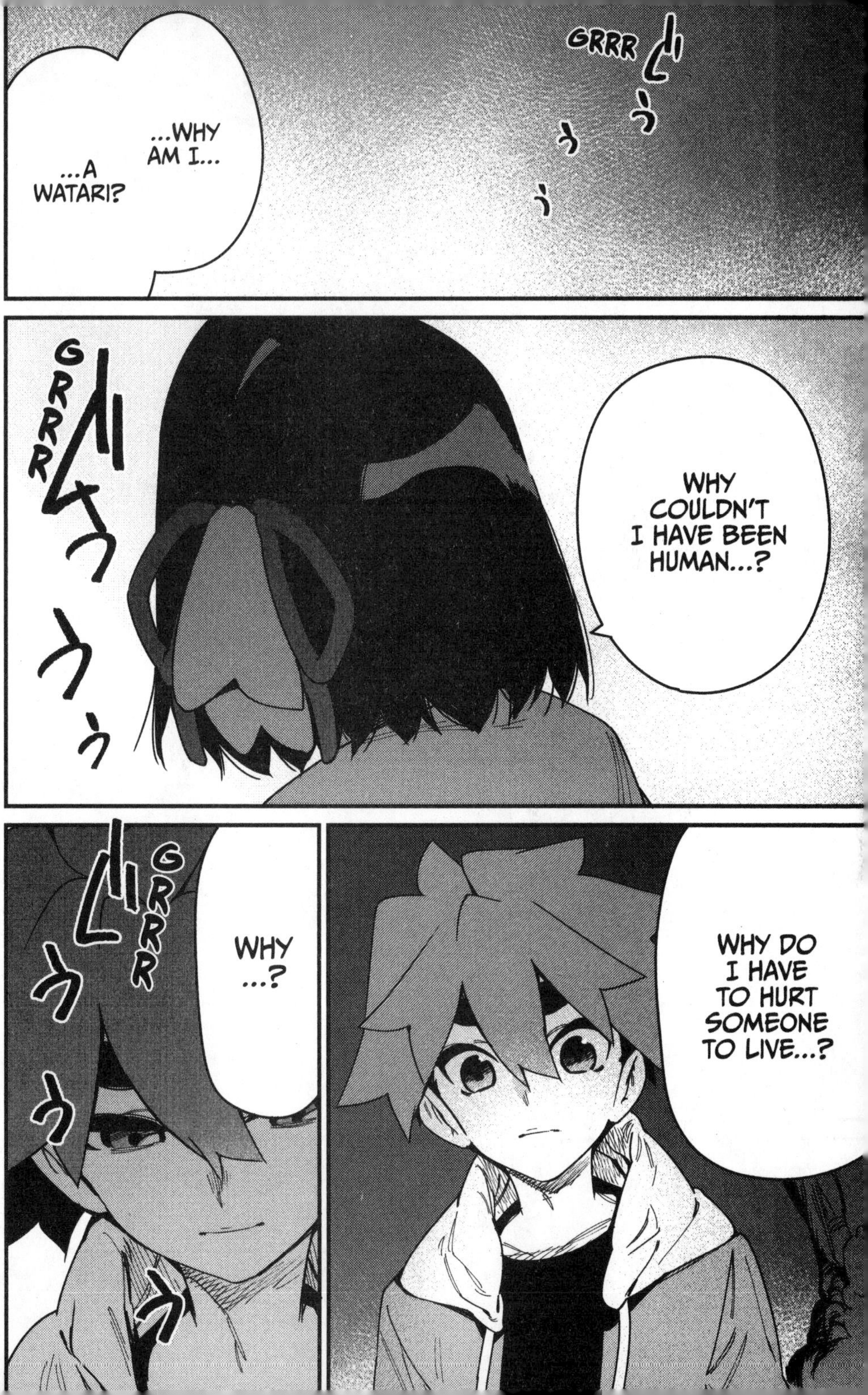
GRRR
...WHY AM I...
...A WATARI?
WHY COULDN'T I HAVE BEEN HUMAN...?
GRRR
WHY DO I HAVE TO HURT SOMEONE TO LIVE...?
WHY ...?
GRRR

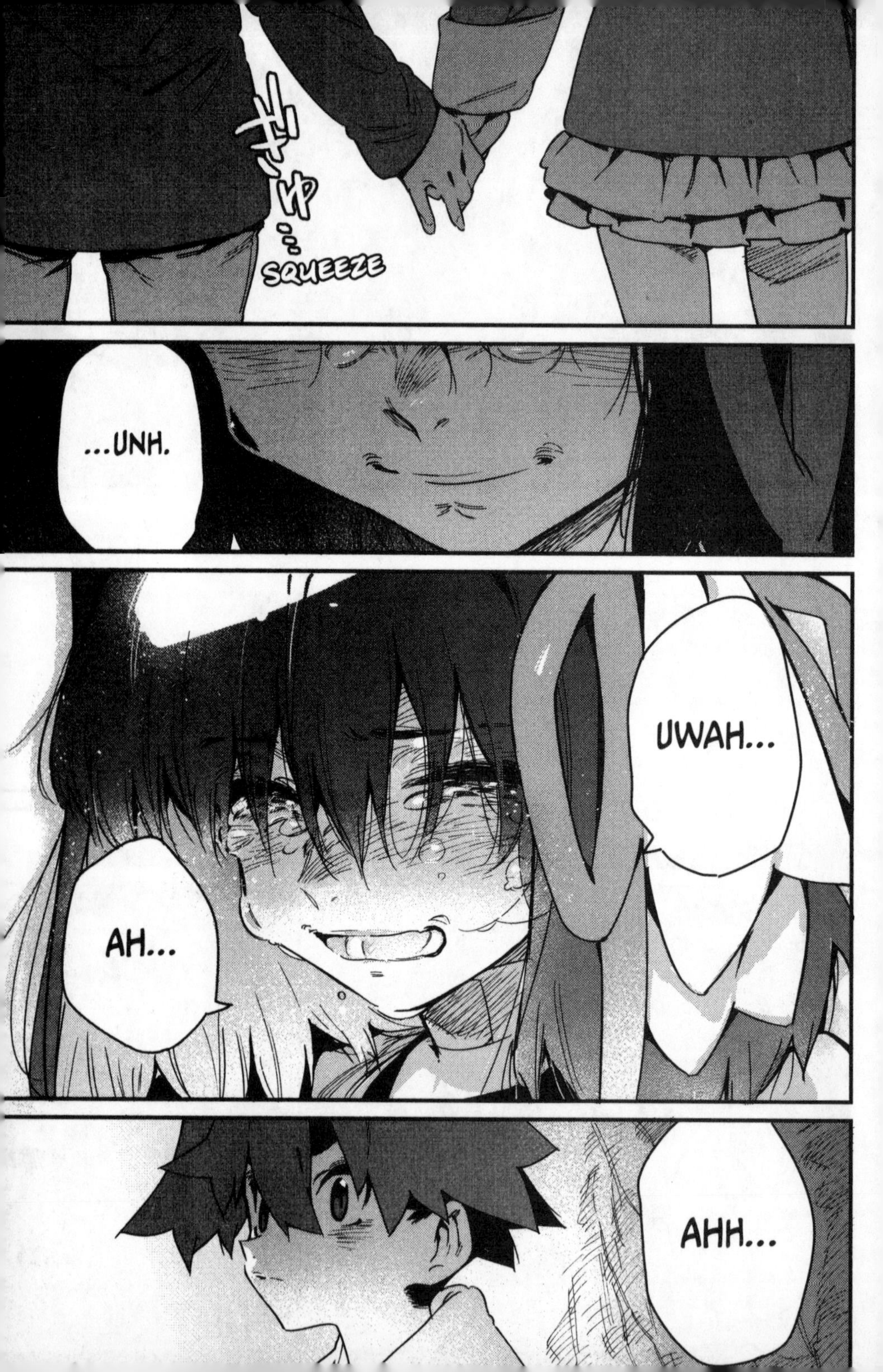
ぎゅ…
SQUEEZE
...UNH.
UWAH...
AH...
AHH...

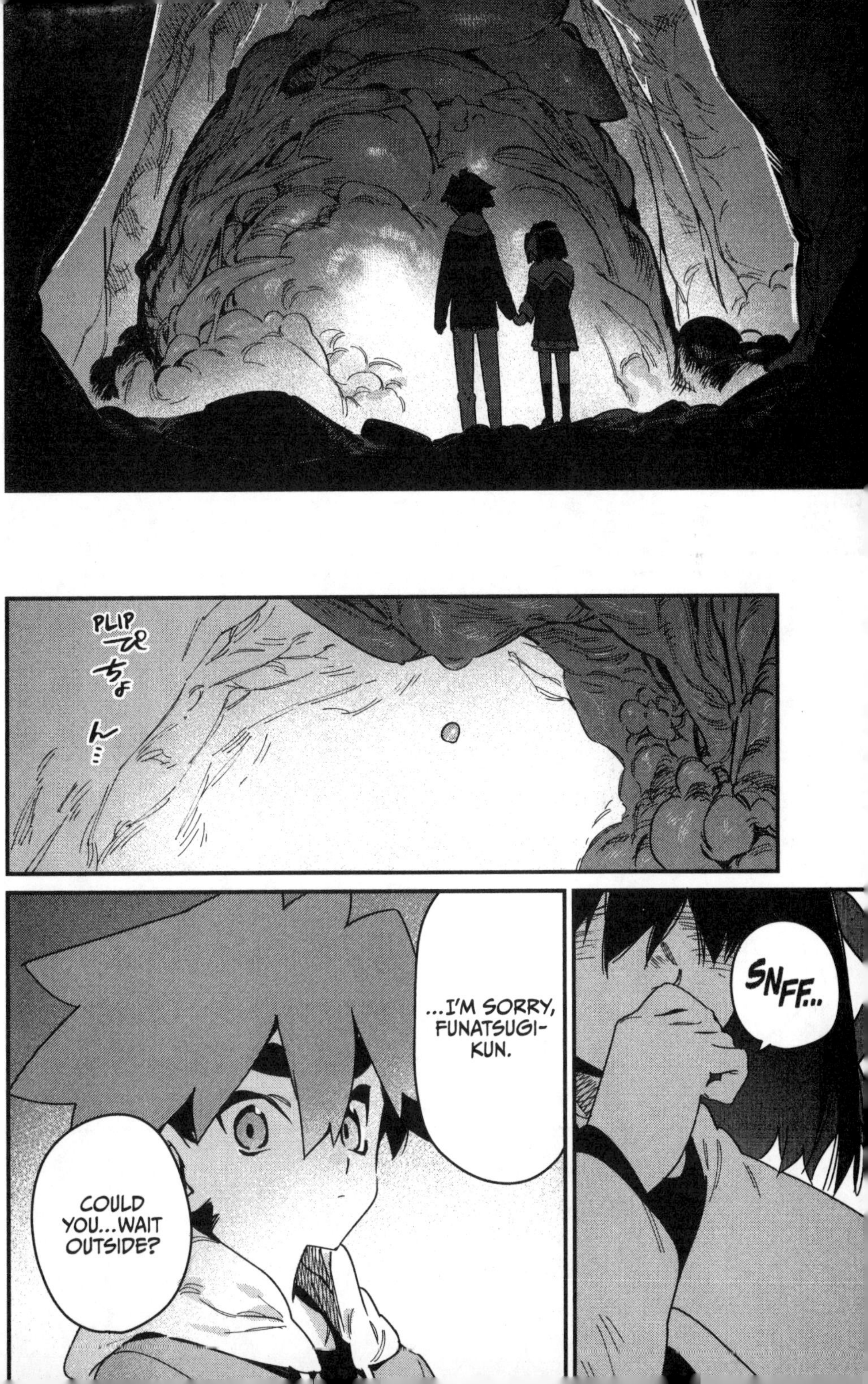
PLIP
ぴちょん…
SNFF...
...I'M SORRY, FUNATSUGI-KUN.
COULD YOU...WAIT OUTSIDE?

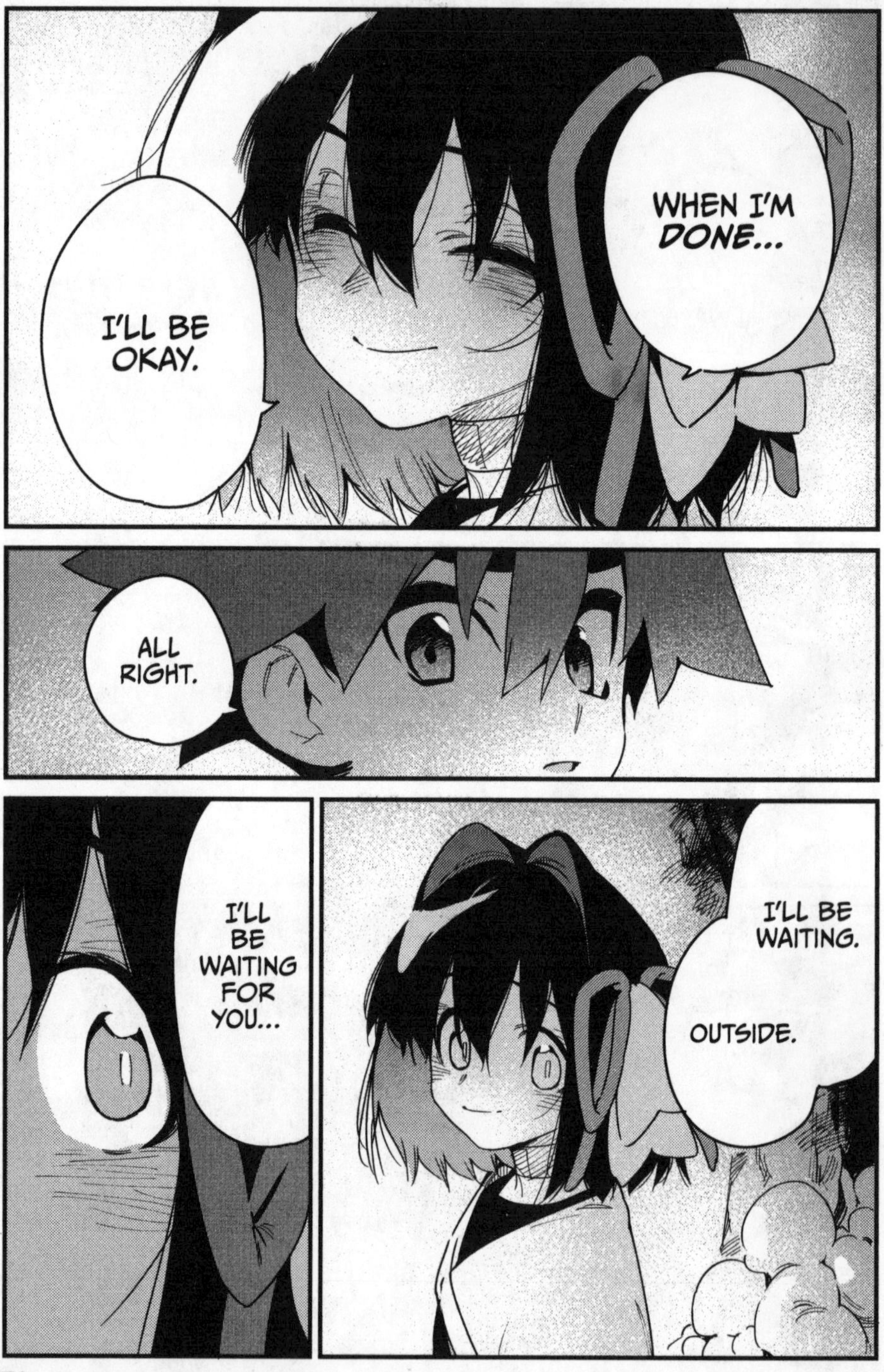
WHEN I'M *DONE*...
I'LL BE OKAY.
ALL RIGHT.
I'LL BE WAITING.
OUTSIDE.
I'LL BE WAITING FOR YOU...

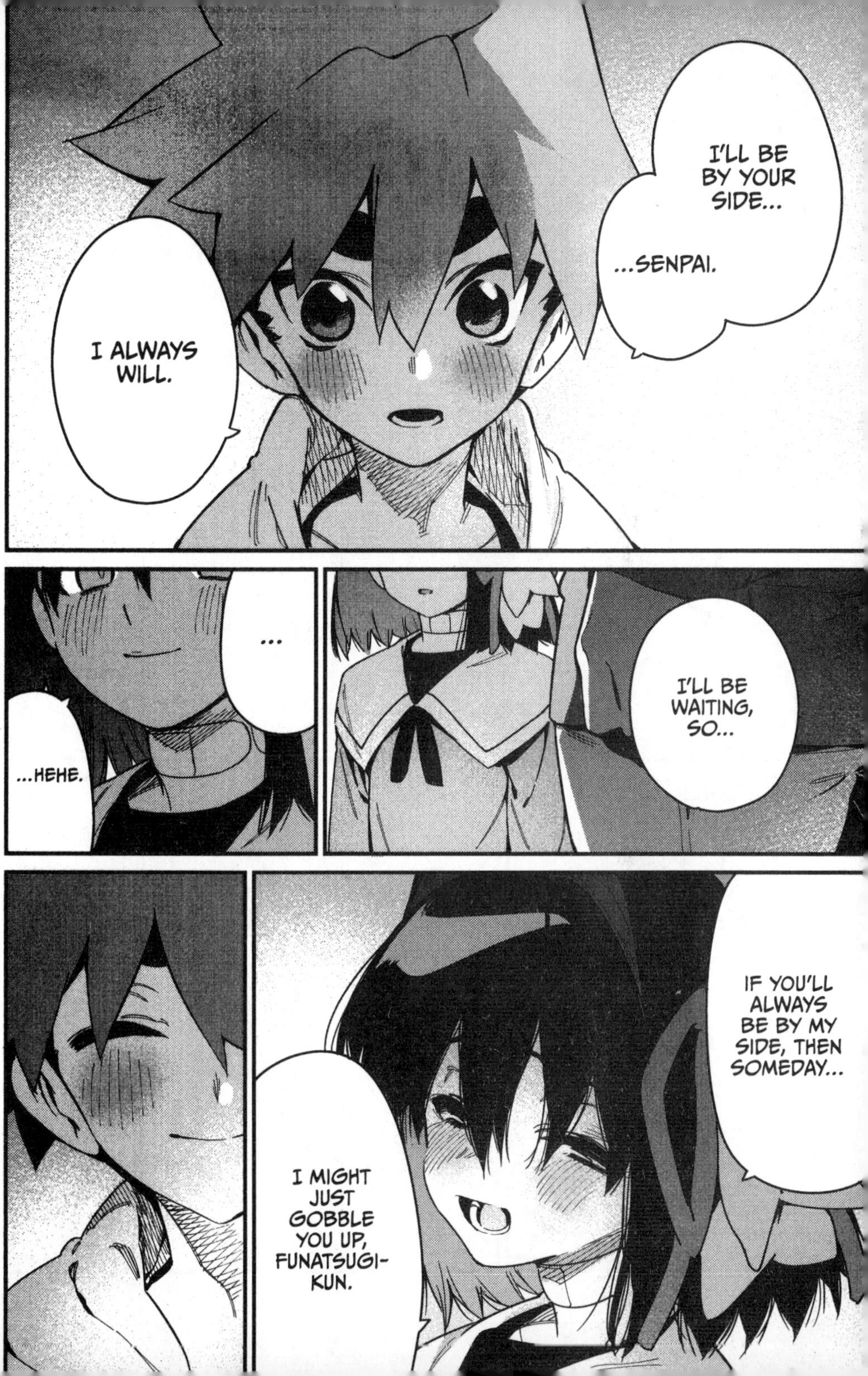
I'LL BE BY YOUR SIDE...
...SENPAI.
I ALWAYS WILL.
I'LL BE WAITING, SO...
...
...HEHE.
IF YOU'LL ALWAYS BE BY MY SIDE, THEN SOMEDAY...
I MIGHT JUST GOBBLE YOU UP, FUNATSUGI-KUN.

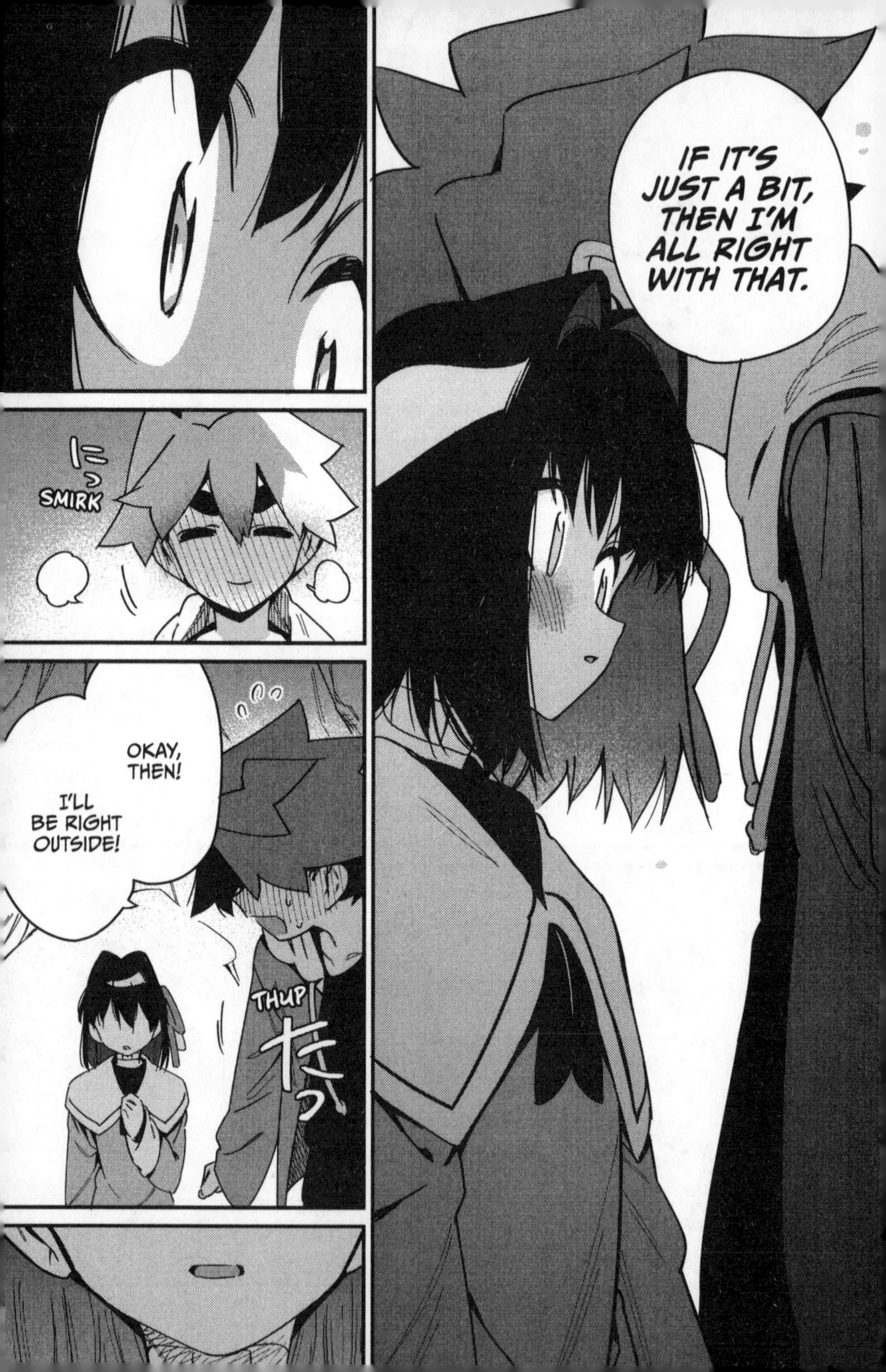
IF IT'S JUST A BIT, THEN I'M ALL RIGHT WITH THAT.
にっ
SMIRK
OKAY, THEN!
I'LL BE RIGHT OUTSIDE!
THUP
たっ

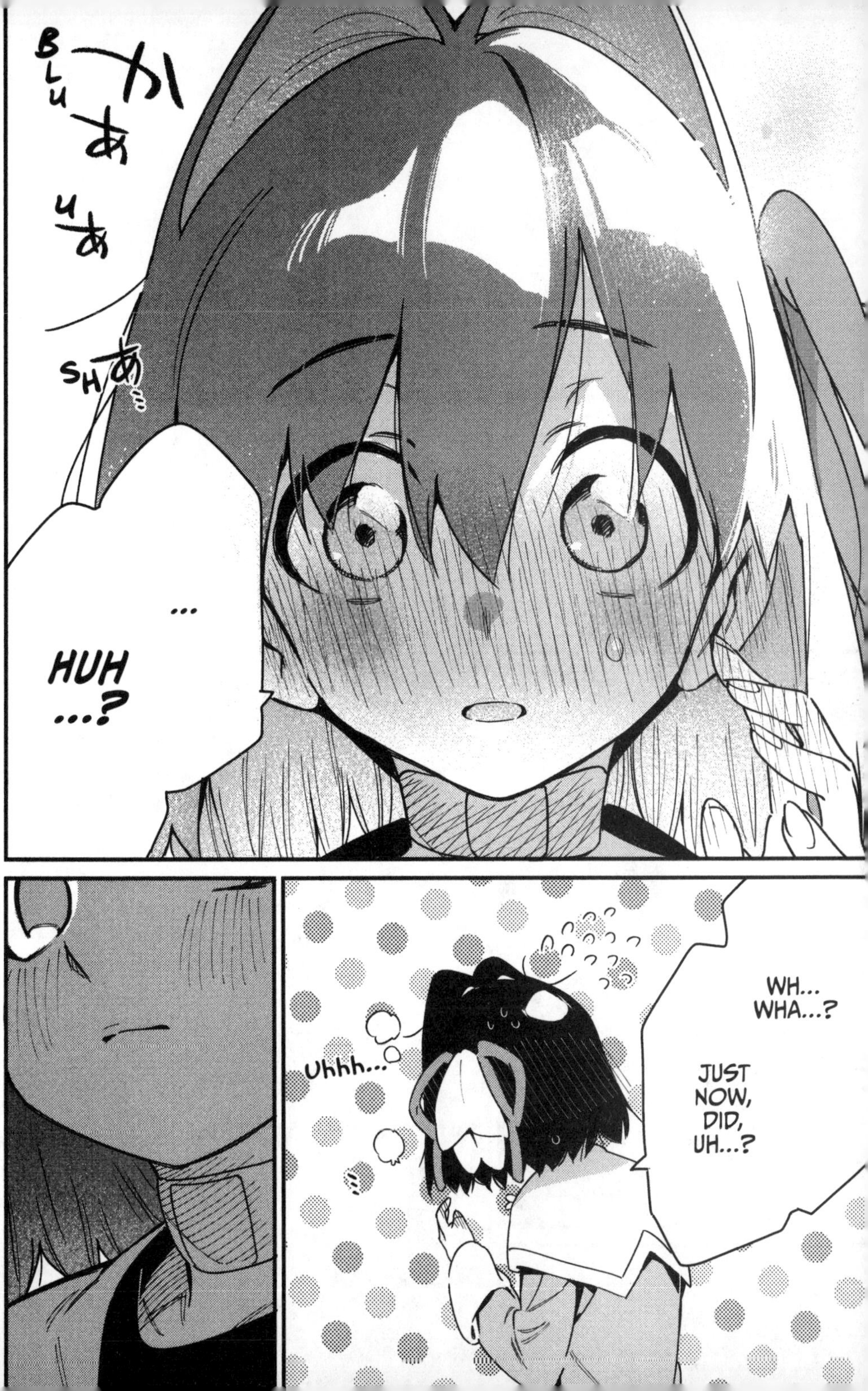
BLU かあ
u あ
SH あ...
... HUH ...?
WH... WHA...?
JUST NOW, DID, UH...?
Uhhh...

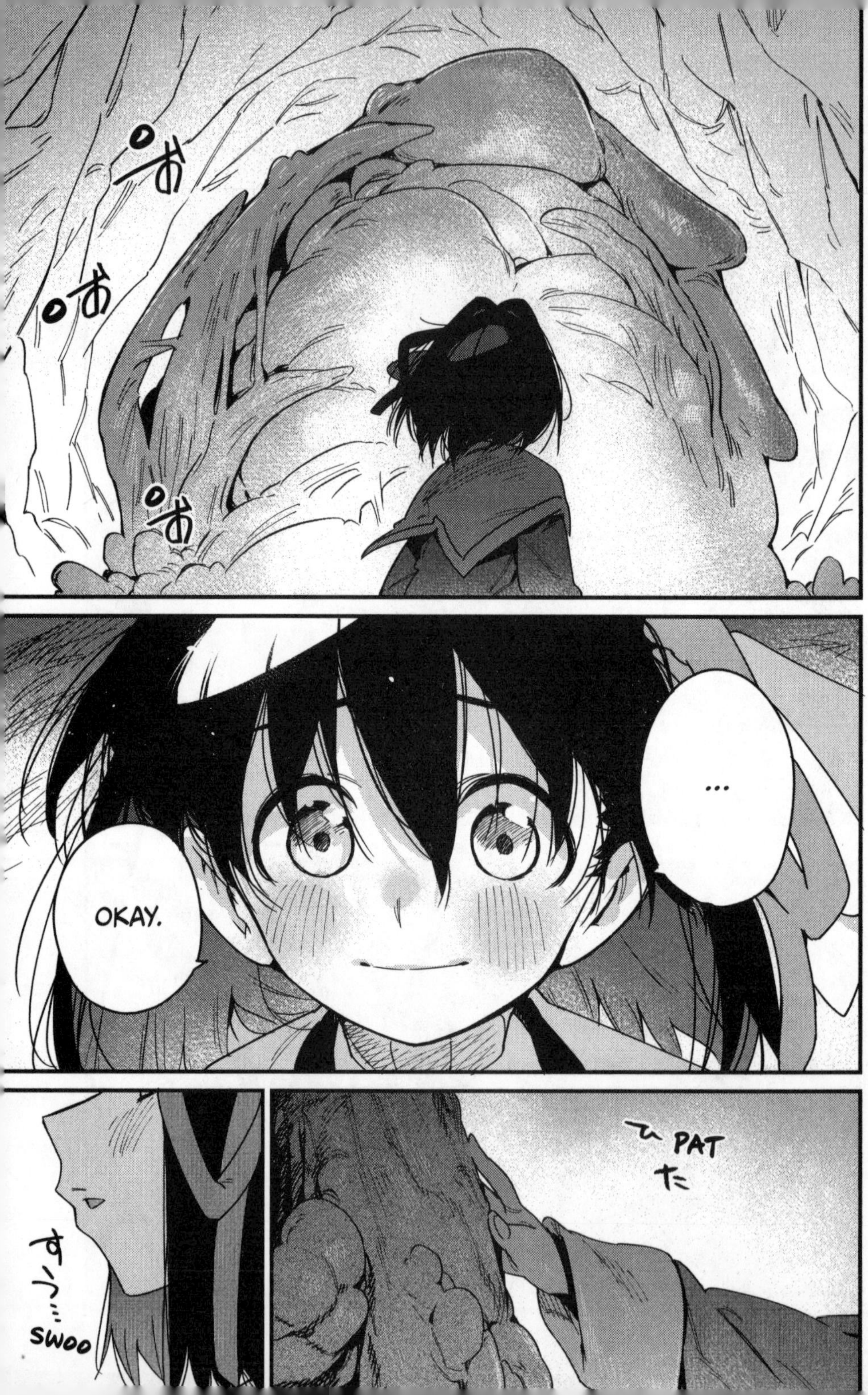
お
お
お
...
OKAY.
PAT
すう
SWOO

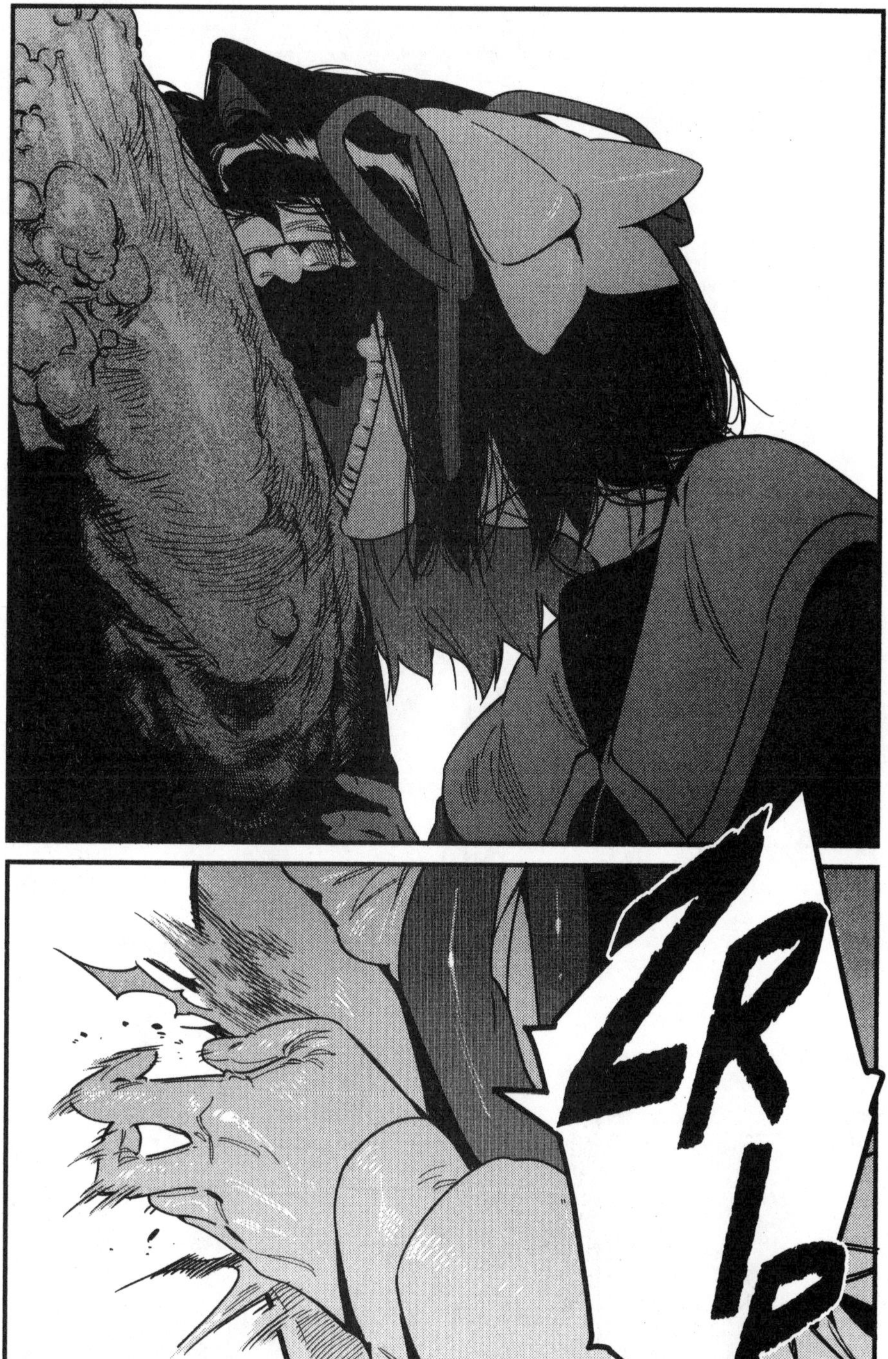
ZRIP

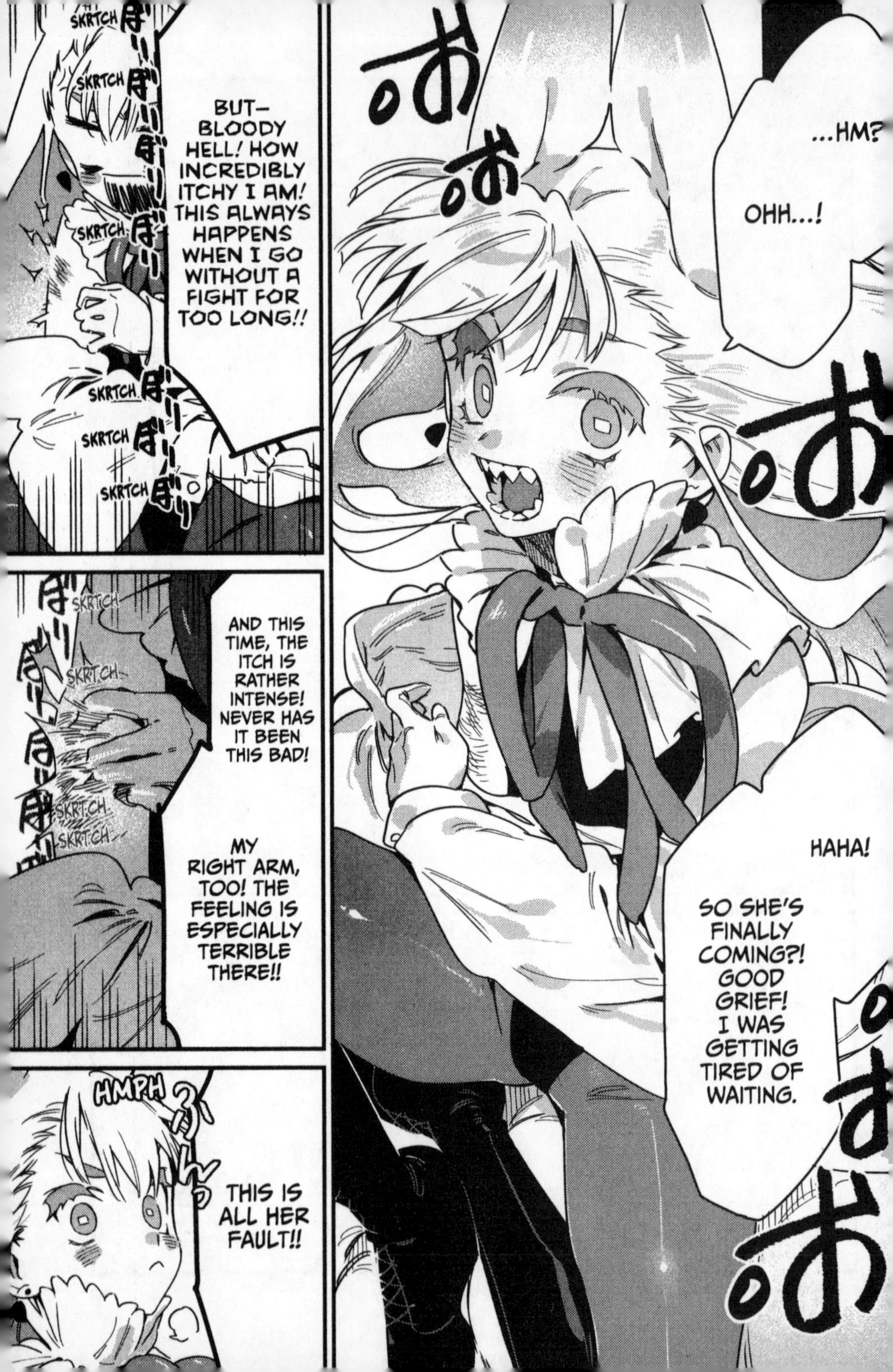
...HM?
OHH...!
HAHA!
SO SHE'S FINALLY COMING?! GOOD GRIEF! I WAS GETTING TIRED OF WAITING.
SKRTCH
SKRTCH
SKRTCH
BUT—BLOODY HELL! HOW INCREDIBLY ITCHY I AM! THIS ALWAYS HAPPENS WHEN I GO WITHOUT A FIGHT FOR TOO LONG!!
SKRTCH
SKRTCH
SKRTCH
SKRTCH
SKRTCH
SKRTCH
SKRTCH
AND THIS TIME, THE ITCH IS RATHER INTENSE! NEVER HAS IT BEEN THIS BAD!
MY RIGHT ARM, TOO! THE FEELING IS ESPECIALLY TERRIBLE THERE!!
HMPH
THIS IS ALL HER FAULT!!

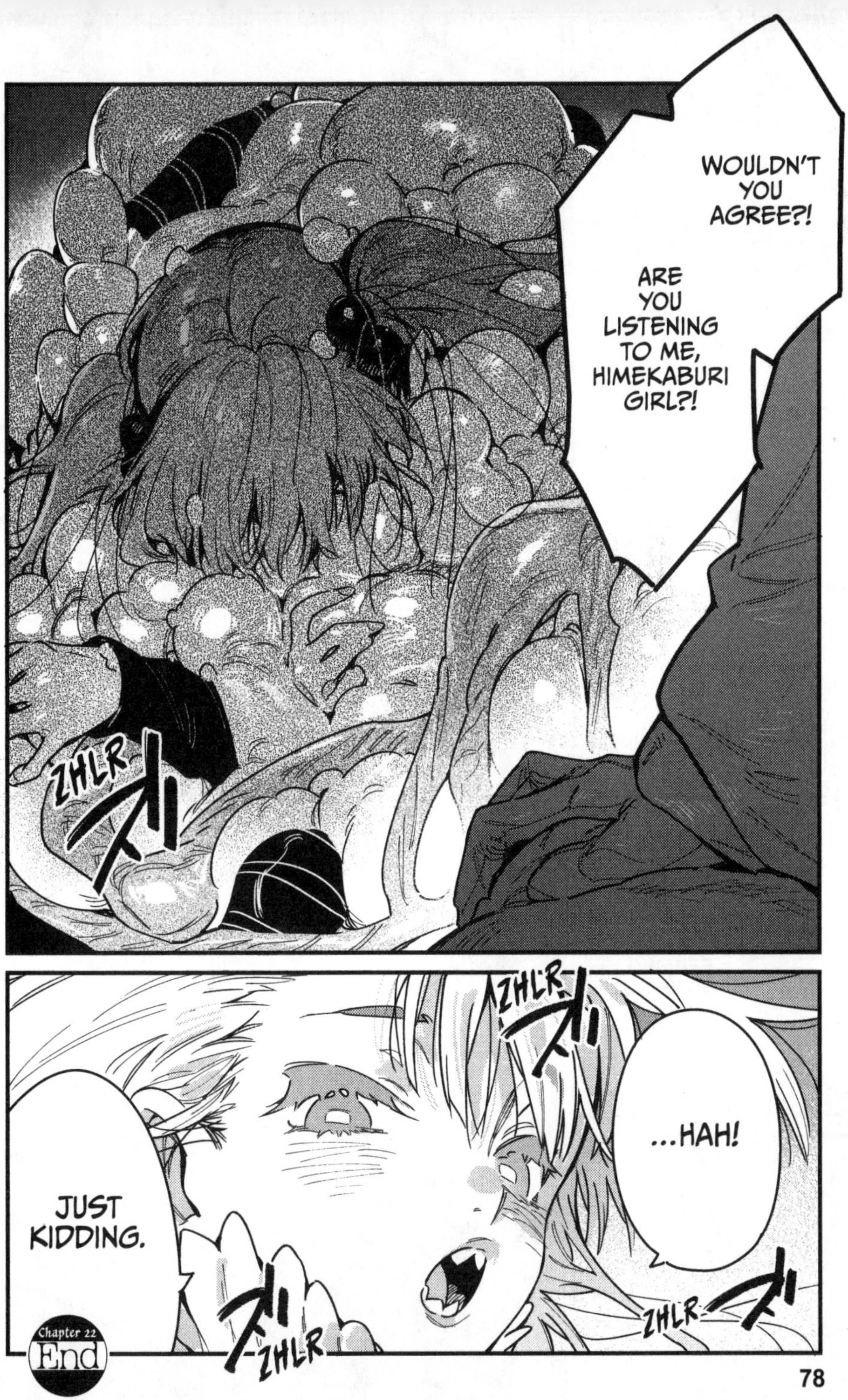
WOULDN'T YOU AGREE?!
ARE YOU LISTENING TO ME, HIMEKABURI GIRL?!
ZHLR
ZHLR
...HAH!
ZHLR
JUST KIDDING.
ZHLR
Chapter 22 End

Sachi's
MONSTROUS
Appetite

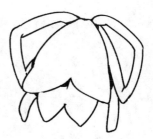

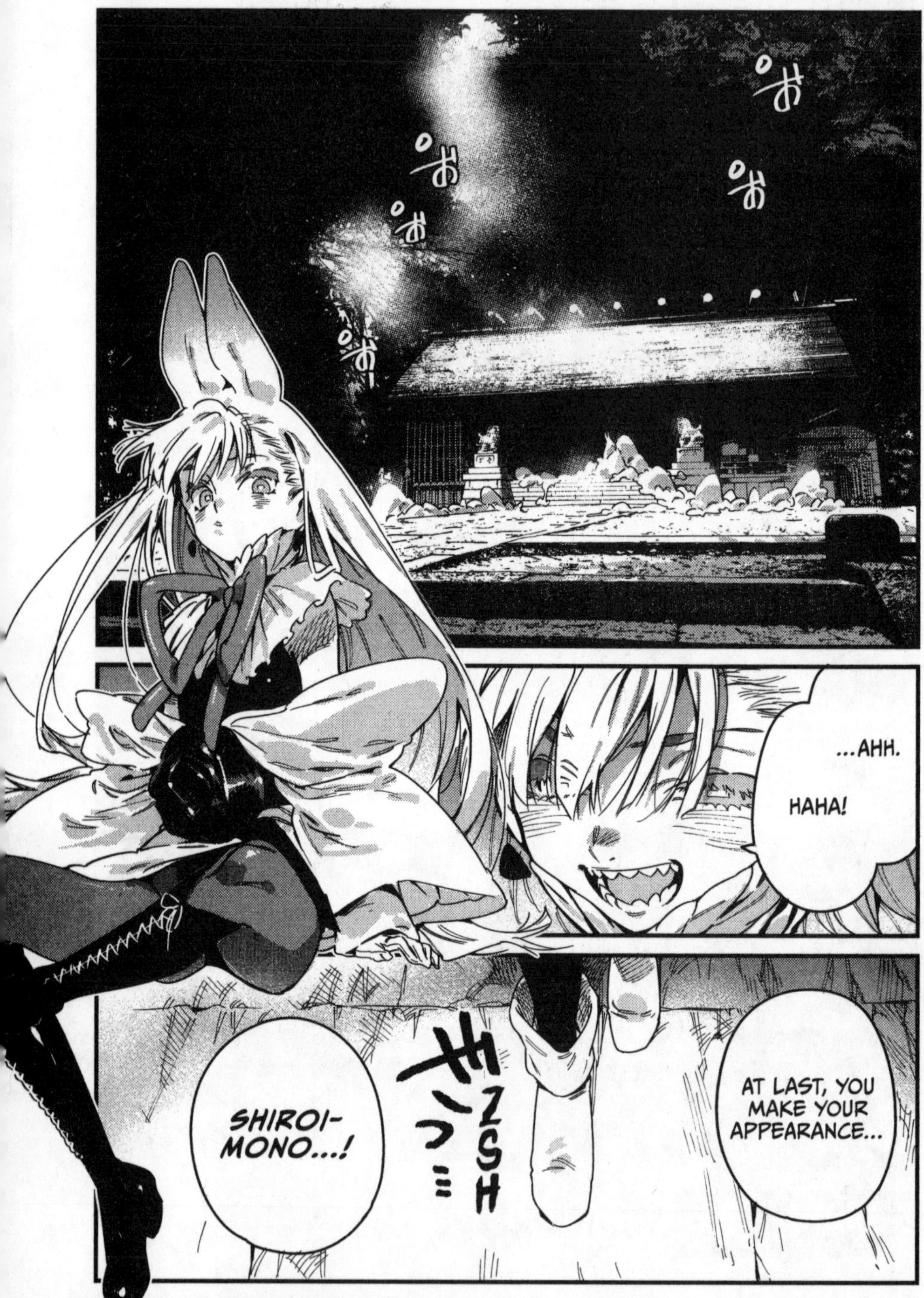
...AHH.
HAHA!
AT LAST, YOU MAKE YOUR APPEARANCE...
ZSH
SHIROI-MONO...!

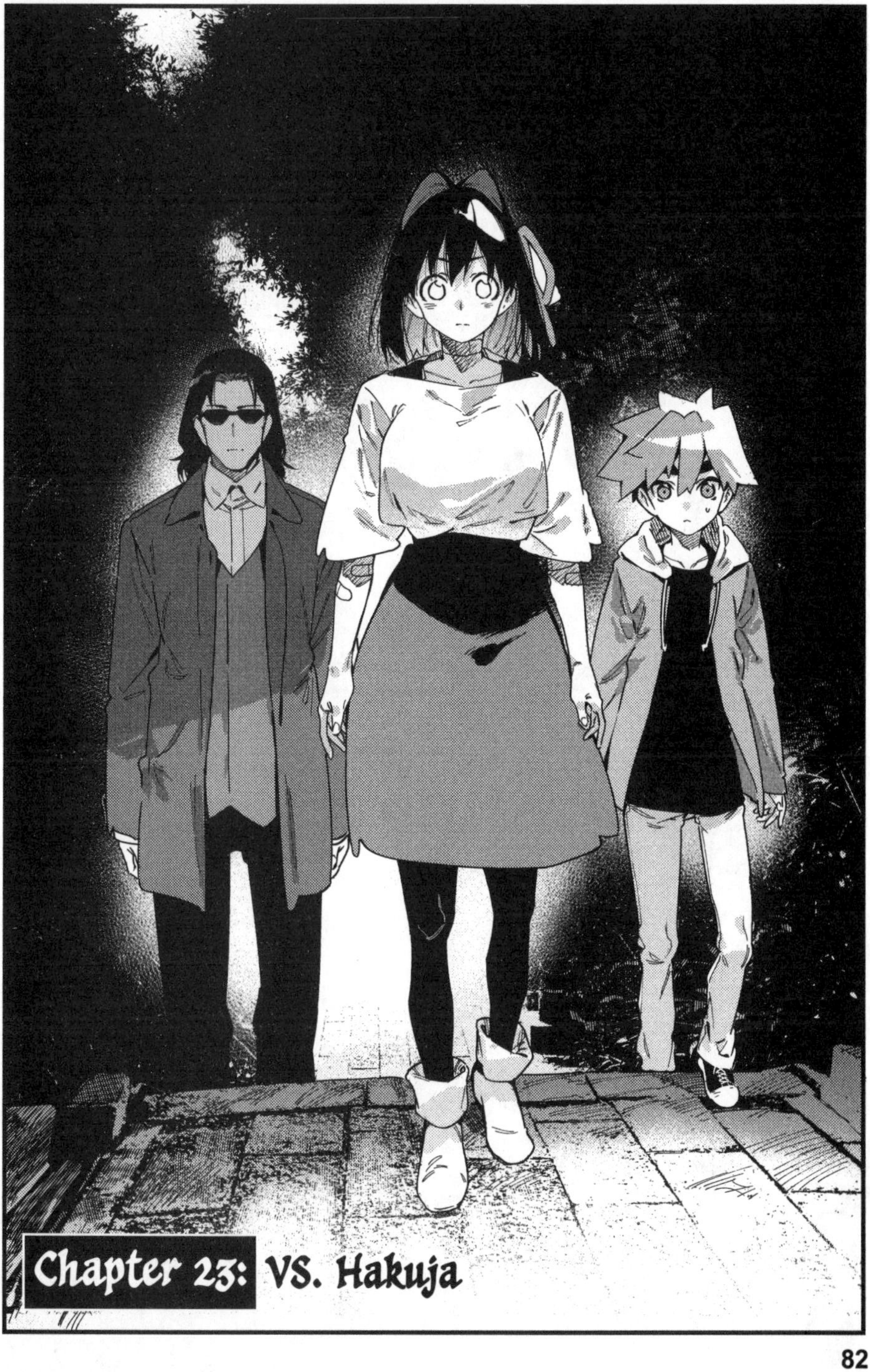
Chapter 23: VS. Hakuja

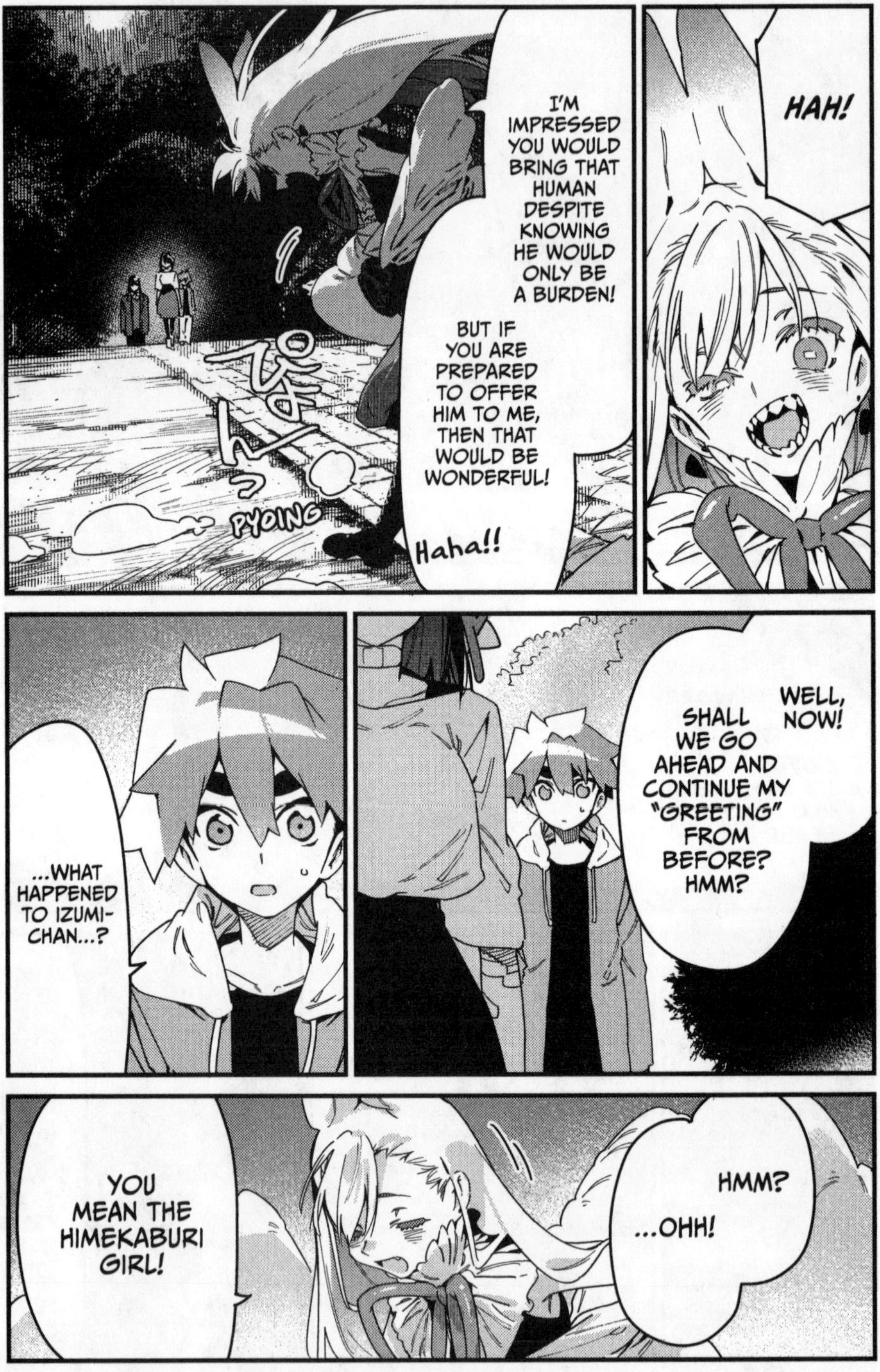
HAH!
I'M IMPRESSED YOU WOULD BRING THAT HUMAN DESPITE KNOWING HE WOULD ONLY BE A BURDEN!
BUT IF YOU ARE PREPARED TO OFFER HIM TO ME, THEN THAT WOULD BE WONDERFUL!
Haha!!
ぴょんっ
PYOING
WELL, NOW!
SHALL WE GO AHEAD AND CONTINUE MY "GREETING" FROM BEFORE? HMM?
...WHAT HAPPENED TO IZUMI-CHAN...?
HMM?
...OHH!
YOU MEAN THE HIMEKABURI GIRL!

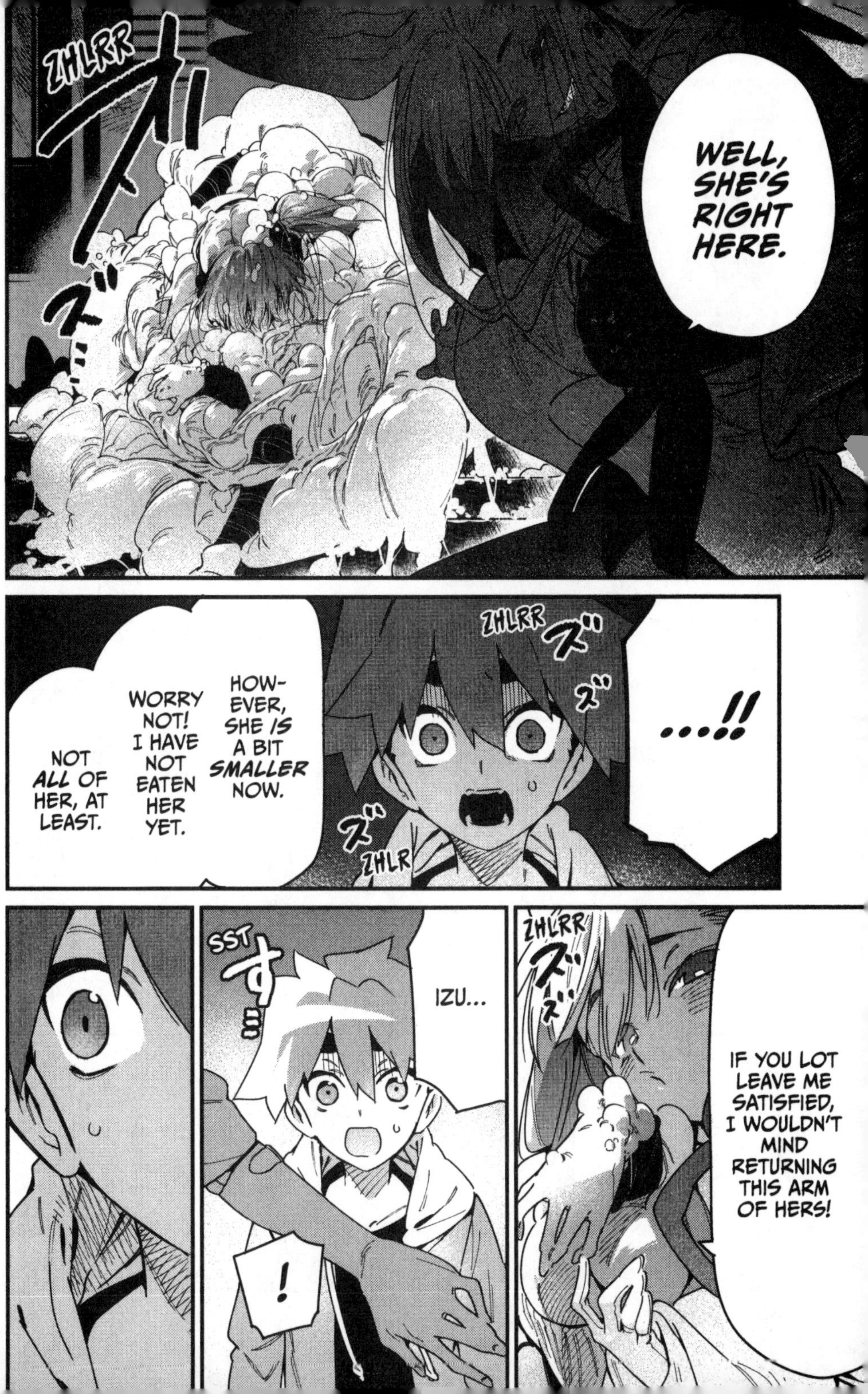

WELL, SHE'S RIGHT HERE.
ZHLRR
...!!
ZHLRR
ZHLR
HOW-EVER, SHE IS A BIT SMALLER NOW.
WORRY NOT! I HAVE NOT EATEN HER YET.
NOT ALL OF HER, AT LEAST.
ZHLRR
IF YOU LOT LEAVE ME SATISFIED, I WOULDN'T MIND RETURNING THIS ARM OF HERS!
SST
IZU...
!

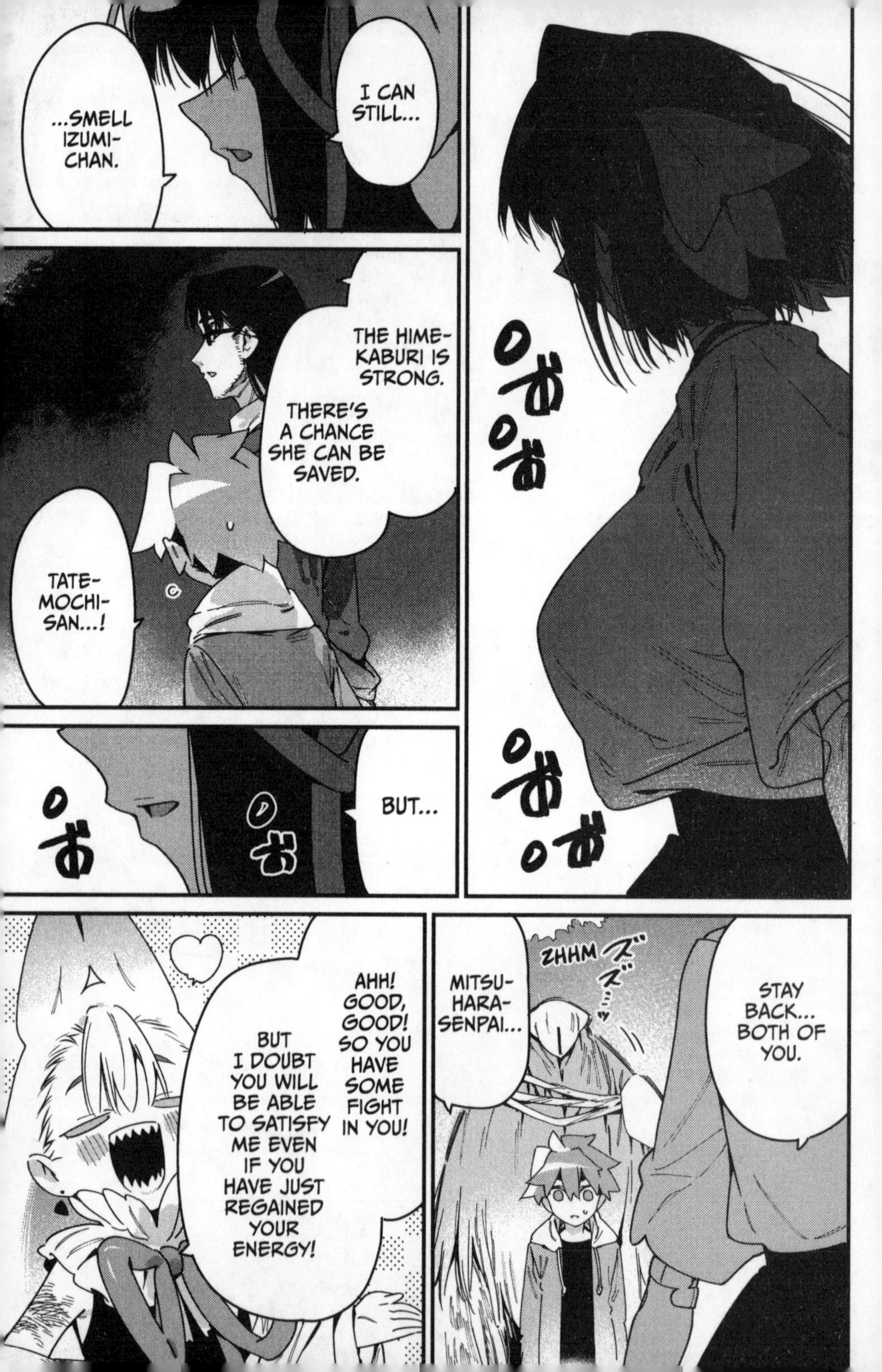
おお
おお
I CAN STILL...
...SMELL IZUMI-CHAN.
THE HIME-KABURI IS STRONG.
THERE'S A CHANCE SHE CAN BE SAVED.
TATE-MOCHI-SAN...!
BUT...
お
お
STAY BACK... BOTH OF YOU.
ZHHM
MITSU-HARA-SENPAI...
AHH! GOOD, GOOD! SO YOU HAVE SOME FIGHT IN YOU!
BUT I DOUBT YOU WILL BE ABLE TO SATISFY ME EVEN IF YOU HAVE JUST REGAINED YOUR ENERGY!

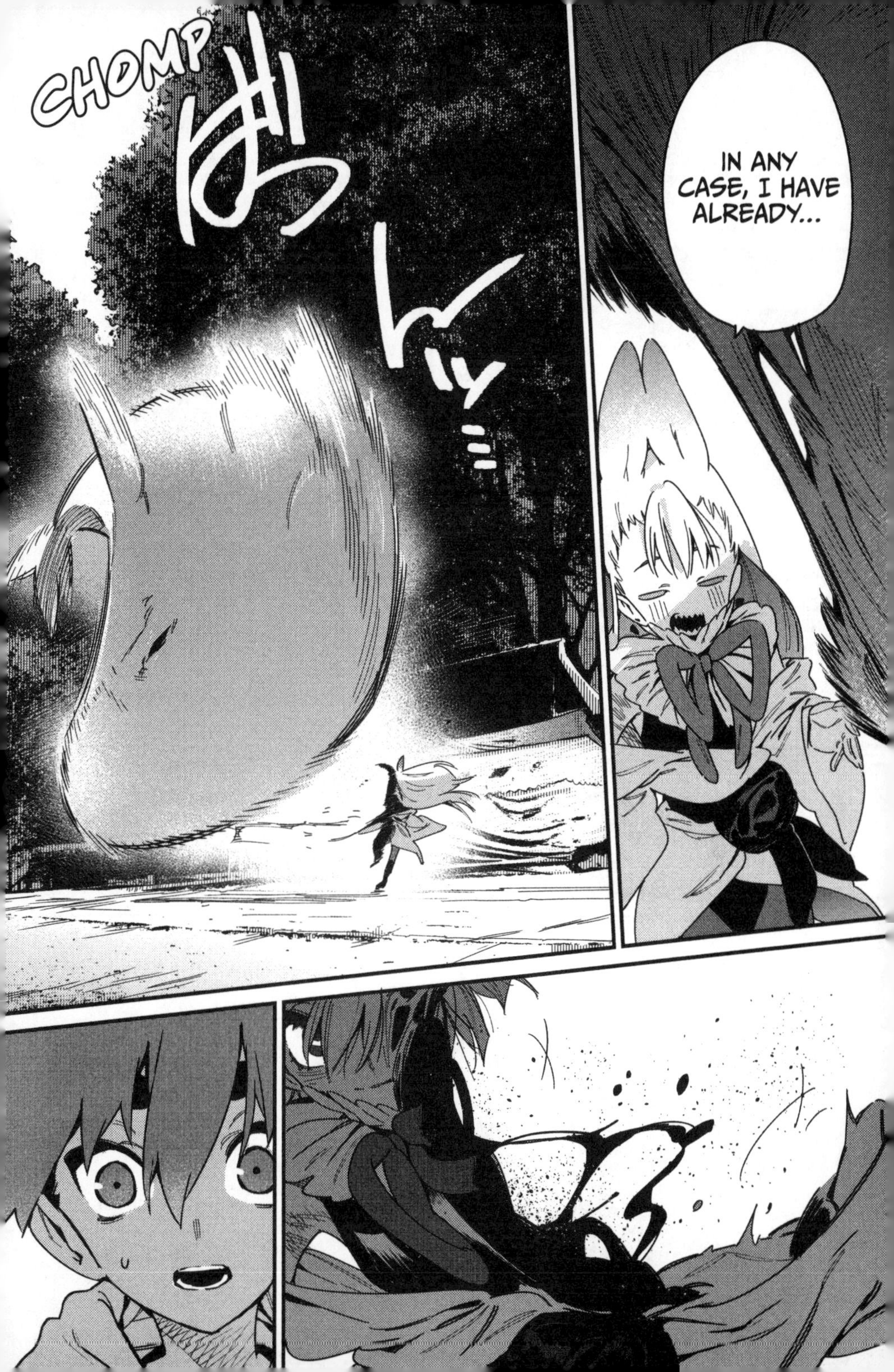
IN ANY CASE, I HAVE ALREADY...
CHOMP

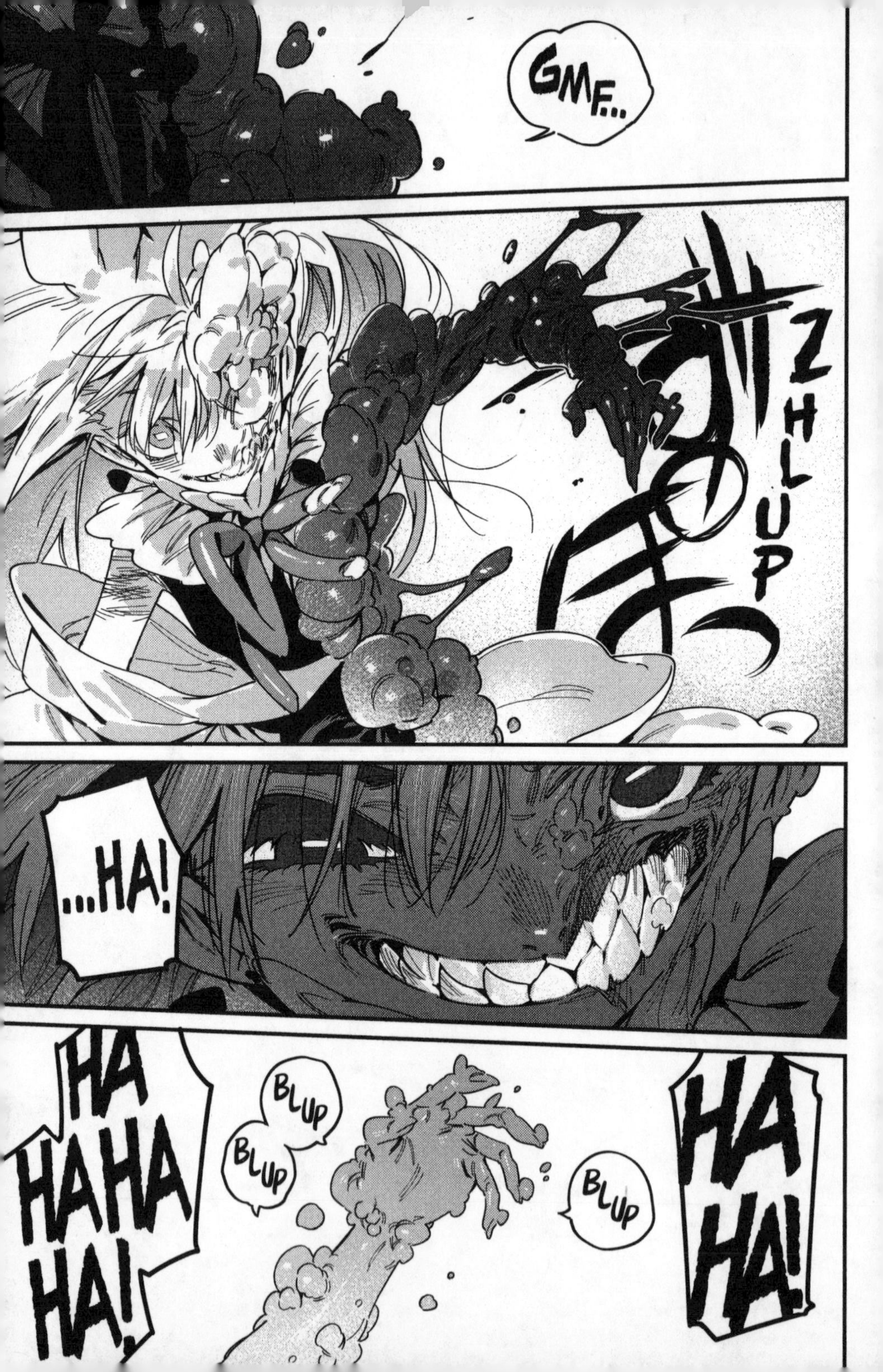
GMF...
ZHLLUP
...HA!
HA HA HA!
BLUP
BLUP
BLUP
HA HAHA HAHA HA!

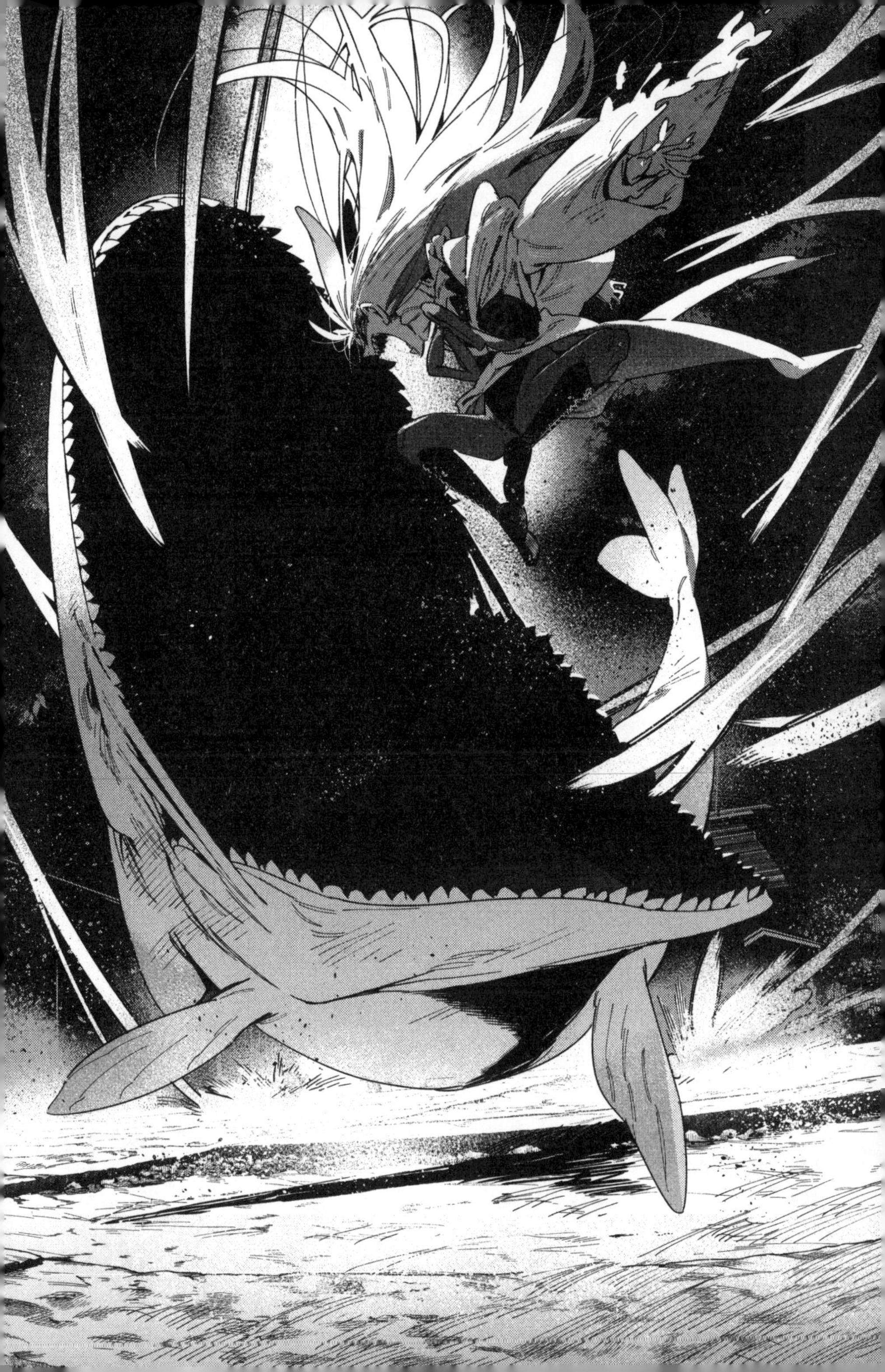

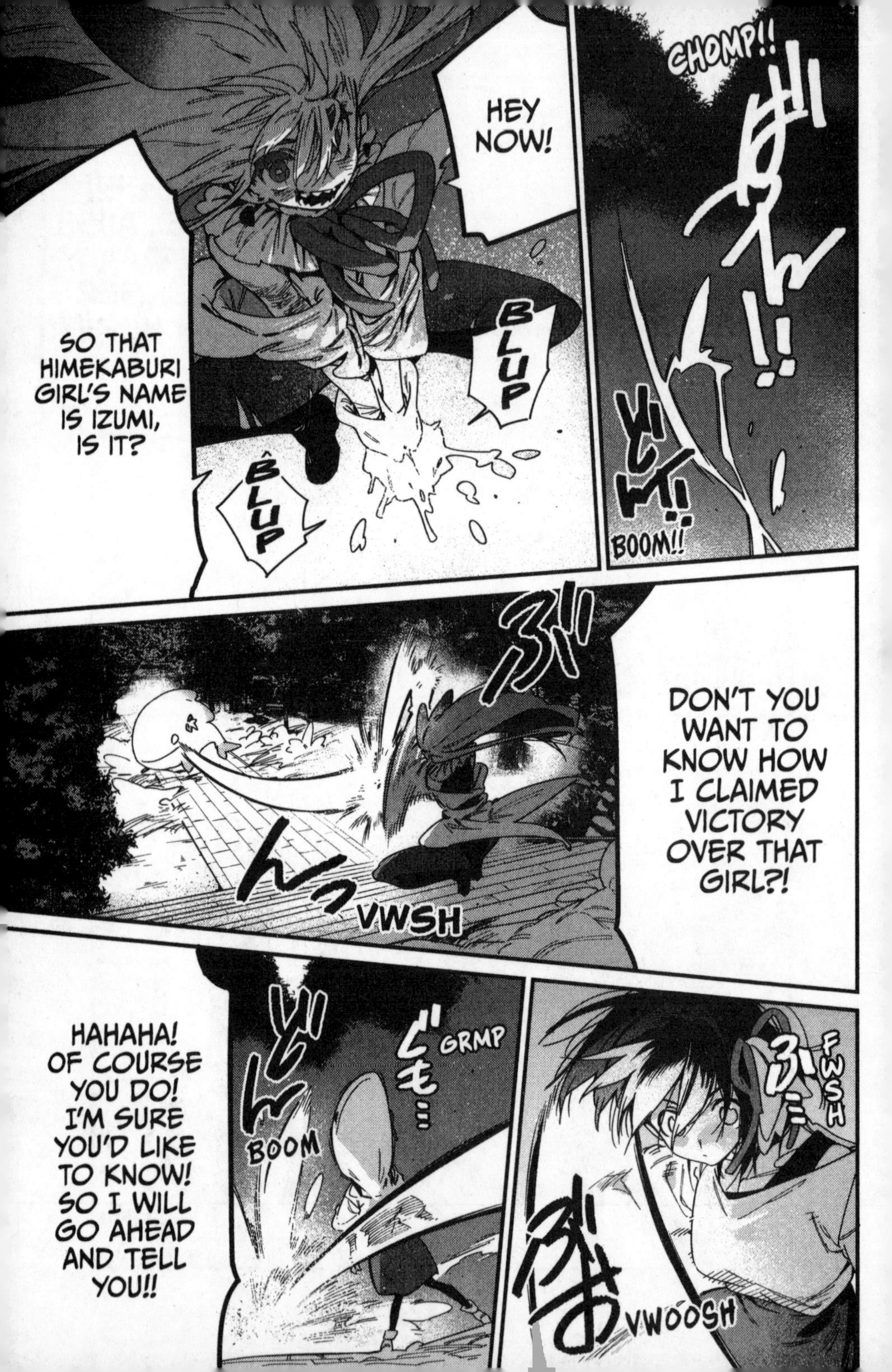

CHOMP!!
BOOM!!
HEY NOW!
BLUP
SO THAT HIMEKABURI GIRL'S NAME IS IZUMI, IS IT?
BLUP
DON'T YOU WANT TO KNOW HOW I CLAIMED VICTORY OVER THAT GIRL?!
VWSH
FWSH
VWOOSH
GRMP
BOOM
HAHAHA! OF COURSE YOU DO! I'M SURE YOU'D LIKE TO KNOW! SO I WILL GO AHEAD AND TELL YOU!!

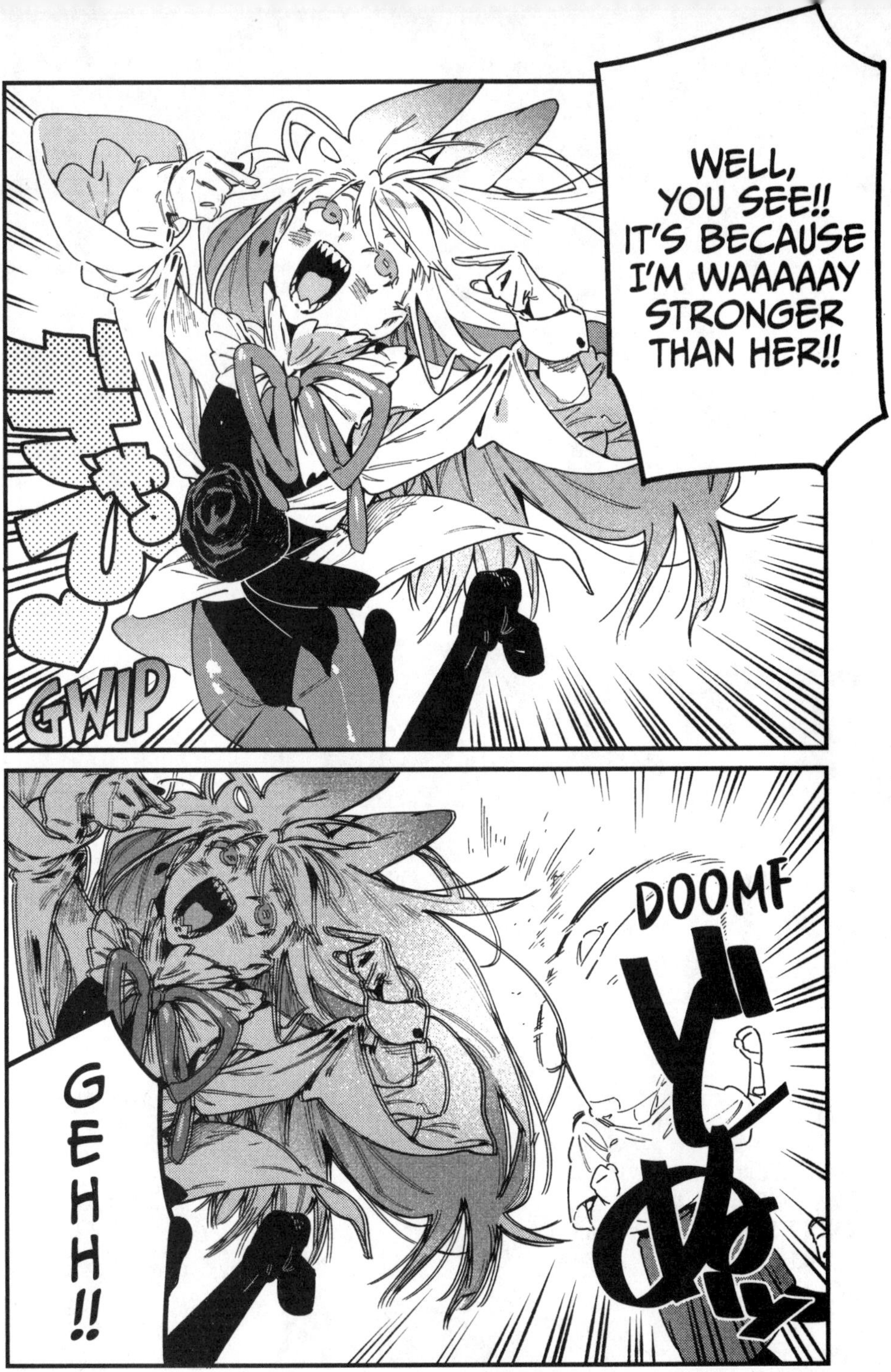
WELL, YOU SEE!! IT'S BECAUSE I'M WAAAAAY STRONGER THAN HER!!
GWIP
DOOMF
GEHH!!

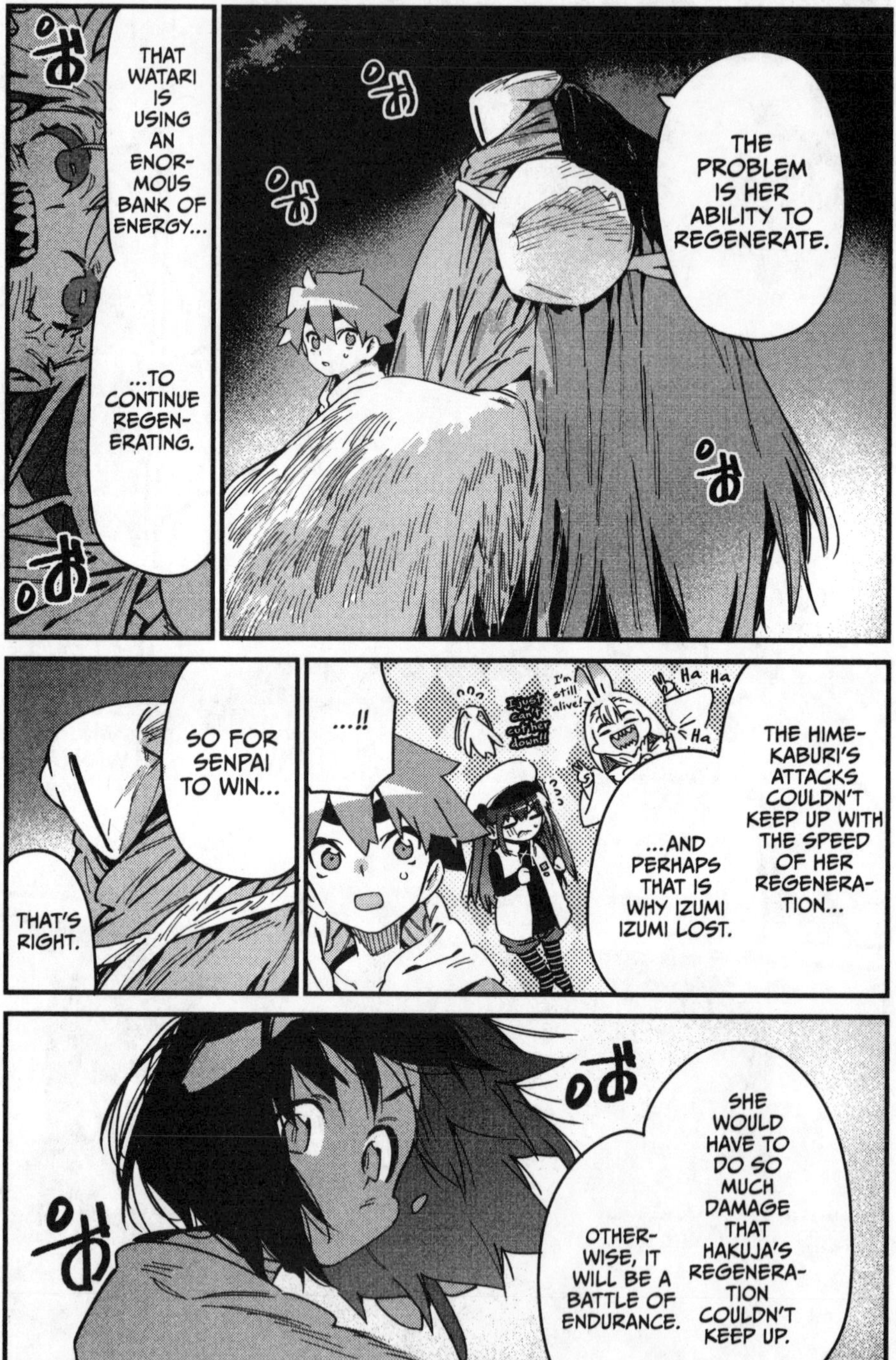
ぉお
THE PROBLEM IS HER ABILITY TO REGENERATE.
THAT WATARI IS USING AN ENORMOUS BANK OF ENERGY...
...TO CONTINUE REGENERATING.
THE HIME-KABURI'S ATTACKS COULDN'T KEEP UP WITH THE SPEED OF HER REGENERATION...
Ha Ha Ha
I'm still alive!
I just can't cut her down!!
...AND PERHAPS THAT IS WHY IZUMI IZUMI LOST.
...!!
SO FOR SENPAI TO WIN...
THAT'S RIGHT.
SHE WOULD HAVE TO DO SO MUCH DAMAGE THAT HAKUJA'S REGENERATION COULDN'T KEEP UP.
OTHERWISE, IT WILL BE A BATTLE OF ENDURANCE.

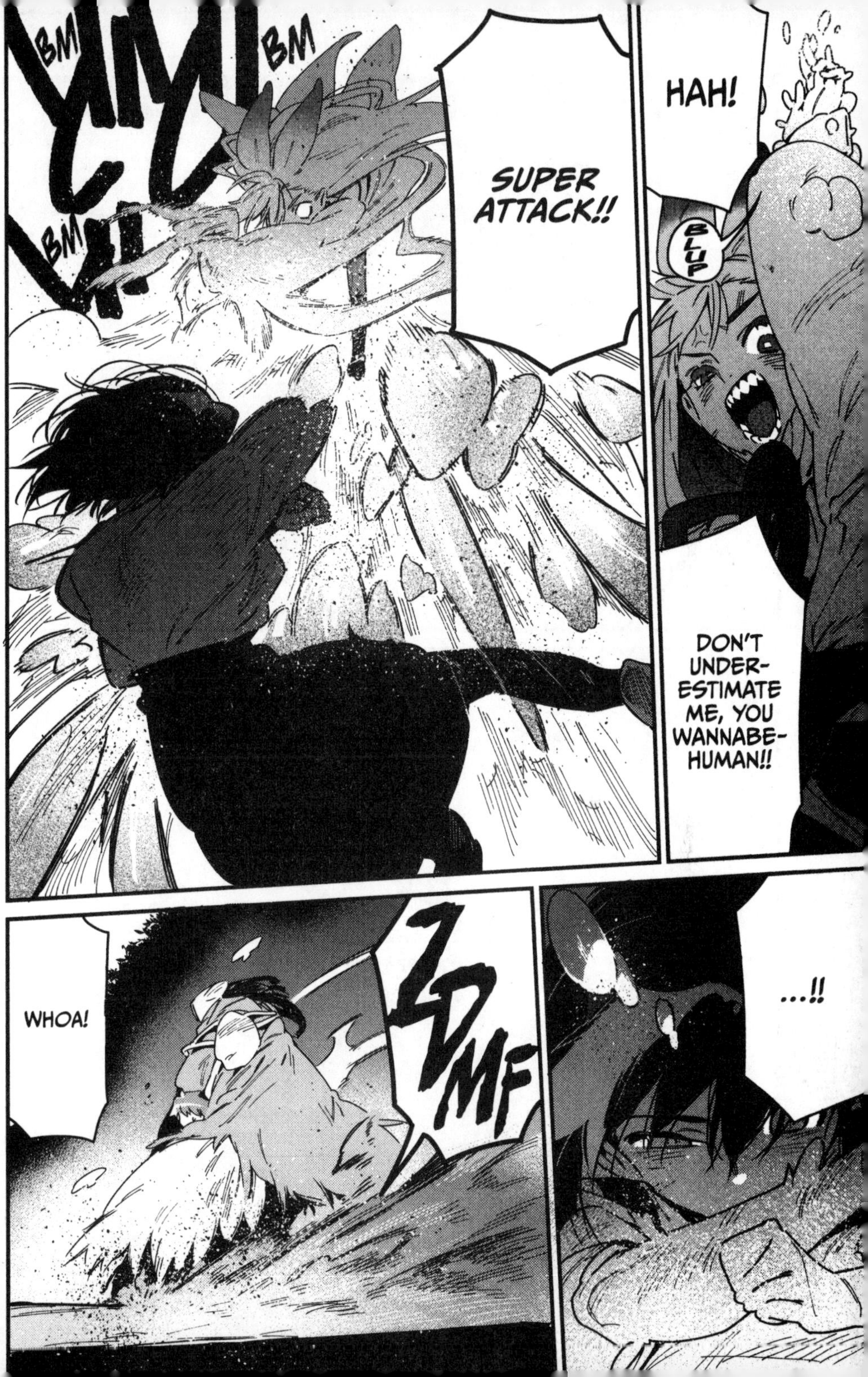
HAH!
BLUP
DON'T UNDER-ESTIMATE ME, YOU WANNABE-HUMAN!!
BM
BM
BM
SUPER ATTACK!!
...!!
ZDMF
WHOA!

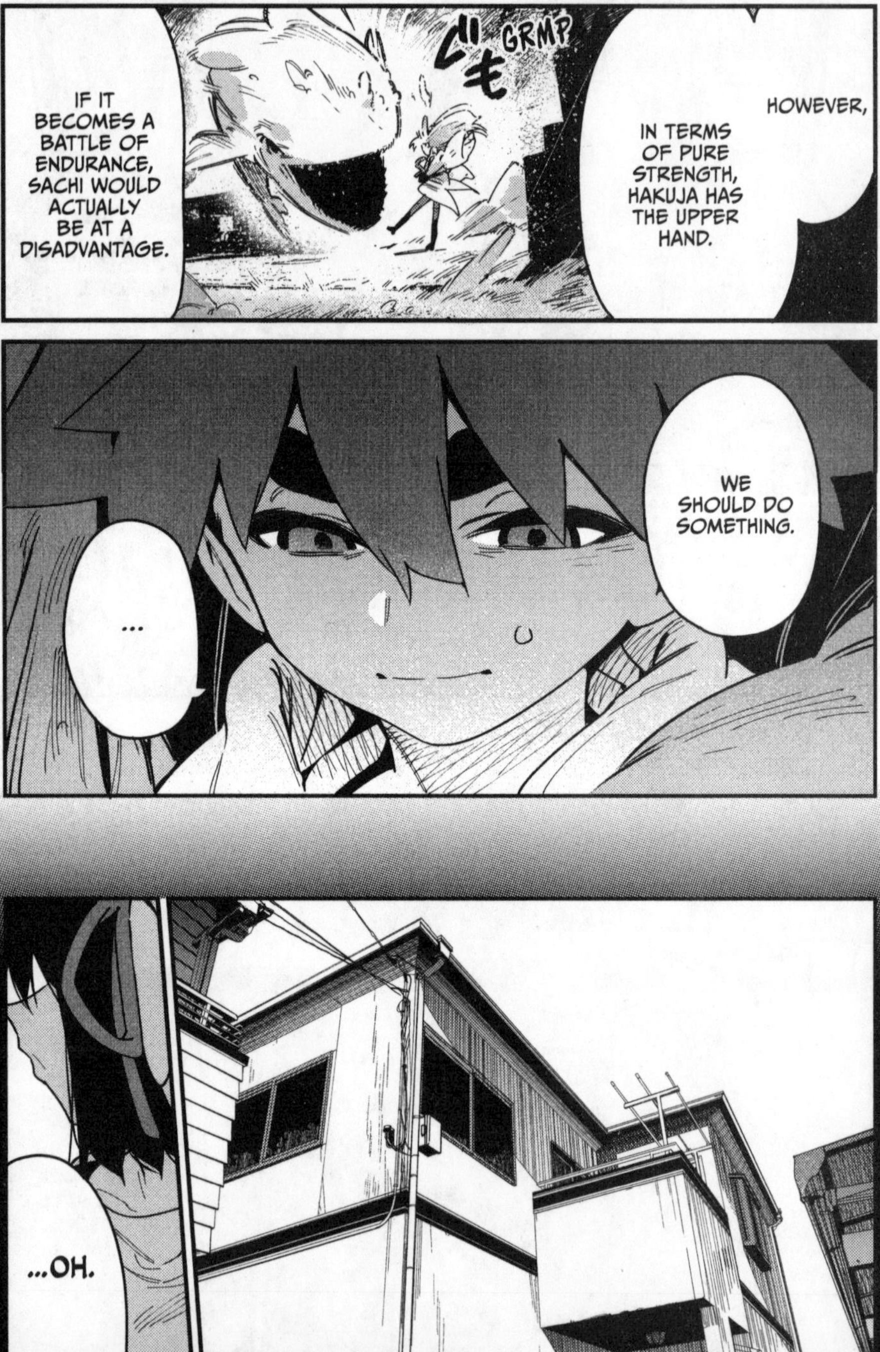
HOWEVER,
IN TERMS OF PURE STRENGTH, HAKUJA HAS THE UPPER HAND.
ぐも GRMP
IF IT BECOMES A BATTLE OF ENDURANCE, SACHI WOULD ACTUALLY BE AT A DISADVANTAGE.
WE SHOULD DO SOMETHING.
...
...OH.

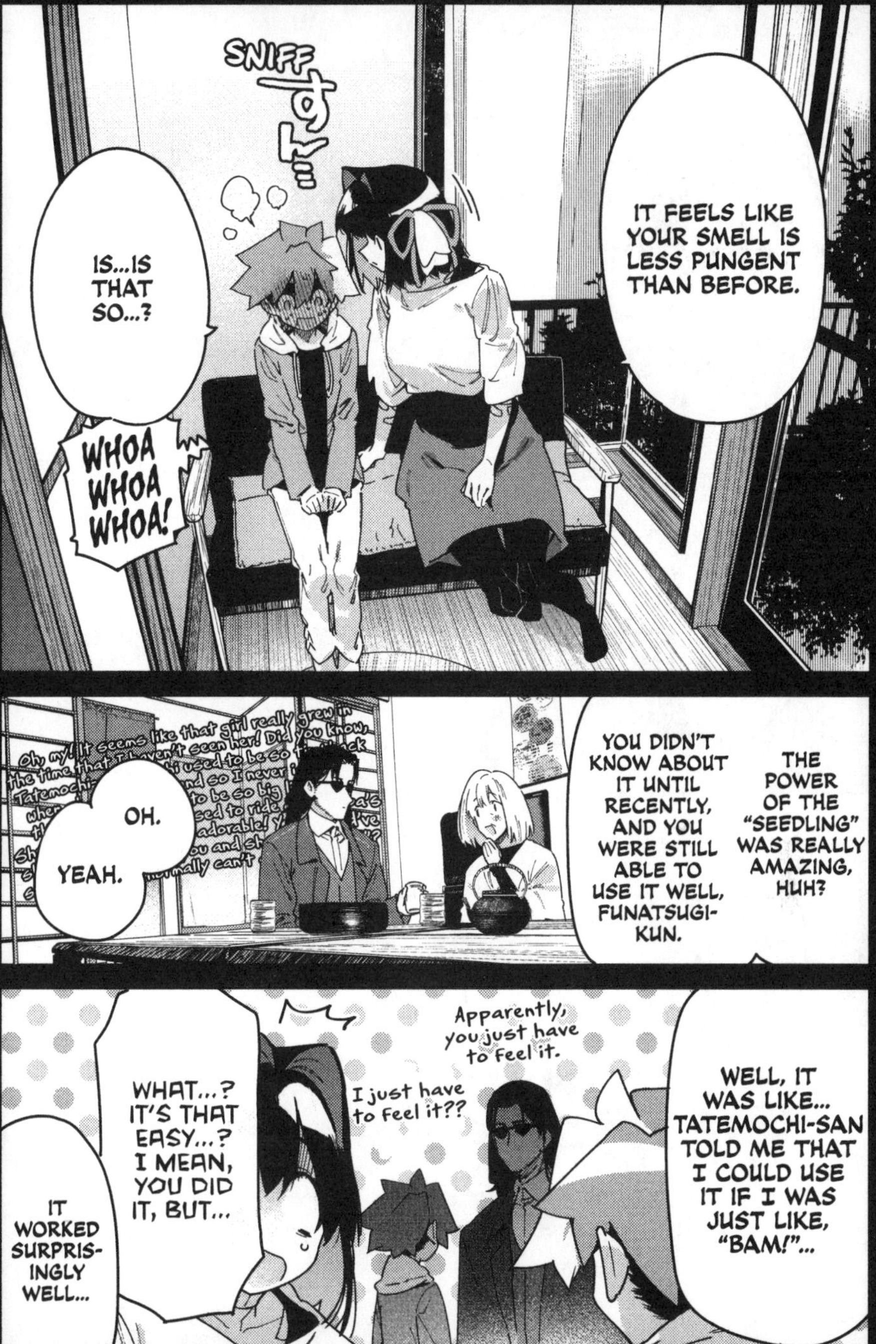
IT FEELS LIKE YOUR SMELL IS LESS PUNGENT THAN BEFORE.
SNIFF
すん
IS...IS THAT SO...?
WHOA WHOA WHOA!
THE POWER OF THE "SEEDLING" WAS REALLY AMAZING, HUH?
YOU DIDN'T KNOW ABOUT IT UNTIL RECENTLY, AND YOU WERE STILL ABLE TO USE IT WELL, FUNATSUGI-KUN.
OH.
YEAH.
WELL, IT WAS LIKE... TATEMOCHI-SAN TOLD ME THAT I COULD USE IT IF I WAS JUST LIKE, "BAM!"...
Apparently, you just have to feel it.
I just have to feel it??
WHAT...? IT'S THAT EASY...? I MEAN, YOU DID IT, BUT...
IT WORKED SURPRISINGLY WELL...

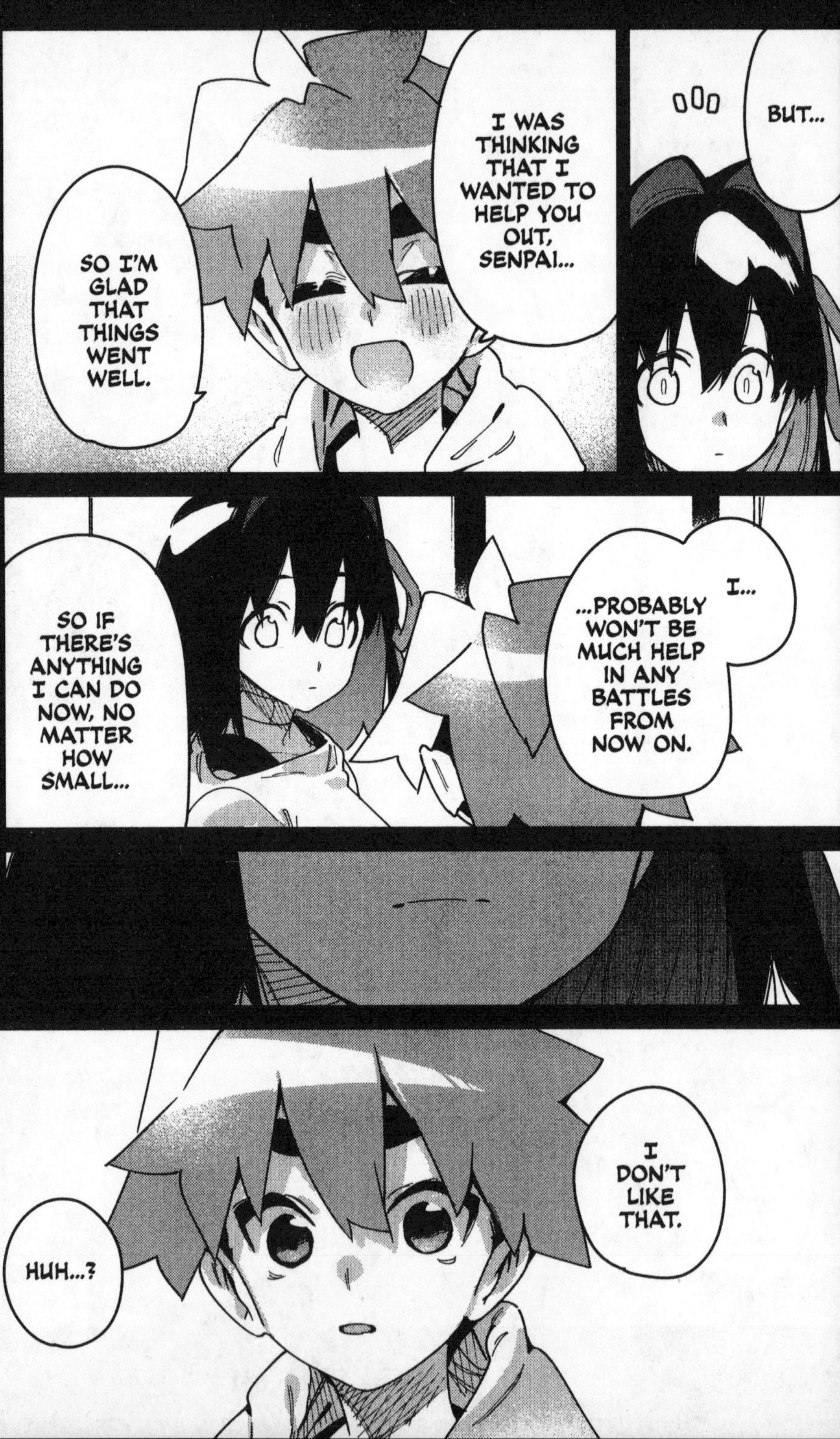

BUT...
OOO
I WAS THINKING THAT I WANTED TO HELP YOU OUT, SENPAI...
SO I'M GLAD THAT THINGS WENT WELL.
I...
...PROBABLY WON'T BE MUCH HELP IN ANY BATTLES FROM NOW ON.
SO IF THERE'S ANYTHING I CAN DO NOW, NO MATTER HOW SMALL...
I DON'T LIKE THAT.
HUH...?

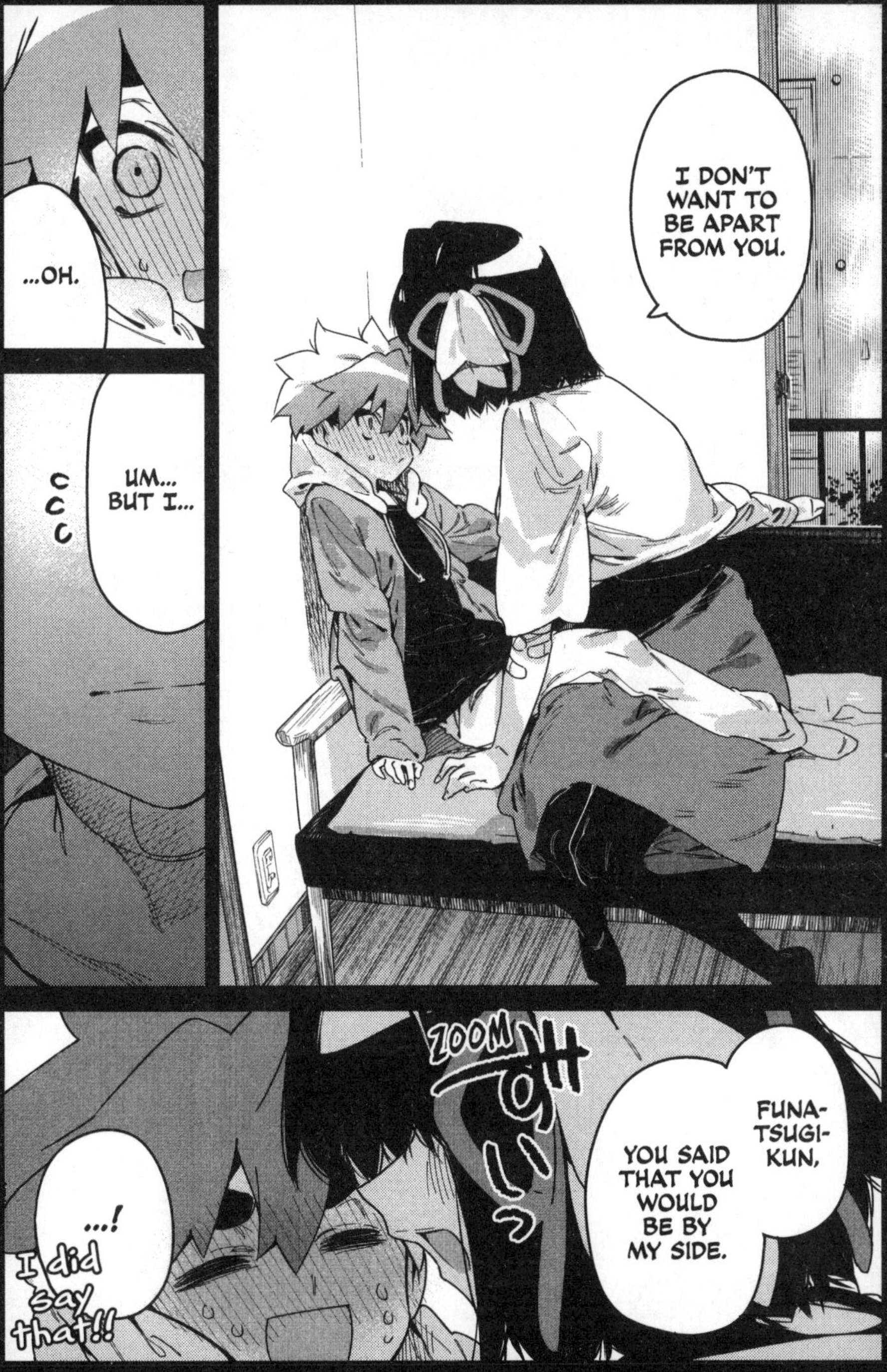
I DON'T WANT TO BE APART FROM YOU.
...OH.
UM... BUT I...
CCC
ZOOM
FUNA-TSUGI-KUN, YOU SAID THAT YOU WOULD BE BY MY SIDE.
...!
I did say that!!

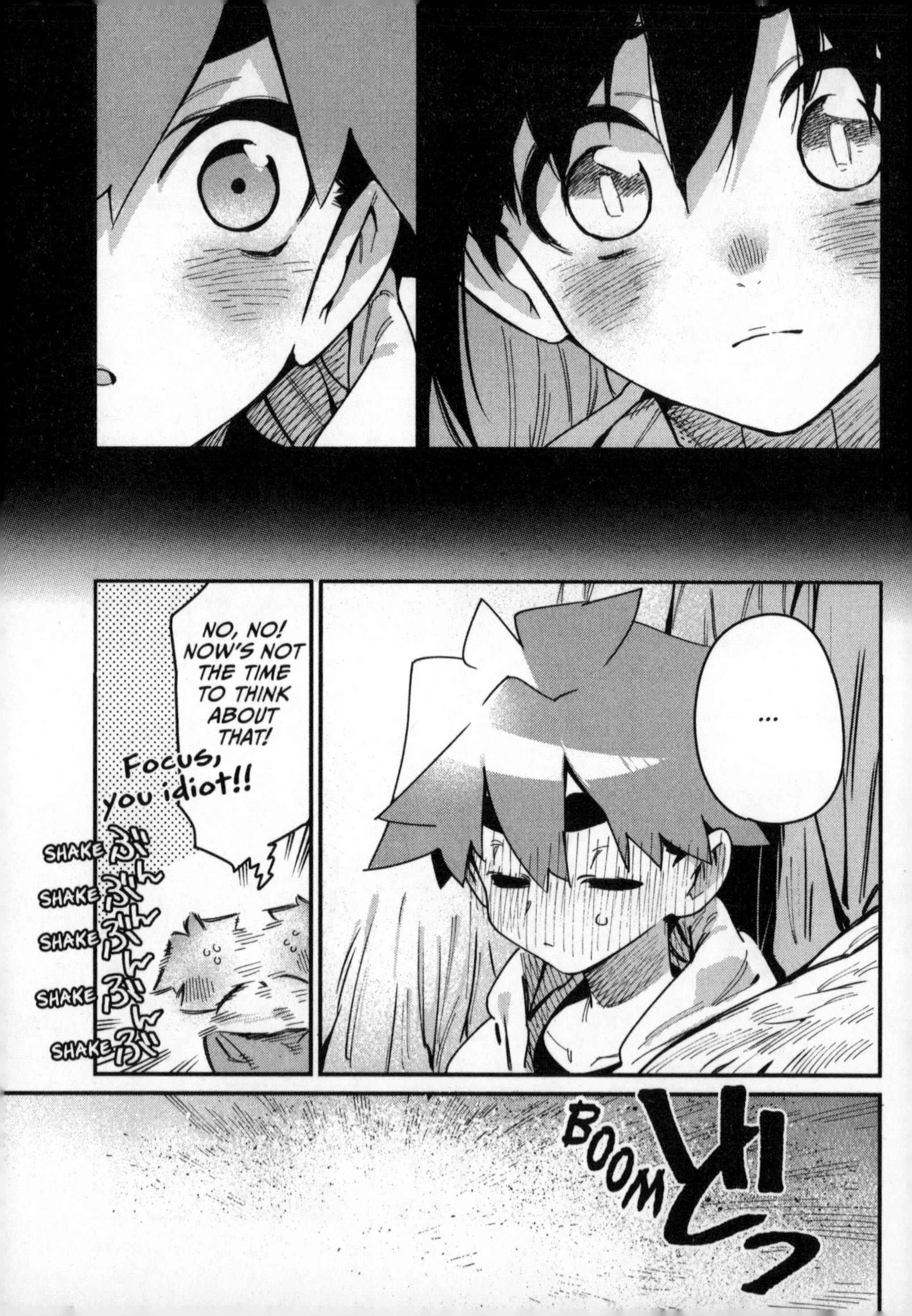
...
NO, NO! NOW'S NOT THE TIME TO THINK ABOUT THAT!
Focus, you idiot!!
SHAKE
SHAKE
SHAKE
SHAKE
SHAKE
BOOM

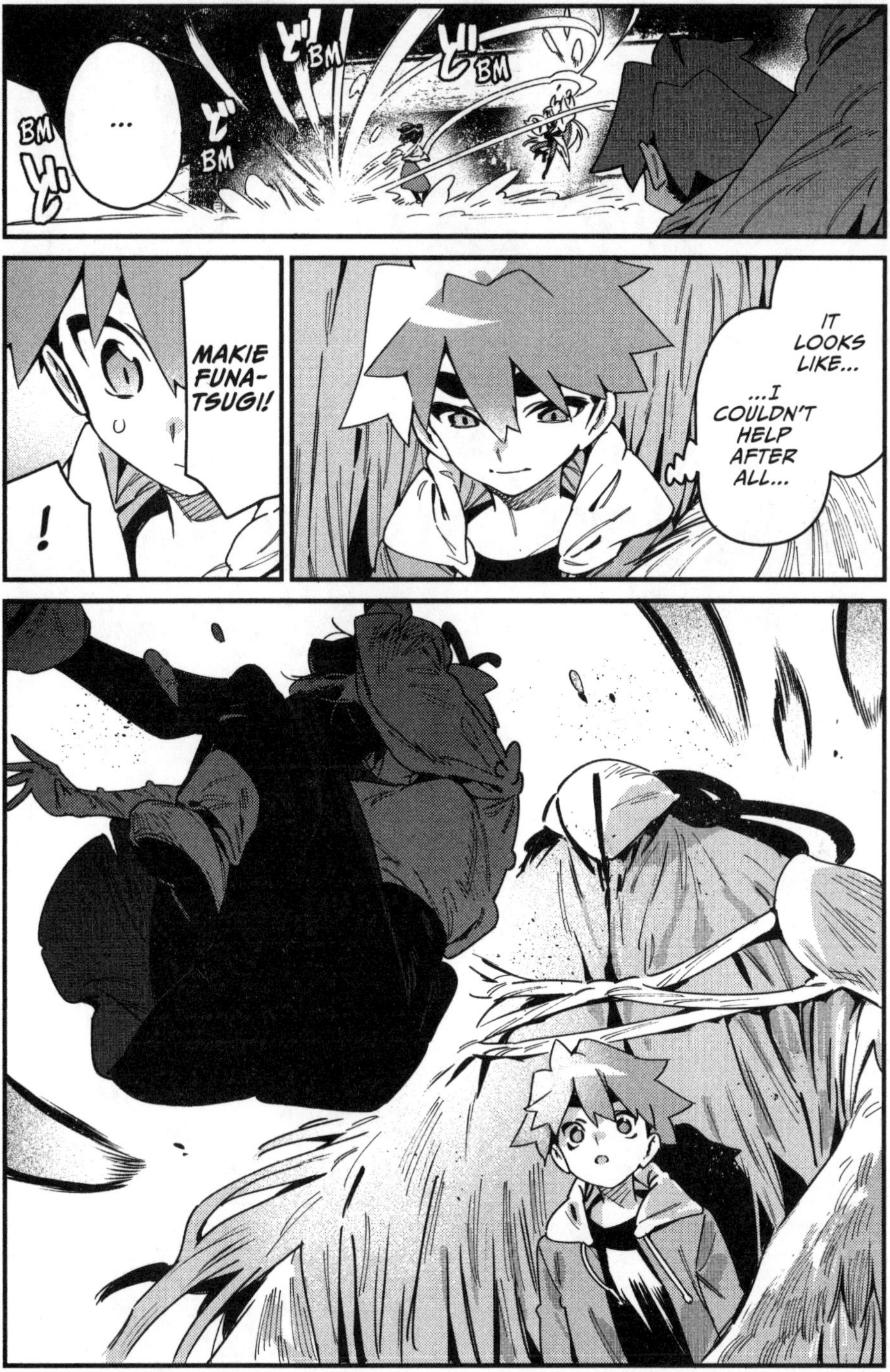

ど BM
ど BM
ど BM
...
BM ど
IT LOOKS LIKE...
...I COULDN'T HELP AFTER ALL...
MAKIE FUNA-TSUGI!
!

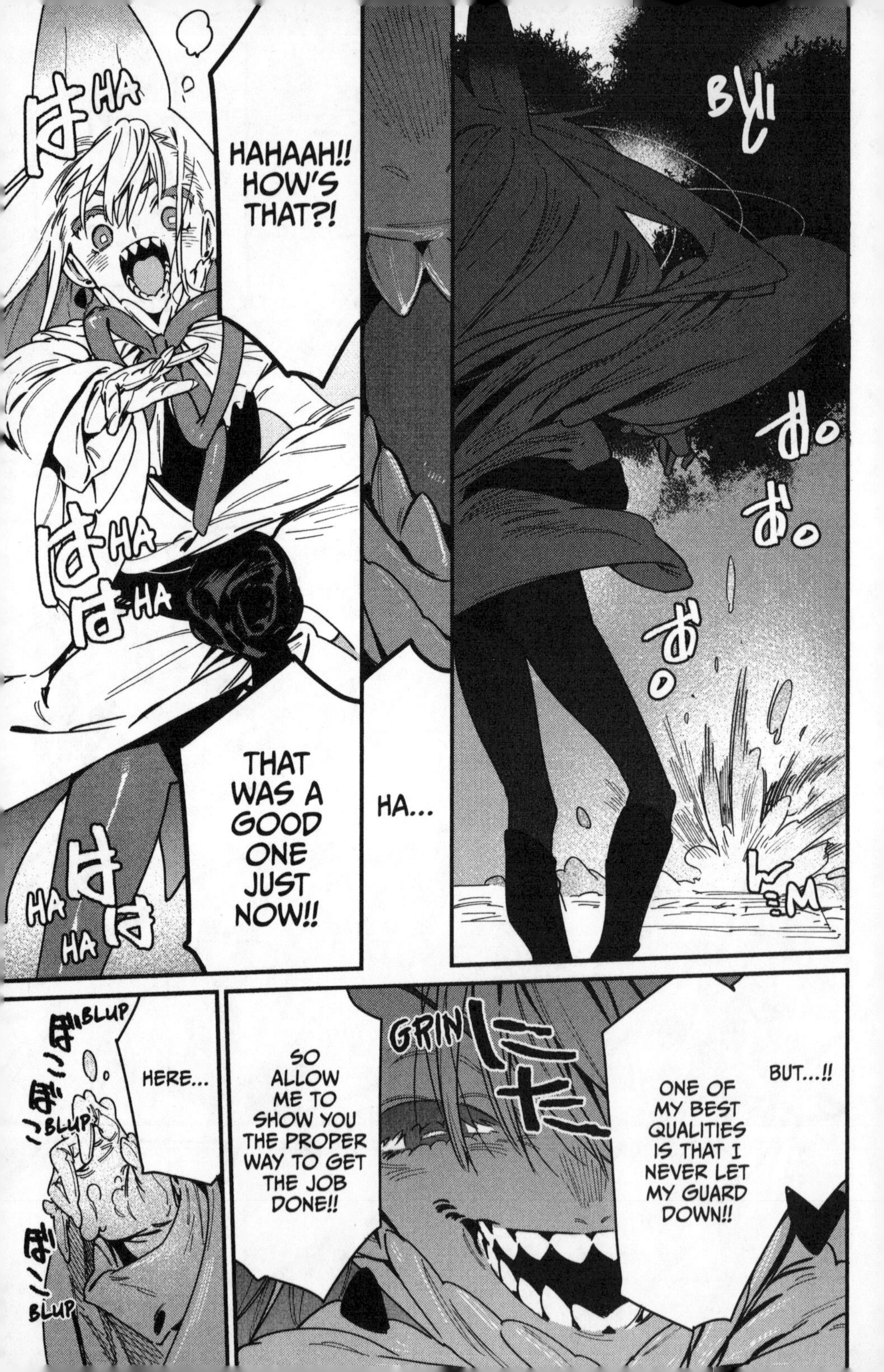
BYU
お。お。お。
ん M
HA...
HAHAAH!! HOW'S THAT?!
は HA
はは HA HA
THAT WAS A GOOD ONE JUST NOW!!
はは HA HA
BUT...!!
ONE OF MY BEST QUALITIES IS THAT I NEVER LET MY GUARD DOWN!!
GRIN にたー
SO ALLOW ME TO SHOW YOU THE PROPER WAY TO GET THE JOB DONE!!
HERE...
BLUP
BLUP
BLUP

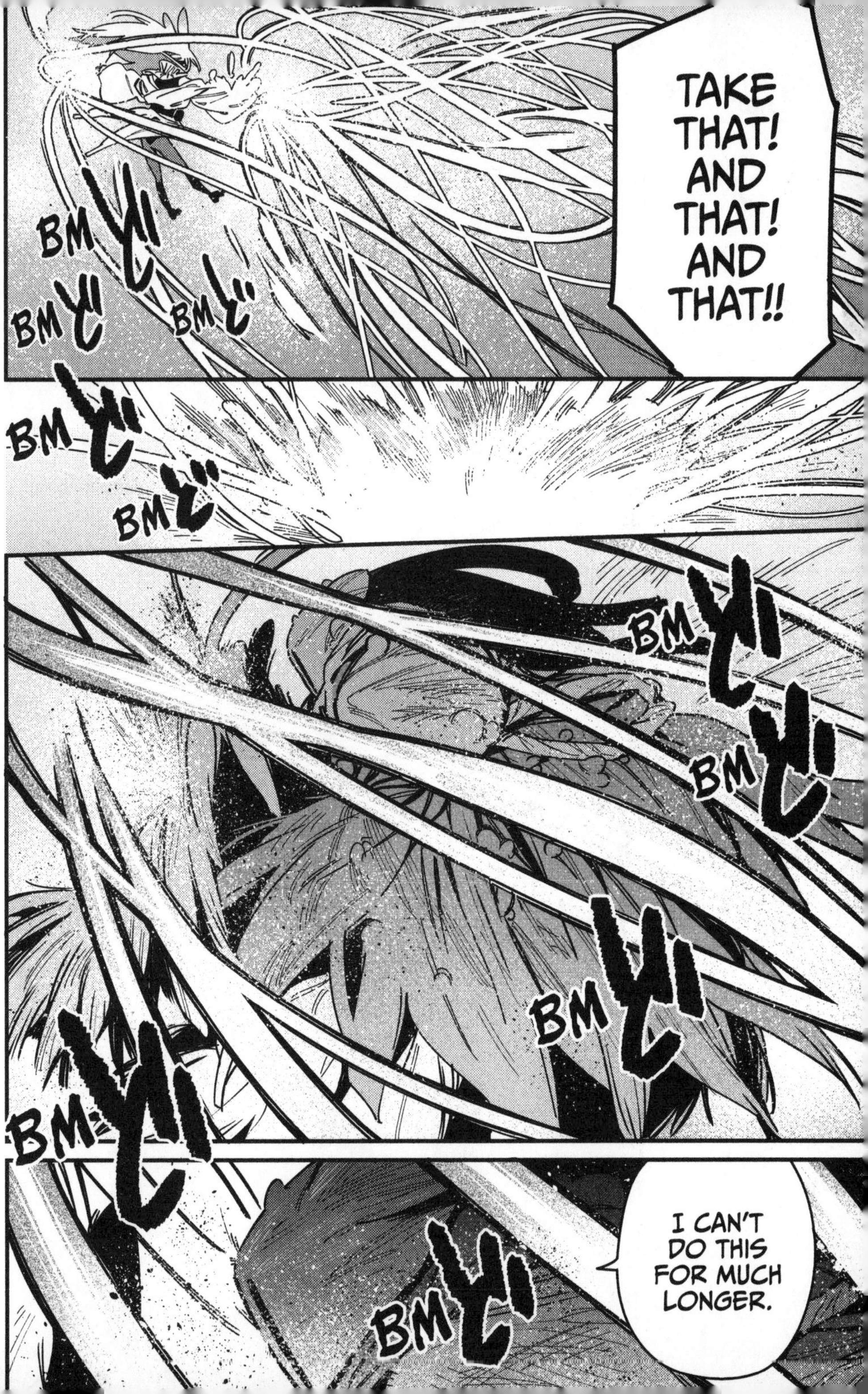
TAKE THAT! AND THAT! AND THAT!!
BM
BM
BM
BM
BM
BM
BM
BM
BM
I CAN'T DO THIS FOR MUCH LONGER.
BM

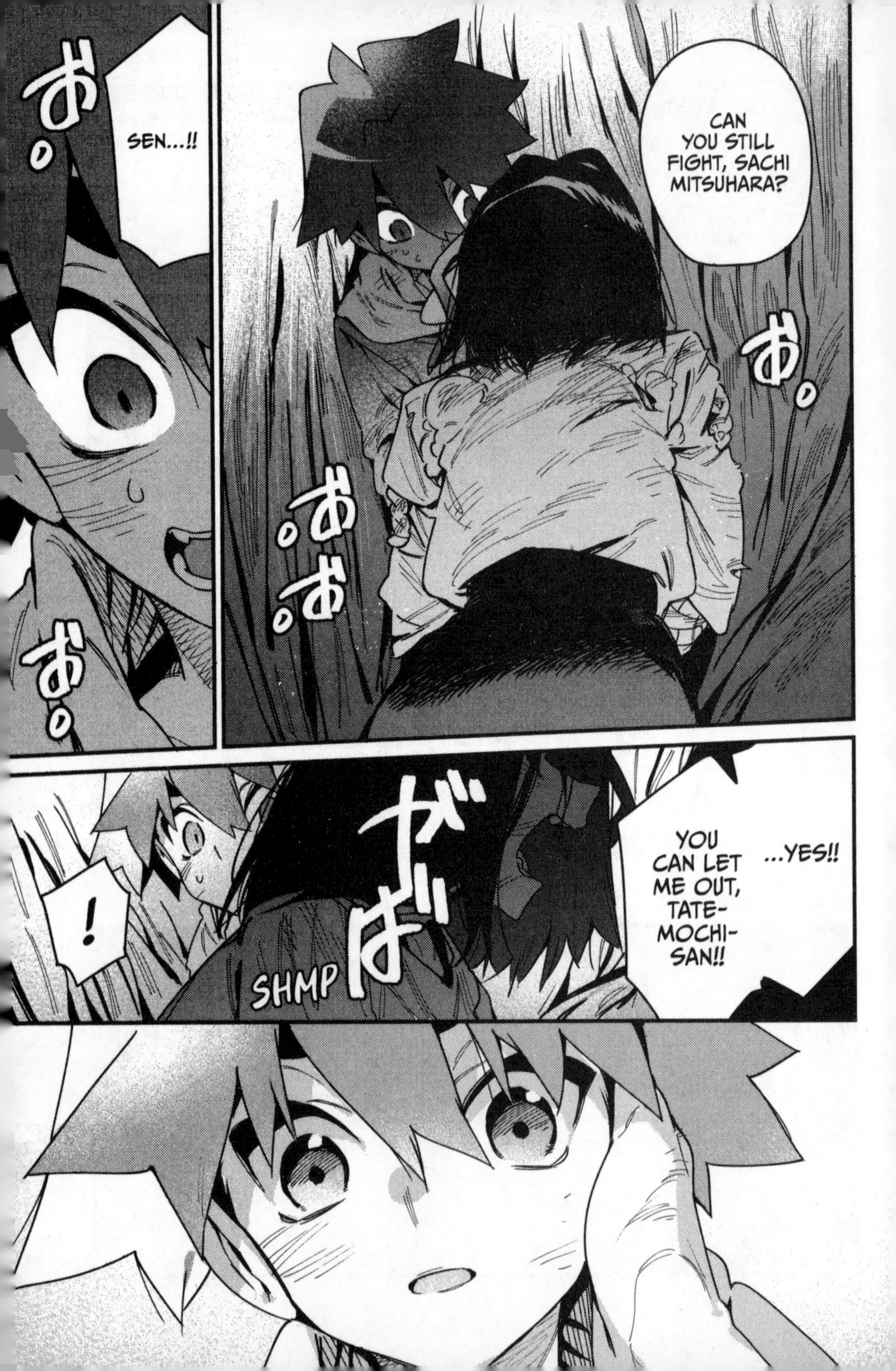
CAN YOU STILL FIGHT, SACHI MITSUHARA?
お。
おお。
SEN...!!
お。
お。
...YES!!
YOU CAN LET ME OUT, TATE-MOCHI-SAN!!
がば
SHMP
!

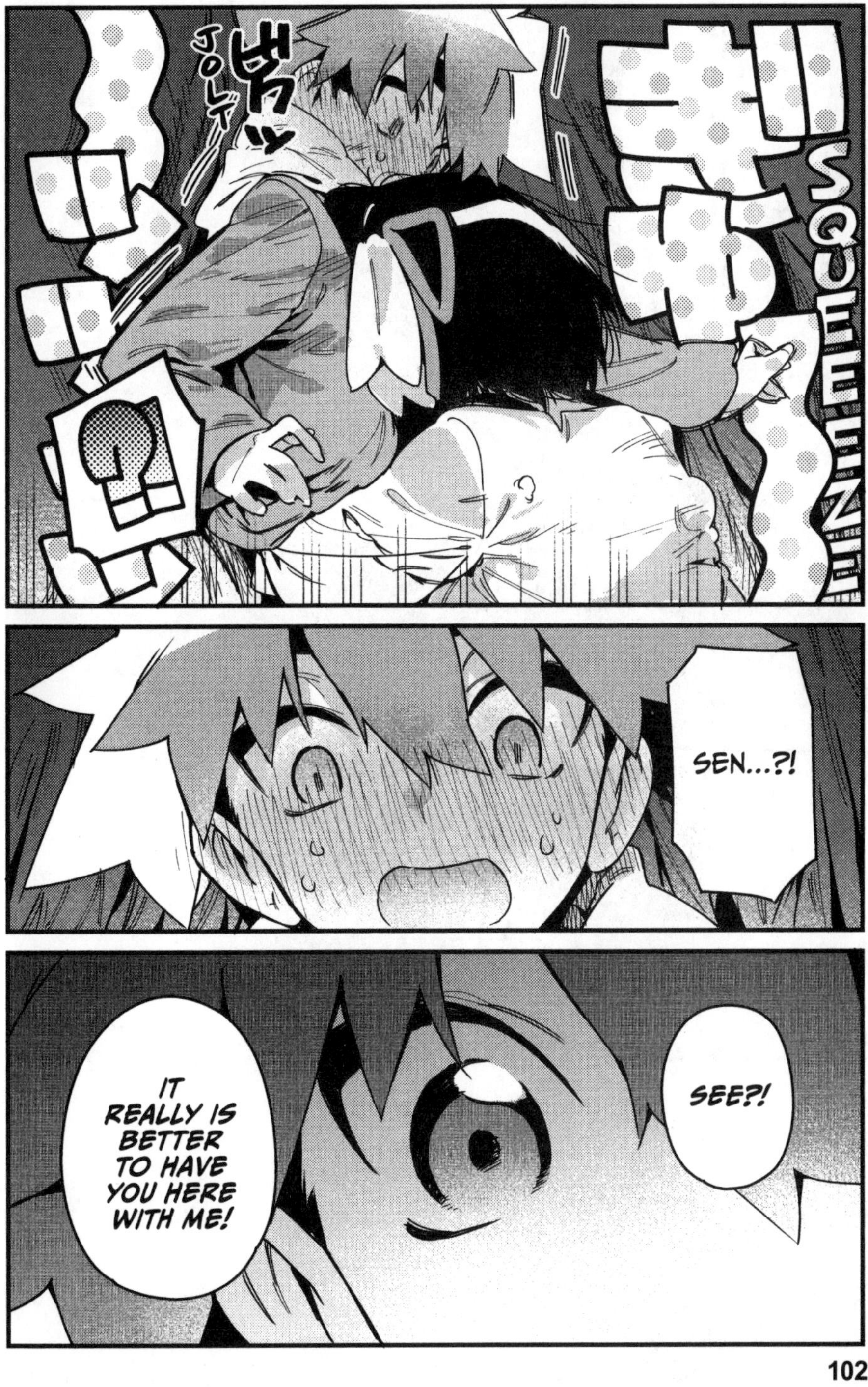
SQUEEEEZE!!
JOLT
SEN...?!
SEE?!
IT REALLY IS BETTER TO HAVE YOU HERE WITH ME!

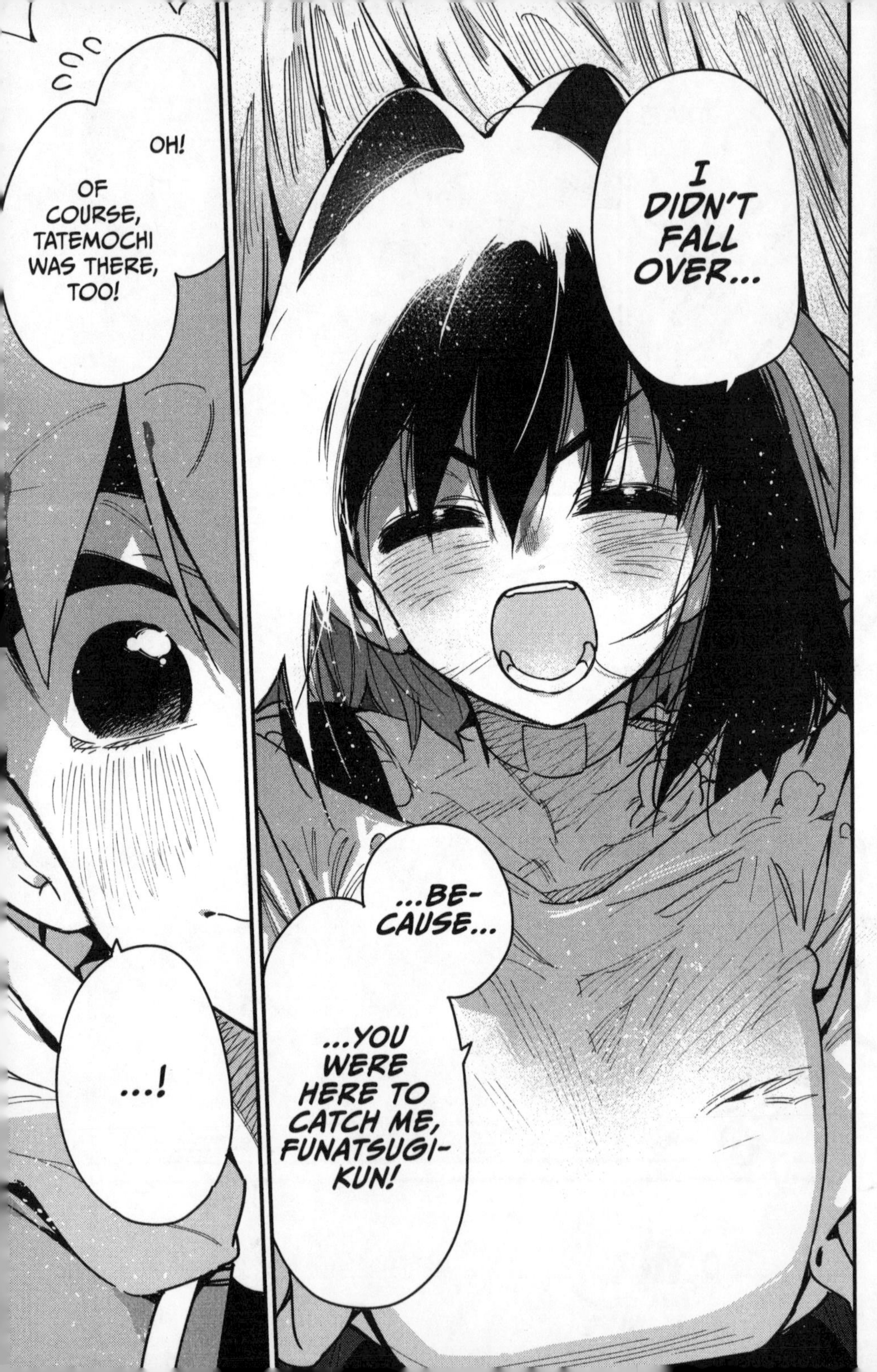
I DIDN'T FALL OVER...
...BE-CAUSE...
...YOU WERE HERE TO CATCH ME, FUNATSUGI-KUN!
OH! OF COURSE, TATEMOCHI WAS THERE, TOO!
...!

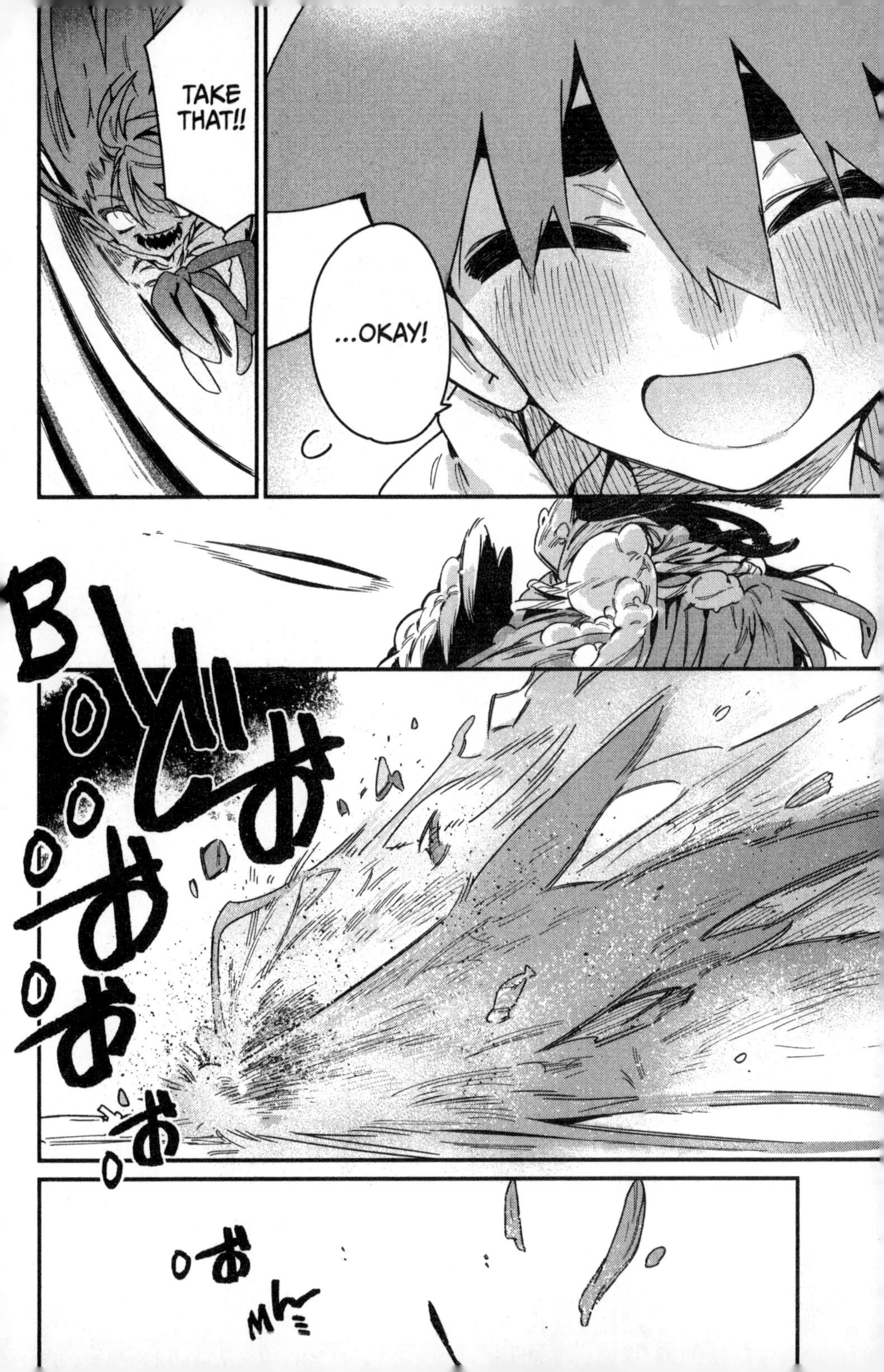
...OKAY!
TAKE THAT!!

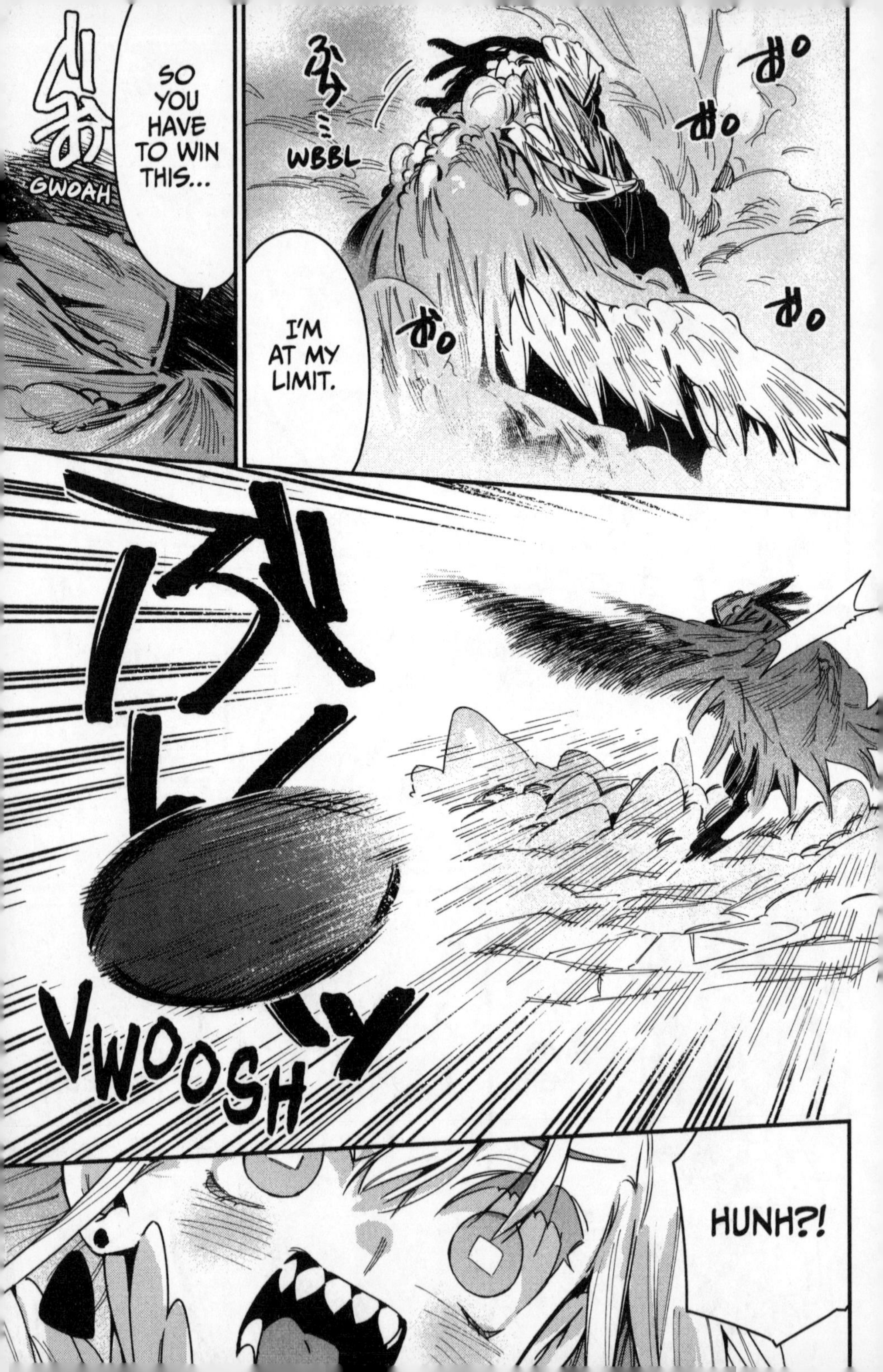
WBBL
I'M AT MY LIMIT.
SO YOU HAVE TO WIN THIS...
GWOAH
VWOOSH
HUNH?!

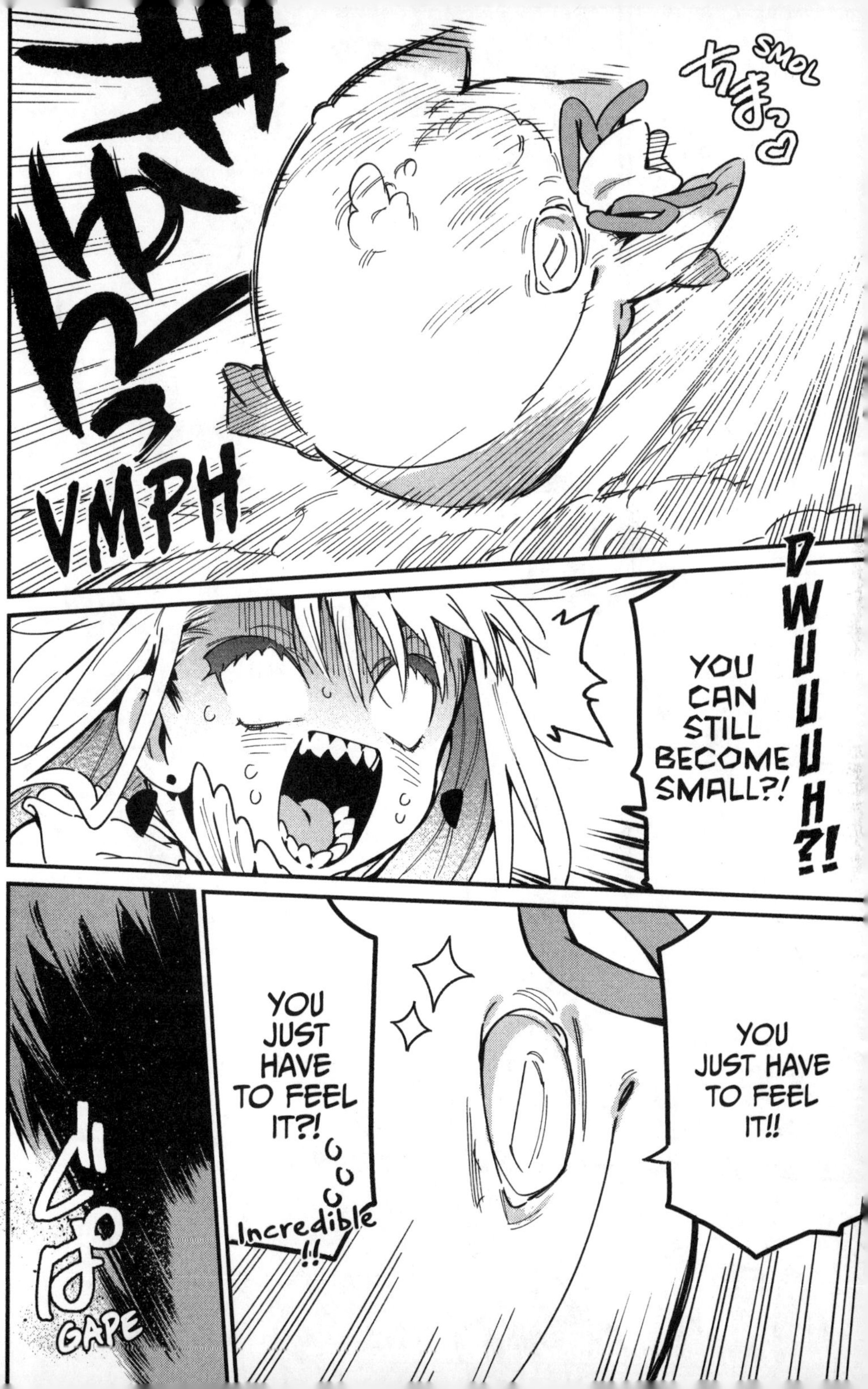
ちまっ♡
SMOL
ぎゅわっ
VMPH
DWUUUH?!
YOU CAN STILL BECOME SMALL?!
YOU JUST HAVE TO FEEL IT!!
YOU JUST HAVE TO FEEL IT?!
Incredible !!
くぱ
GAPE

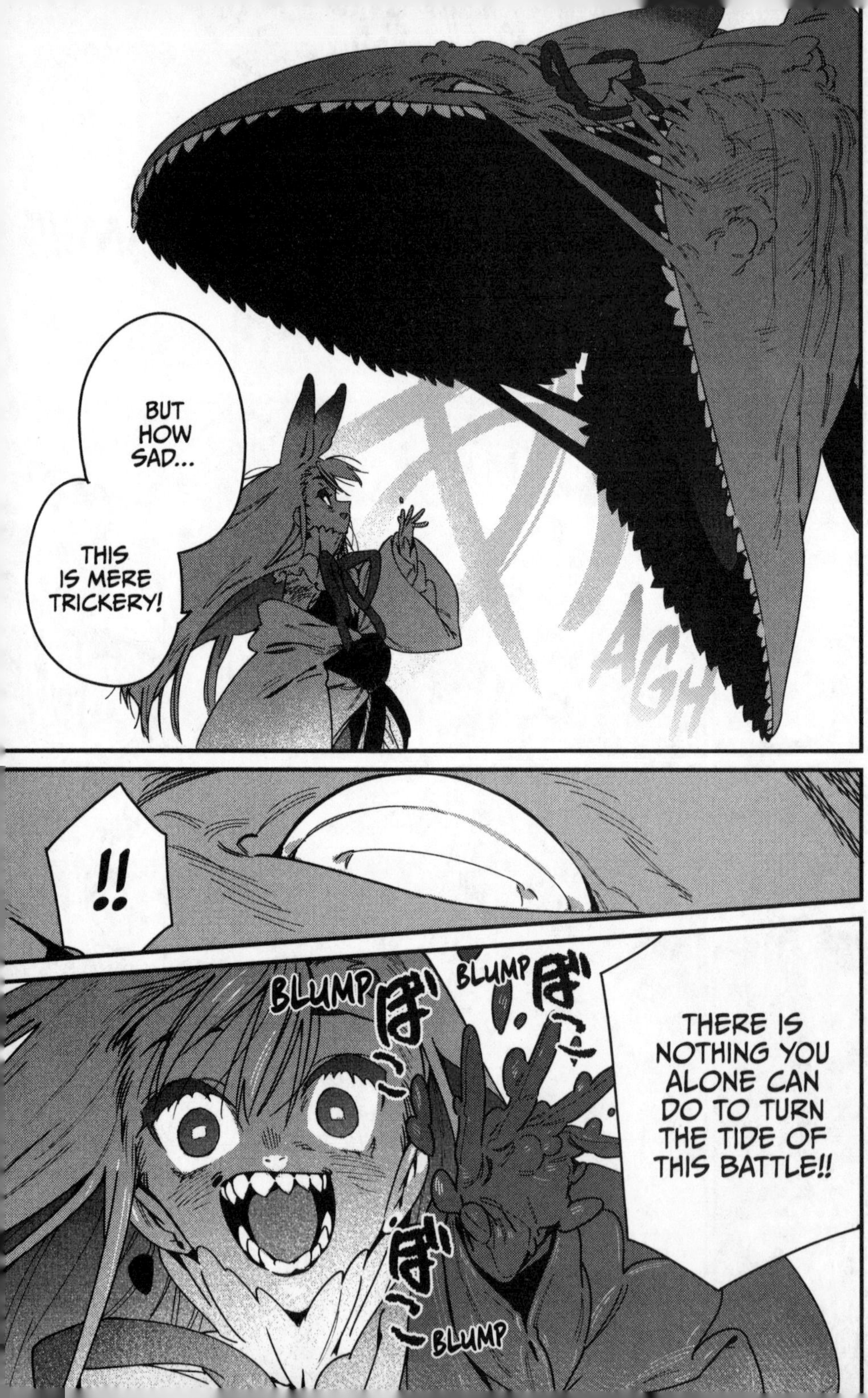
BUT HOW SAD...
THIS IS MERE TRICKERY!
AGH
!!
THERE IS NOTHING YOU ALONE CAN DO TO TURN THE TIDE OF THIS BATTLE!!
ぼこ
BLUMP
ぼこ
BLUMP
ぼこ
BLUMP

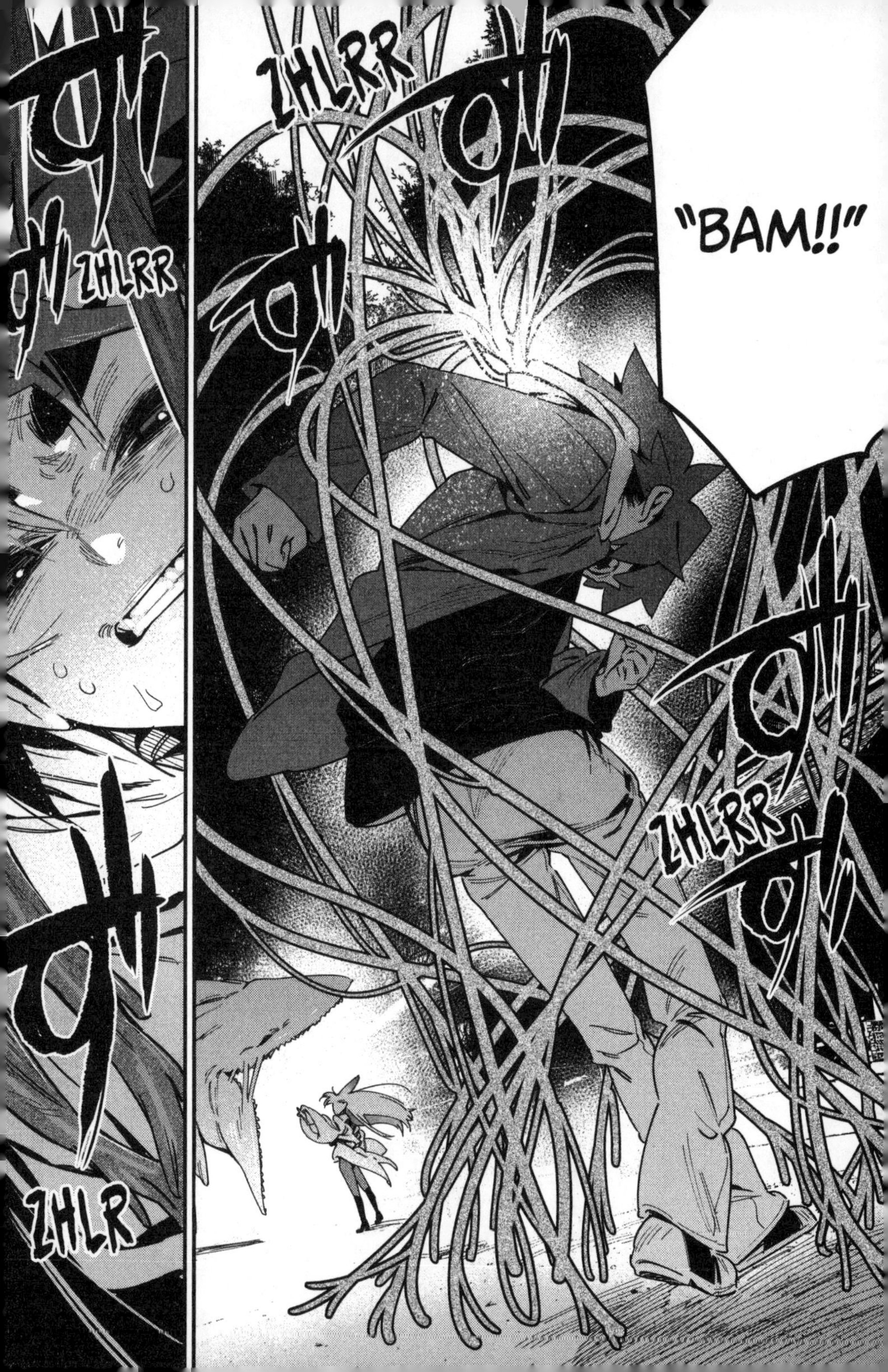
"BAM!!"
ZHLRR
ZHLRR
ZHLRR
ZHLR

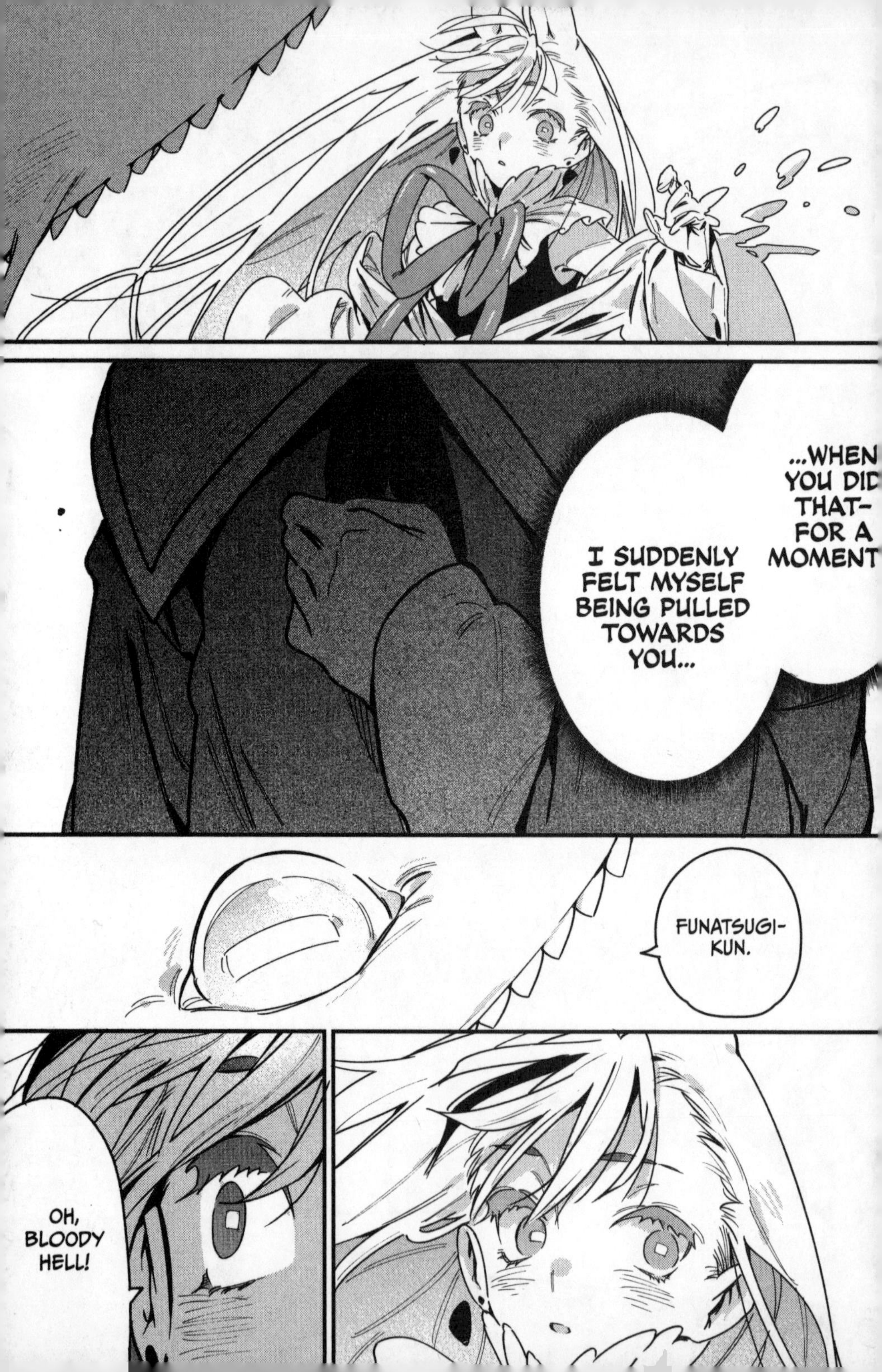
...WHEN YOU DID THAT- FOR A MOMENT
I SUDDENLY FELT MYSELF BEING PULLED TOWARDS YOU...
FUNATSUGI-KUN.
OH, BLOODY HELL!

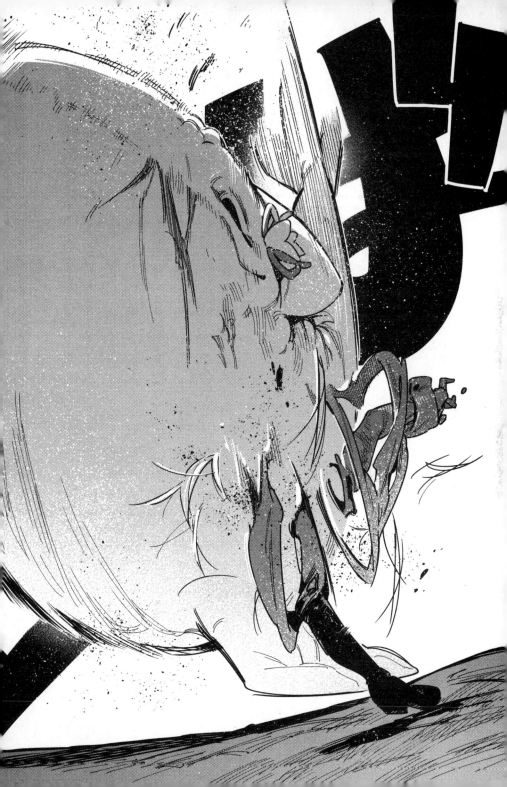

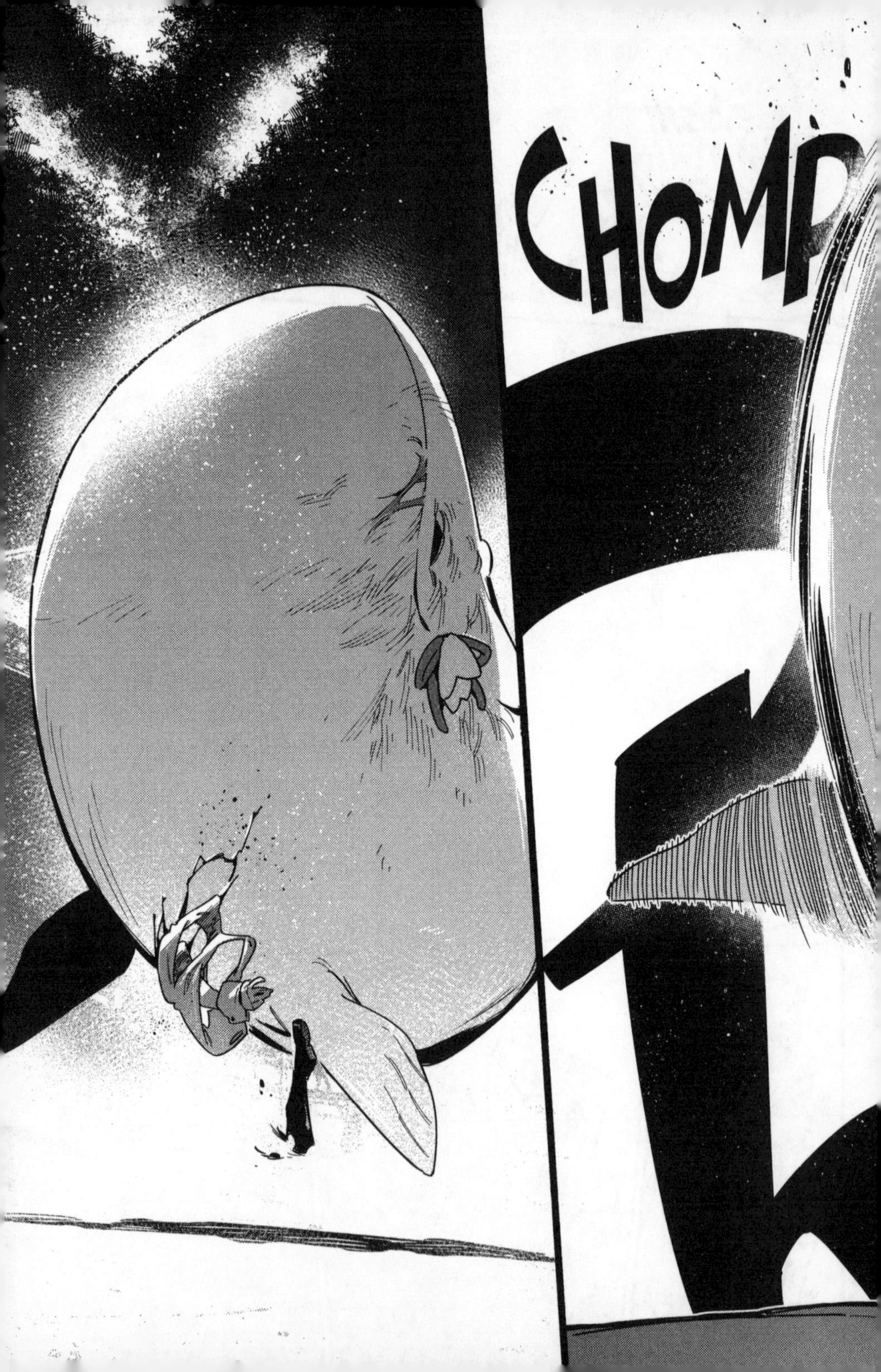
CHOMP

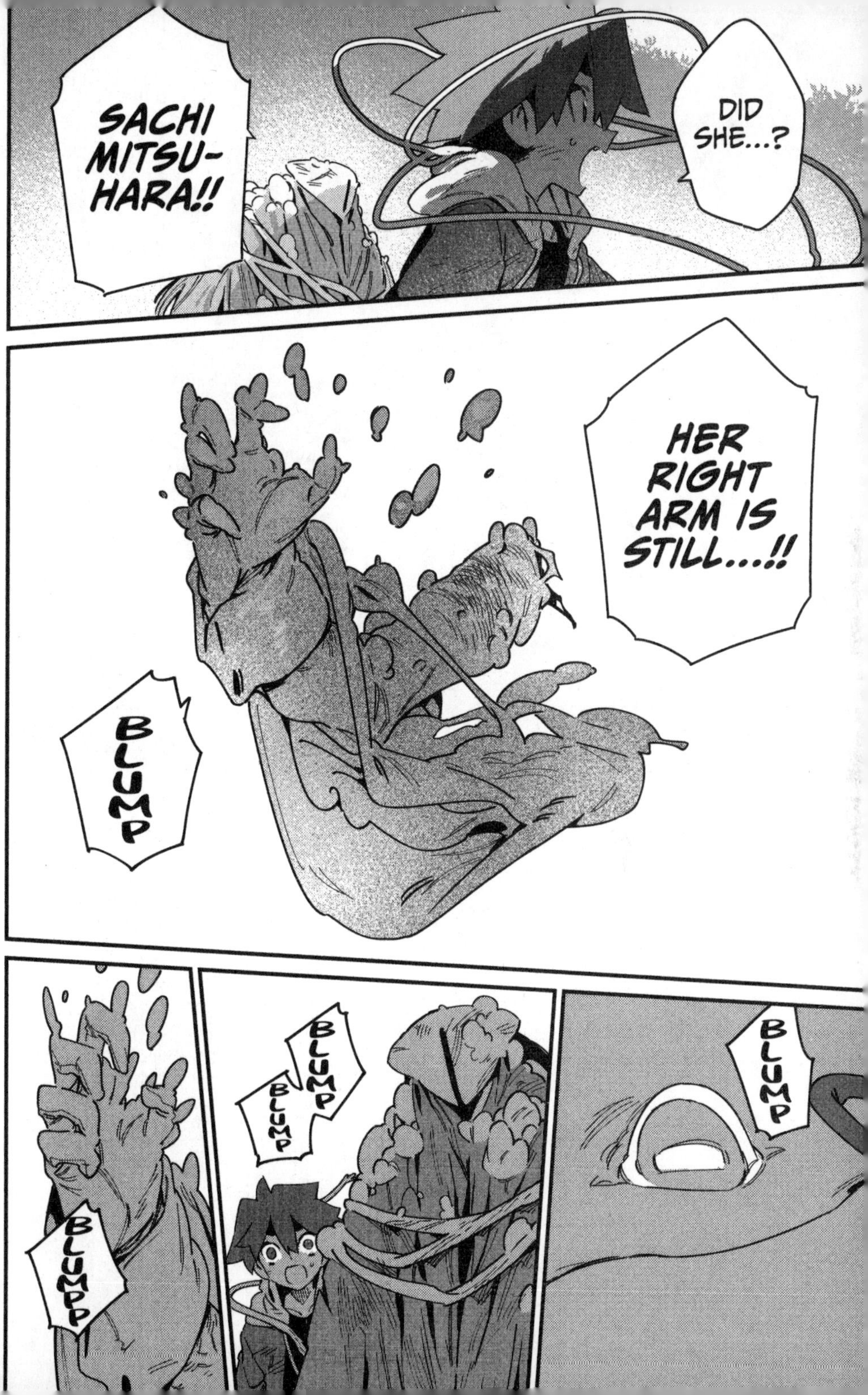
DID SHE...?
SACHI MITSU-HARA!!
HER RIGHT ARM IS STILL...!!
BLUMP
BLUMP
BLUMP
BLUMP
BLUMPP

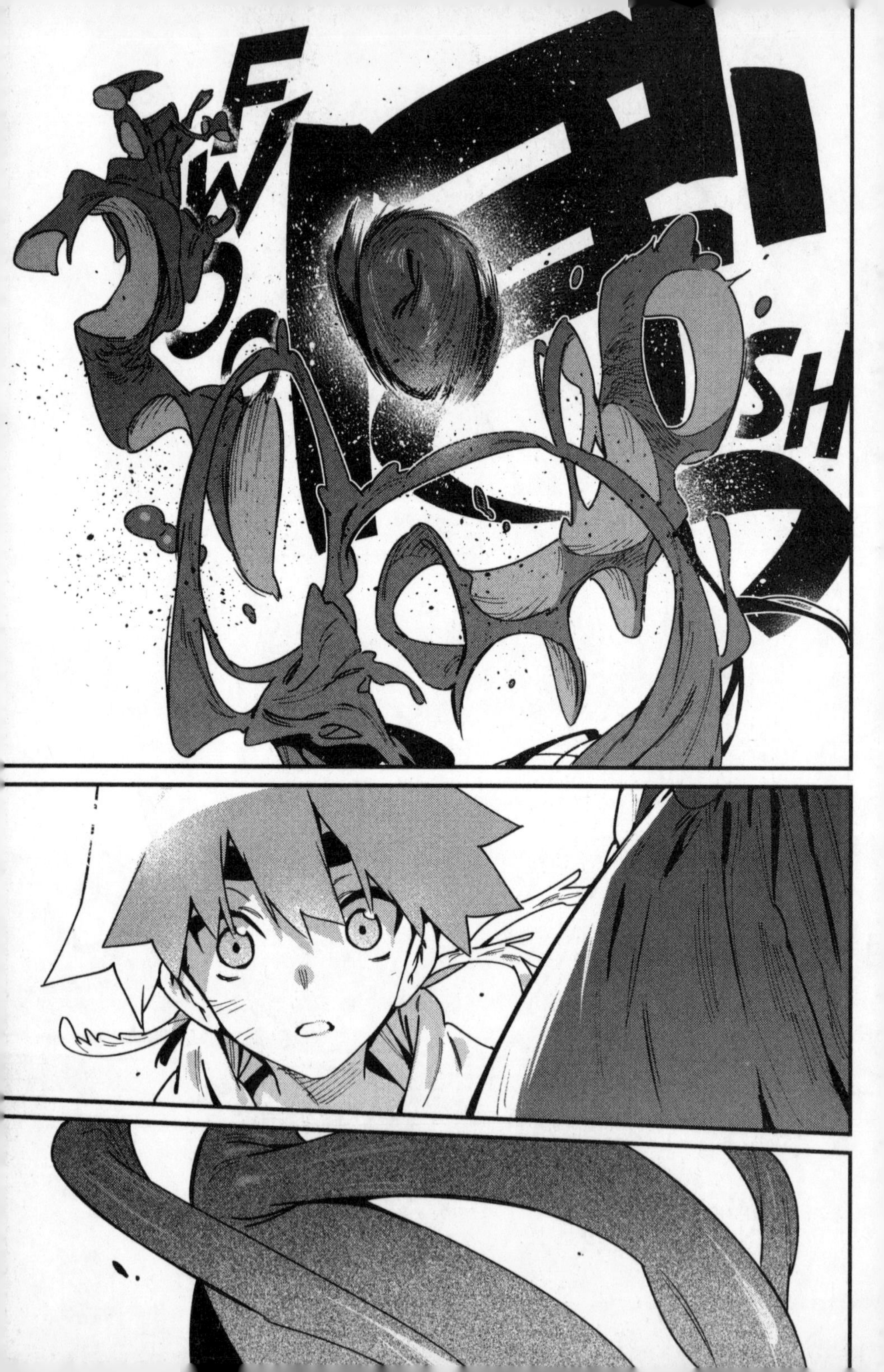
FWOOOSH

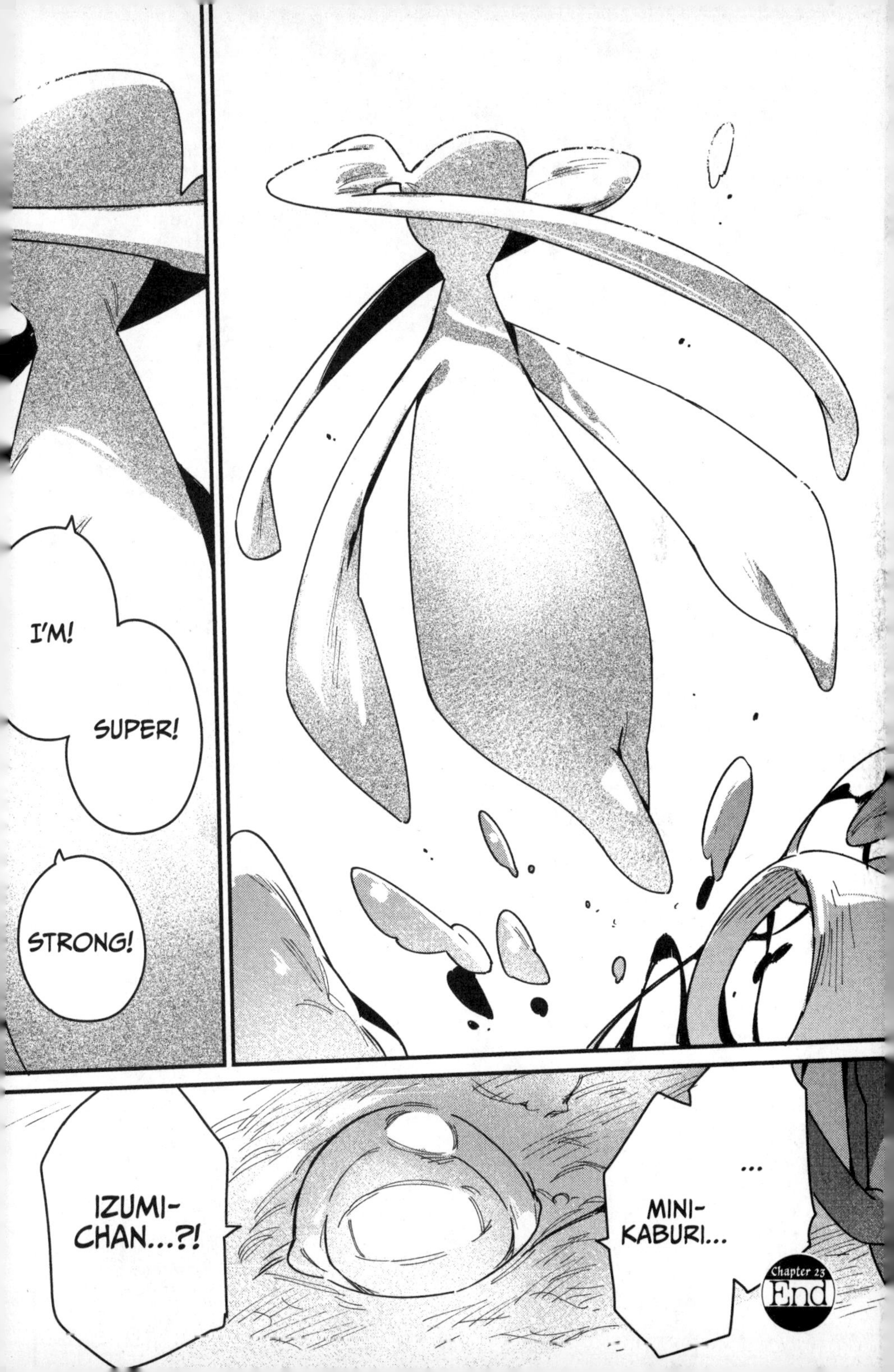
I'M!
SUPER!
STRONG!
...
MINI-KABURI...
IZUMI-CHAN...?!
Chapter 23 End

Sachi's MONSTROUS Appetite

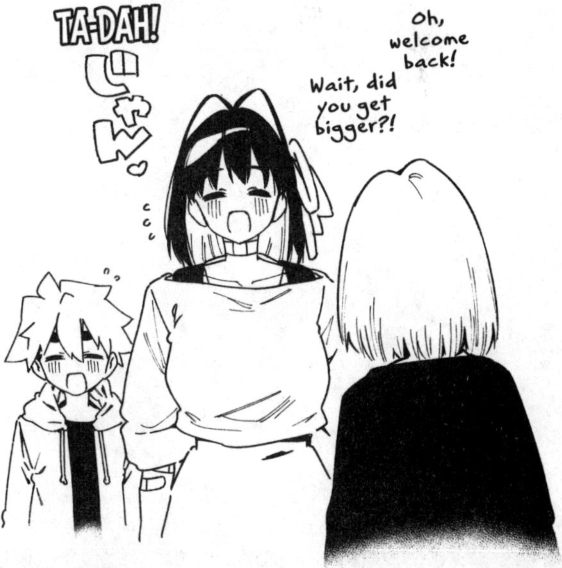
Oh, welcome back!
Wait, did you get bigger?!
TA-DAH!
じゃん

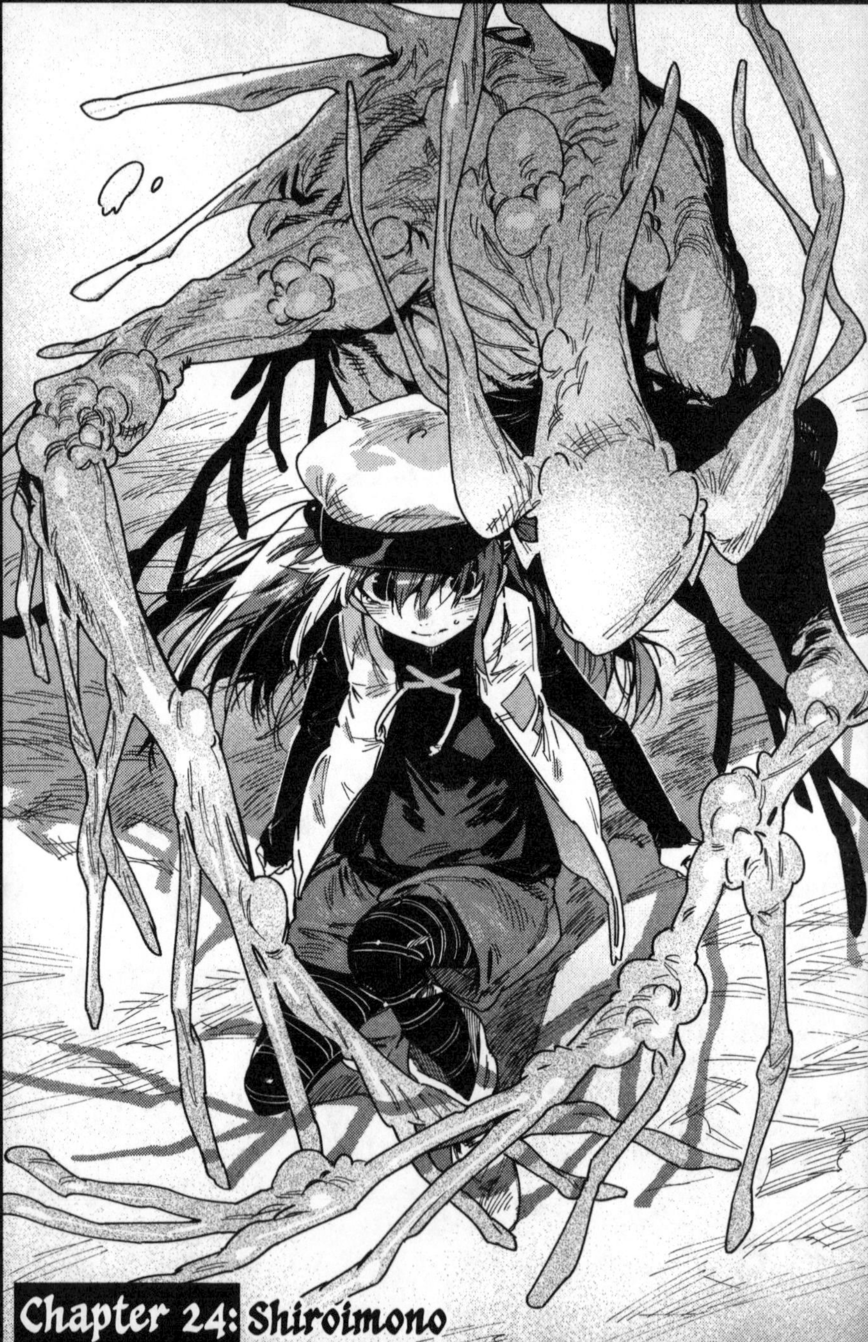
Chapter 24: Shiroimono

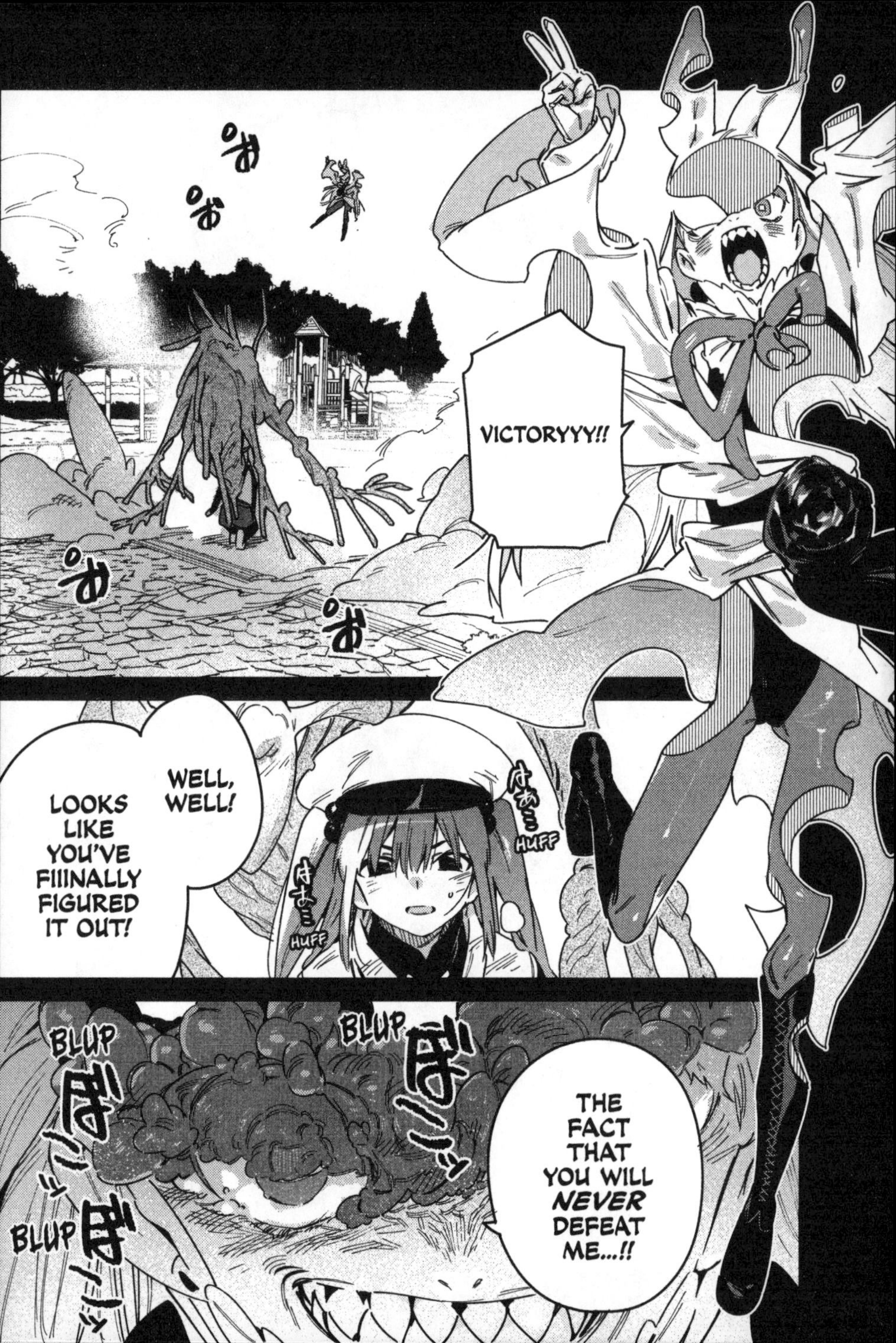
VICTORYYY!!
HUFF
HUFF
WELL, WELL!
LOOKS LIKE YOU'VE FIIINALLY FIGURED IT OUT!
BLUP
THE FACT THAT YOU WILL *NEVER* DEFEAT ME...!!
BLUP
BLUP

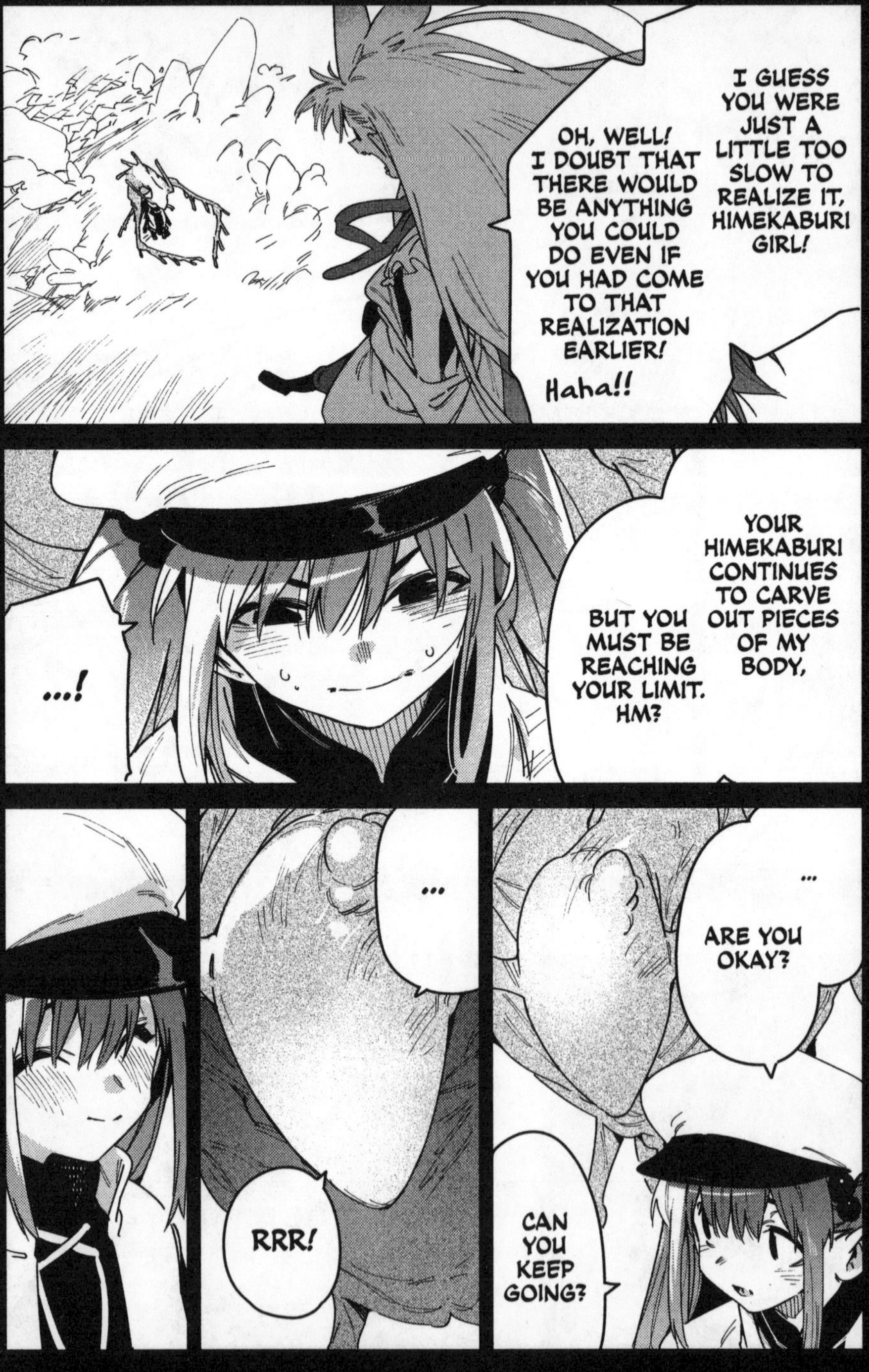
I GUESS YOU WERE JUST A LITTLE TOO SLOW TO REALIZE IT, HIMEKABURI GIRL!
OH, WELL! I DOUBT THAT THERE WOULD BE ANYTHING YOU COULD DO EVEN IF YOU HAD COME TO THAT REALIZATION EARLIER!
Haha!!
YOUR HIMEKABURI CONTINUES TO CARVE OUT PIECES OF MY BODY,
BUT YOU MUST BE REACHING YOUR LIMIT. HM?
...!
...
ARE YOU OKAY?
CAN YOU KEEP GOING?
...
RRR!

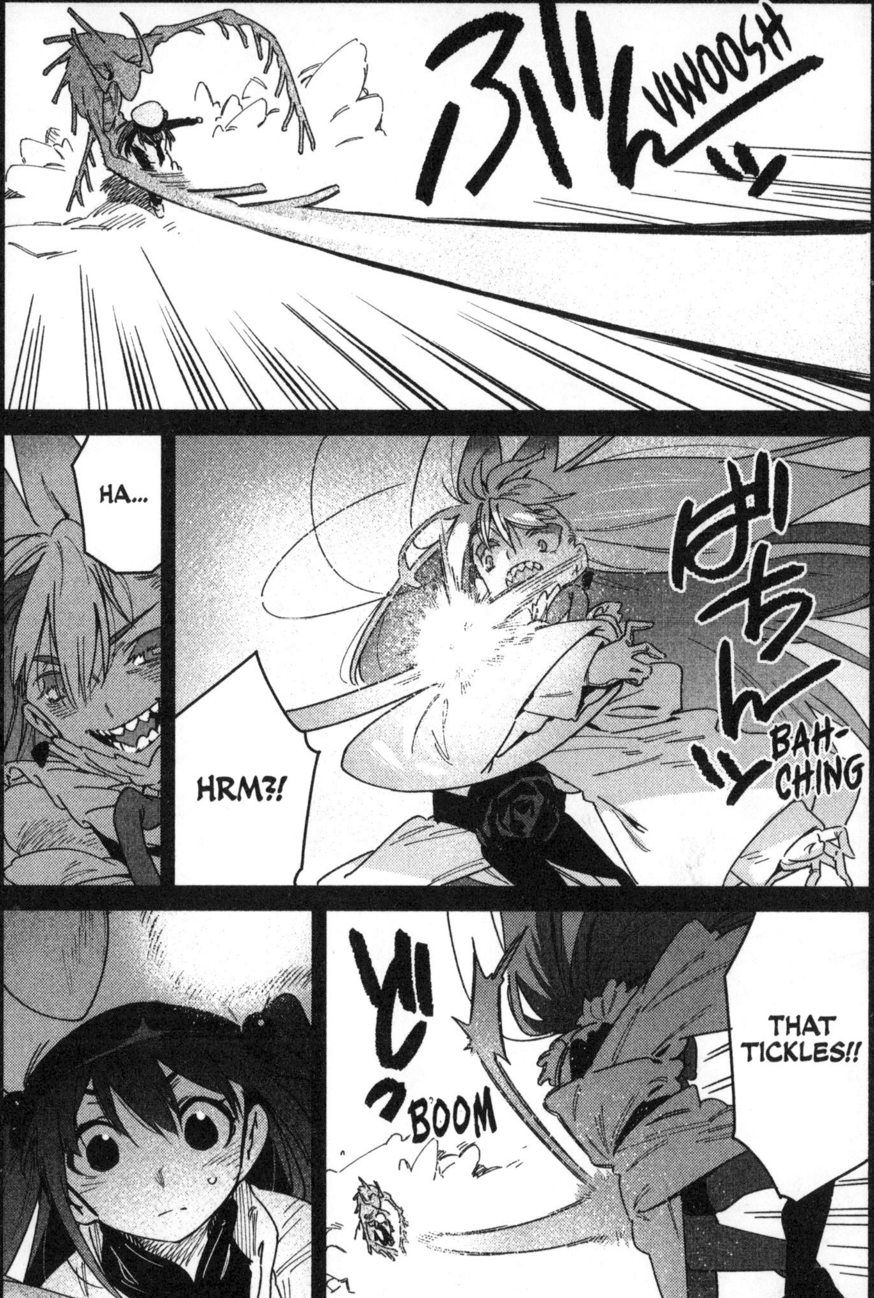
VWOOSH
BAH-CHING
HRM?!
HA...
THAT TICKLES!!
BOOM

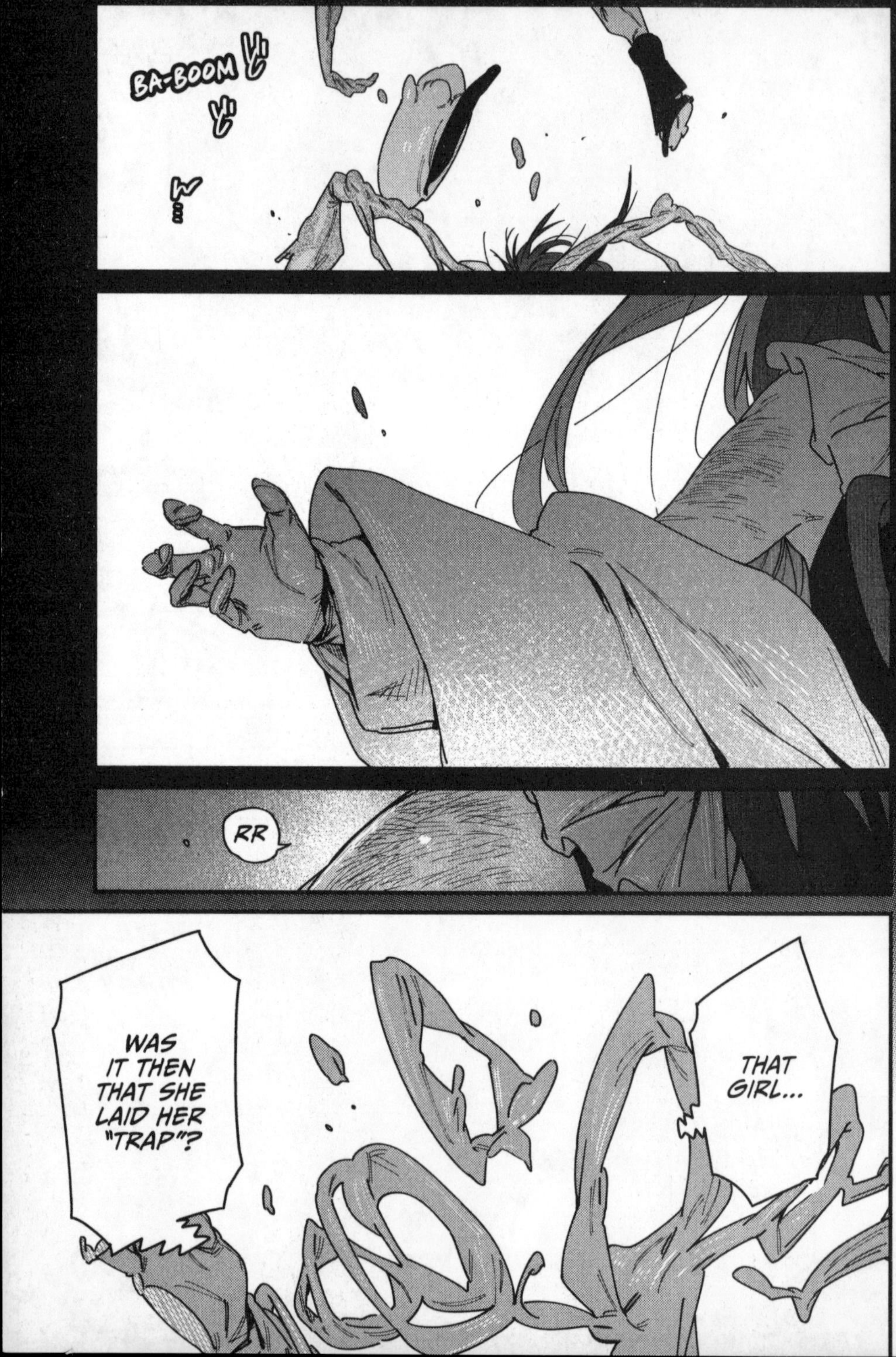
BA-BOOM
RR
THAT GIRL...
WAS IT THEN THAT SHE LAID HER "TRAP"?

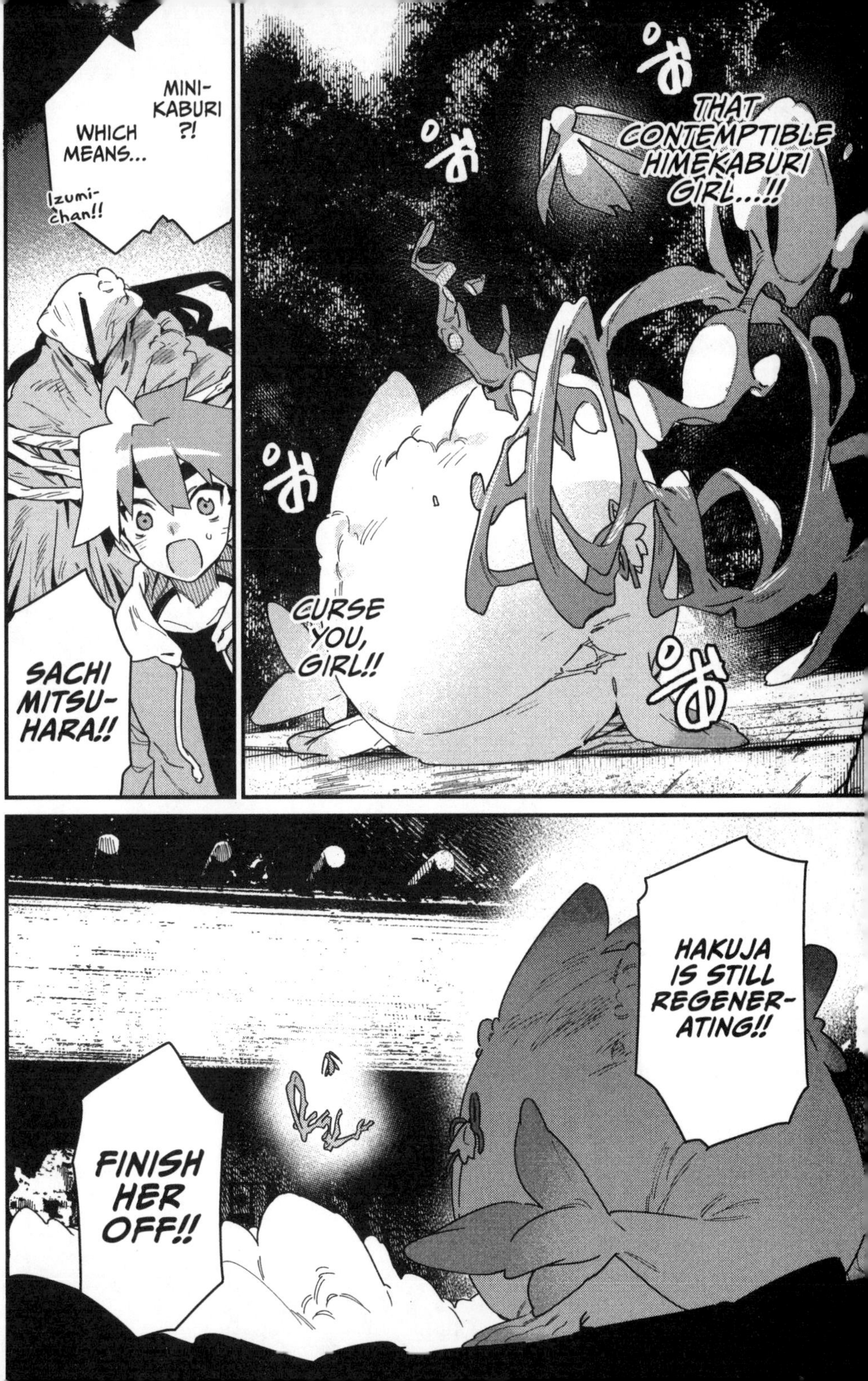
ぉ
ぉ
THAT CONTEMPTIBLE HIMEKABURI GIRL...!!
ぉ
CURSE YOU, GIRL!!
ぉ
MINI-KABURI ?!
WHICH MEANS...
Izumi-chan!!
SACHI MITSU-HARA!!
HAKUJA IS STILL REGENER-ATING!!
FINISH HER OFF!!

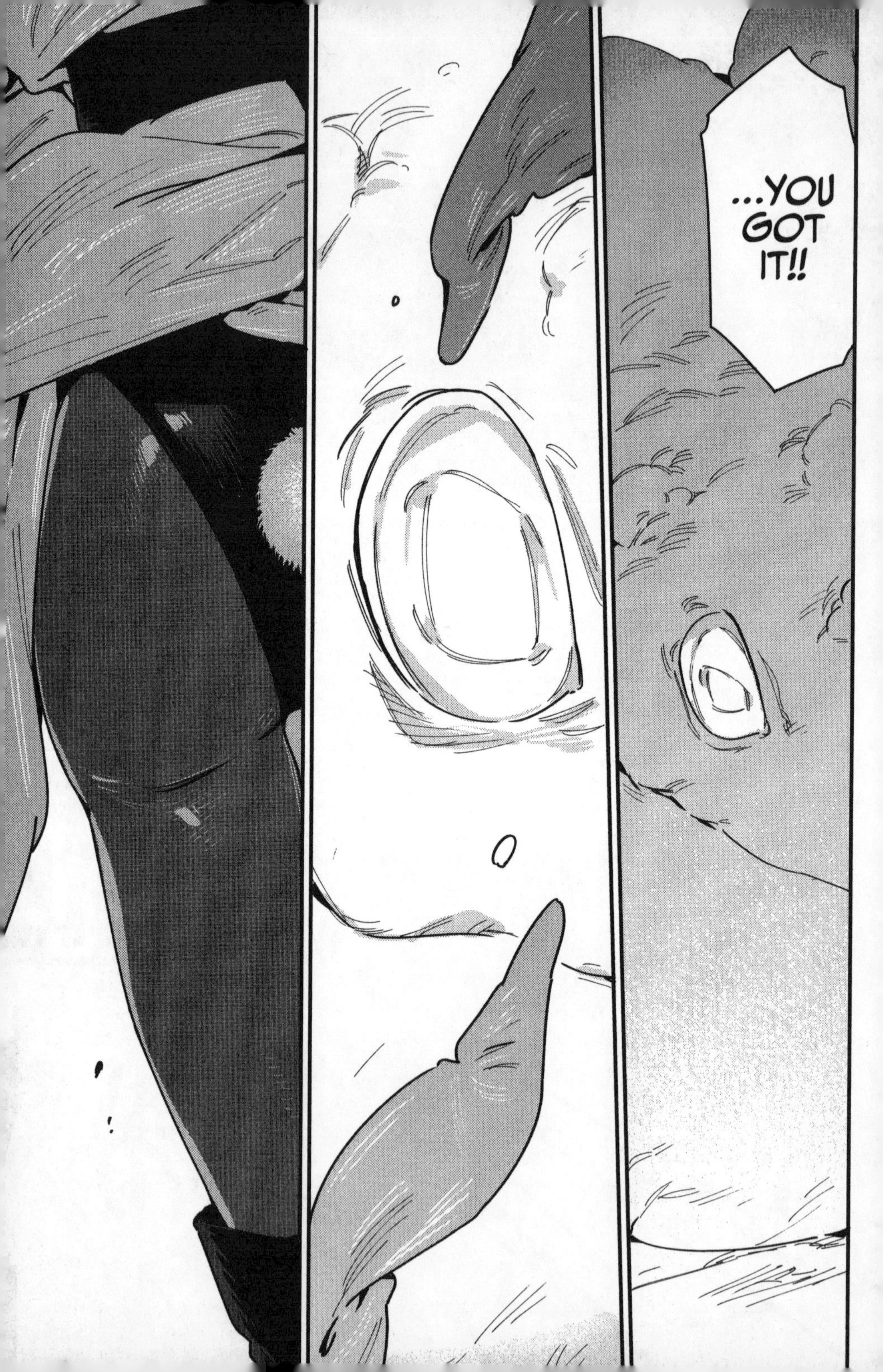
...YOU GOT IT!!

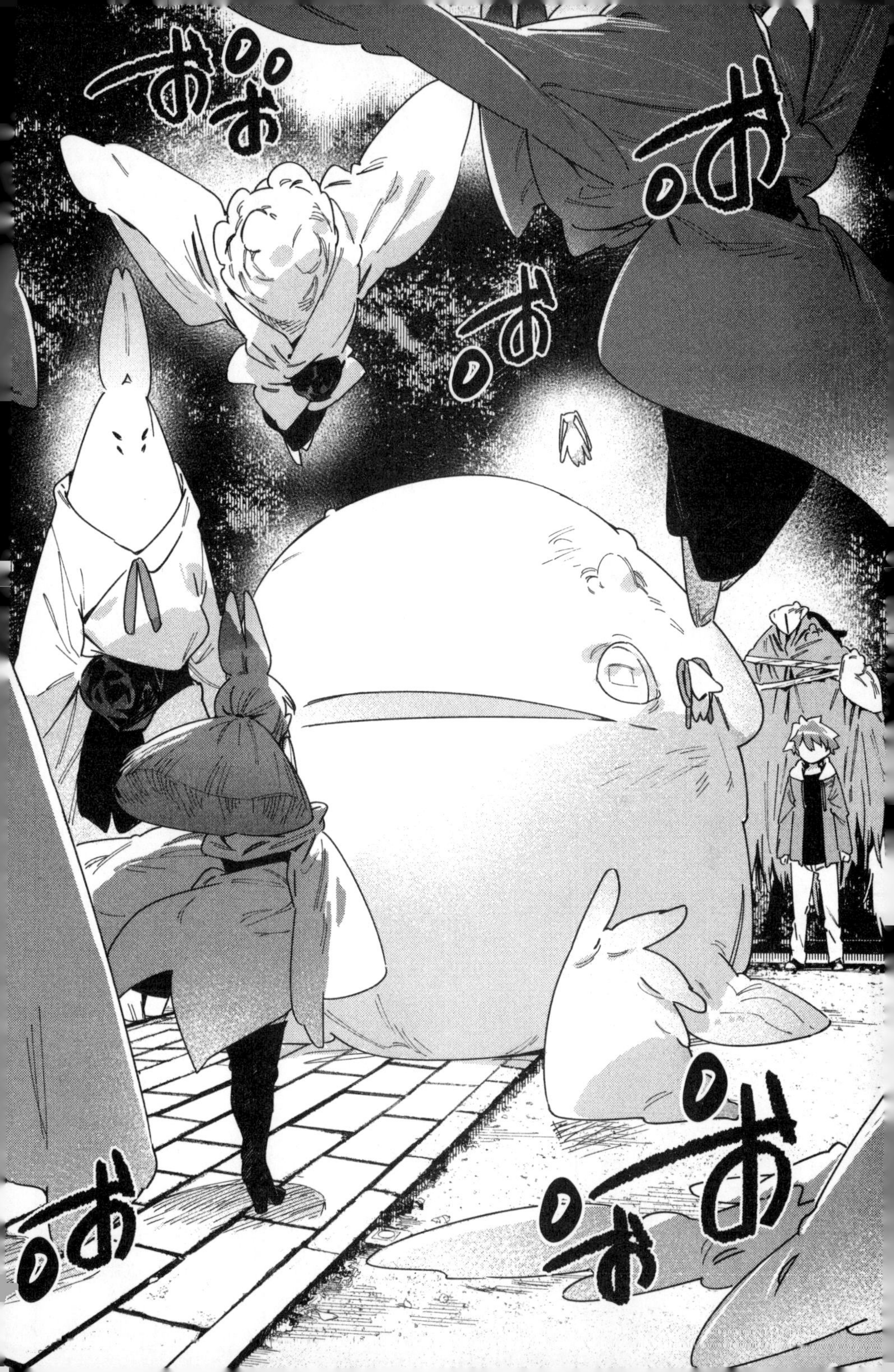
お
お
おぉぉ
おぉ
お

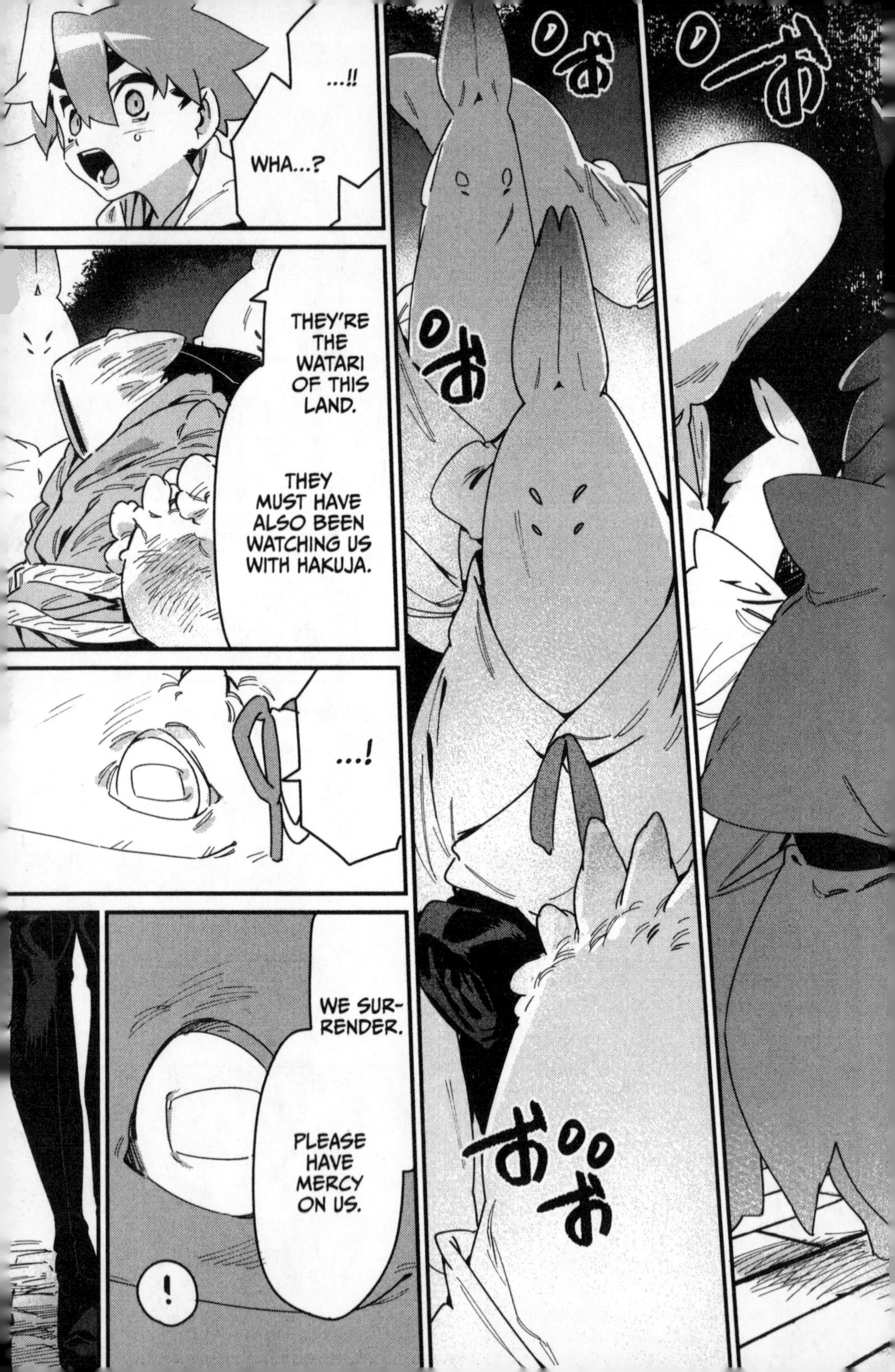
...!!
WHA...?
THEY'RE THE WATARI OF THIS LAND.
THEY MUST HAVE ALSO BEEN WATCHING US WITH HAKUJA.
...!
WE SUR-RENDER.
PLEASE HAVE MERCY ON US.
!

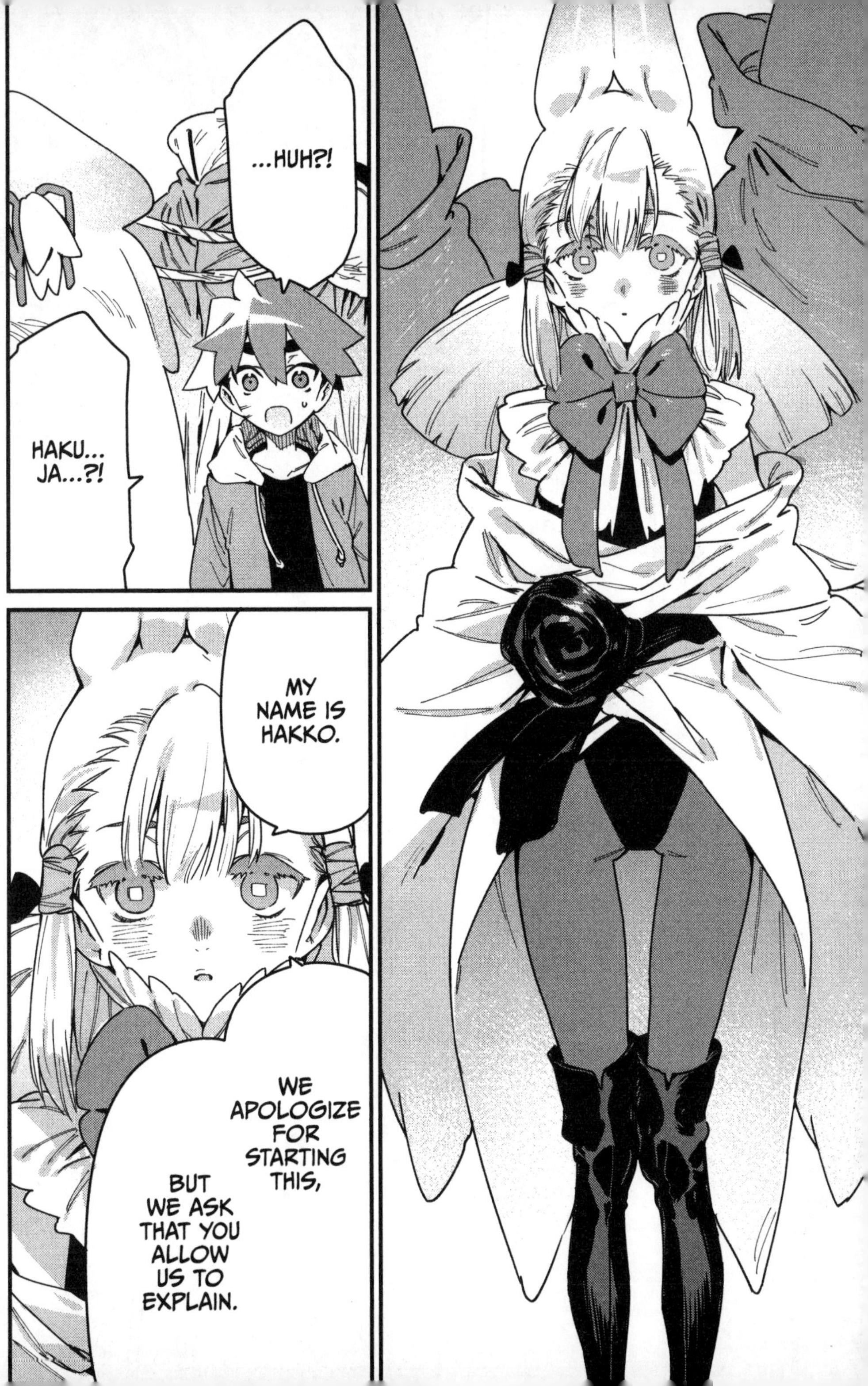
...HUH?!
HAKU... JA...?!
MY NAME IS HAKKO.
WE APOLOGIZE FOR STARTING THIS,
BUT WE ASK THAT YOU ALLOW US TO EXPLAIN.

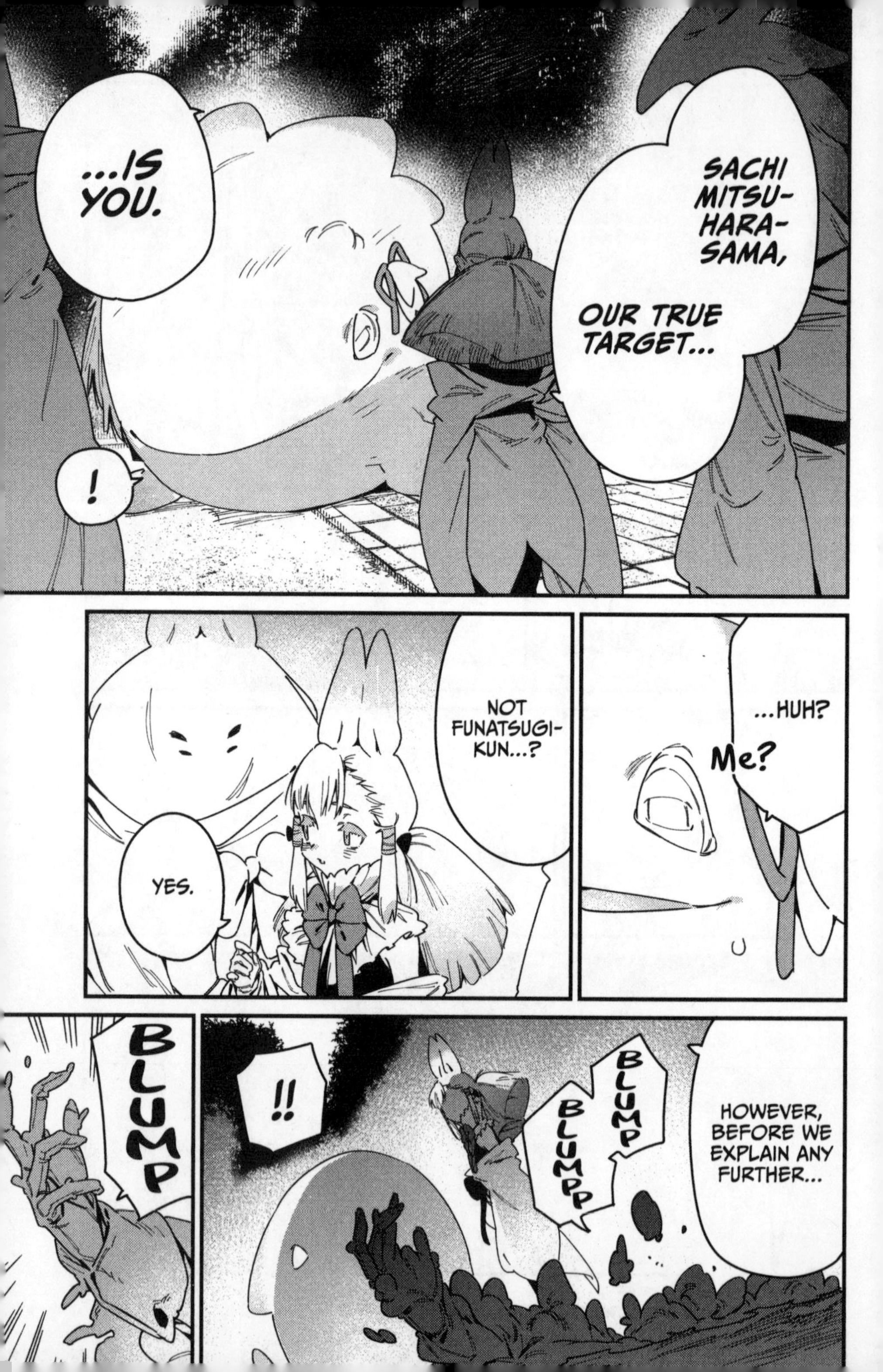
SACHI MITSU-HARA-SAMA, OUR TRUE TARGET...
...IS YOU.
!
...HUH? Me?
NOT FUNATSUGI-KUN...?
YES.
HOWEVER, BEFORE WE EXPLAIN ANY FURTHER...
BLUMP BLUMP BLUMPP
!!
BLUMP

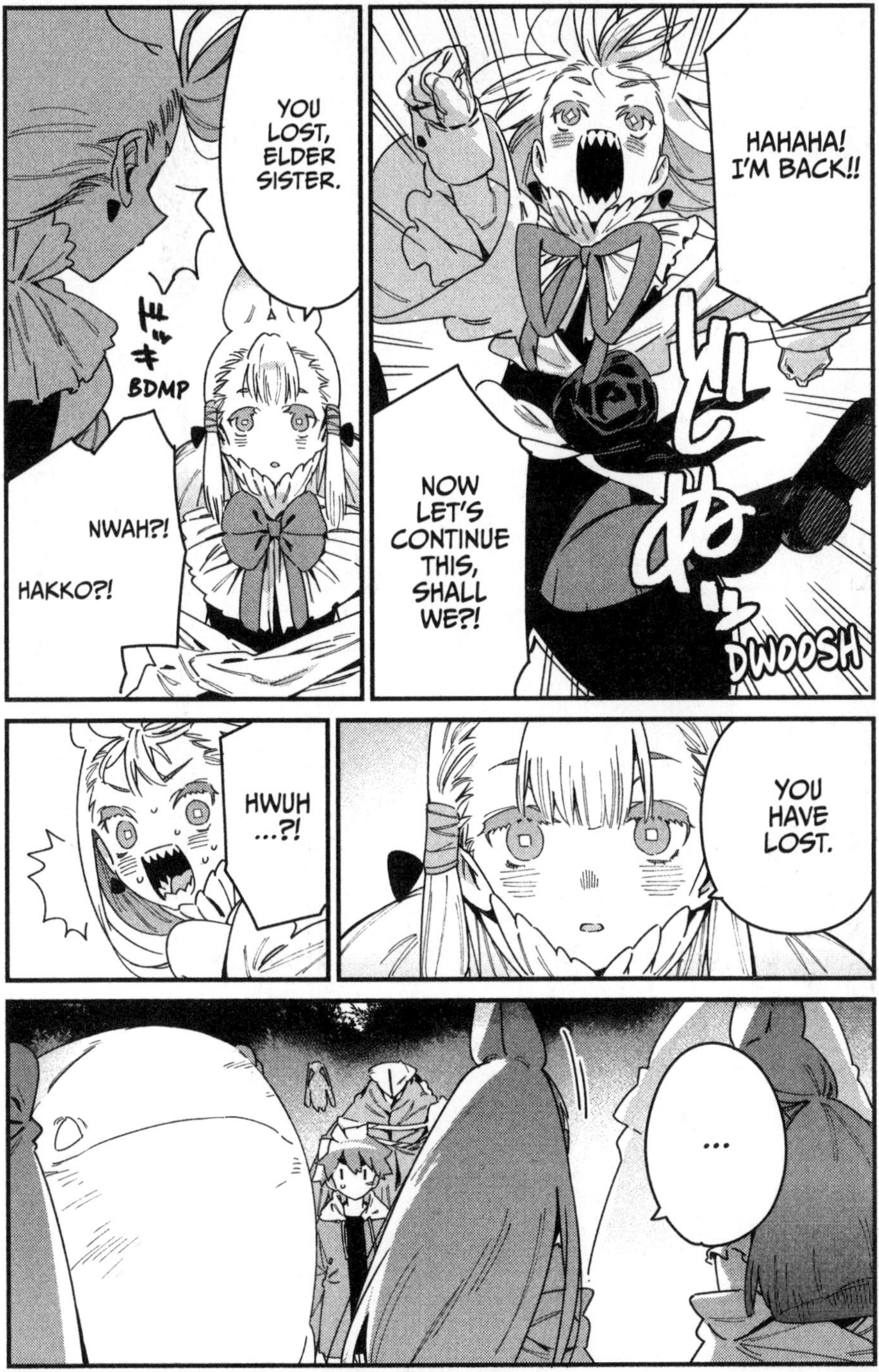
HAHAHA! I'M BACK!!
NOW LET'S CONTINUE THIS, SHALL WE?!
DWOOSH
YOU LOST, ELDER SISTER.
BDMP
NWAH?!
HAKKO?!
YOU HAVE LOST.
HWUH ...?!
...

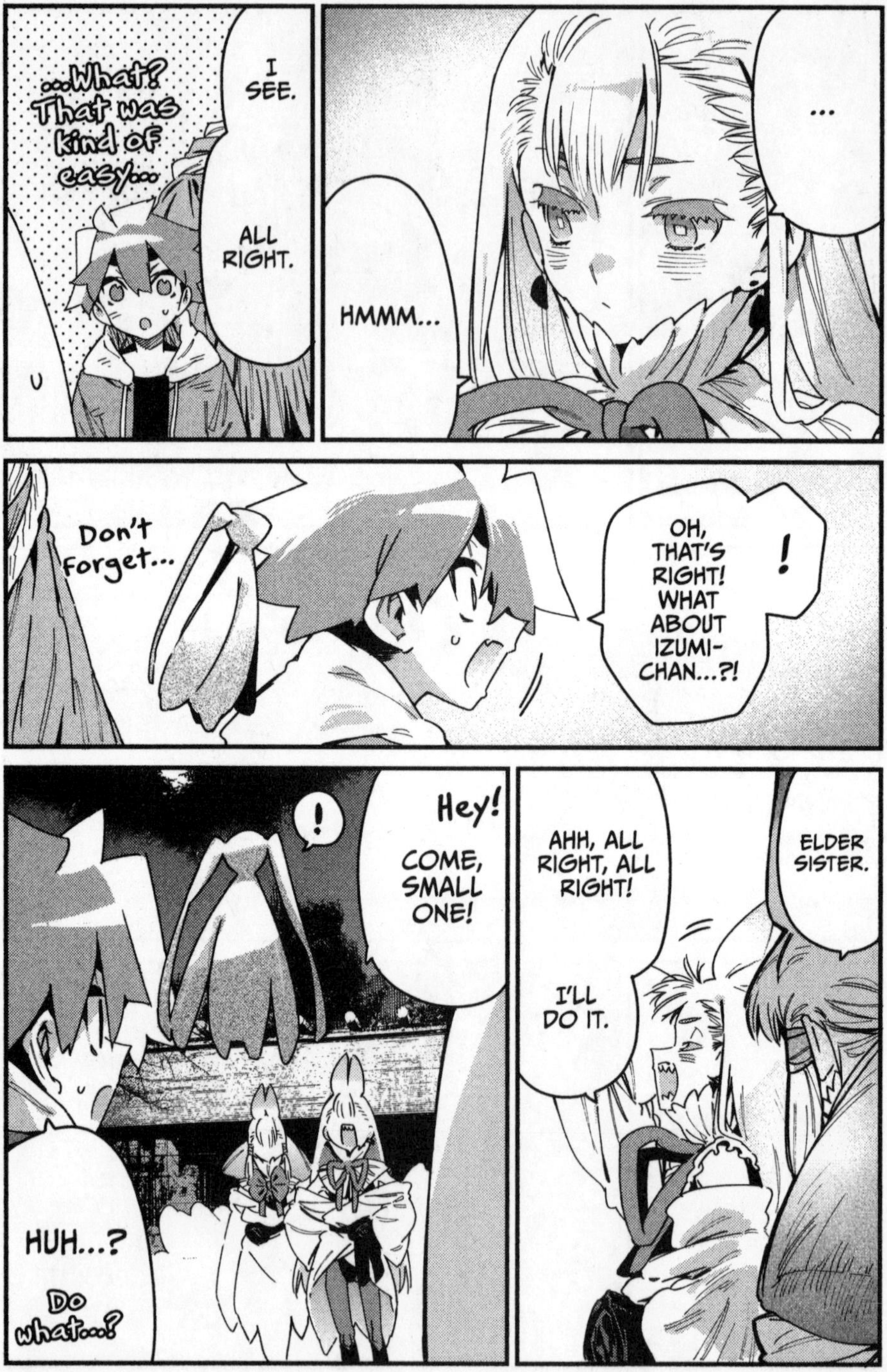
...
HMMM...
I SEE.
ALL RIGHT.
...What? That was kind of easy...
!
OH, THAT'S RIGHT! WHAT ABOUT IZUMI-CHAN...?!
Don't forget...
ELDER SISTER.
AHH, ALL RIGHT, ALL RIGHT!
I'LL DO IT.
Hey!
COME, SMALL ONE!
!
HUH...?
Do what...?

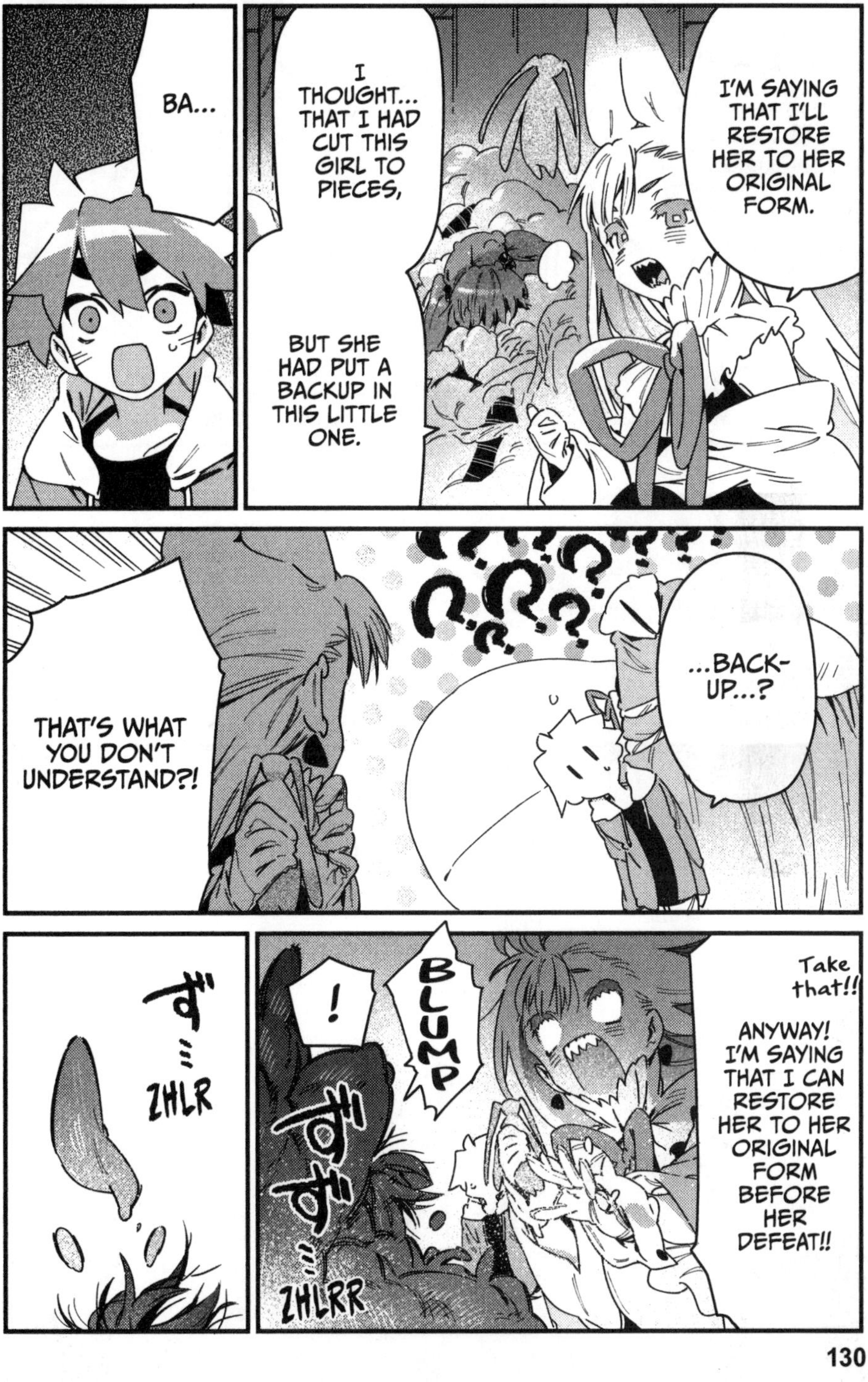

I'M SAYING THAT I'LL RESTORE HER TO HER ORIGINAL FORM.
I THOUGHT... THAT I HAD CUT THIS GIRL TO PIECES,
BUT SHE HAD PUT A BACKUP IN THIS LITTLE ONE.
BA...
...BACK-UP...?
THAT'S WHAT YOU DON'T UNDERSTAND?!
Take that!!
ANYWAY! I'M SAYING THAT I CAN RESTORE HER TO HER ORIGINAL FORM BEFORE HER DEFEAT!!
BLUMP
!
ずず
ZHLRR
ず
ZHLR

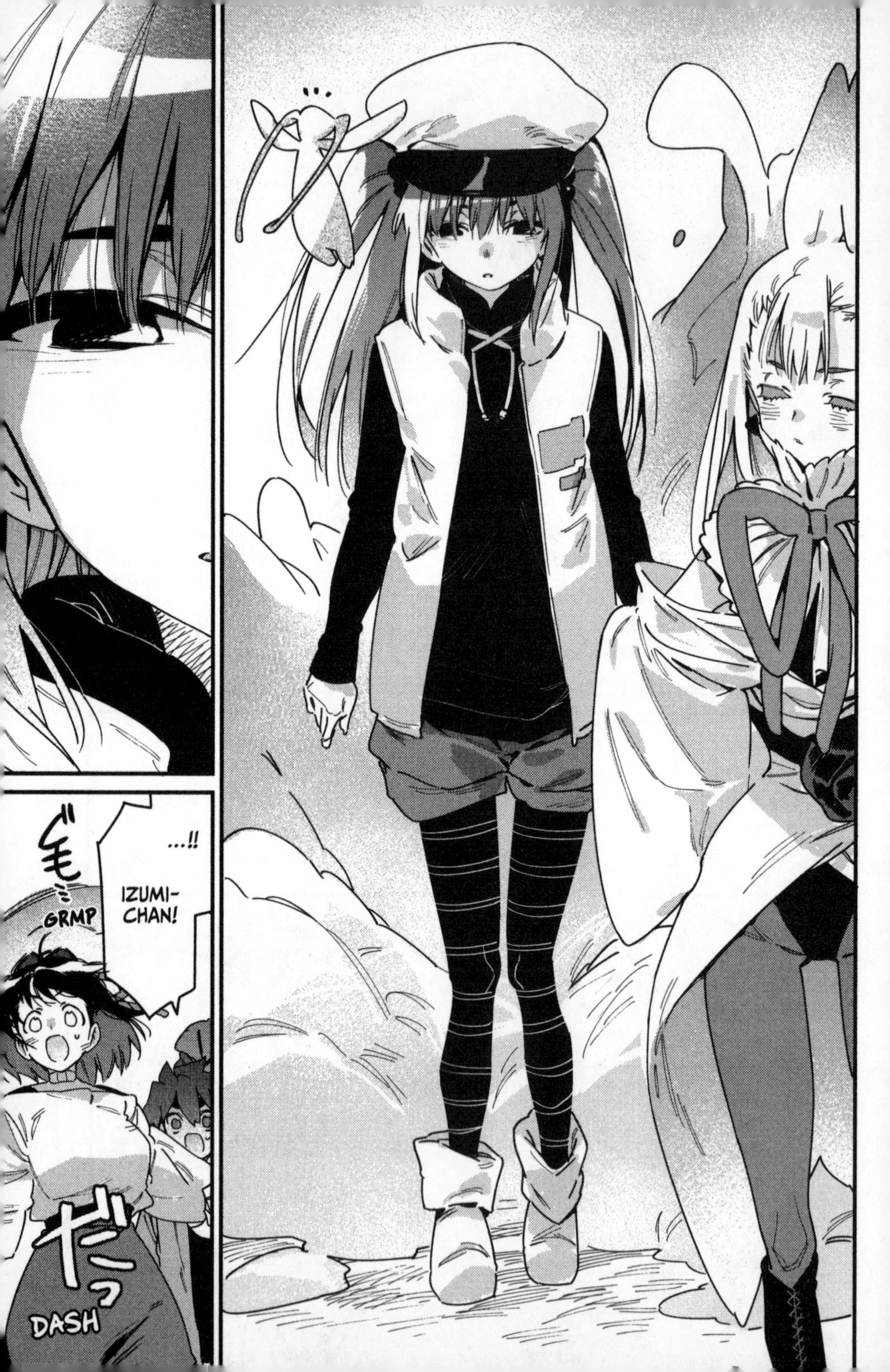
...
...!!
IZUMI-CHAN!
ぐも
GRMP
ダッ
DASH

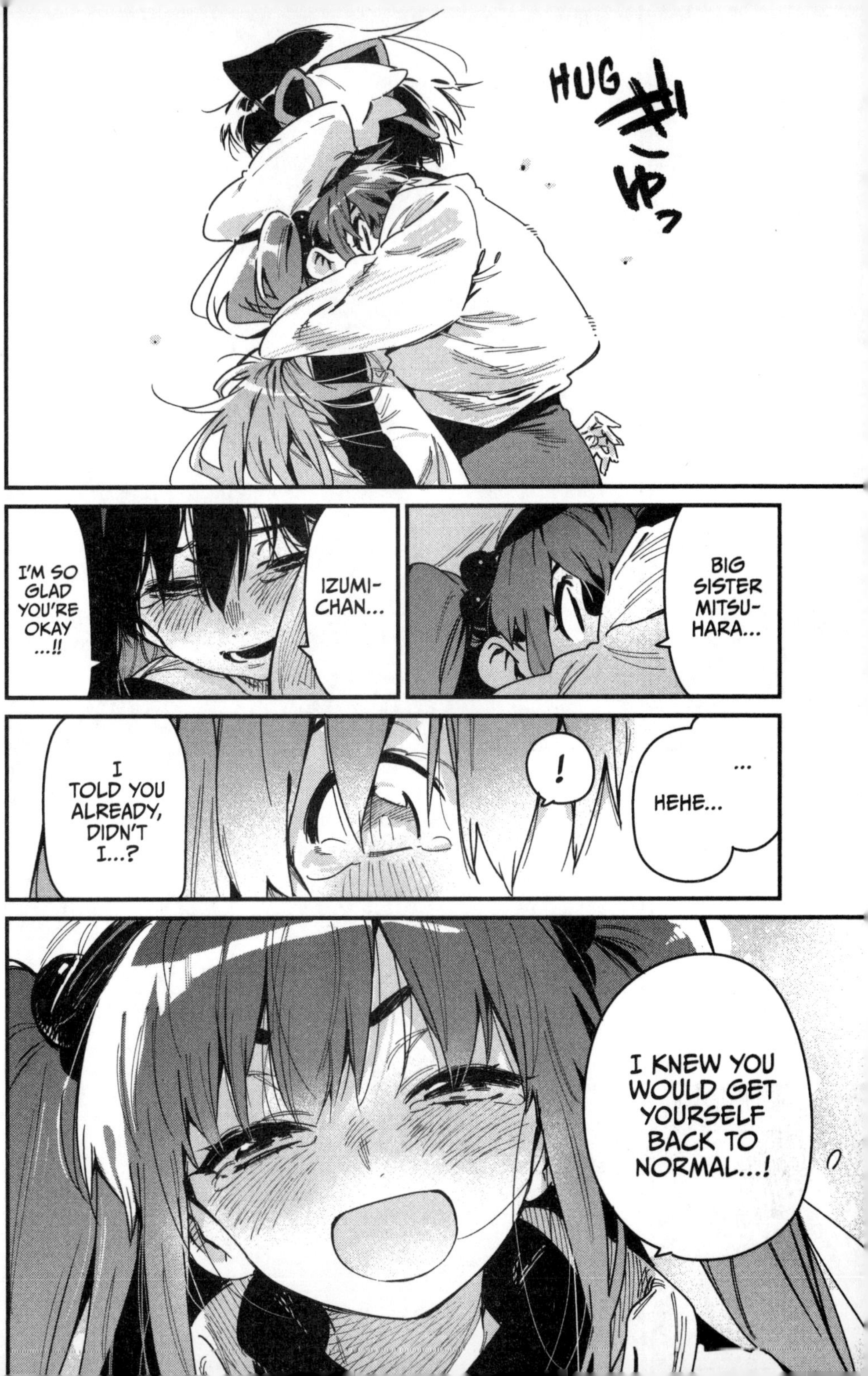
HUG
ぎゅっ
BIG SISTER MITSU-HARA...
IZUMI-CHAN...
I'M SO GLAD YOU'RE OKAY ...!!
... HEHE...
!
I TOLD YOU ALREADY, DIDN'T I...?
I KNEW YOU WOULD GET YOURSELF BACK TO NORMAL...!

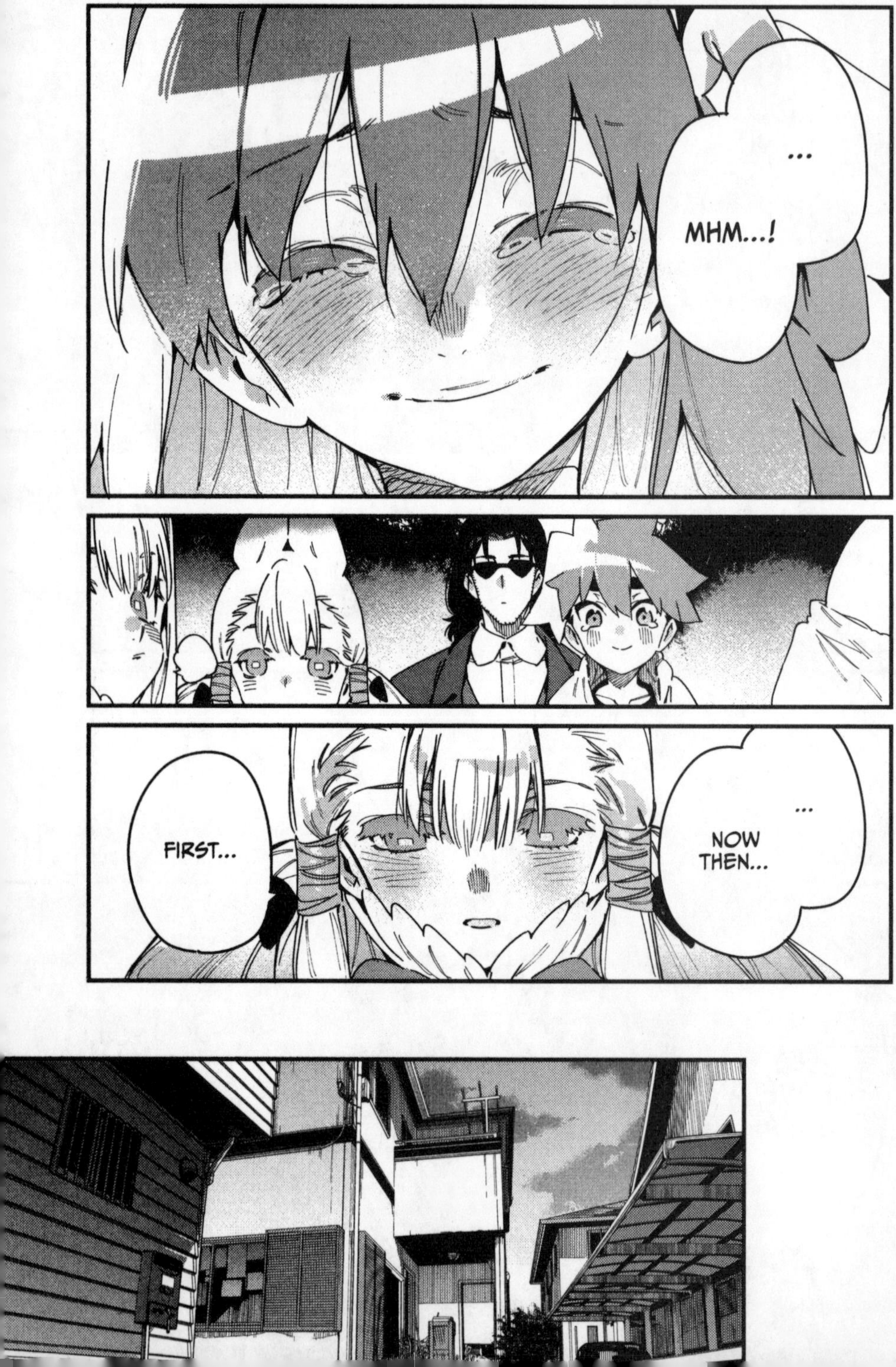
... MHM...!
... NOW THEN...
FIRST...

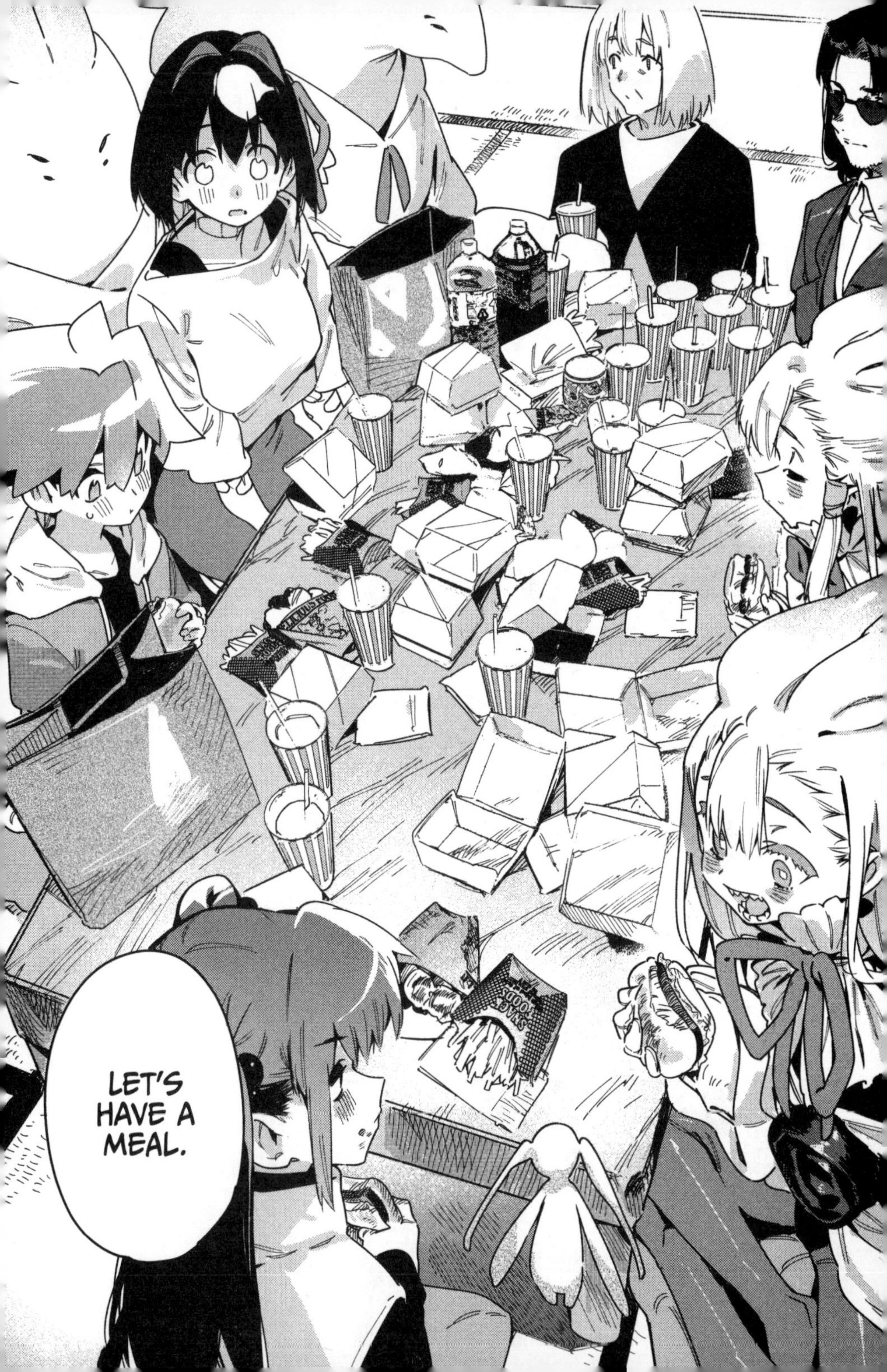
LET'S HAVE A MEAL.

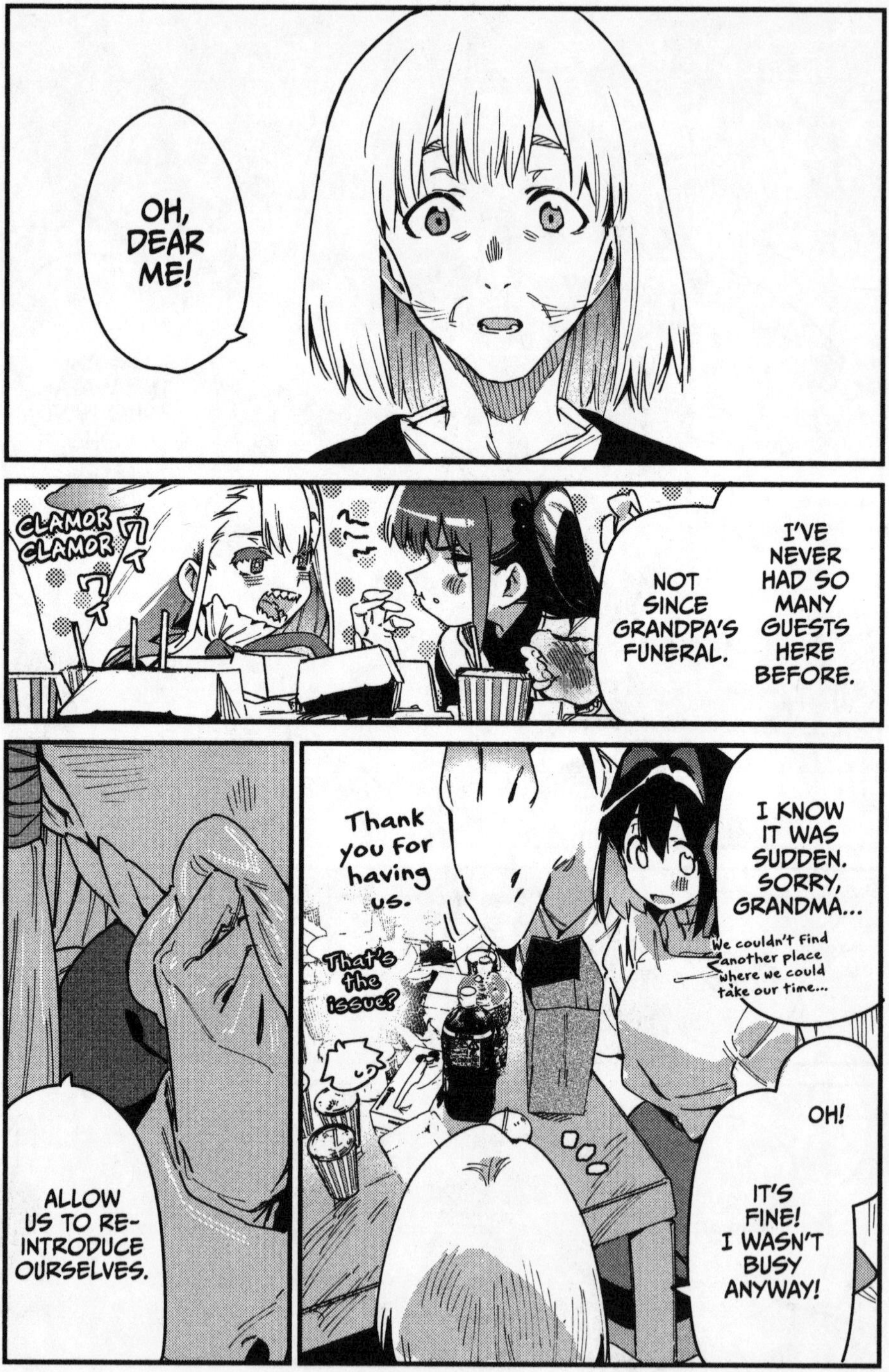
OH, DEAR ME!
I'VE NEVER HAD SO MANY GUESTS HERE BEFORE.
NOT SINCE GRANDPA'S FUNERAL.
CLAMOR CLAMOR
I KNOW IT WAS SUDDEN. SORRY, GRANDMA...
We couldn't find another place where we could take our time...
Thank you for having us.
That's the issue?
OH!
IT'S FINE! I WASN'T BUSY ANYWAY!
ALLOW US TO RE-INTRODUCE OURSELVES.

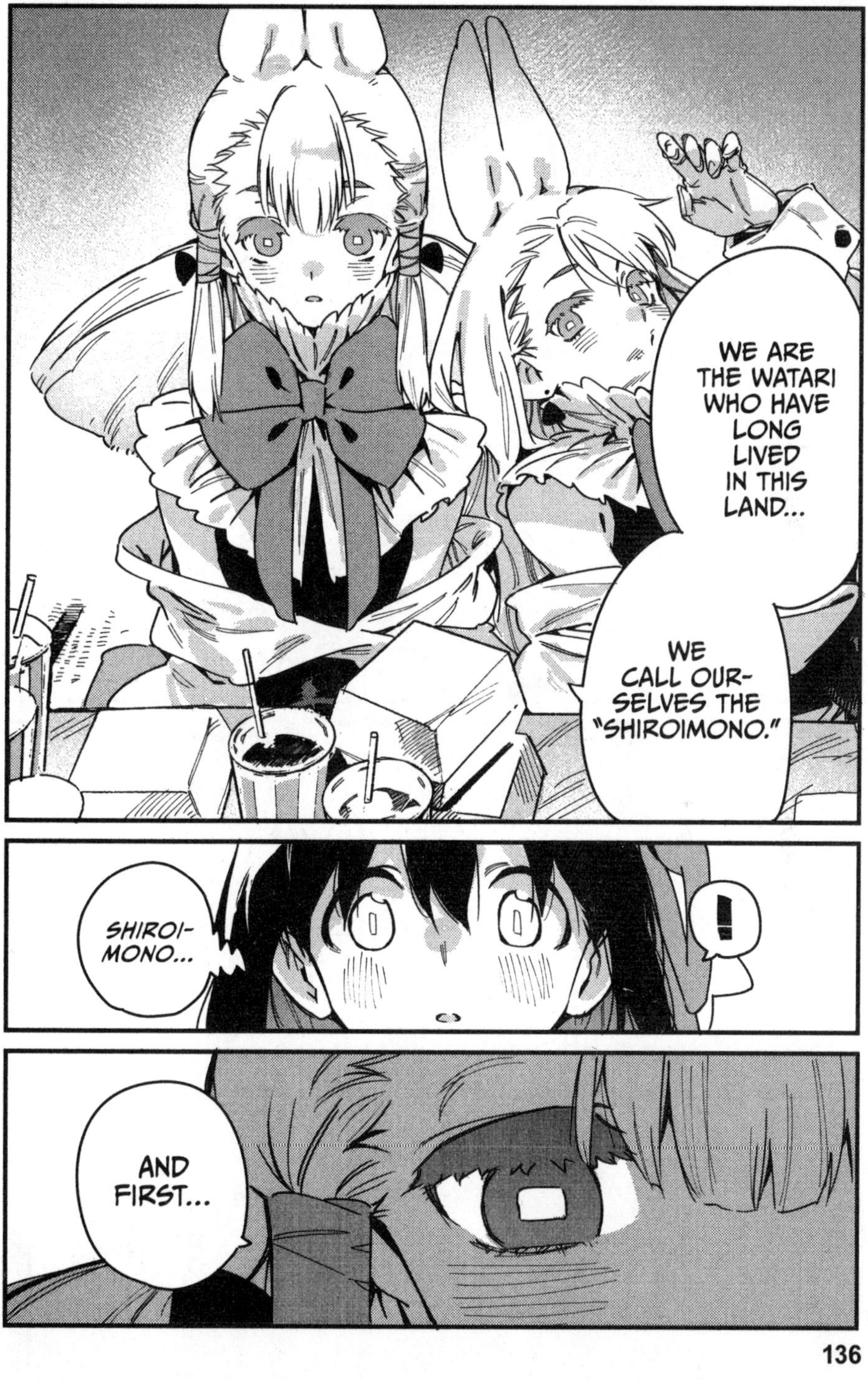
WE ARE THE WATARI WHO HAVE LONG LIVED IN THIS LAND...
WE CALL OUR-SELVES THE "SHIROIMONO."
!
SHIROI-MONO...
AND FIRST...

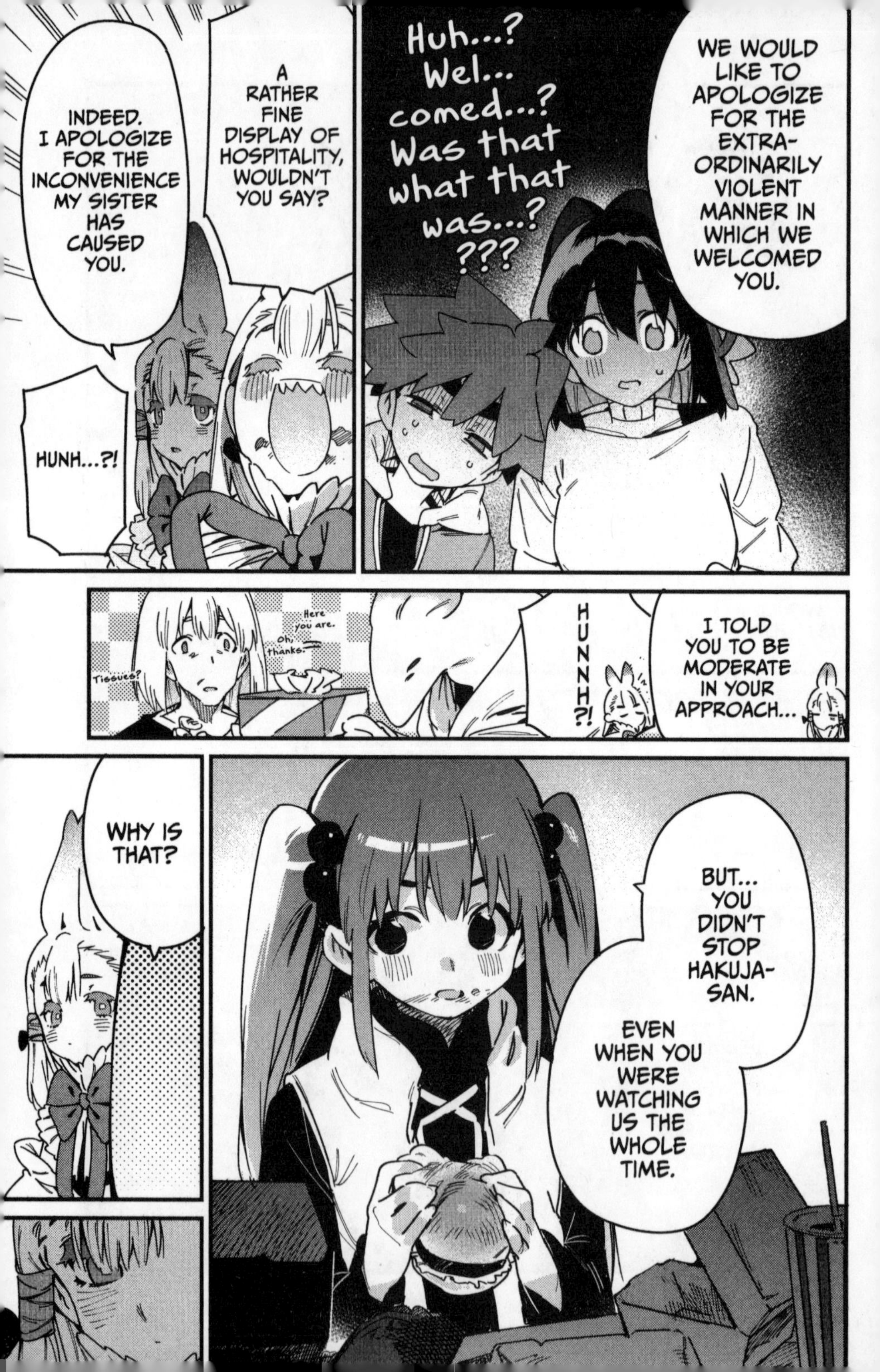
WE WOULD LIKE TO APOLOGIZE FOR THE EXTRA-ORDINARILY VIOLENT MANNER IN WHICH WE WELCOMED YOU.
Huh...? Wel... comed...? Was that what that was...? ???
A RATHER FINE DISPLAY OF HOSPITALITY, WOULDN'T YOU SAY?
INDEED. I APOLOGIZE FOR THE INCONVENIENCE MY SISTER HAS CAUSED YOU.
HUNH...?!
I TOLD YOU TO BE MODERATE IN YOUR APPROACH...
HUNNH?!
Here you are.
Oh, thanks.
Tissues?
BUT... YOU DIDN'T STOP HAKUJA-SAN.
EVEN WHEN YOU WERE WATCHING US THE WHOLE TIME.
WHY IS THAT?

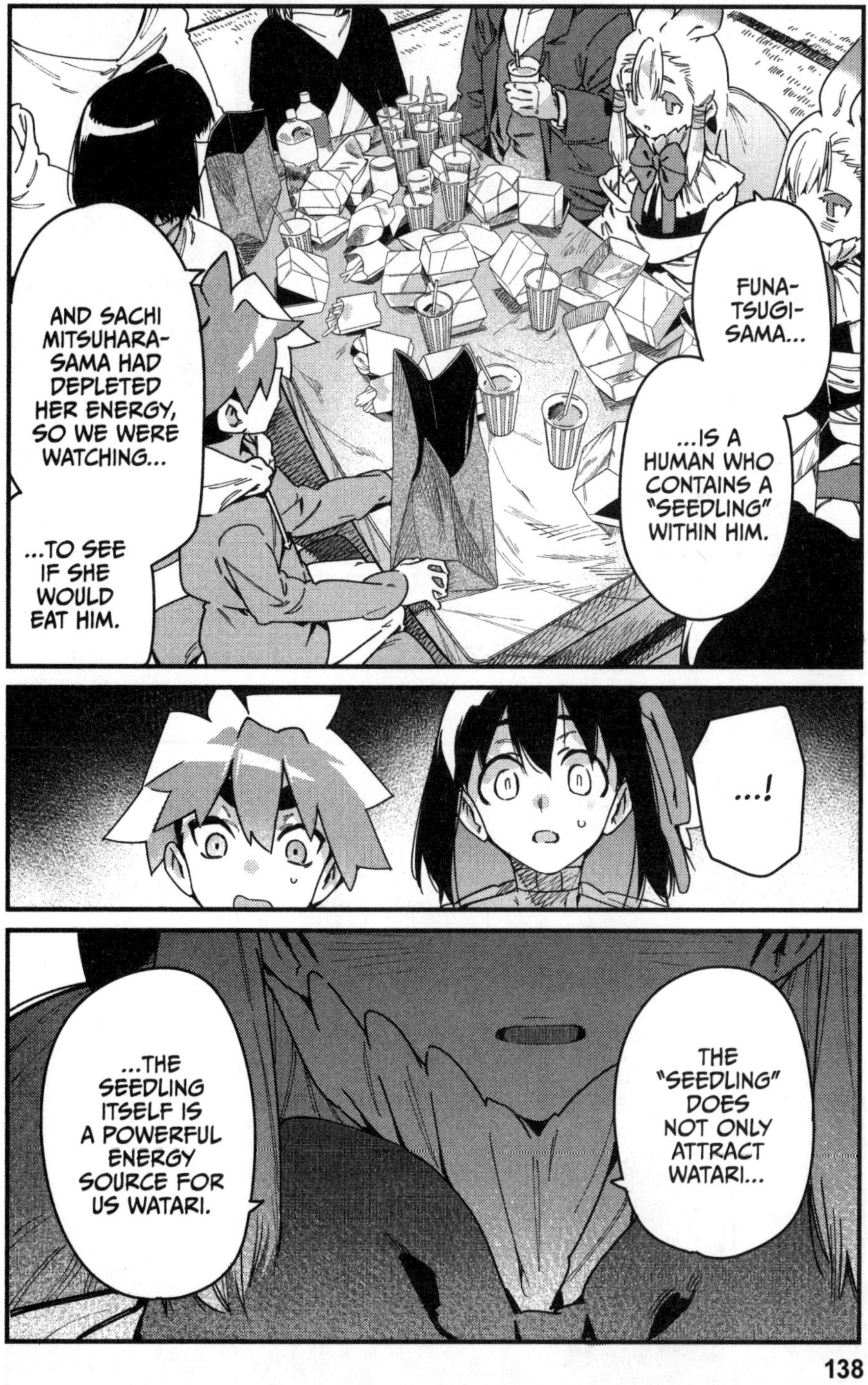
FUNA-TSUGI-SAMA...
...IS A HUMAN WHO CONTAINS A "SEEDLING" WITHIN HIM.
AND SACHI MITSUHARA-SAMA HAD DEPLETED HER ENERGY, SO WE WERE WATCHING...
...TO SEE IF SHE WOULD EAT HIM.
...!
THE "SEEDLING" DOES NOT ONLY ATTRACT WATARI...
...THE SEEDLING ITSELF IS A POWERFUL ENERGY SOURCE FOR US WATARI.

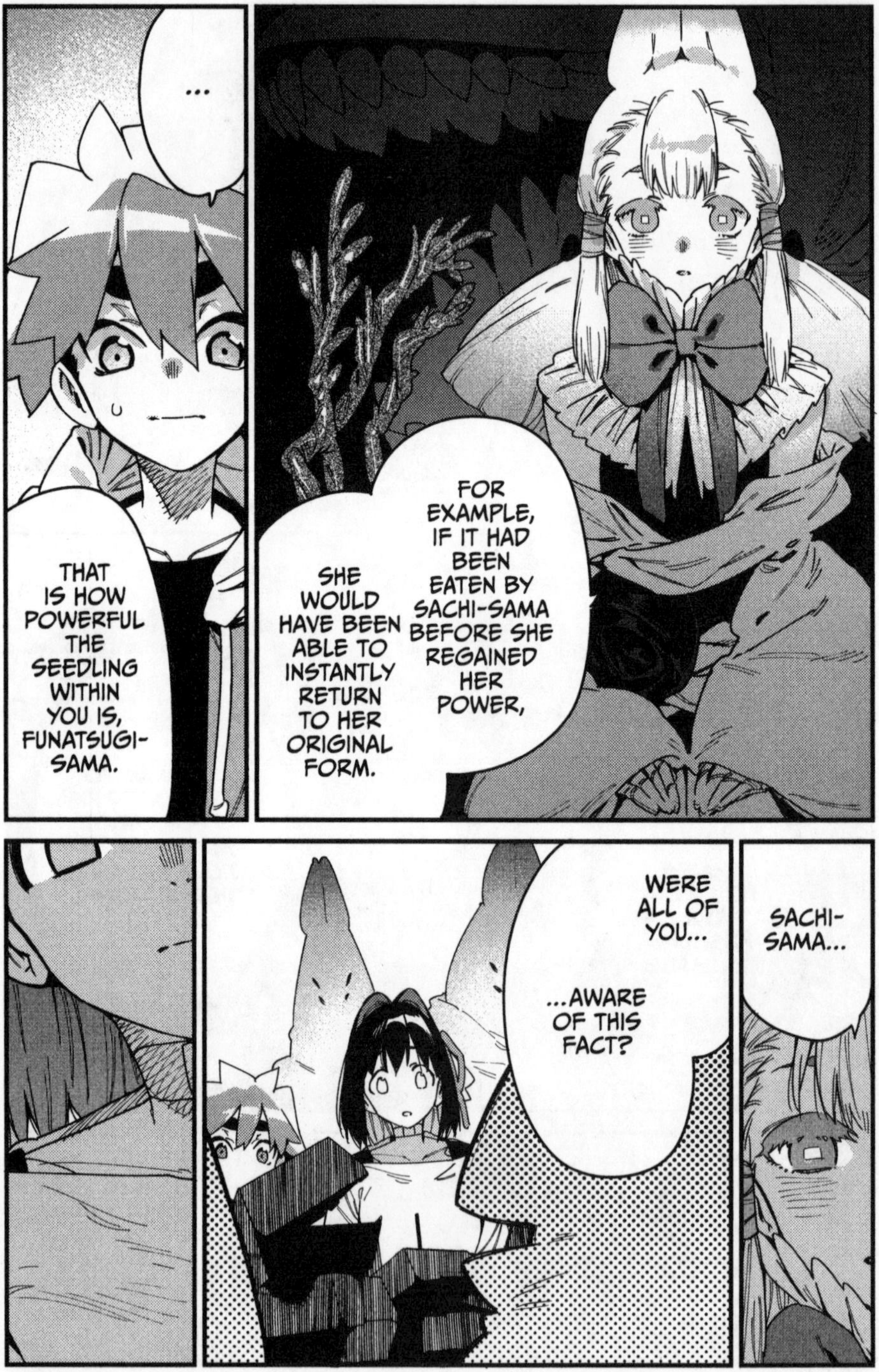
FOR EXAMPLE, IF IT HAD BEEN EATEN BY SACHI-SAMA BEFORE SHE REGAINED HER POWER,
SHE WOULD HAVE BEEN ABLE TO INSTANTLY RETURN TO HER ORIGINAL FORM.
...
THAT IS HOW POWERFUL THE SEEDLING WITHIN YOU IS, FUNATSUGI-SAMA.
SACHI-SAMA...
WERE ALL OF YOU...
...AWARE OF THIS FACT?

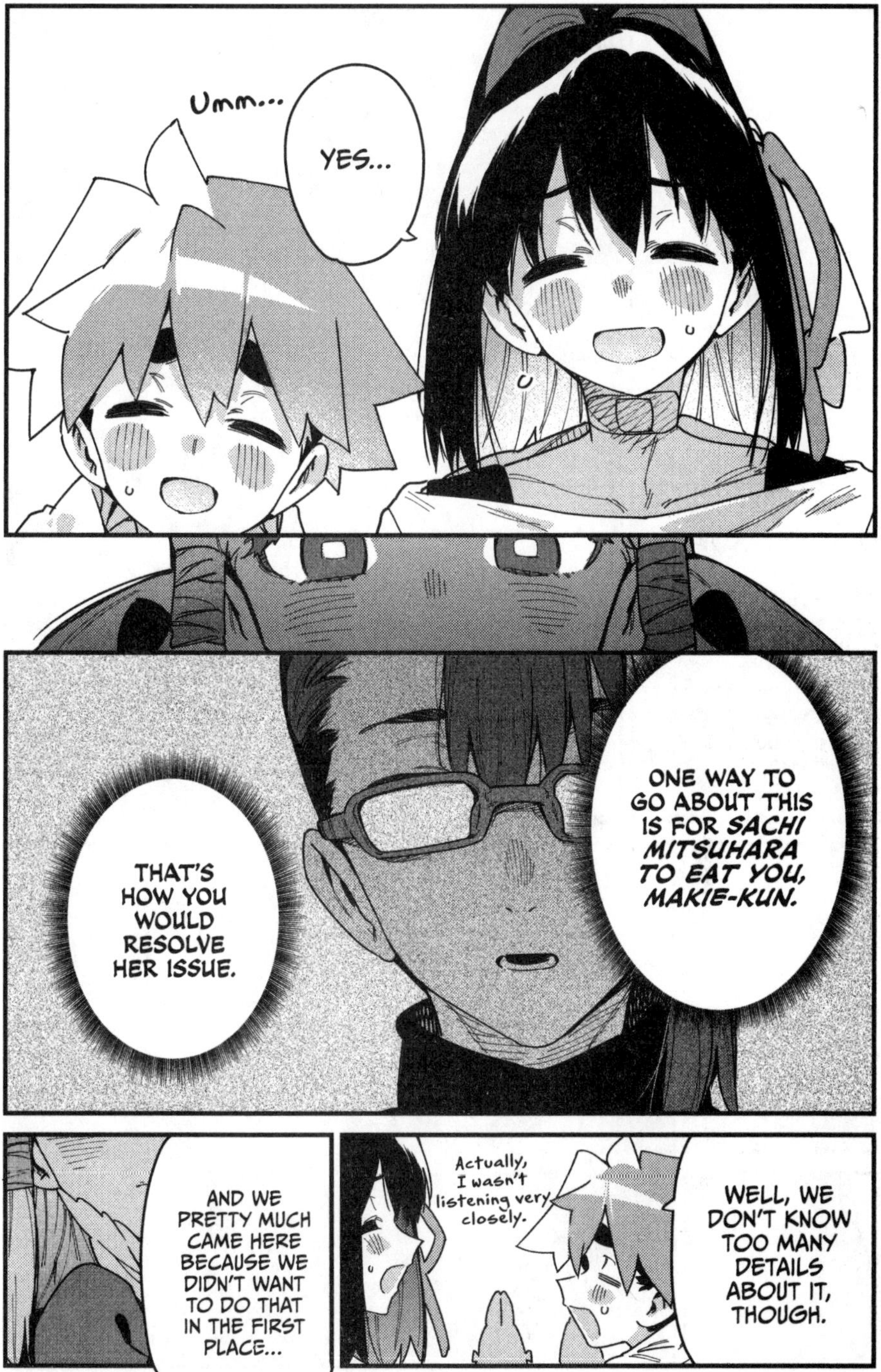
YES...
Umm...
ONE WAY TO GO ABOUT THIS IS FOR *SACHI MITSUHARA TO EAT YOU, MAKIE-KUN.*
THAT'S HOW YOU WOULD RESOLVE HER ISSUE.
WELL, WE DON'T KNOW TOO MANY DETAILS ABOUT IT, THOUGH.
Actually, I wasn't listening very closely.
AND WE PRETTY MUCH CAME HERE BECAUSE WE DIDN'T WANT TO DO THAT IN THE FIRST PLACE...

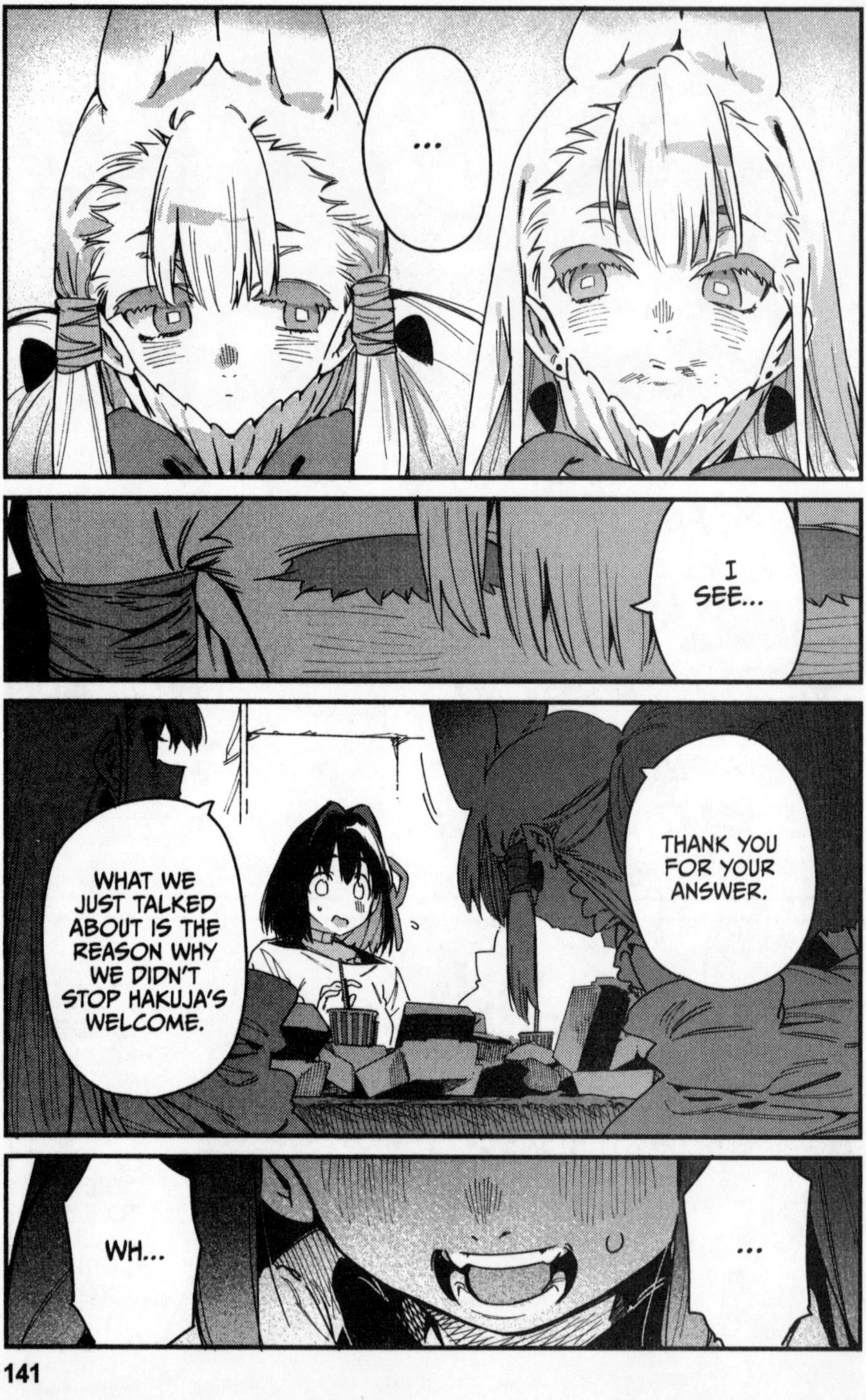
...
I SEE...
THANK YOU FOR YOUR ANSWER.
WHAT WE JUST TALKED ABOUT IS THE REASON WHY WE DIDN'T STOP HAKUJA'S WELCOME.
...
WH...

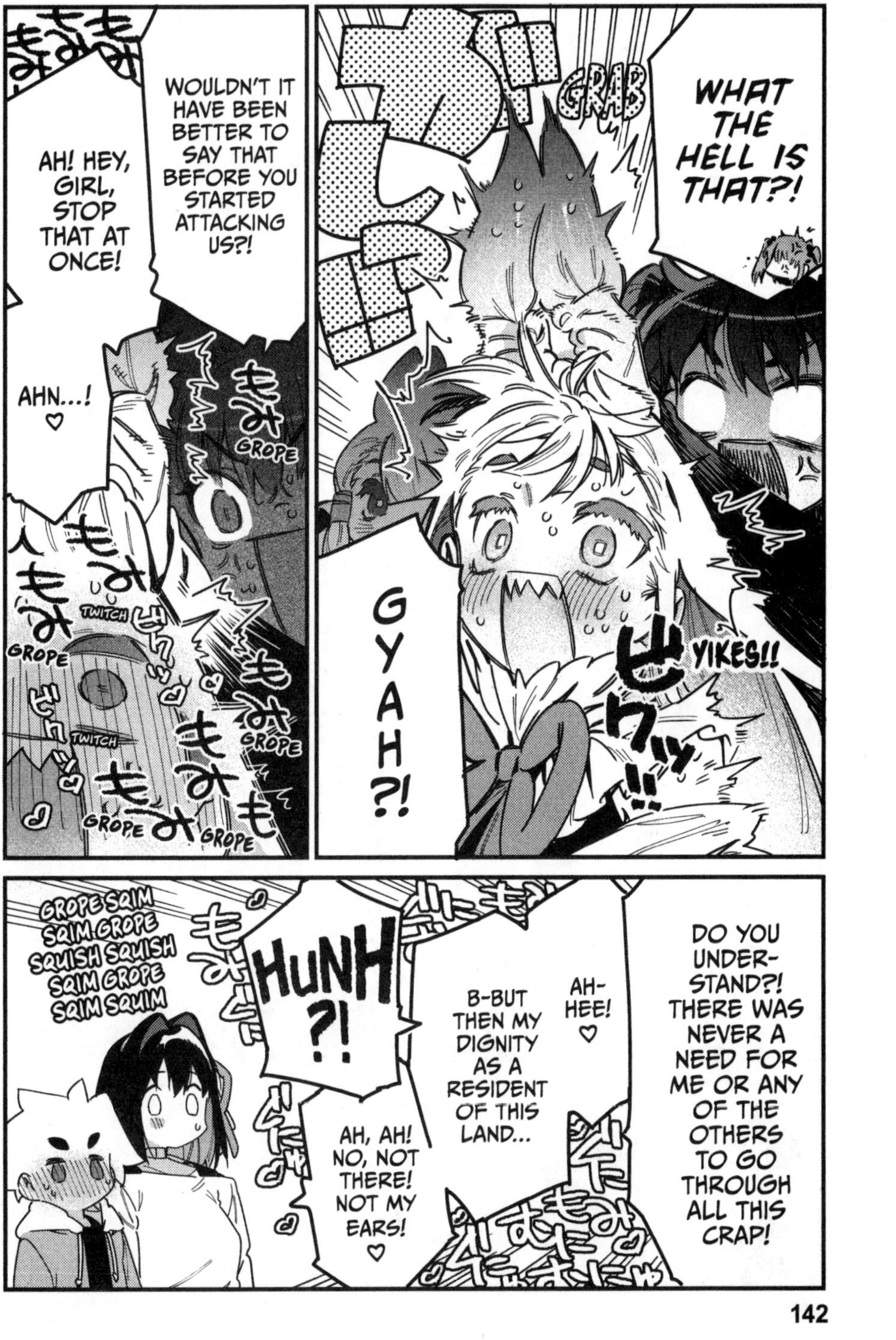
WHAT THE HELL IS THAT?!
GRAB
YIKES!!
GYAH?!
WOULDN'T IT HAVE BEEN BETTER TO SAY THAT BEFORE YOU STARTED ATTACKING US?!
AH! HEY, GIRL, STOP THAT AT ONCE!
AHN...! ♡
GROPE
TWITCH
GROPE
TWITCH
GROPE
GROPE
GROPE
DO YOU UNDERSTAND?! THERE WAS NEVER A NEED FOR ME OR ANY OF THE OTHERS TO GO THROUGH ALL THIS CRAP!
AH-HEE! ♡
B-BUT THEN MY DIGNITY AS A RESIDENT OF THIS LAND...
HUNH?!
AH, AH! NO, NOT THERE! NOT MY EARS! ♡
GROPE SQIM SQIM GROPE SQUISH SQUISH SQIM GROPE SQIM SQUIM

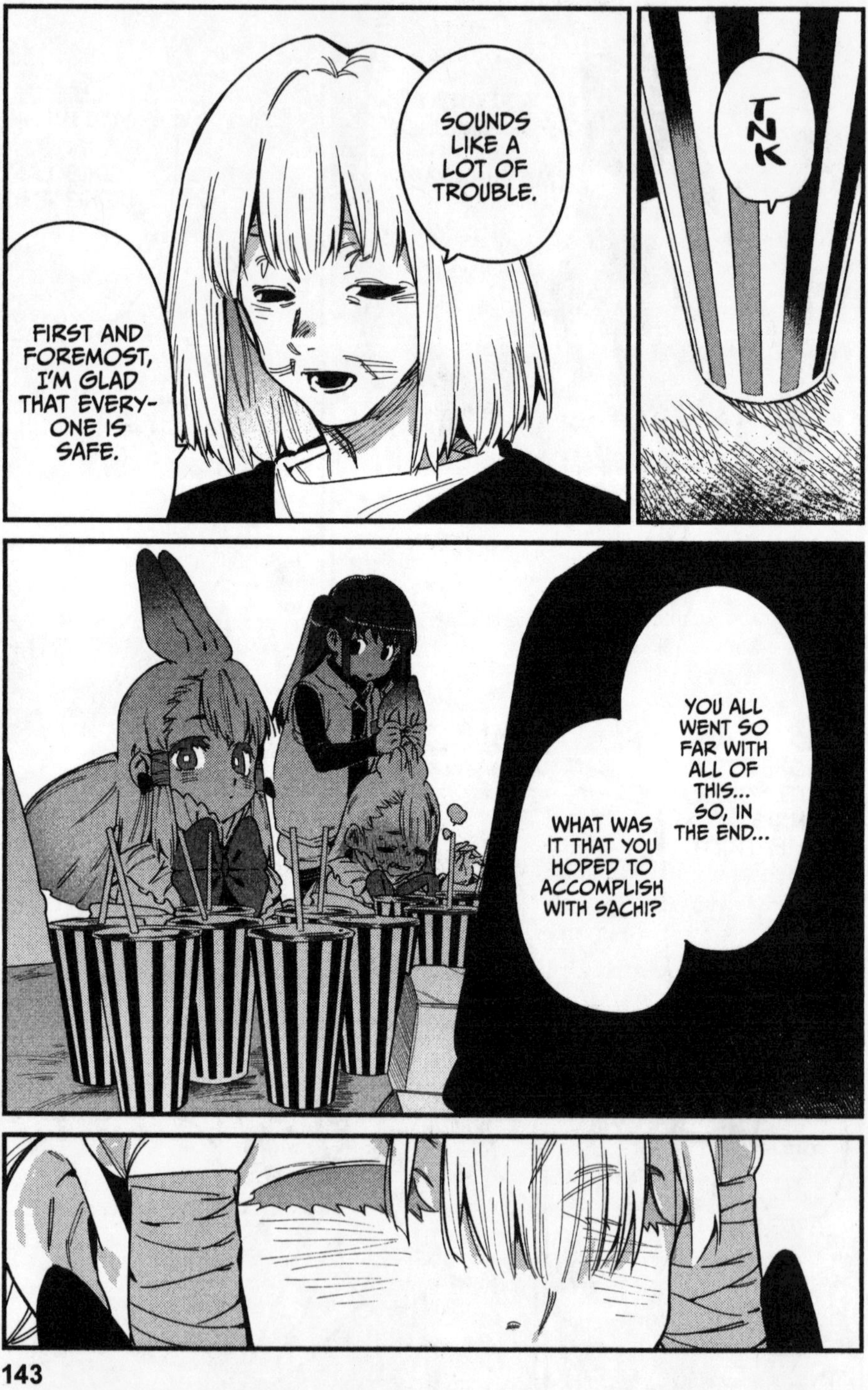
TNK
SOUNDS LIKE A LOT OF TROUBLE.
FIRST AND FOREMOST, I'M GLAD THAT EVERY-ONE IS SAFE.
YOU ALL WENT SO FAR WITH ALL OF THIS... SO, IN THE END...
WHAT WAS IT THAT YOU HOPED TO ACCOMPLISH WITH SACHI?

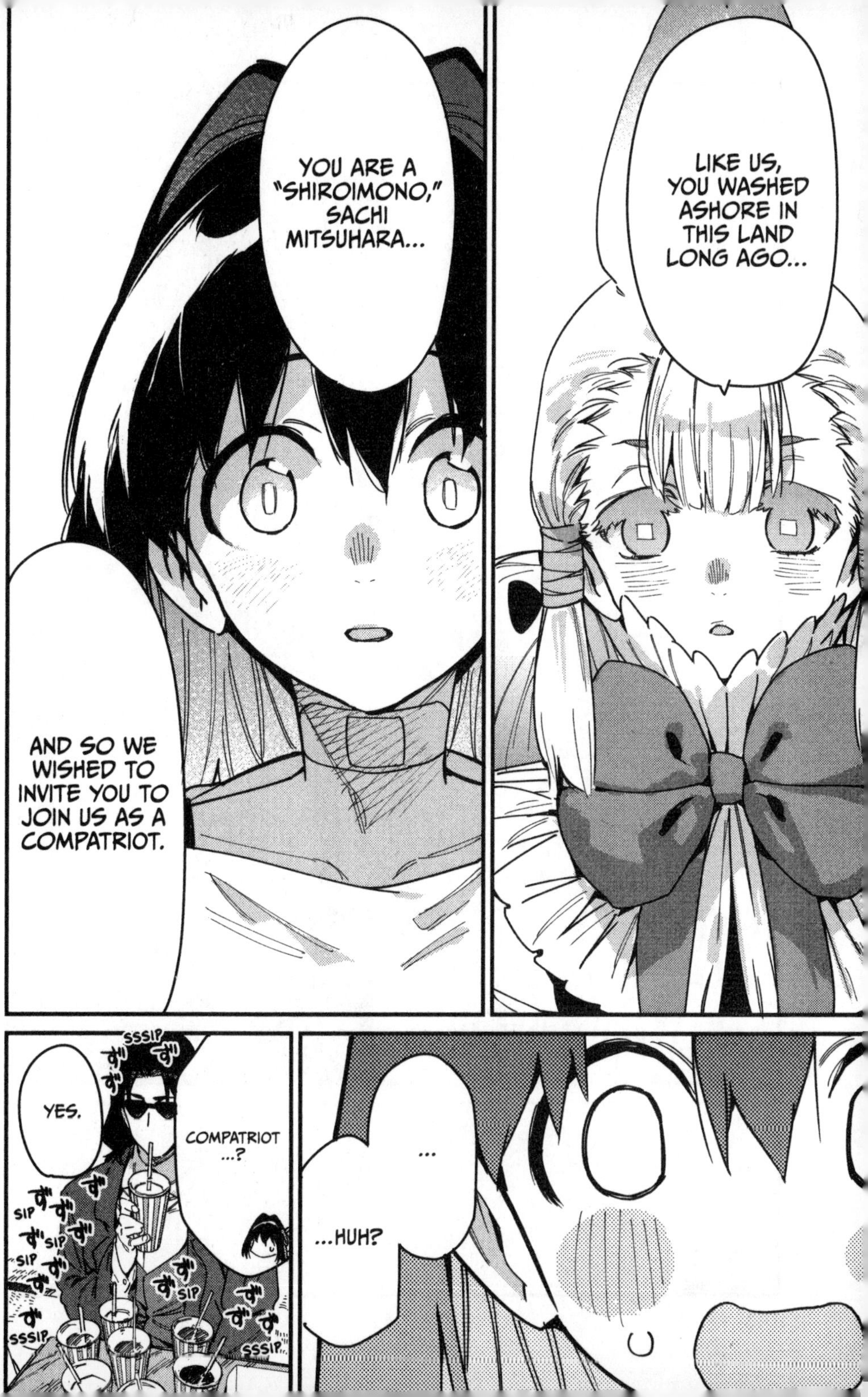

LIKE US, YOU WASHED ASHORE IN THIS LAND LONG AGO...
YOU ARE A "SHIROIMONO," SACHI MITSUHARA...
AND SO WE WISHED TO INVITE YOU TO JOIN US AS A COMPATRIOT.
...
...HUH?
COMPATRIOT ...?
SSSIP
YES.
SIP
SIP
SIP
SIP
SSSIP
SSSIP

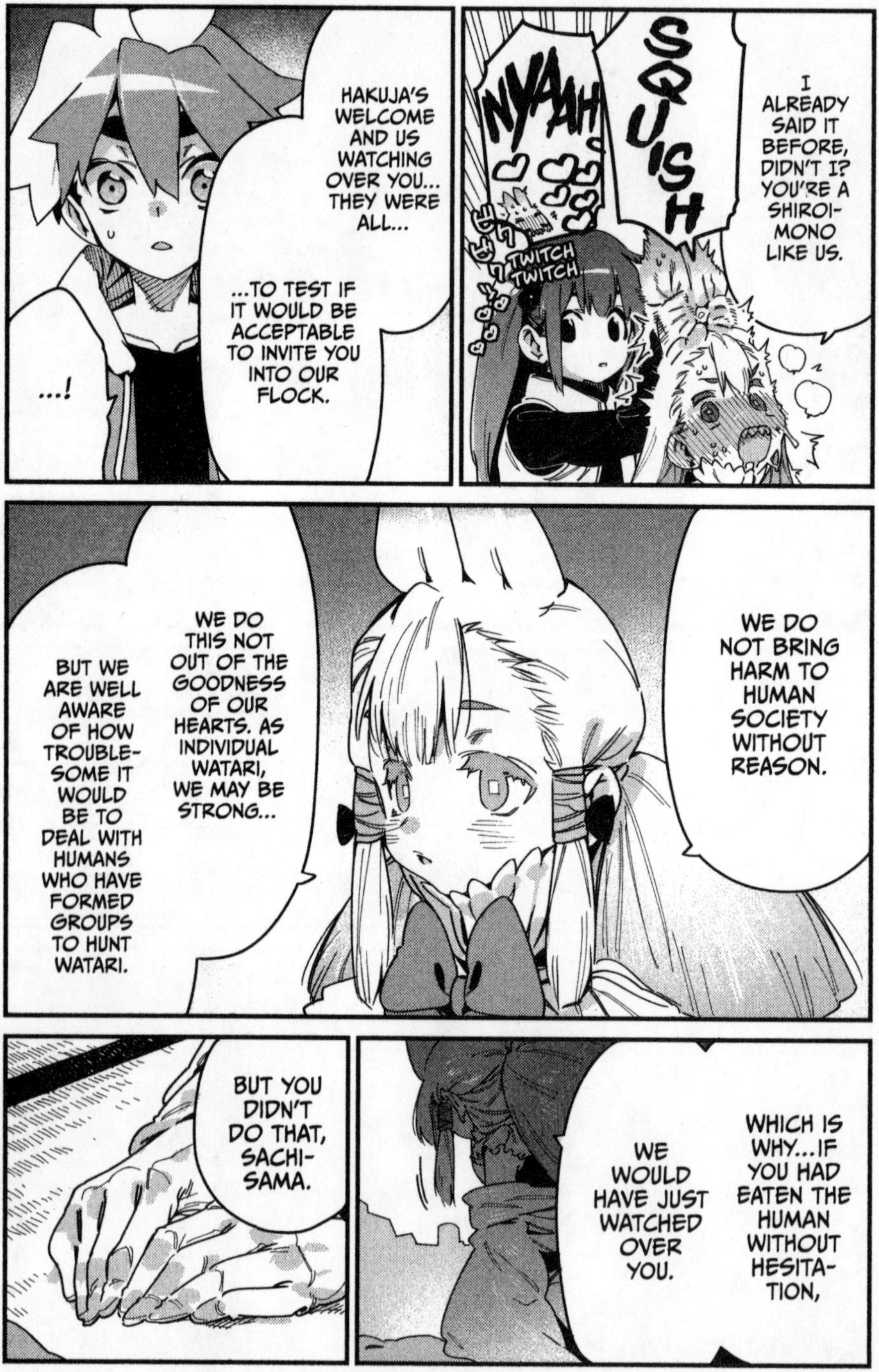
I ALREADY SAID IT BEFORE, DIDN'T I? YOU'RE A SHIROI-MONO LIKE US.
SQUISH
NYAAH
TWITCH TWITCH
HAKUJA'S WELCOME AND US WATCHING OVER YOU... THEY WERE ALL...
...TO TEST IF IT WOULD BE ACCEPTABLE TO INVITE YOU INTO OUR FLOCK.
...!
WE DO NOT BRING HARM TO HUMAN SOCIETY WITHOUT REASON.
WE DO THIS NOT OUT OF THE GOODNESS OF OUR HEARTS. AS INDIVIDUAL WATARI, WE MAY BE STRONG...
BUT WE ARE WELL AWARE OF HOW TROUBLE-SOME IT WOULD BE TO DEAL WITH HUMANS WHO HAVE FORMED GROUPS TO HUNT WATARI.
WHICH IS WHY...IF YOU HAD EATEN THE HUMAN WITHOUT HESITA-TION,
WE WOULD HAVE JUST WATCHED OVER YOU.
BUT YOU DIDN'T DO THAT, SACHI-SAMA.

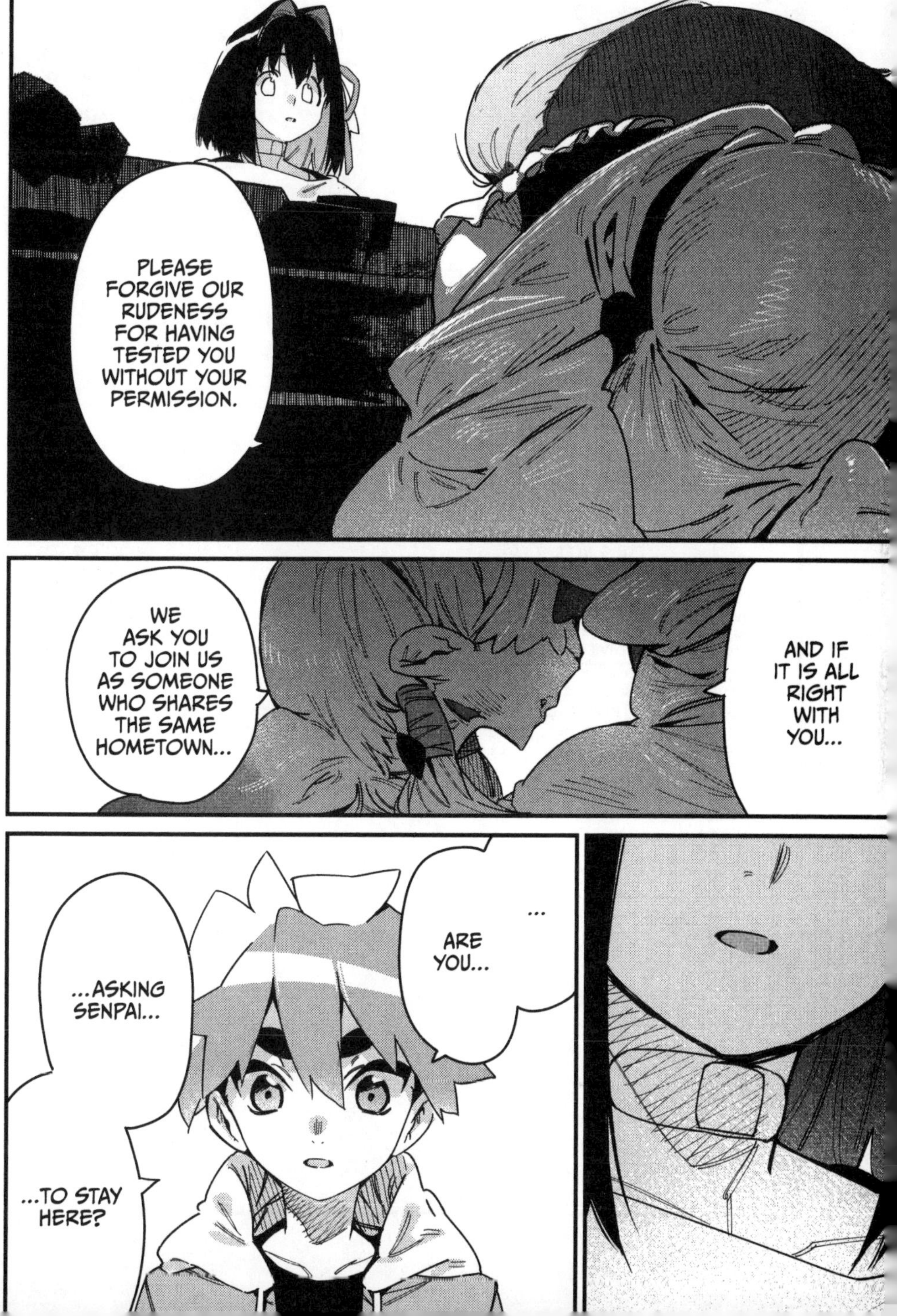
PLEASE FORGIVE OUR RUDENESS FOR HAVING TESTED YOU WITHOUT YOUR PERMISSION.
AND IF IT IS ALL RIGHT WITH YOU...
WE ASK YOU TO JOIN US AS SOMEONE WHO SHARES THE SAME HOMETOWN...
...
ARE YOU...
...ASKING SENPAI...
...TO STAY HERE?

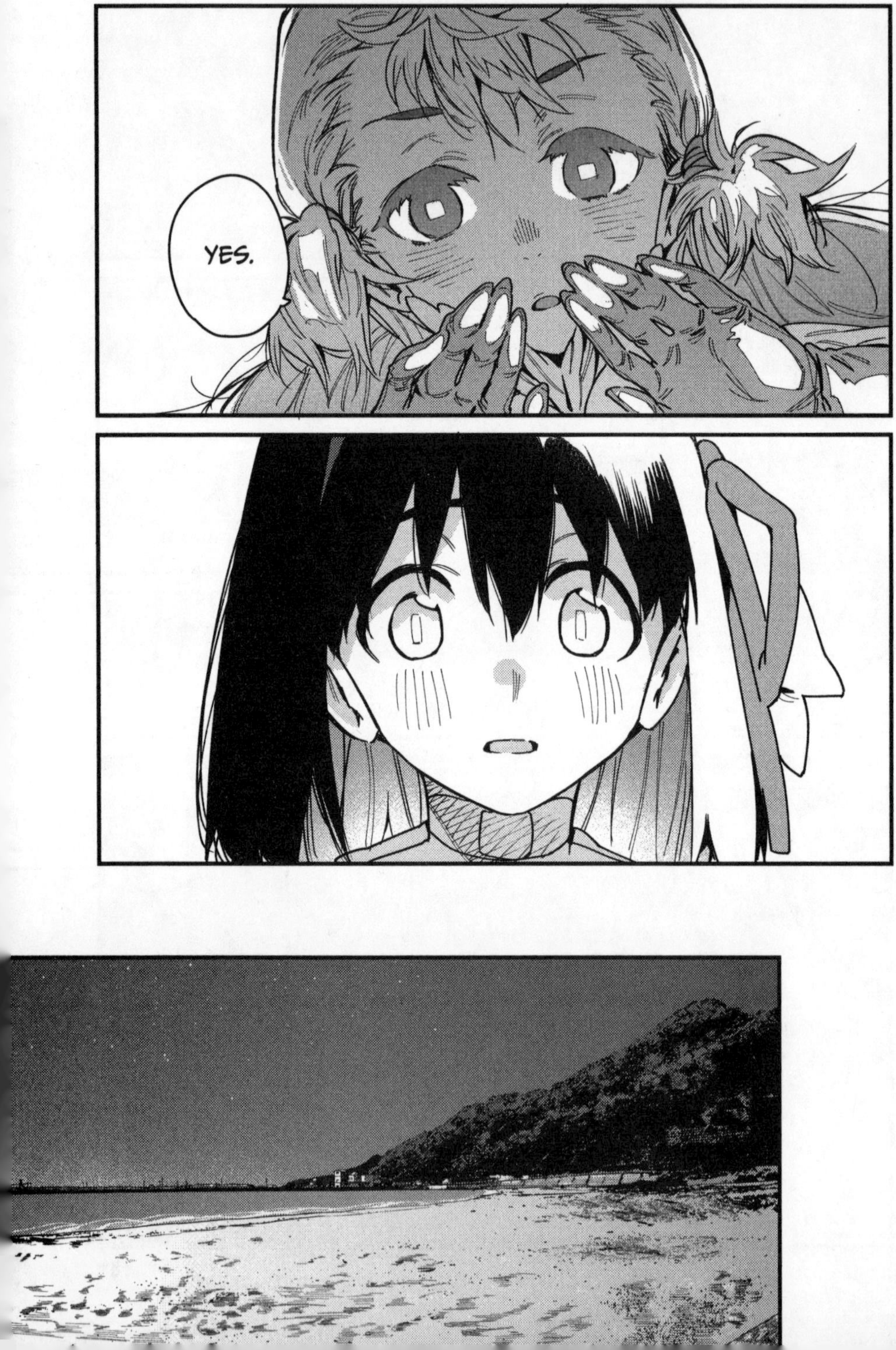
YES.

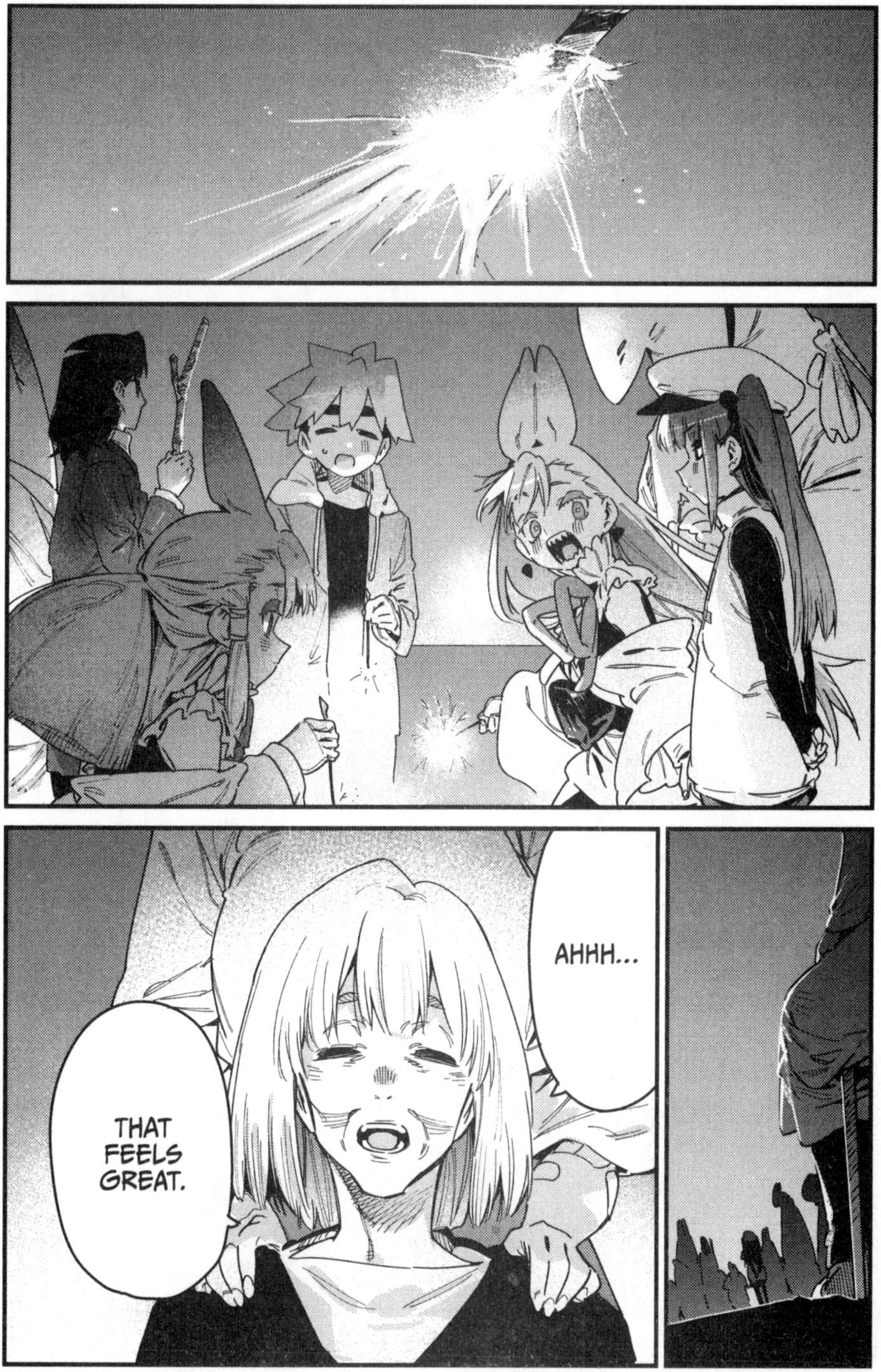
AHHH...
THAT FEELS GREAT.

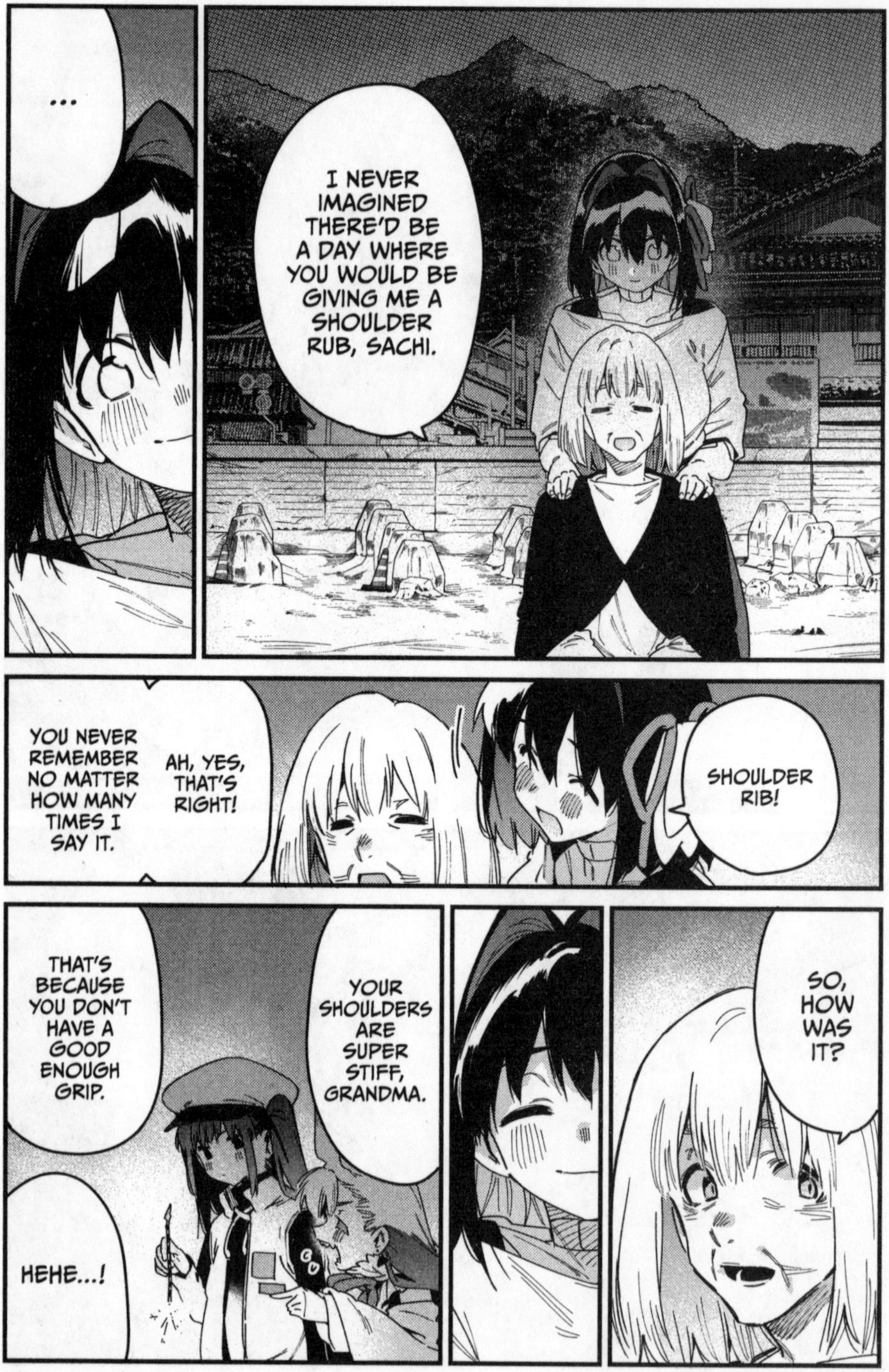
I NEVER IMAGINED THERE'D BE A DAY WHERE YOU WOULD BE GIVING ME A SHOULDER RUB, SACHI.
...
SHOULDER RIB!
AH, YES, THAT'S RIGHT!
YOU NEVER REMEMBER NO MATTER HOW MANY TIMES I SAY IT.
SO, HOW WAS IT?
YOUR SHOULDERS ARE SUPER STIFF, GRANDMA.
THAT'S BECAUSE YOU DON'T HAVE A GOOD ENOUGH GRIP.
HEHE...!

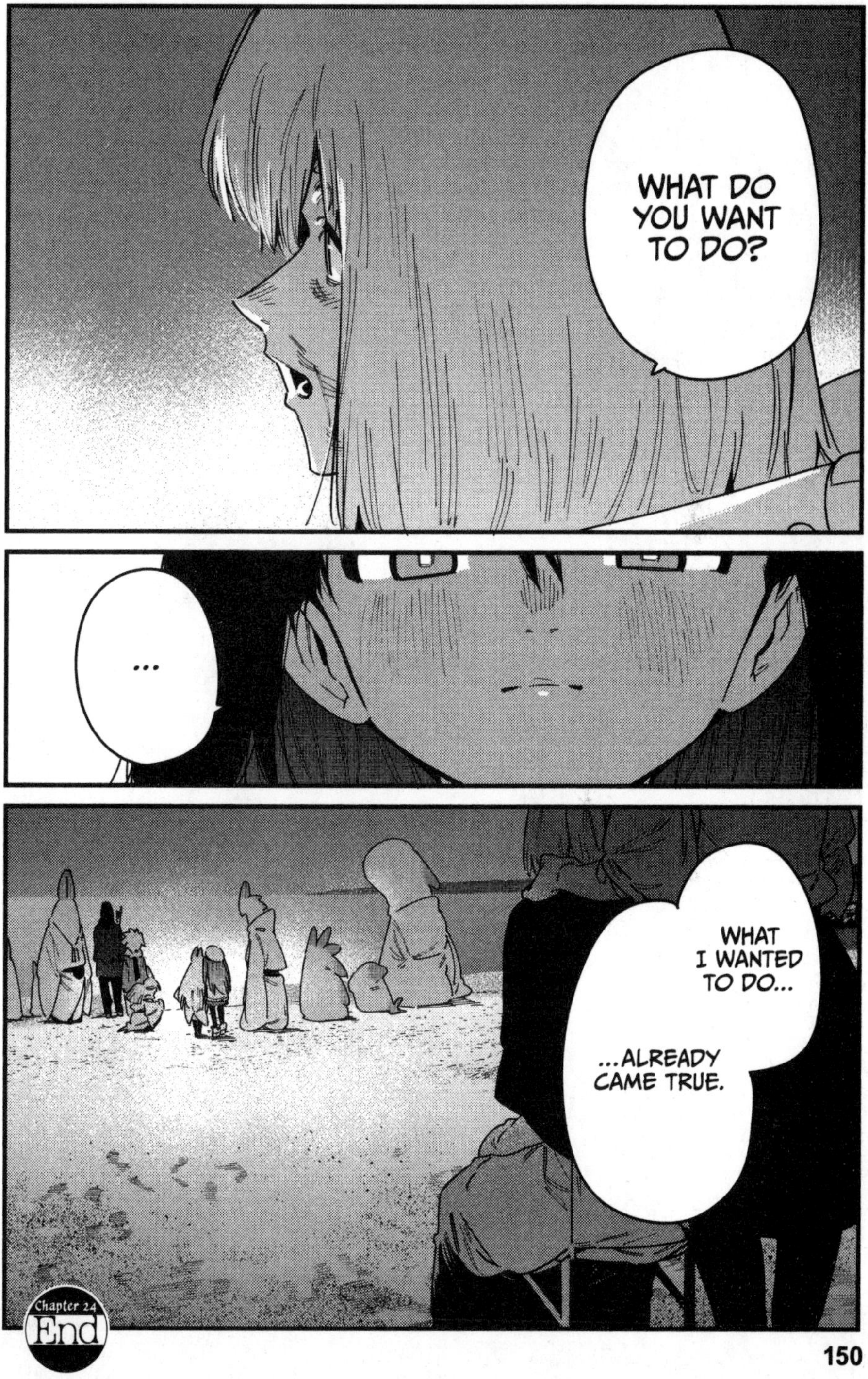
WHAT DO YOU WANT TO DO?
...
WHAT I WANTED TO DO...
...ALREADY CAME TRUE.
Chapter 24 End

Sachi's
MONSTROUS
Appetite

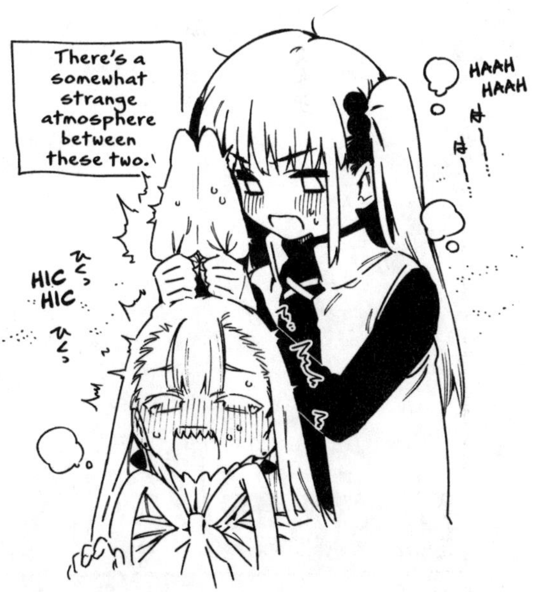
HAAH HAAH
There's a somewhat strange atmosphere between these two.
HIC HIC

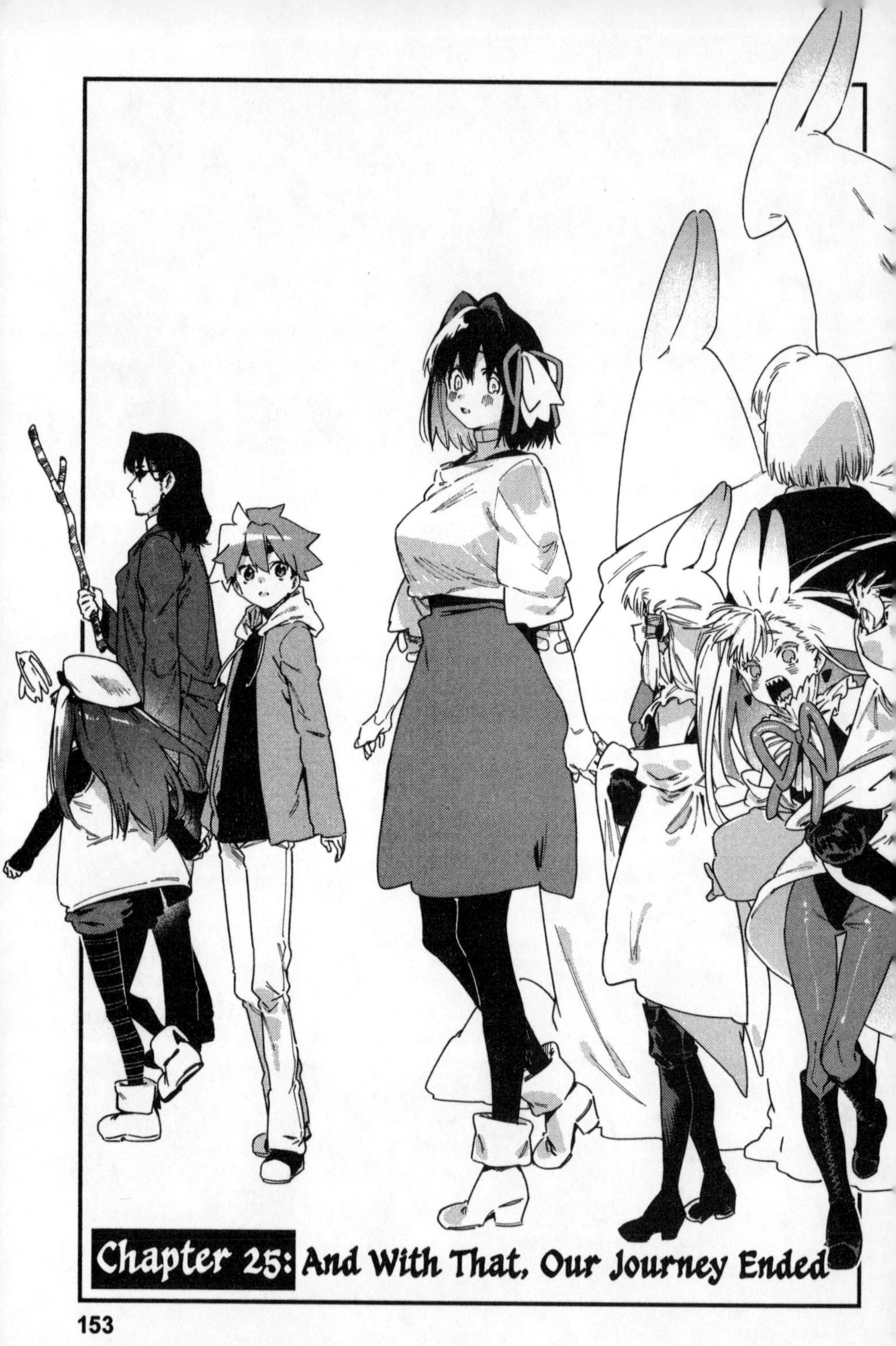
Chapter 25: And With That, Our Journey Ended

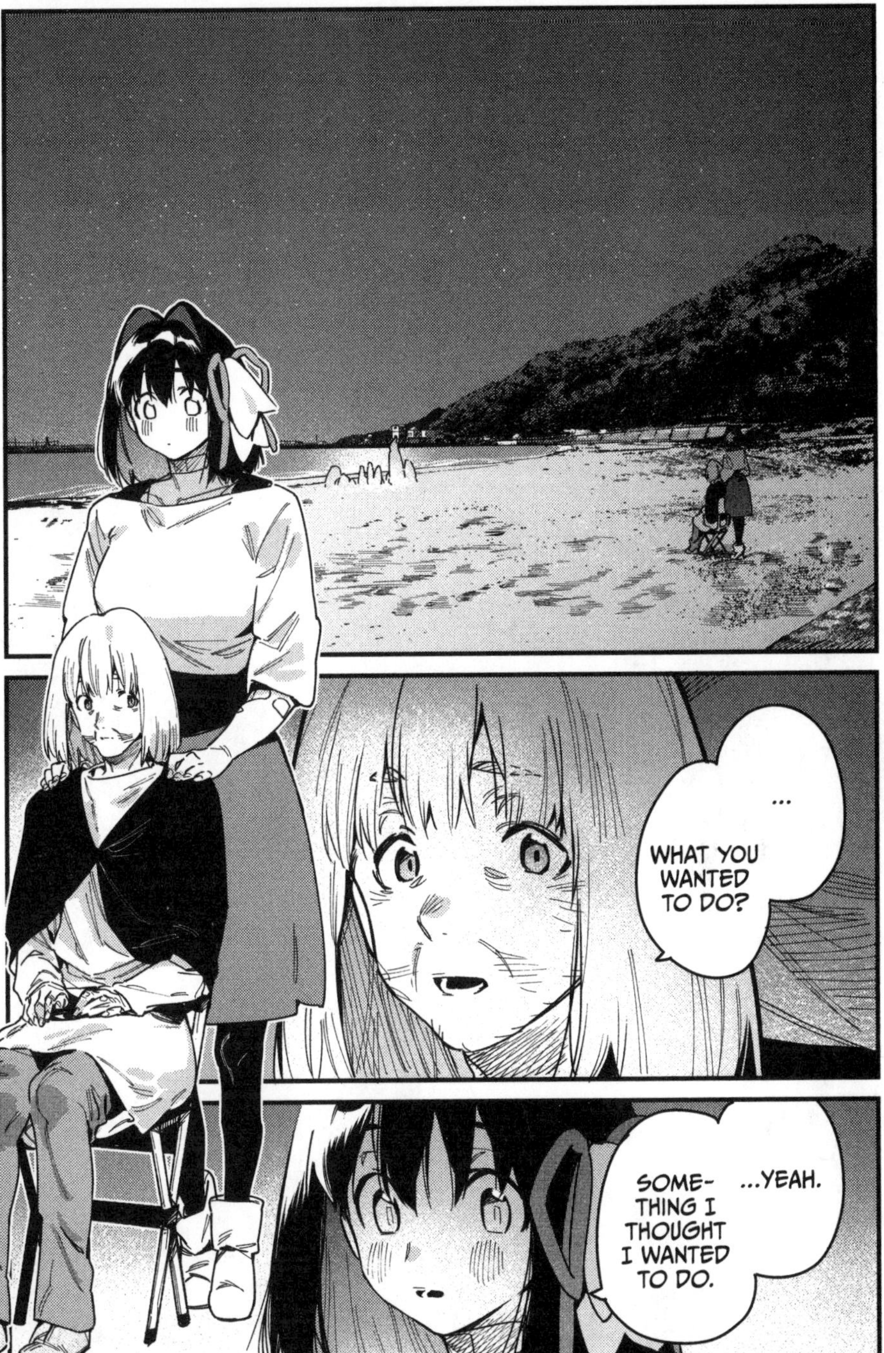
...
WHAT YOU WANTED TO DO?
...YEAH.
SOME-THING I THOUGHT I WANTED TO DO.

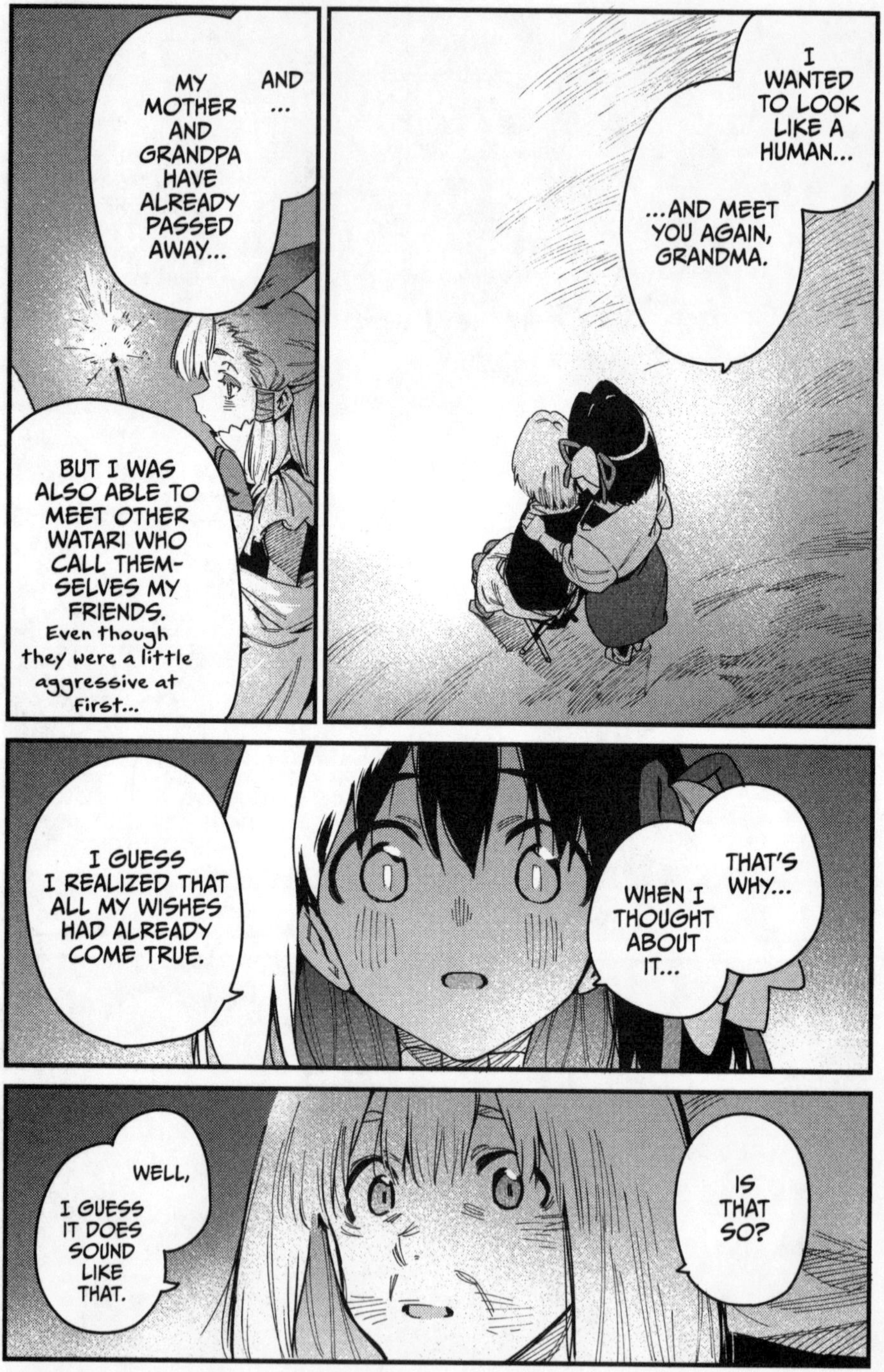
I WANTED TO LOOK LIKE A HUMAN...
...AND MEET YOU AGAIN, GRANDMA.
AND ...
MY MOTHER AND GRANDPA HAVE ALREADY PASSED AWAY...
BUT I WAS ALSO ABLE TO MEET OTHER WATARI WHO CALL THEM-SELVES MY FRIENDS.
Even though they were a little aggressive at first...
THAT'S WHY...
WHEN I THOUGHT ABOUT IT...
I GUESS I REALIZED THAT ALL MY WISHES HAD ALREADY COME TRUE.
IS THAT SO?
WELL,
I GUESS IT DOES SOUND LIKE THAT.

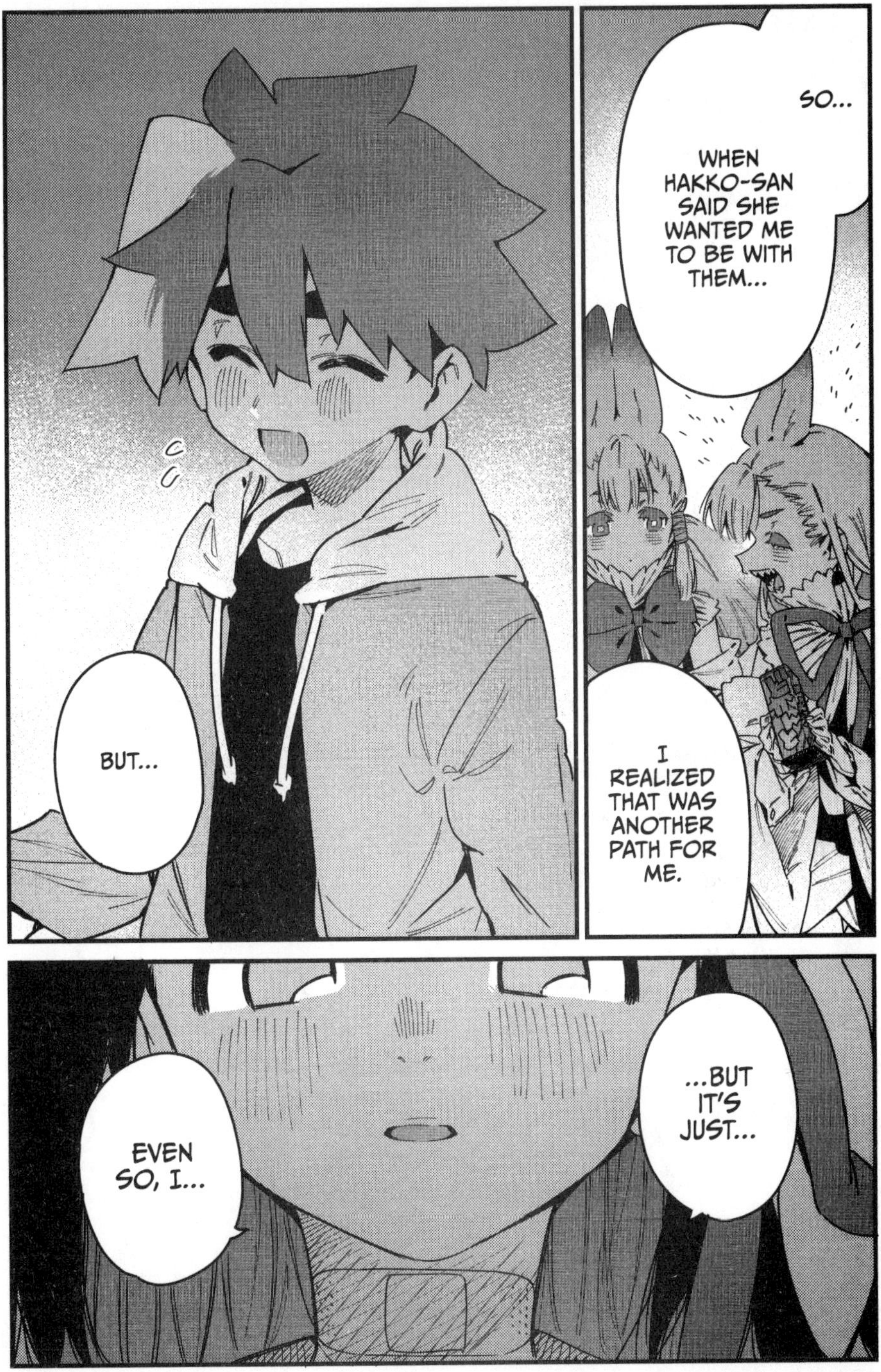
SO...
WHEN HAKKO-SAN SAID SHE WANTED ME TO BE WITH THEM...
I REALIZED THAT WAS ANOTHER PATH FOR ME.
BUT...
...BUT IT'S JUST...
EVEN SO, I...

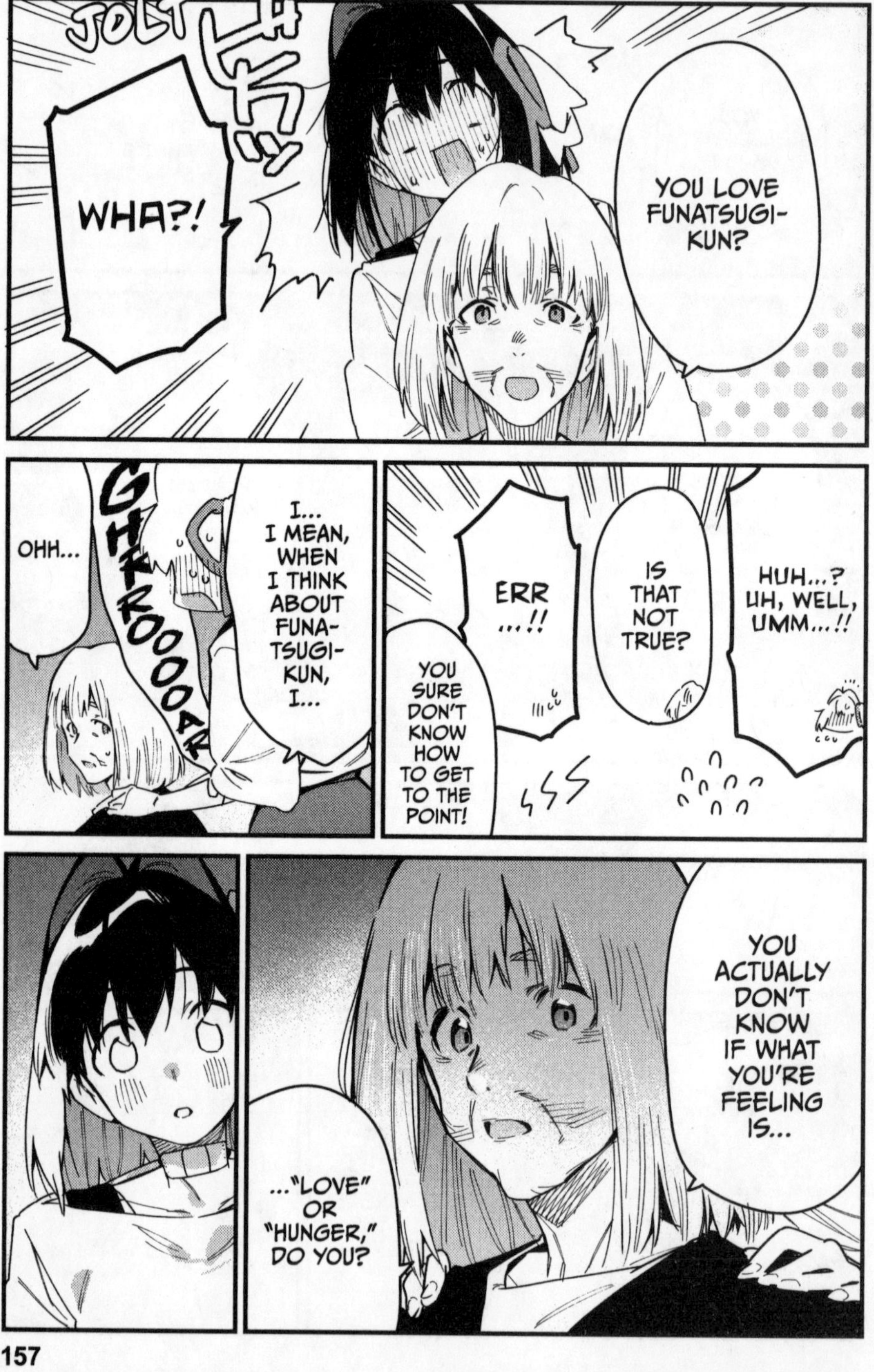
YOU LOVE FUNATSUGI-KUN?
JOLT
ヒクッ
WHA?!
HUH...? UH, WELL, UMM...!!
IS THAT NOT TRUE?
ERR ...!!
YOU SURE DON'T KNOW HOW TO GET TO THE POINT!
I... I MEAN, WHEN I THINK ABOUT FUNA-TSUGI-KUN, I...
GHROOOOAR
OHH...
YOU ACTUALLY DON'T KNOW IF WHAT YOU'RE FEELING IS...
..."LOVE" OR "HUNGER," DO YOU?

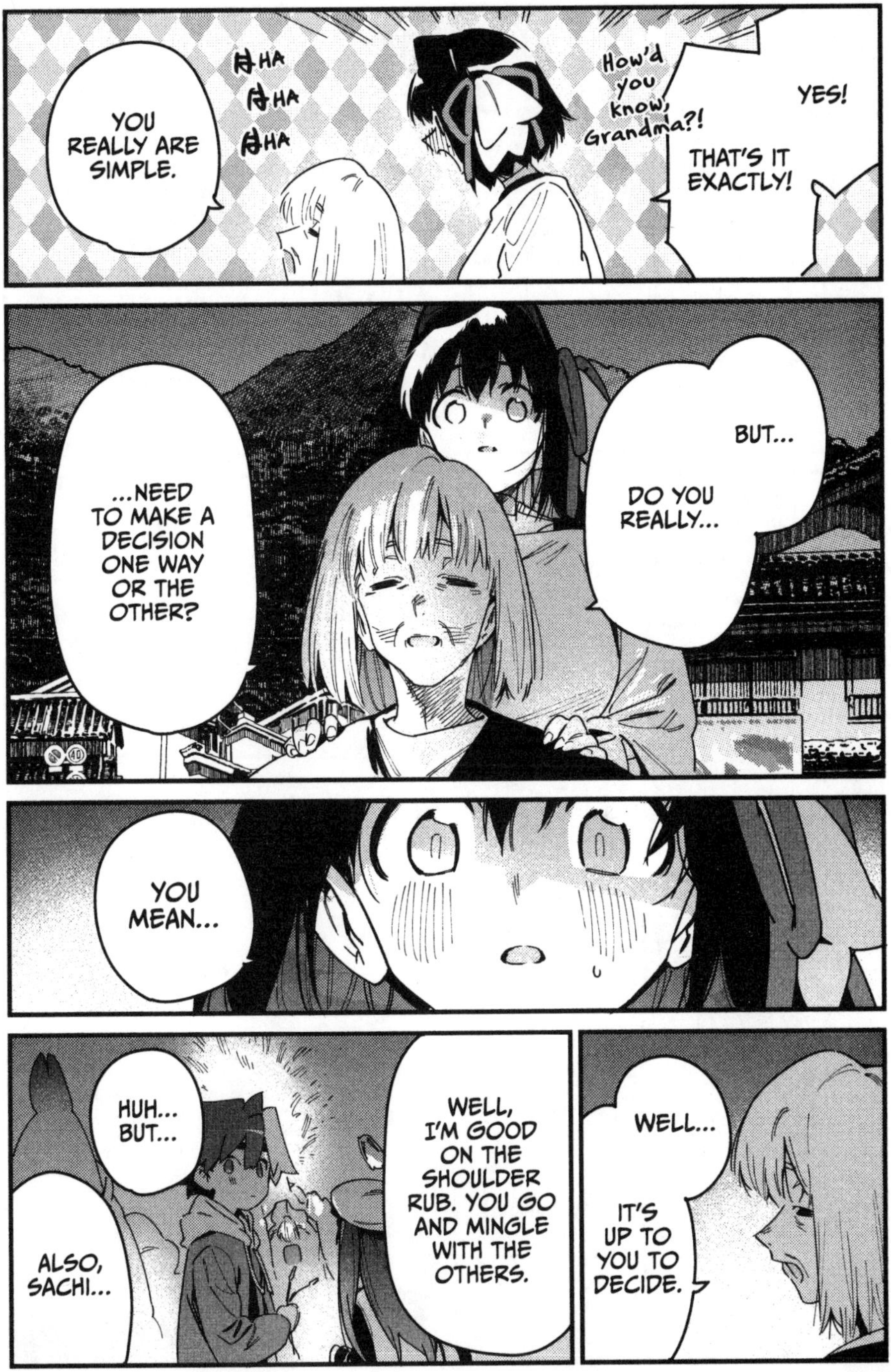
YES!
THAT'S IT EXACTLY!
How'd you know, Grandma?!
HA
HA
HA
YOU REALLY ARE SIMPLE.
BUT...
DO YOU REALLY...
...NEED TO MAKE A DECISION ONE WAY OR THE OTHER?
YOU MEAN...
WELL...
IT'S UP TO YOU TO DECIDE.
WELL, I'M GOOD ON THE SHOULDER RUB. YOU GO AND MINGLE WITH THE OTHERS.
HUH... BUT...
ALSO, SACHI...

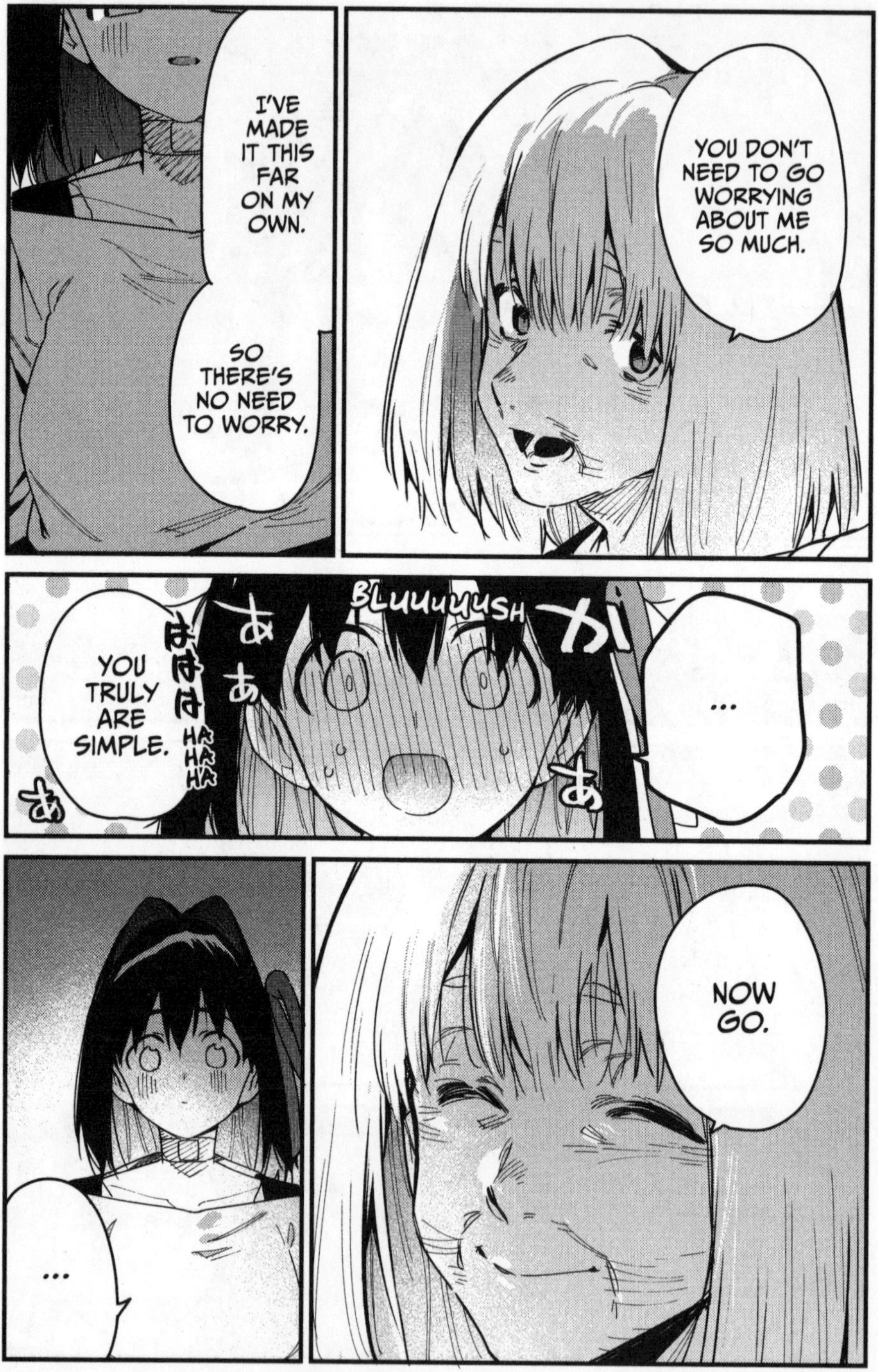
YOU DON'T NEED TO GO WORRYING ABOUT ME SO MUCH.
I'VE MADE IT THIS FAR ON MY OWN.
SO THERE'S NO NEED TO WORRY.
...
BLUUUUUSH
YOU TRULY ARE SIMPLE.
ははは
HA HA HA
NOW GO.
...

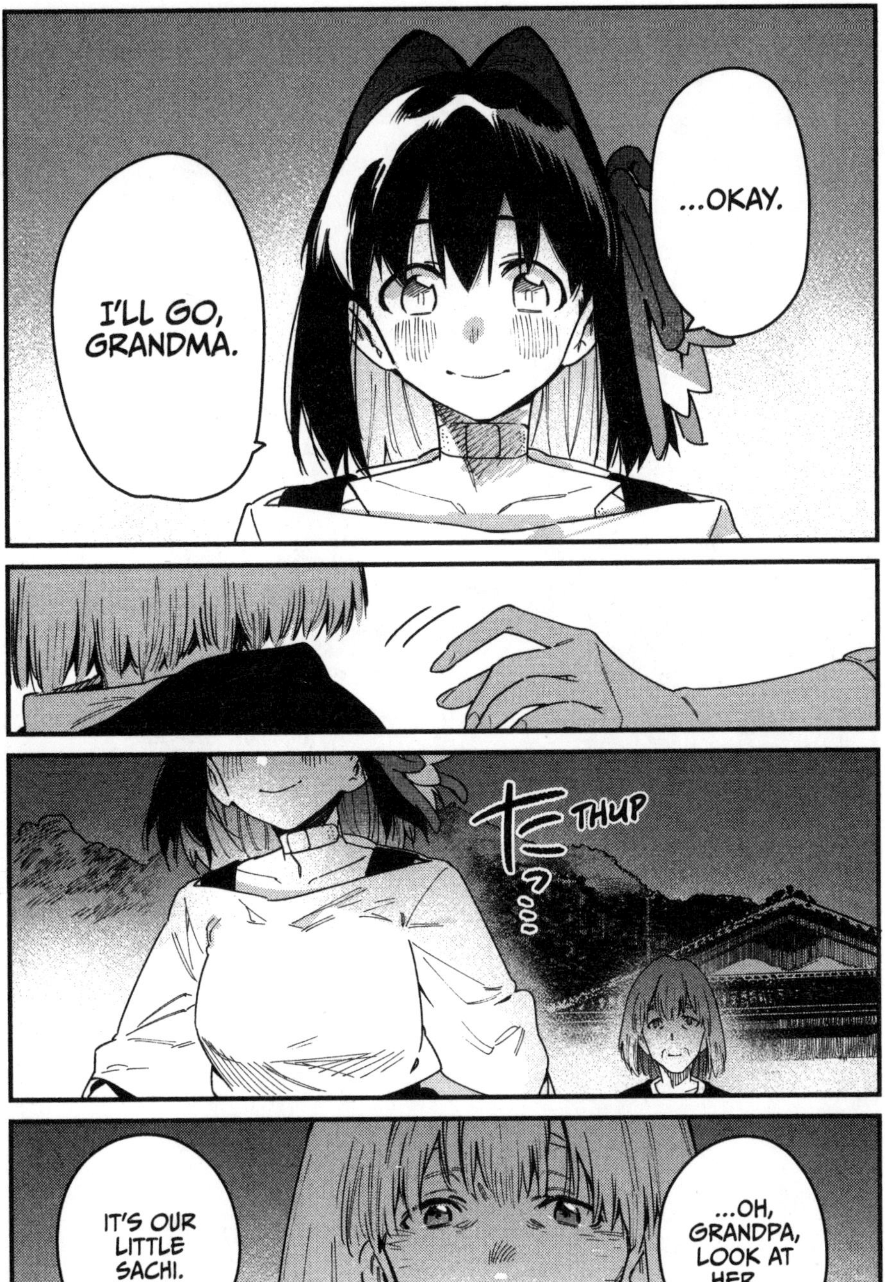
...OKAY.
I'LL GO, GRANDMA.
THUP
...OH, GRANDPA, LOOK AT HER...
IT'S OUR LITTLE SACHI.

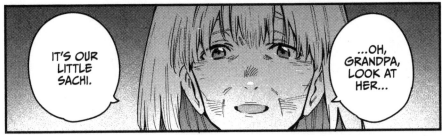

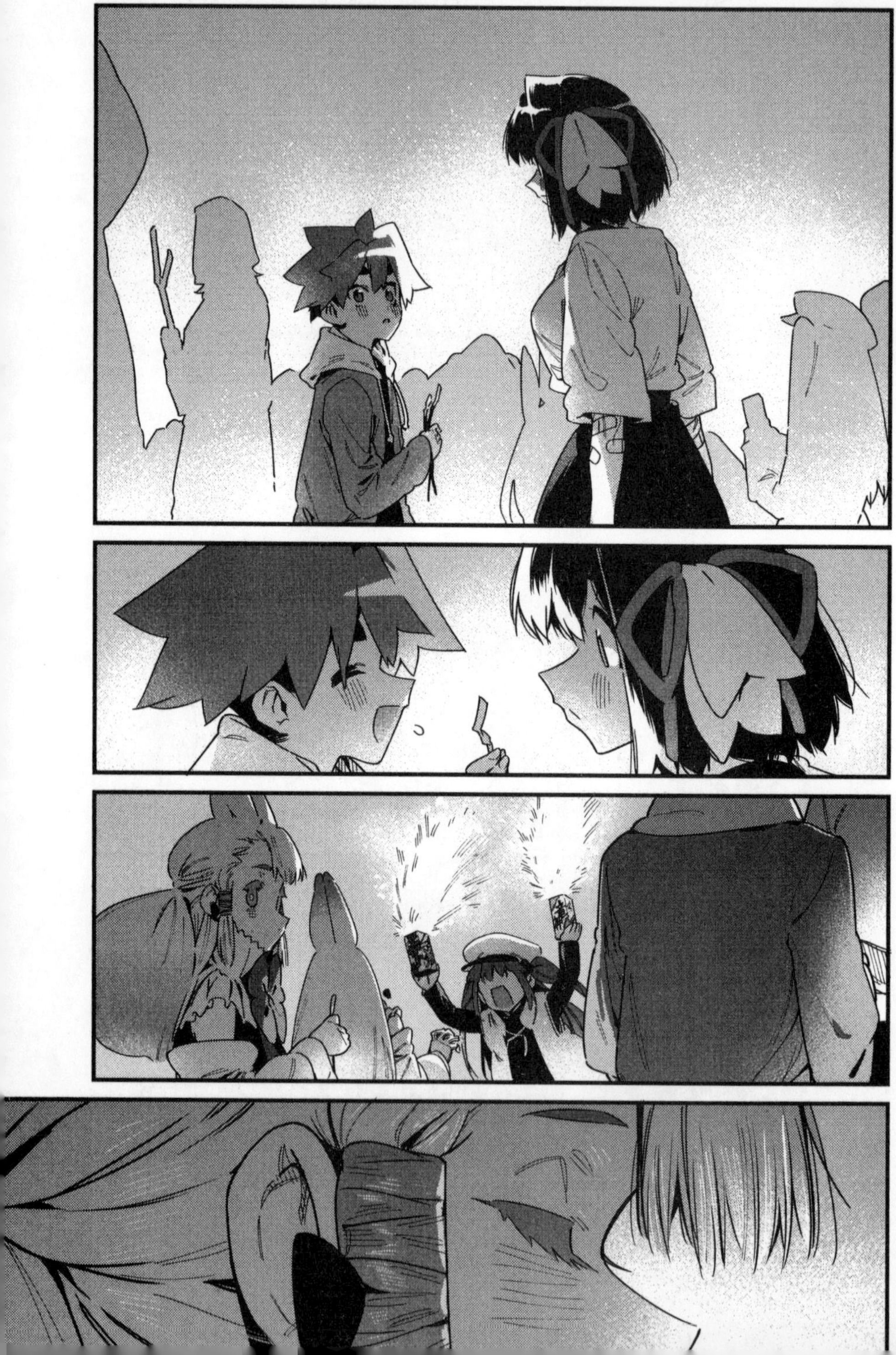

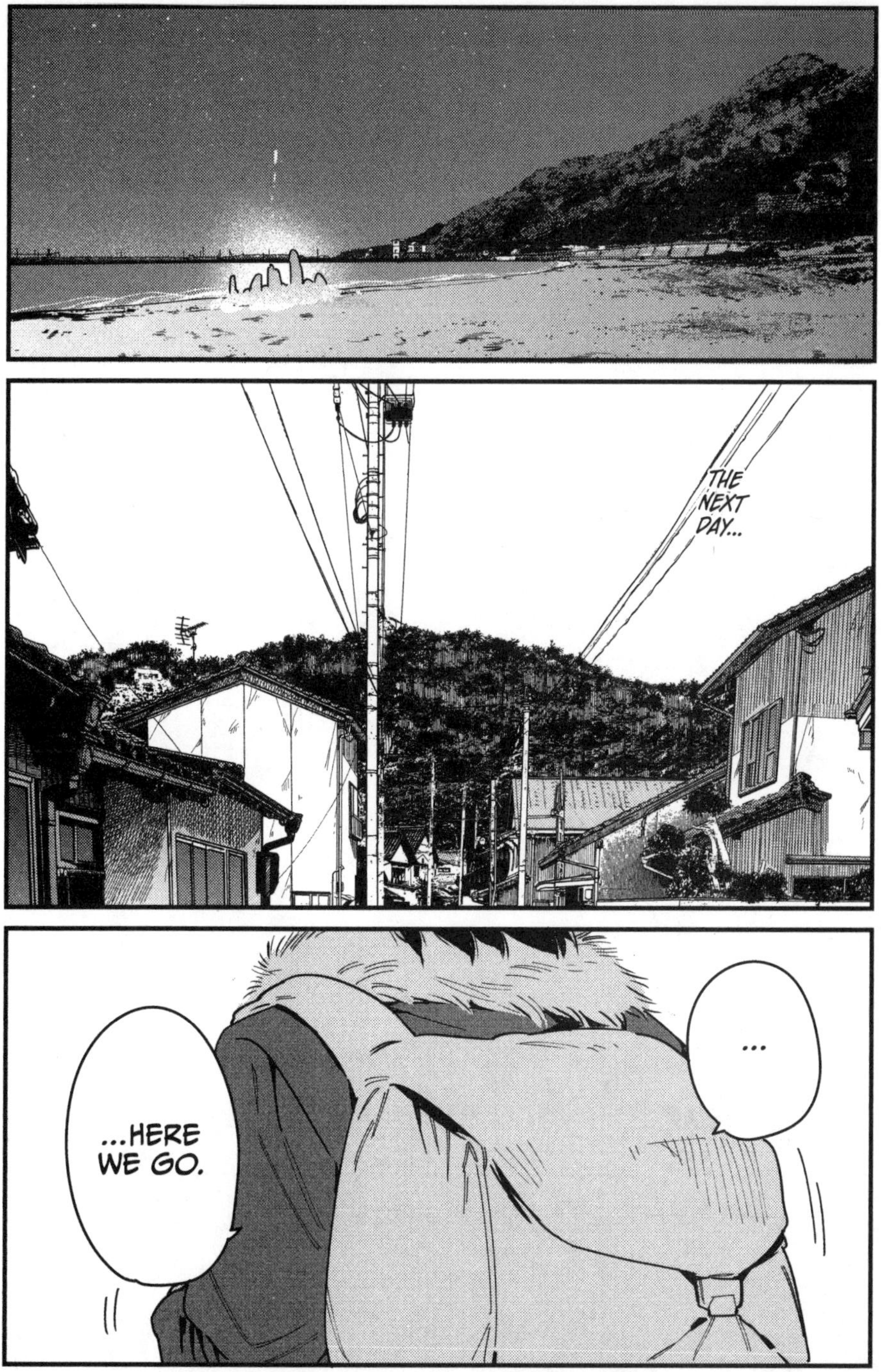
THE NEXT DAY...
...
...HERE WE GO.

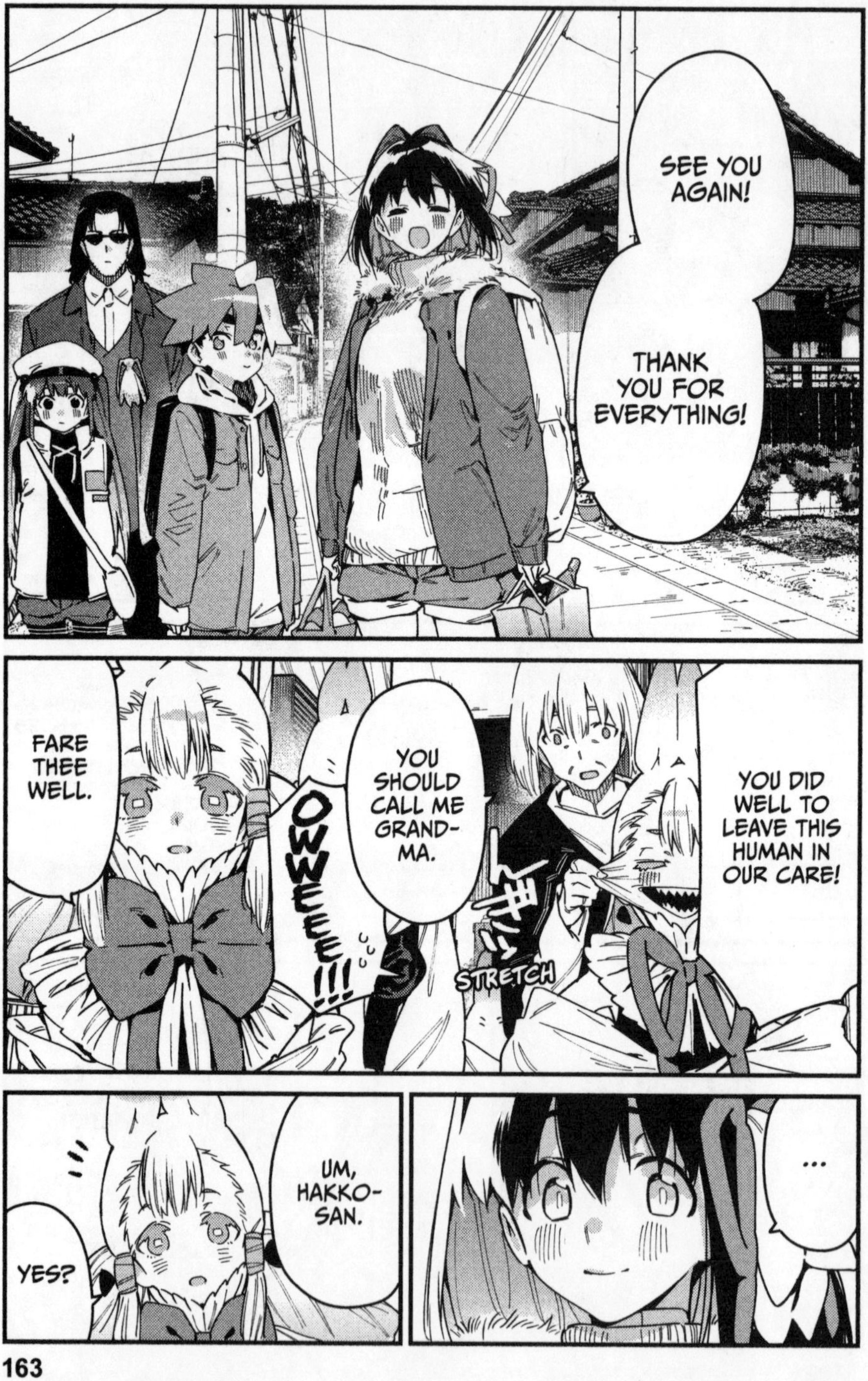
SEE YOU AGAIN!
THANK YOU FOR EVERYTHING!
YOU DID WELL TO LEAVE THIS HUMAN IN OUR CARE!
STRETCH
YOU SHOULD CALL ME GRAND-MA.
OWWEEE!!!
FARE THEE WELL.
...
UM, HAKKO-SAN.
YES?

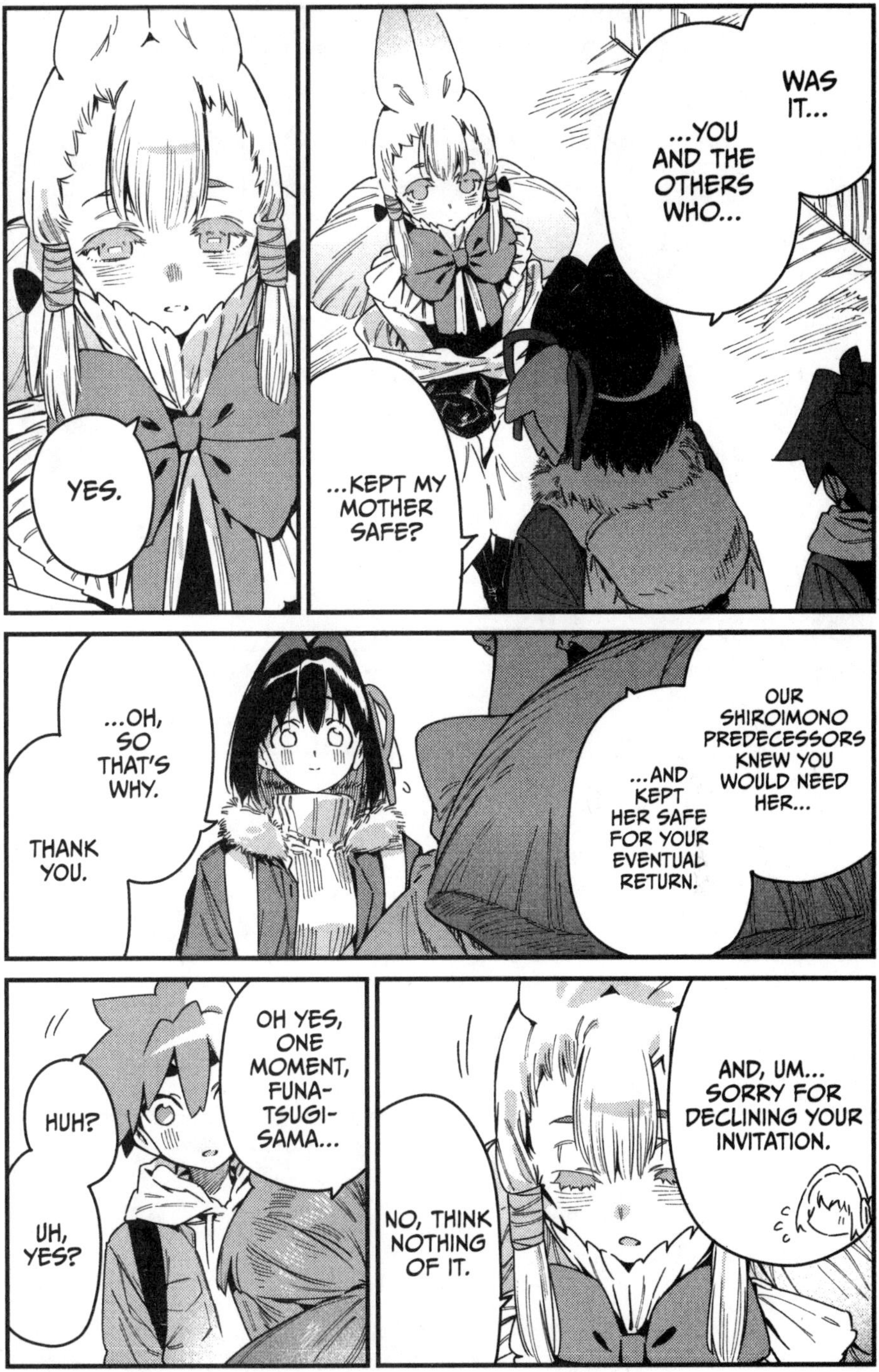
WAS IT...
...YOU AND THE OTHERS WHO...
...KEPT MY MOTHER SAFE?
YES.
OUR SHIROIMONO PREDECESSORS KNEW YOU WOULD NEED HER...
...AND KEPT HER SAFE FOR YOUR EVENTUAL RETURN.
...OH, SO THAT'S WHY.
THANK YOU.
AND, UM... SORRY FOR DECLINING YOUR INVITATION.
NO, THINK NOTHING OF IT.
OH YES, ONE MOMENT, FUNA-TSUGI-SAMA...
HUH?
UH, YES?

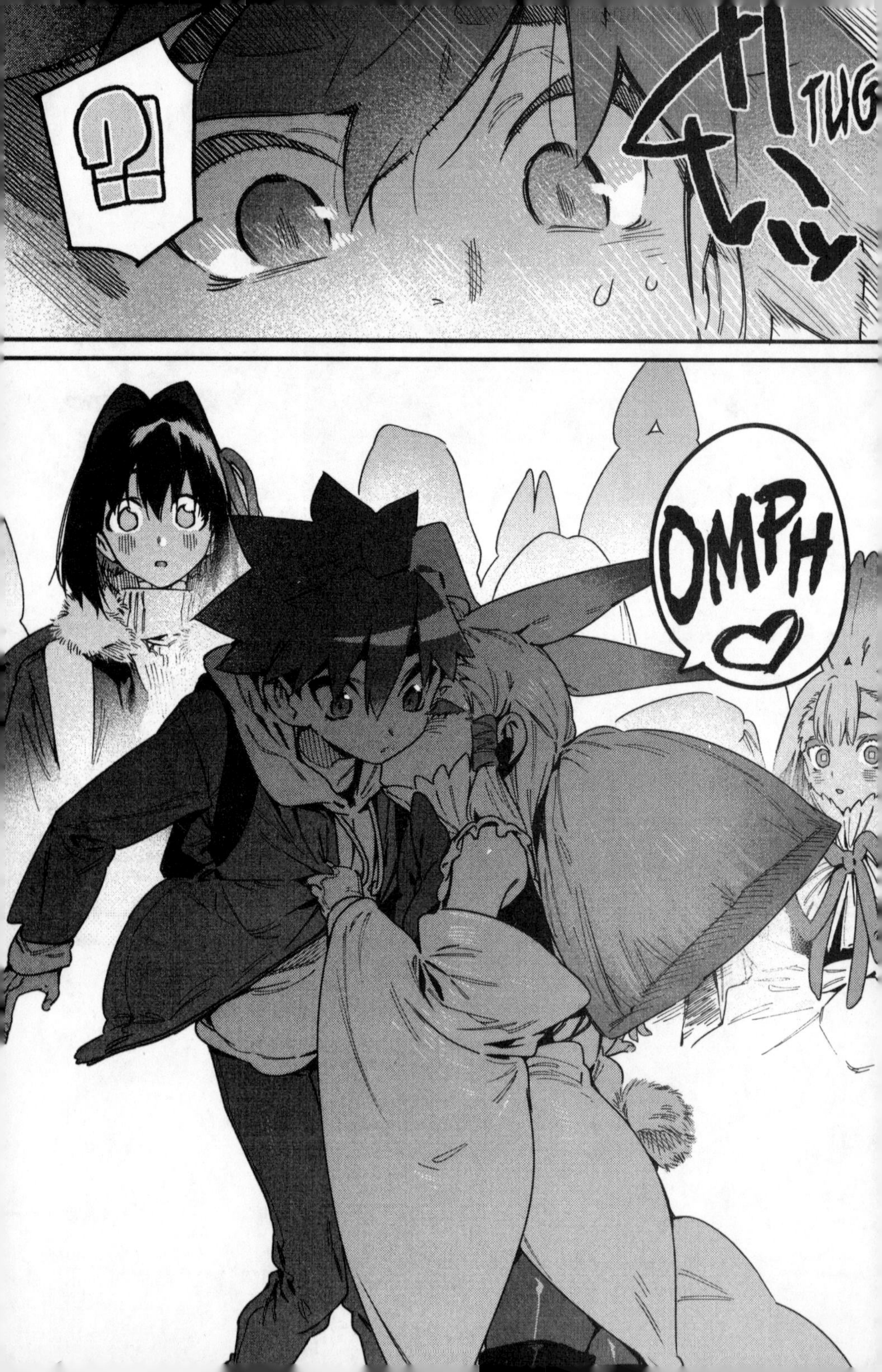
TUG
?!
OMPH ♡

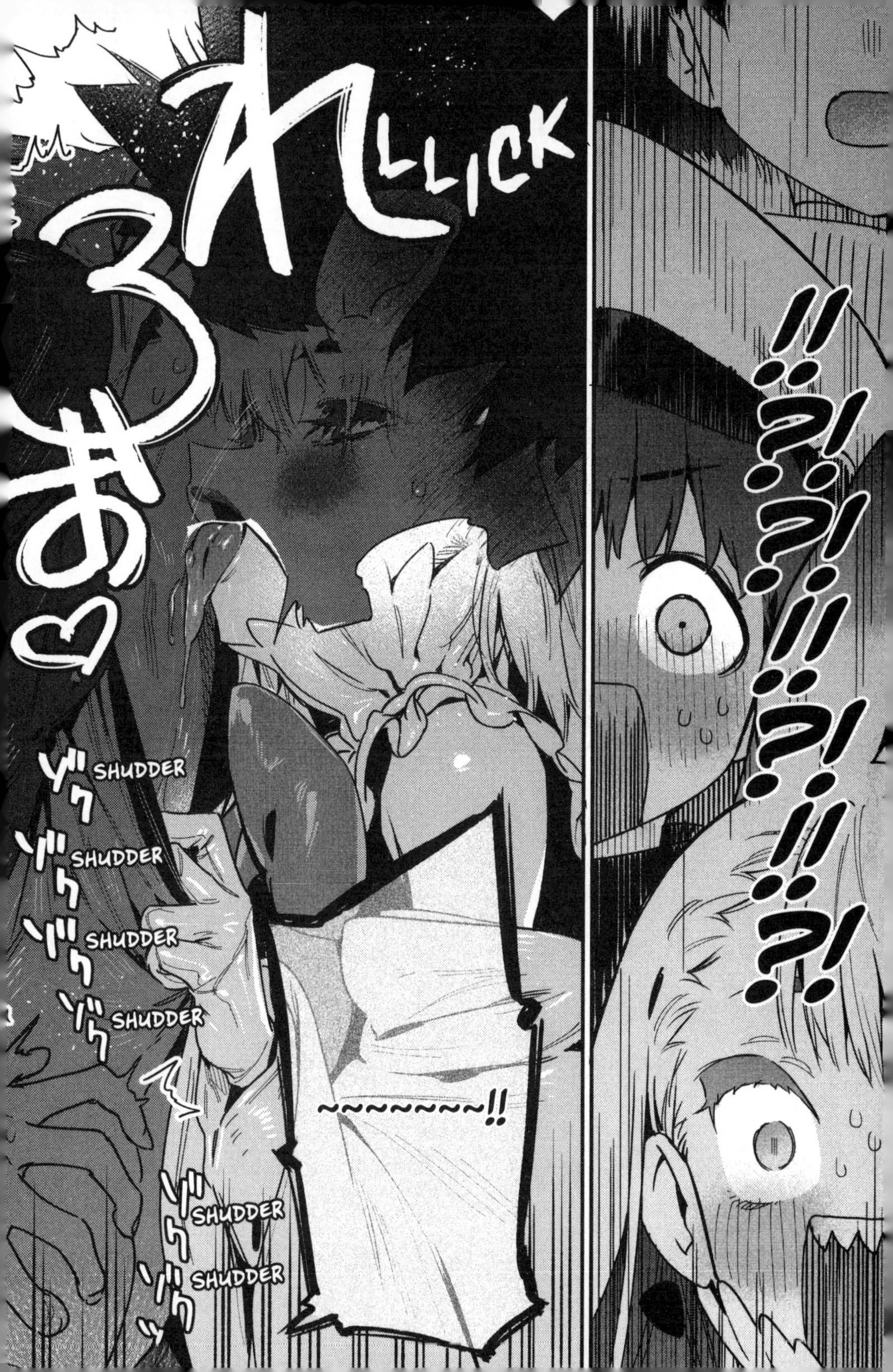

!!?!?!!!?!!!?!
れろお♡
LLICK
ゾク SHUDDER
ゾク SHUDDER
ゾク SHUDDER
ゾク SHUDDER
~~~~~~~~!!
ゾク SHUDDER
ゾク SHUDDER
~~~~~~~~

WHUP
WAIT A...
HAKKO-SA—
ZSH
SHLRP
SHLP
SHLRP
RP
SHLR
SRRP
AAHHH!
SRRP
HEY, HEY, HEY, HEY, HEY, HEY!
SHLRRRRP
WAI...
JOLT

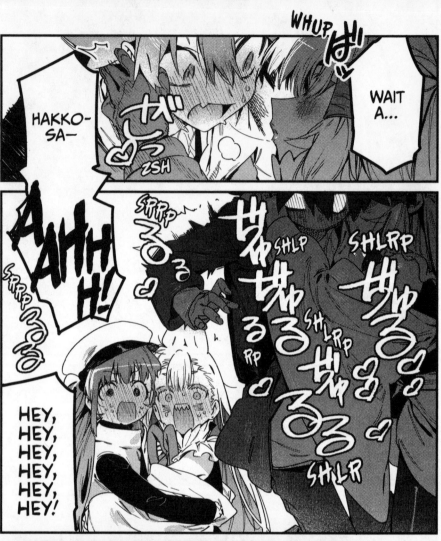

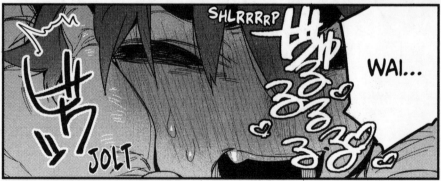

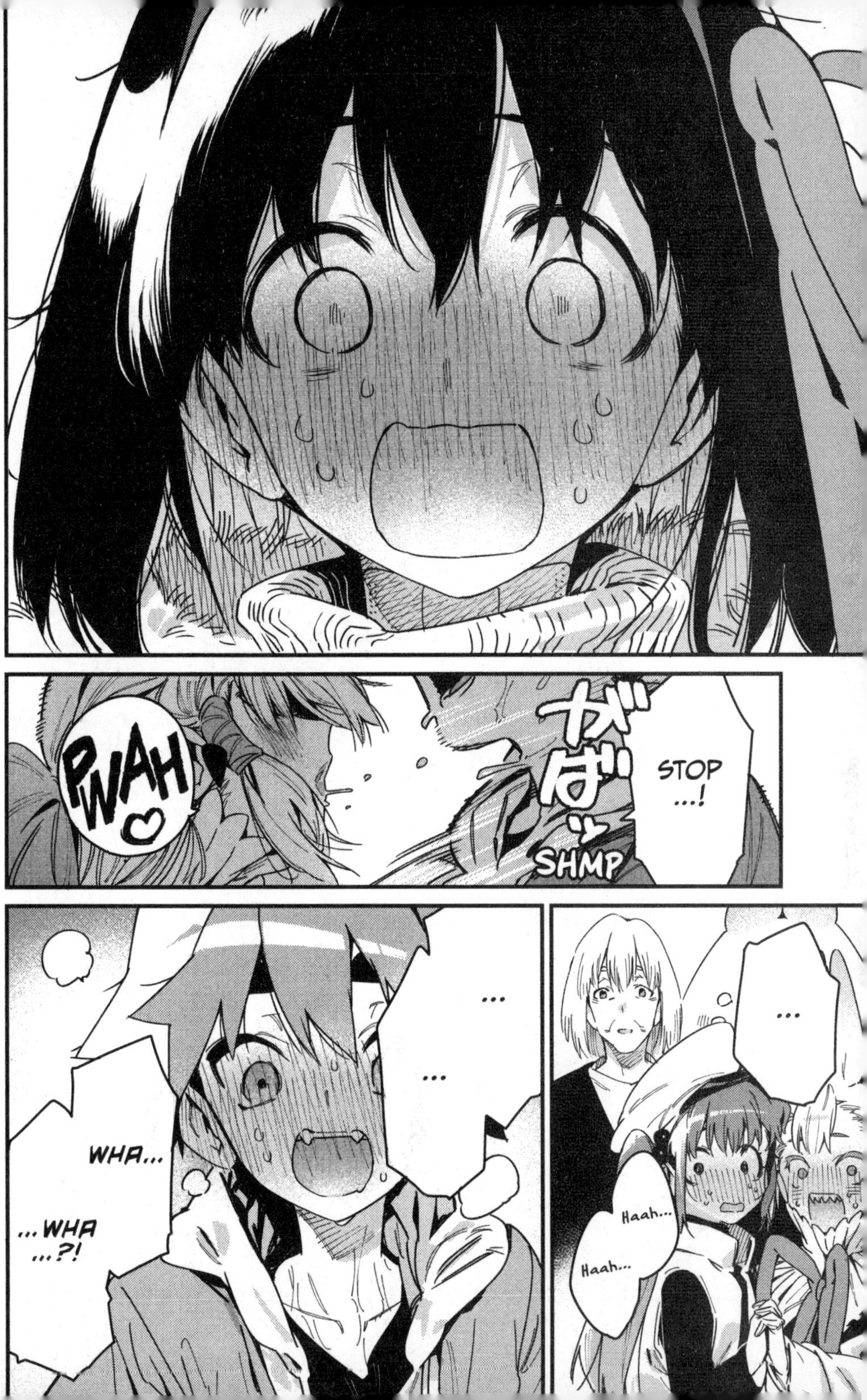
STOP ...!
がばっ
SHMP
PWAH ♡
...
Haah...
Haah...
...
...
WHA...
...WHA ...?!

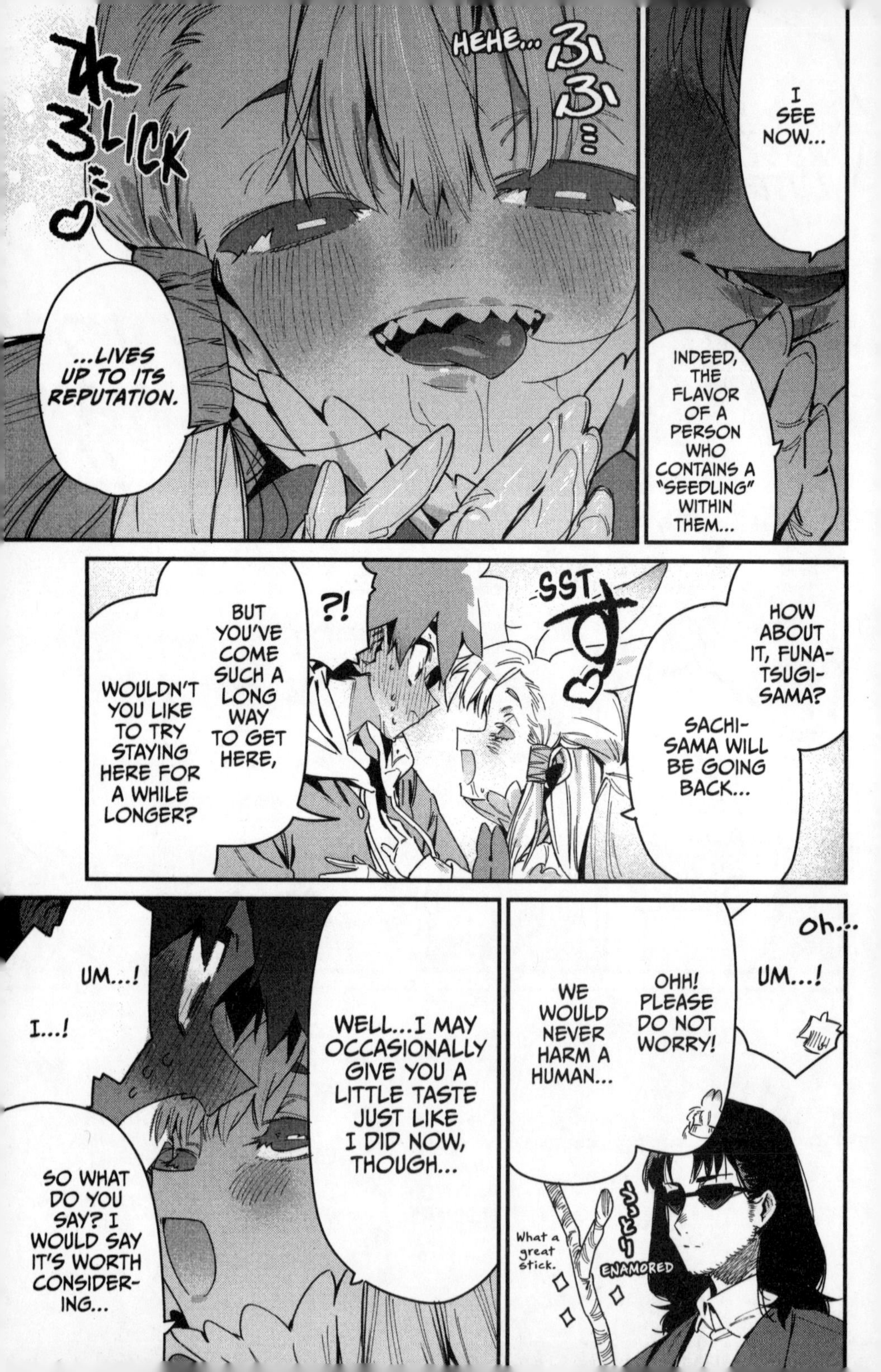
I SEE NOW...
INDEED, THE FLAVOR OF A PERSON WHO CONTAINS A "SEEDLING" WITHIN THEM...
HEHE... ふふ...
れろ LICK ♡
...LIVES UP TO ITS REPUTATION.
SST す♡
HOW ABOUT IT, FUNA-TSUGI-SAMA?
SACHI-SAMA WILL BE GOING BACK...
?!
BUT YOU'VE COME SUCH A LONG WAY TO GET HERE,
WOULDN'T YOU LIKE TO TRY STAYING HERE FOR A WHILE LONGER?
Oh...
UM...!
OHH! PLEASE DO NOT WORRY!
WE WOULD NEVER HARM A HUMAN...
What a great stick.
ENAMORED
WELL...I MAY OCCASIONALLY GIVE YOU A LITTLE TASTE JUST LIKE I DID NOW, THOUGH...
UM...!
I...!
SO WHAT DO YOU SAY? I WOULD SAY IT'S WORTH CONSIDERING...

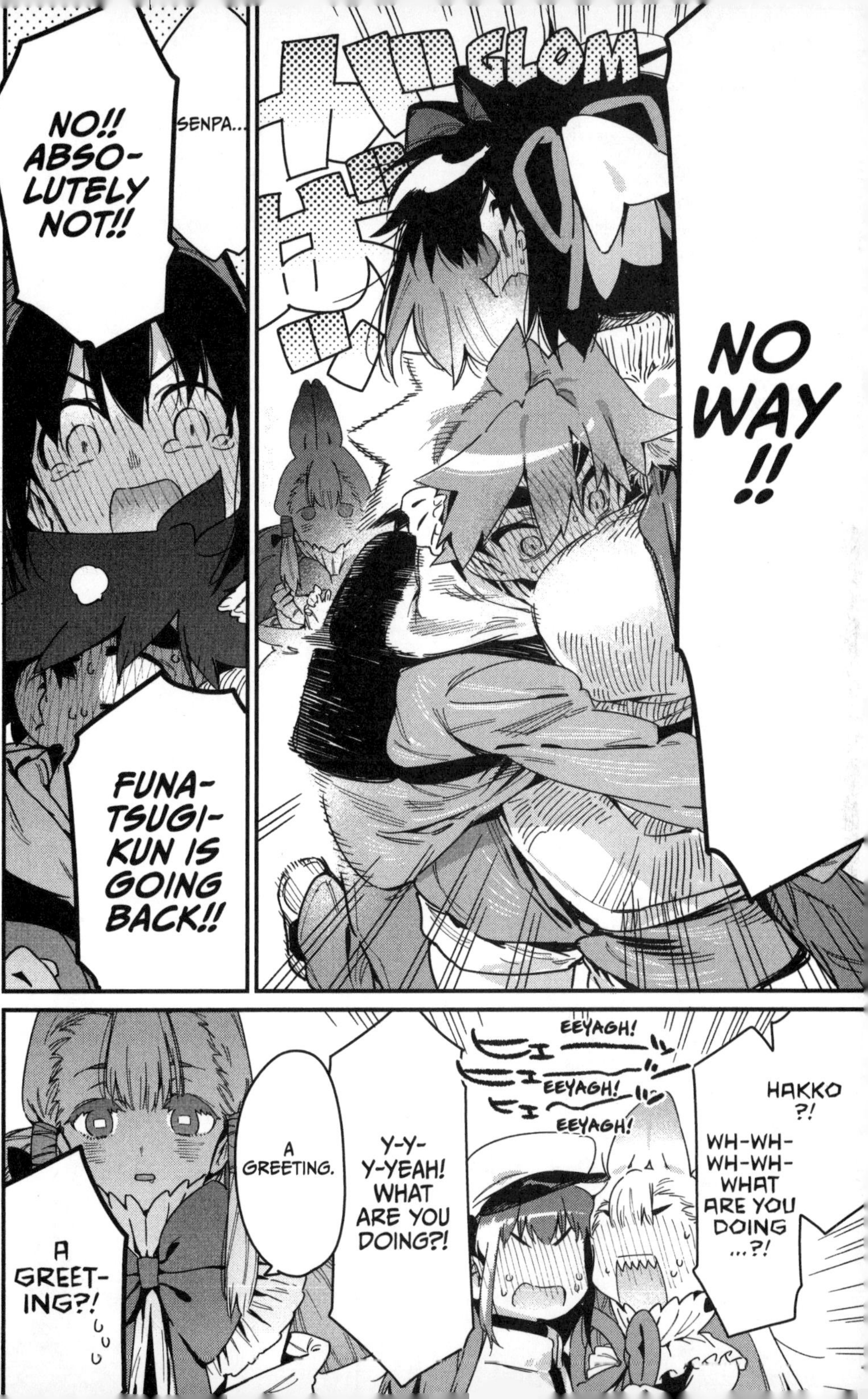
GLOM
NO WAY!!
SENPA...
NO!! ABSO-LUTELY NOT!!
FUNA-TSUGI-KUN IS GOING BACK!!
EEYAGH!
EEYAGH!
EEYAGH!
HAKKO?!
WH-WH-WH-WH-WHAT ARE YOU DOING...?!
Y-Y-Y-YEAH! WHAT ARE YOU DOING?!
A GREETING.
A GREET-ING?!

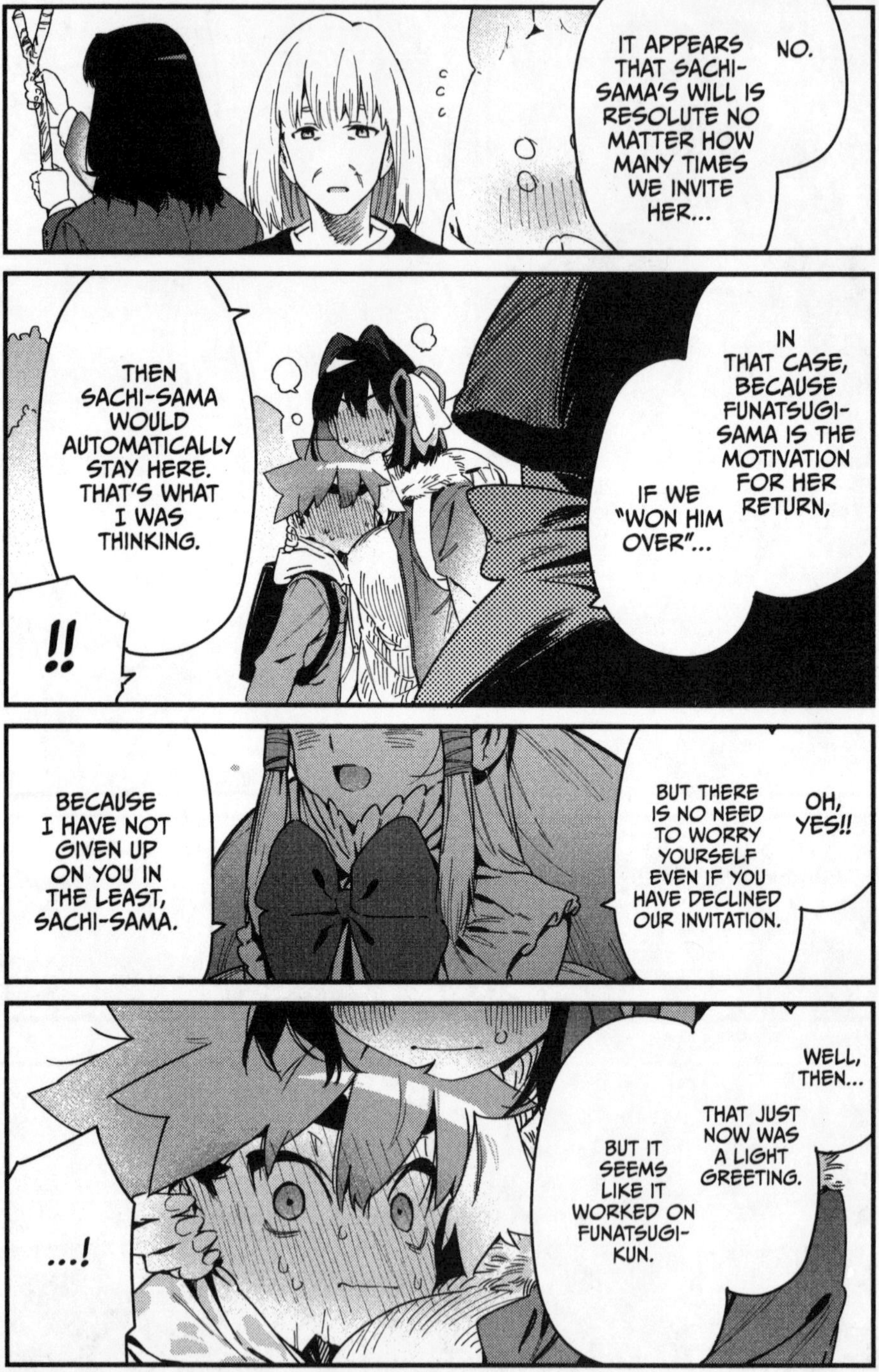
NO.
IT APPEARS THAT SACHI-SAMA'S WILL IS RESOLUTE NO MATTER HOW MANY TIMES WE INVITE HER...
IN THAT CASE, BECAUSE FUNATSUGI-SAMA IS THE MOTIVATION FOR HER RETURN,
IF WE "WON HIM OVER"...
THEN SACHI-SAMA WOULD AUTOMATICALLY STAY HERE. THAT'S WHAT I WAS THINKING.
!!
OH, YES!!
BUT THERE IS NO NEED TO WORRY YOURSELF EVEN IF YOU HAVE DECLINED OUR INVITATION.
BECAUSE I HAVE NOT GIVEN UP ON YOU IN THE LEAST, SACHI-SAMA.
WELL, THEN...
THAT JUST NOW WAS A LIGHT GREETING.
BUT IT SEEMS LIKE IT WORKED ON FUNATSUGI-KUN.
...!

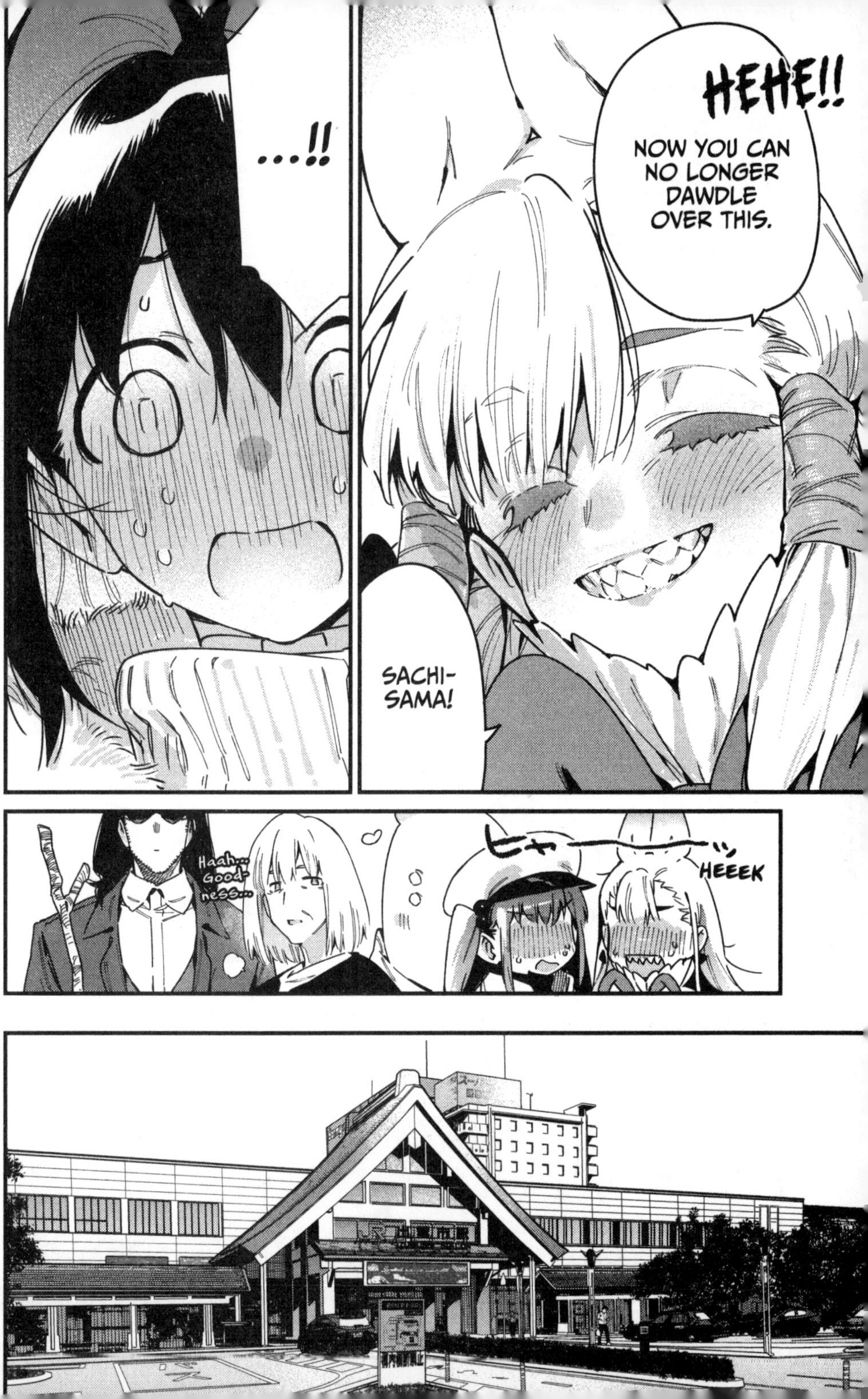
HEHE!!
NOW YOU CAN NO LONGER DAWDLE OVER THIS.
SACHI-SAMA!
...!!
ヒャーーーッ
HEEEK
Haah... Good-ness...

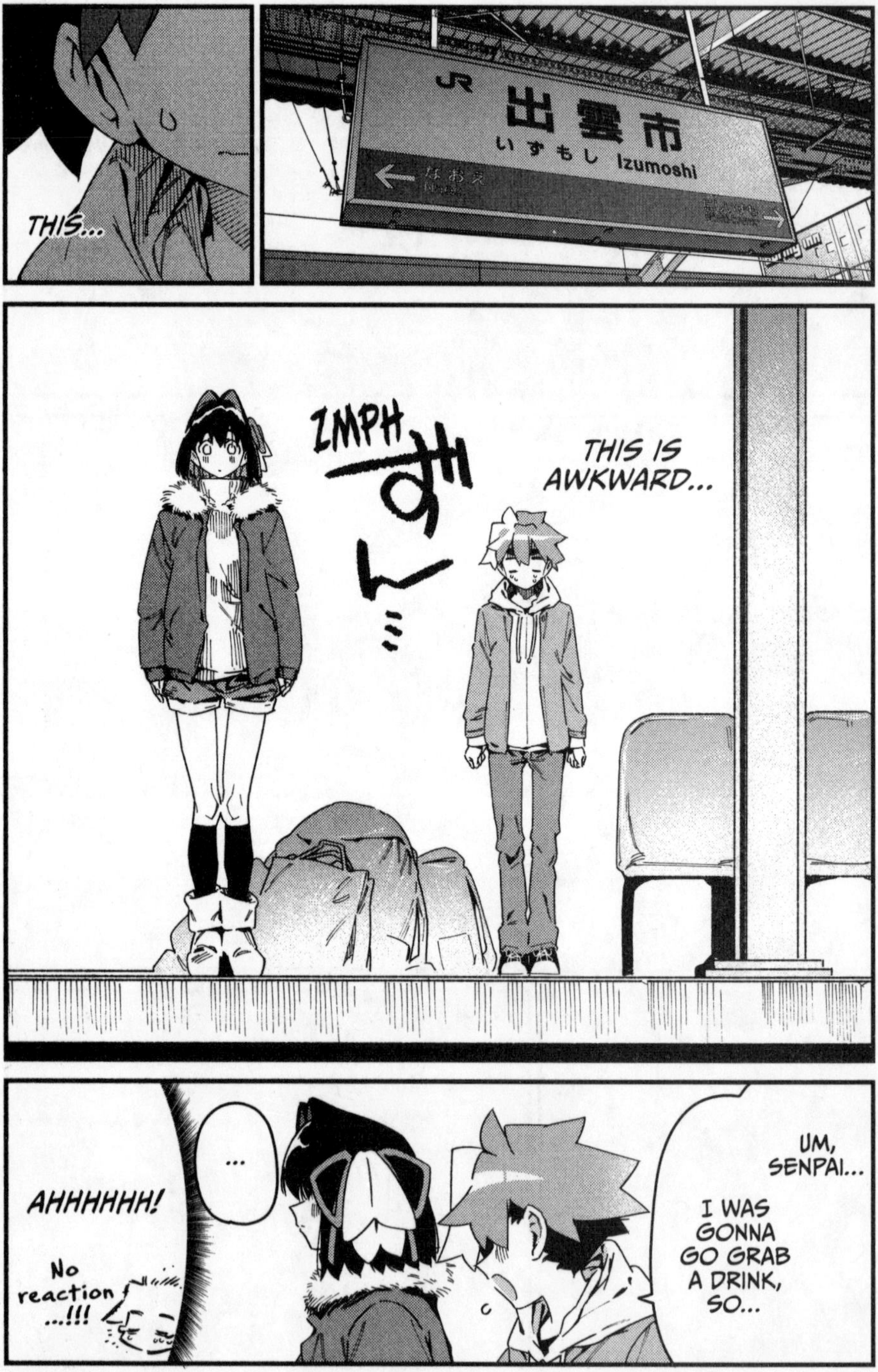
JR
出雲市
いずもし Izumoshi
なおえ
THIS...
THIS IS AWKWARD...
ZMPH
ずん
UM, SENPAI...
I WAS GONNA GO GRAB A DRINK, SO...
...
AHHHHHH!
No reaction ...!!!

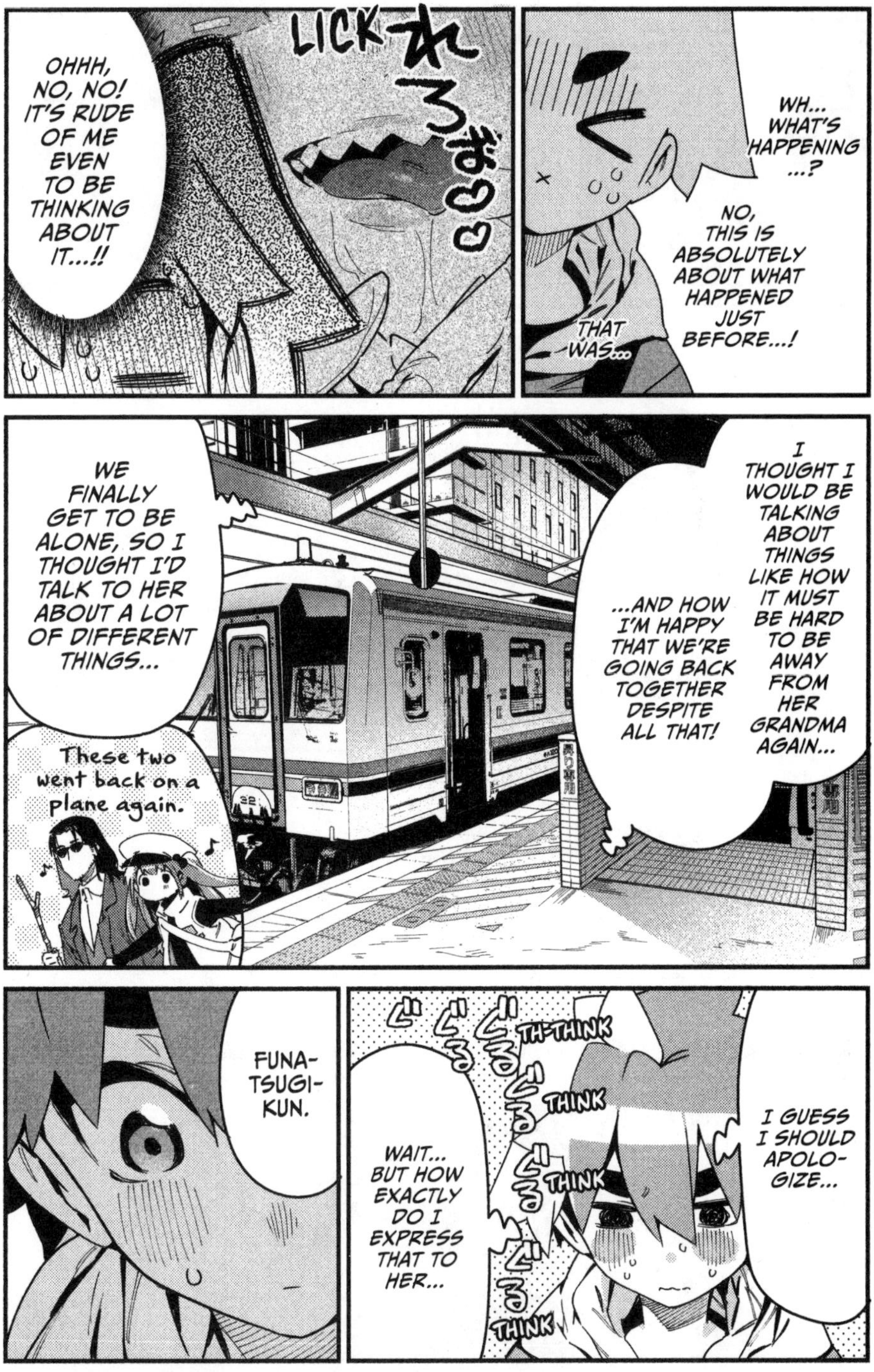
WH... WHAT'S HAPPENING ...?
NO, THIS IS ABSOLUTELY ABOUT WHAT HAPPENED JUST BEFORE...!
THAT WAS...
LICK
れろぉ
OHHH, NO, NO! IT'S RUDE OF ME EVEN TO BE THINKING ABOUT IT...!!
I THOUGHT I WOULD BE TALKING ABOUT THINGS LIKE HOW IT MUST BE HARD TO BE AWAY FROM HER GRANDMA AGAIN...
...AND HOW I'M HAPPY THAT WE'RE GOING BACK TOGETHER DESPITE ALL THAT!
WE FINALLY GET TO BE ALONE, SO I THOUGHT I'D TALK TO HER ABOUT A LOT OF DIFFERENT THINGS...
These two went back on a plane again.
I GUESS I SHOULD APOLO-GIZE...
TH-THINK
THINK
THINK
THINK
WAIT... BUT HOW EXACTLY DO I EXPRESS THAT TO HER...
FUNA-TSUGI-KUN.

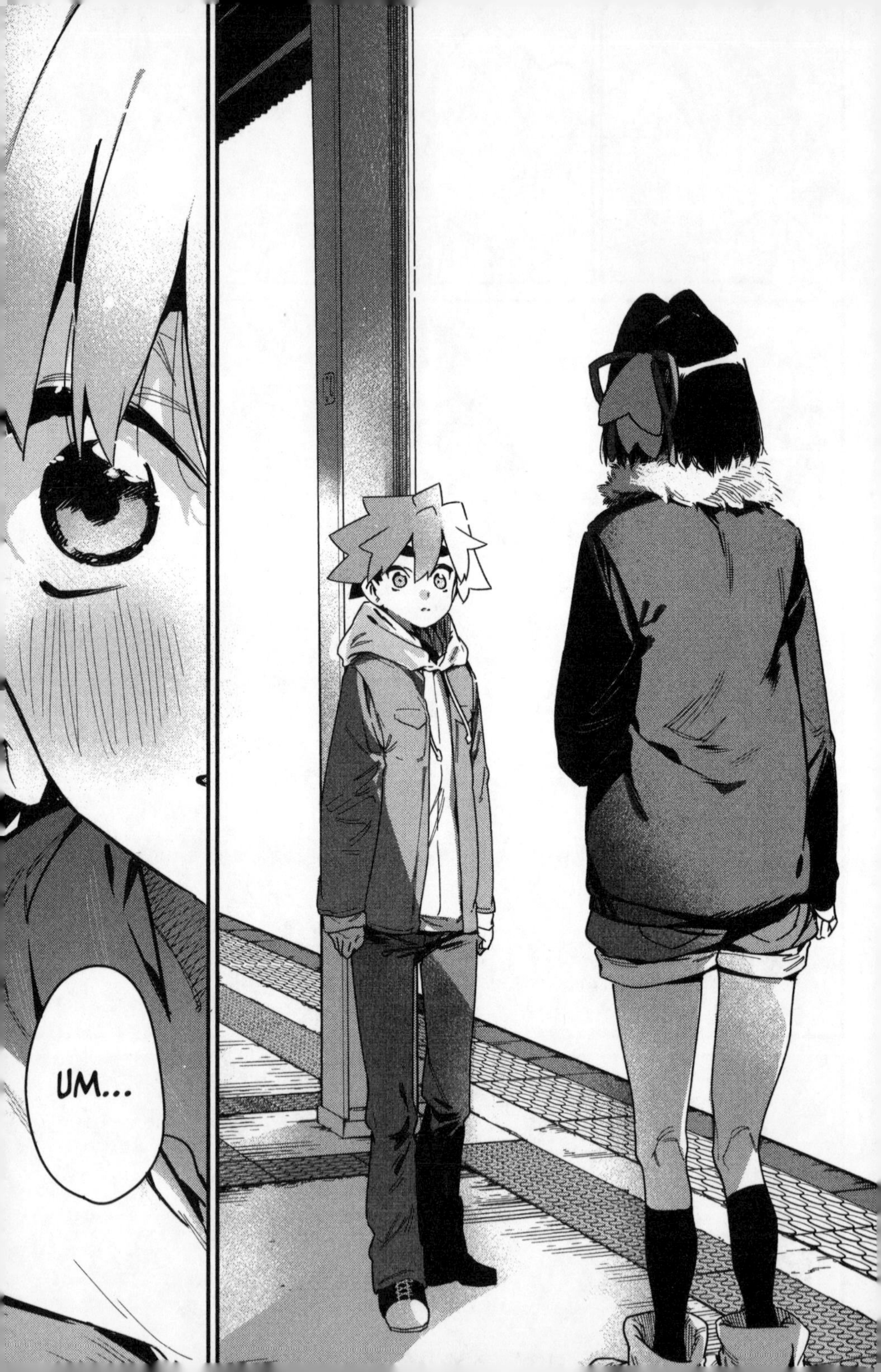
UM...

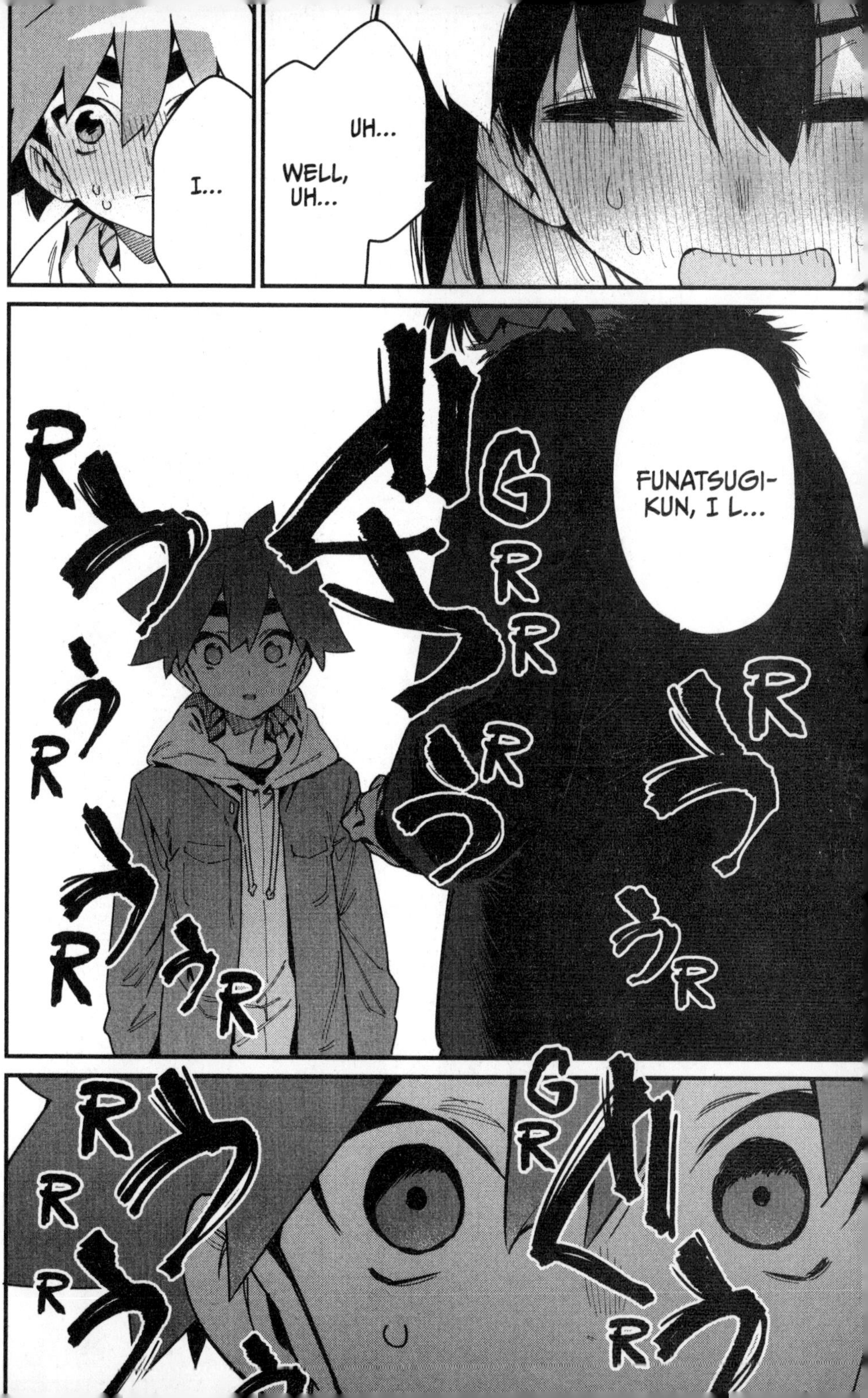
UH...
WELL, UH...
I...
FUNATSUGI-KUN, I L...

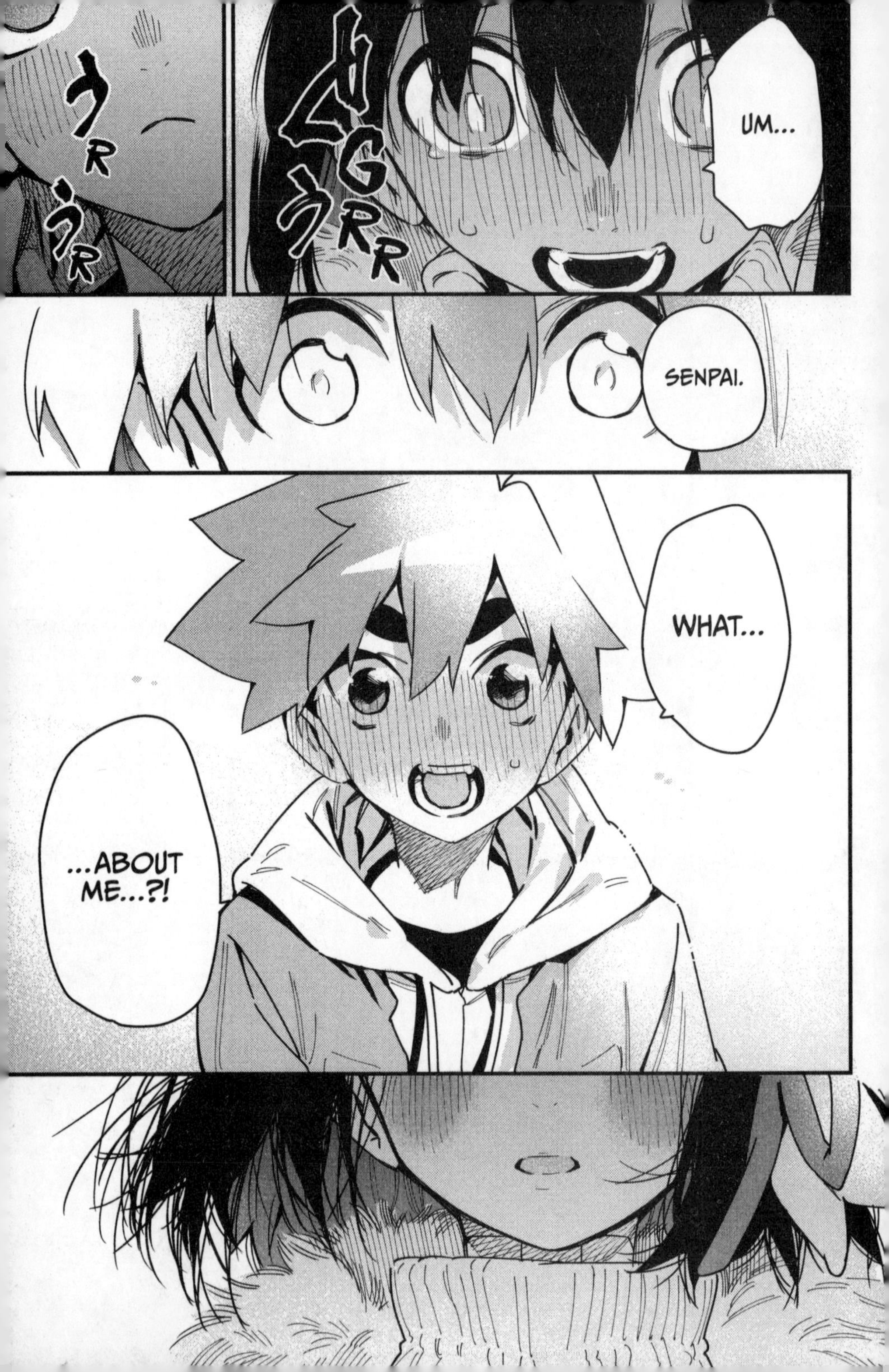

UM...
G
うRR
うR
うR
SENPAI.
WHAT...
...ABOUT ME...?!

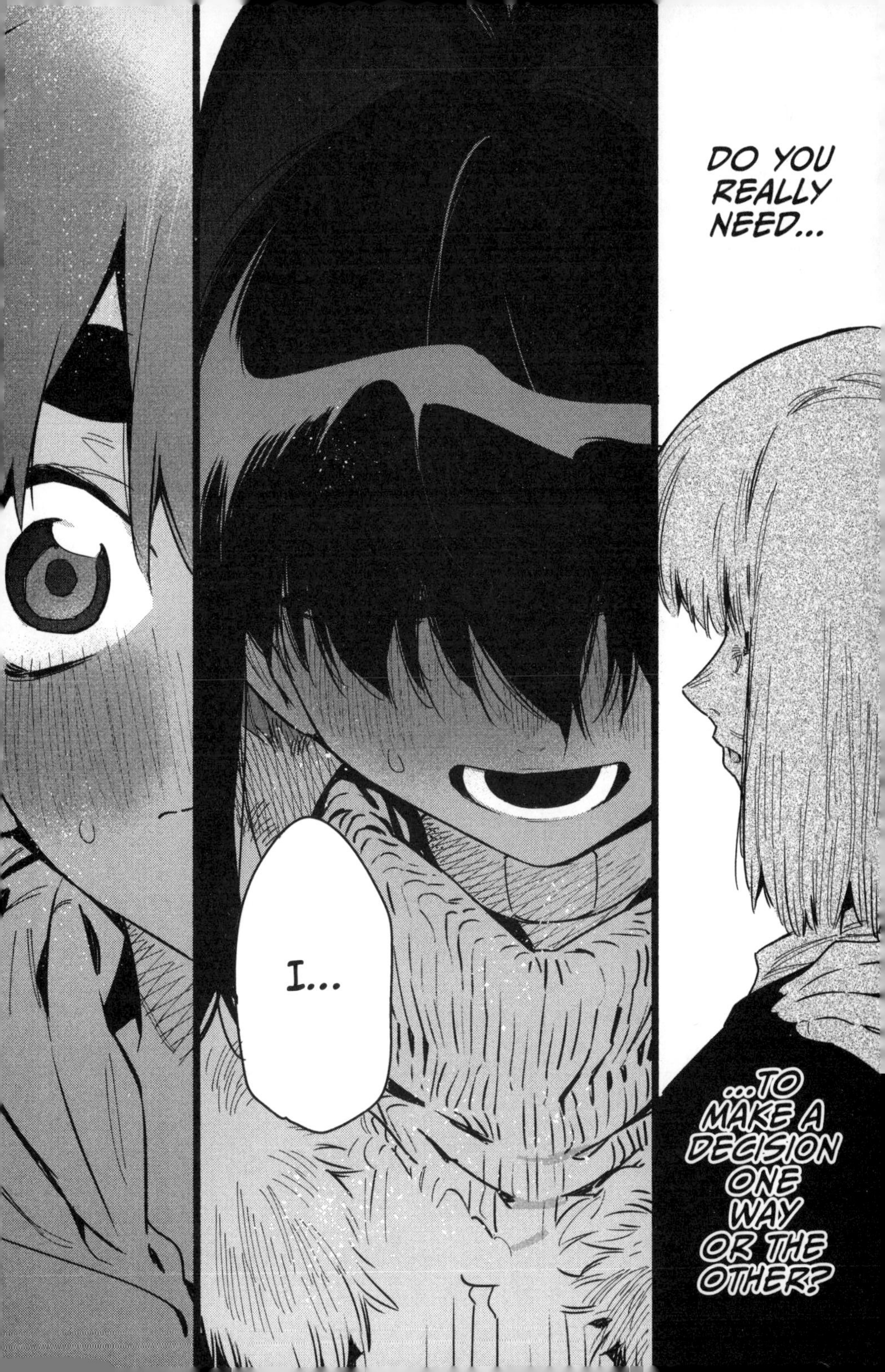
DO YOU REALLY NEED...
...TO MAKE A DECISION ONE WAY OR THE OTHER?
I...

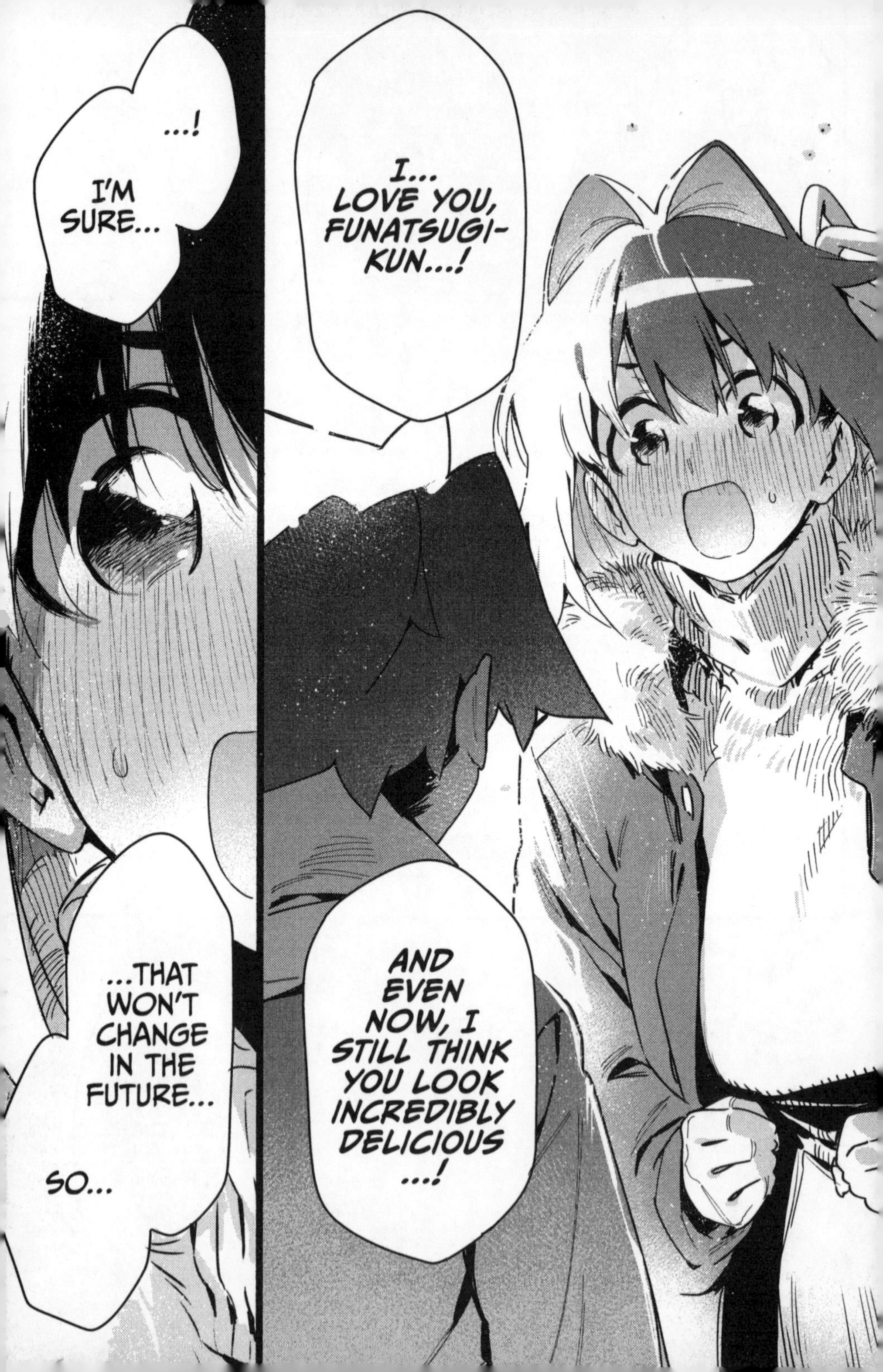
I... LOVE YOU, FUNATSUGI-KUN...!
AND EVEN NOW, I STILL THINK YOU LOOK INCREDIBLY DELICIOUS...!
...! I'M SURE...
...THAT WON'T CHANGE IN THE FUTURE... SO...

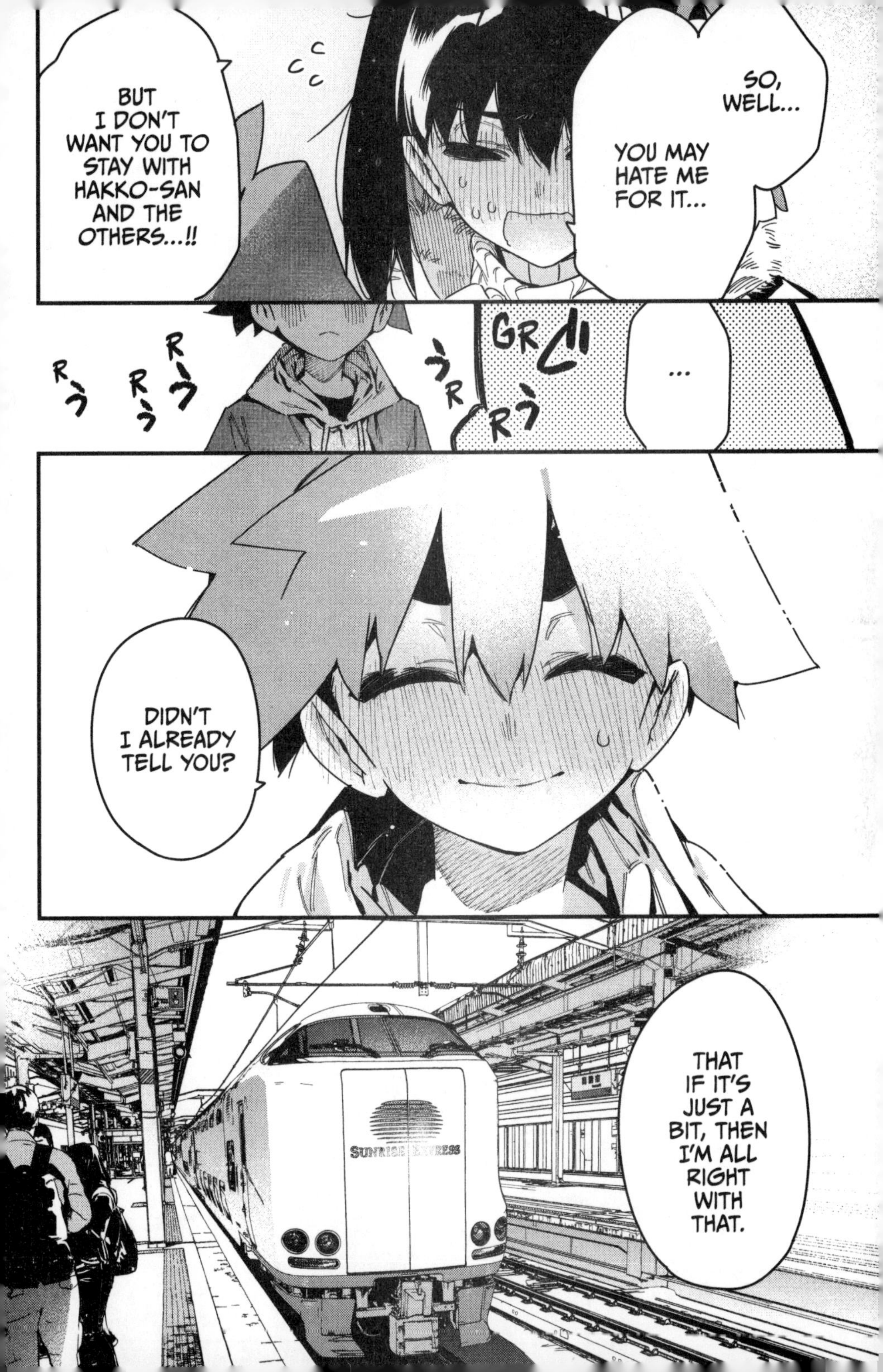
SO, WELL...
YOU MAY HATE ME FOR IT...
BUT I DON'T WANT YOU TO STAY WITH HAKKO-SAN AND THE OTHERS...!!
...
GR
R
R
R
R
R
R
DIDN'T I ALREADY TELL YOU?
THAT IF IT'S JUST A BIT, THEN I'M ALL RIGHT WITH THAT.
SUNRISE

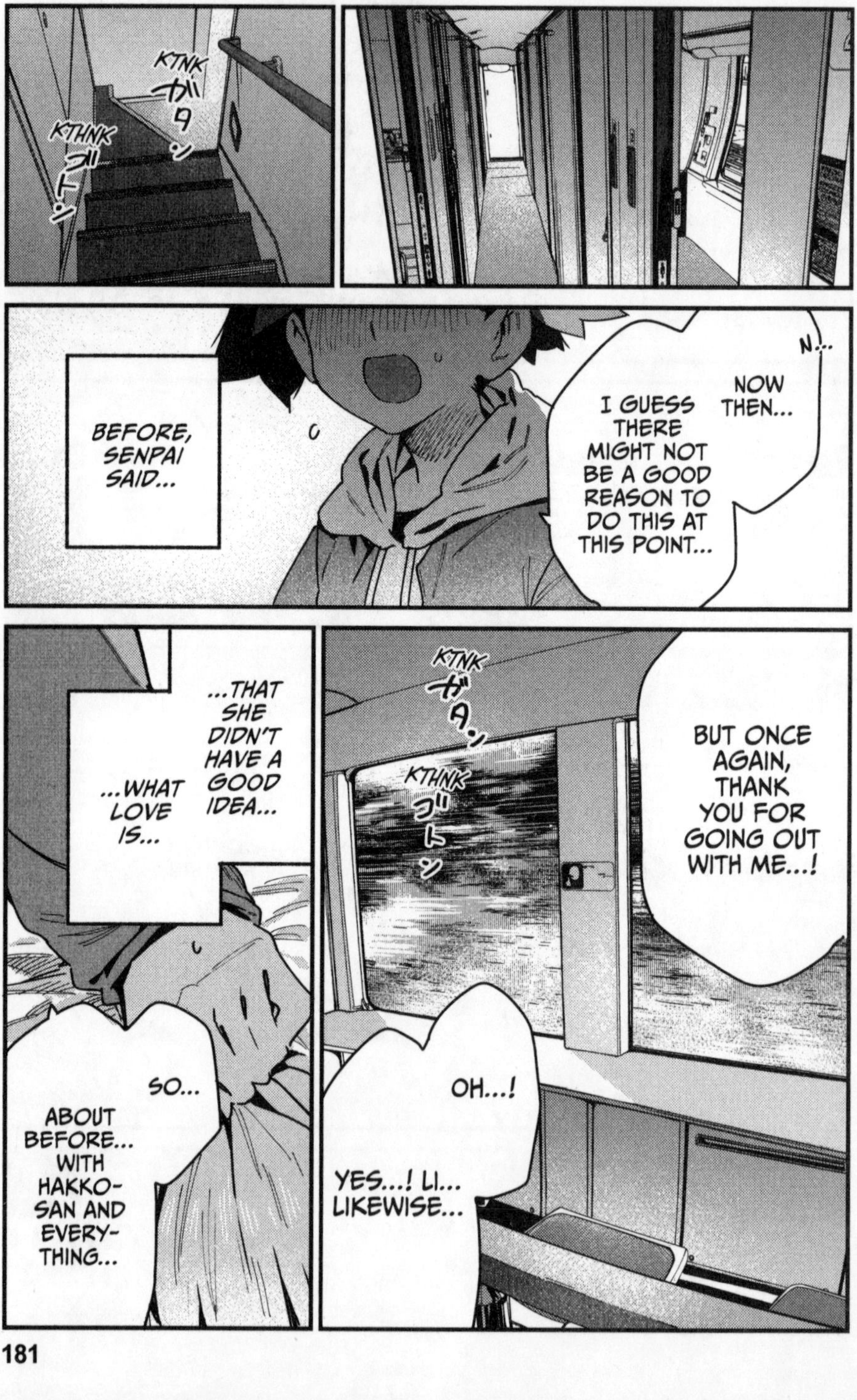
KTNK ガタン
KTHNK ゴトン
N... NOW THEN...
I GUESS THERE MIGHT NOT BE A GOOD REASON TO DO THIS AT THIS POINT...
BEFORE, SENPAI SAID...
KTNK ガタン
KTHNK ゴトン
BUT ONCE AGAIN, THANK YOU FOR GOING OUT WITH ME...!
OH...!
YES...! LI... LIKEWISE...
...THAT SHE DIDN'T HAVE A GOOD IDEA...
...WHAT LOVE IS...
SO...
ABOUT BEFORE... WITH HAKKO-SAN AND EVERY-THING...

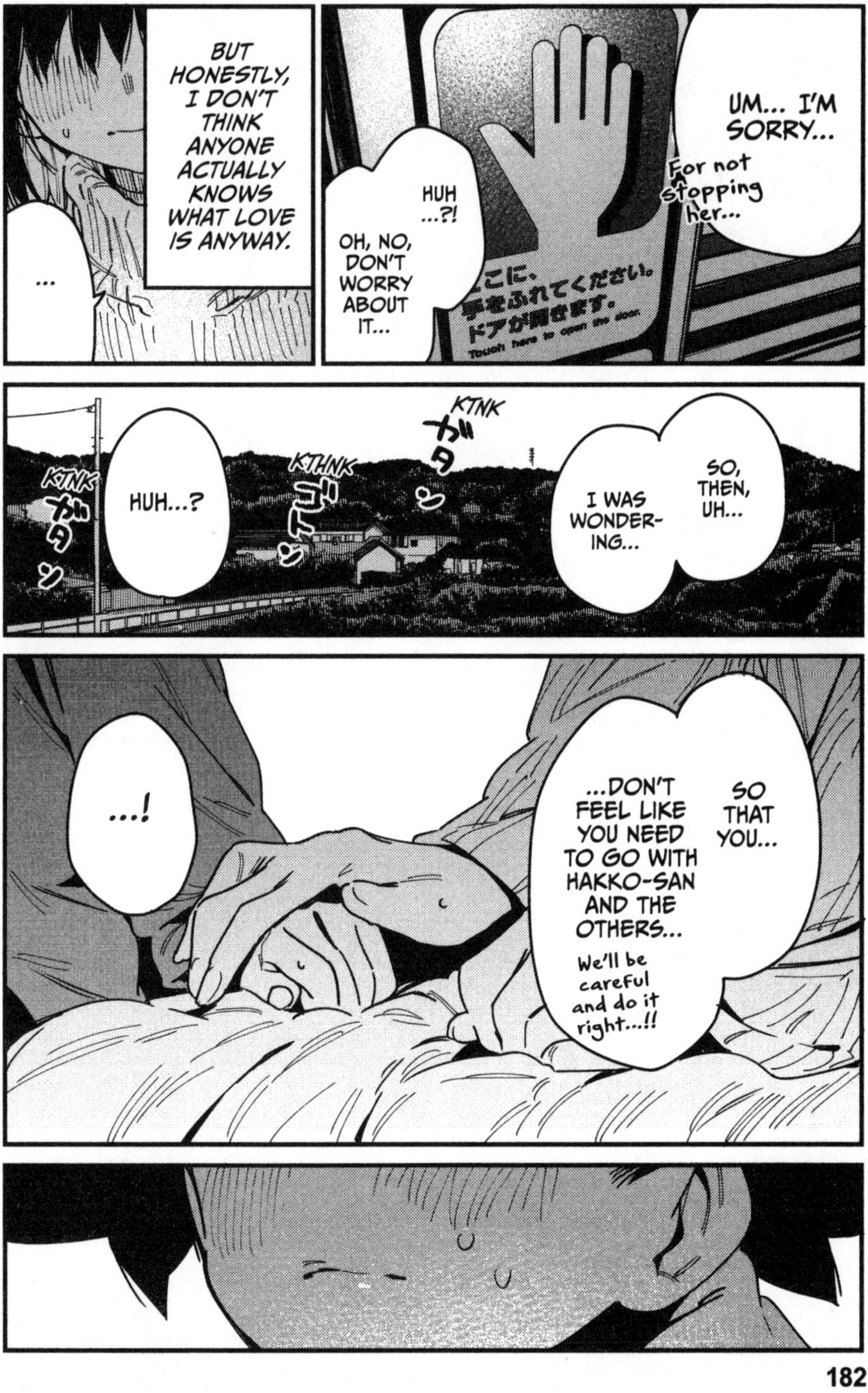
UM... I'M SORRY...
For not stopping her...
こに、手をふれてください。ドアが開きます。
Touch here to open the door
HUH ...?!
OH, NO, DON'T WORRY ABOUT IT...
BUT HONESTLY, I DON'T THINK ANYONE ACTUALLY KNOWS WHAT LOVE IS ANYWAY.
...
SO, THEN, UH...
I WAS WONDERING...
KTNK
ガタン
KTHNK
ゴトン
HUH...?
KTNK
ガタン
SO THAT YOU...
...DON'T FEEL LIKE YOU NEED TO GO WITH HAKKO-SAN AND THE OTHERS...
We'll be careful and do it right...!!
...!

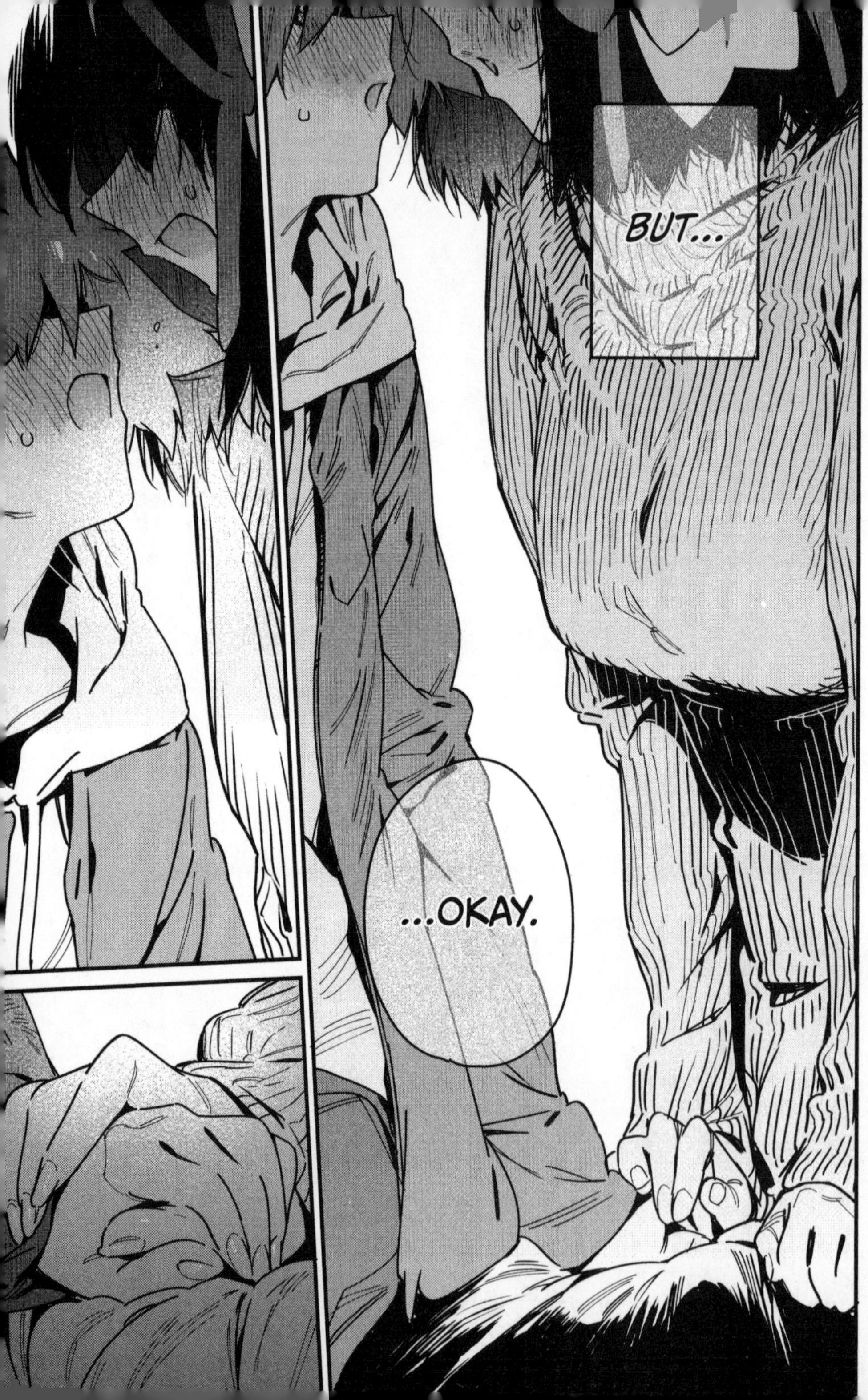
BUT...
...OKAY.

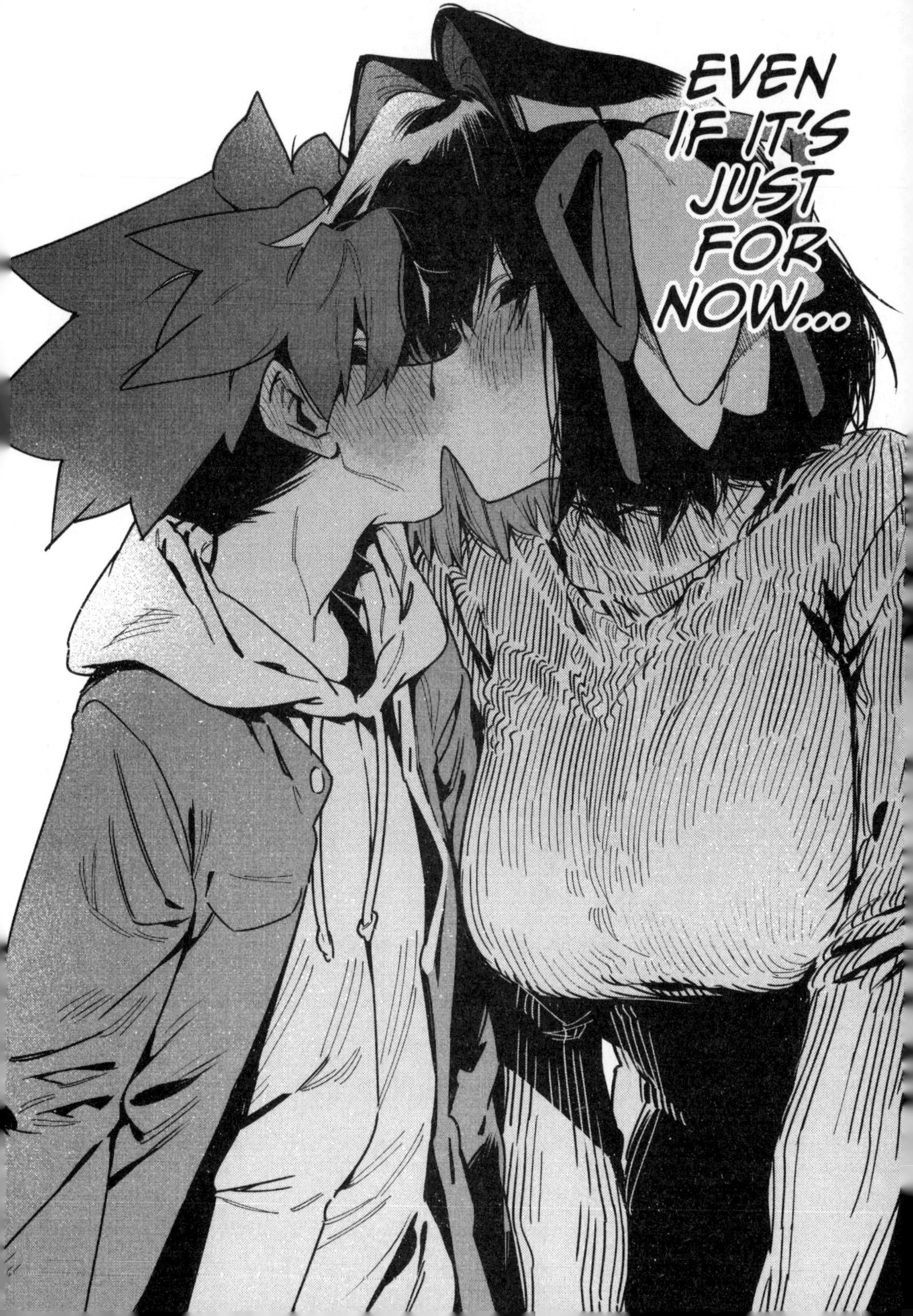
EVEN IF IT'S JUST FOR NOW...

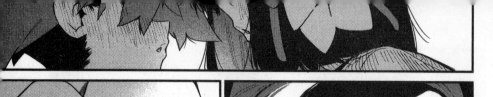

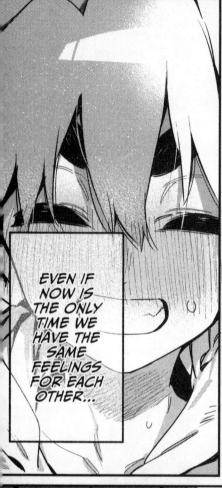

EVEN IF NOW IS THE ONLY TIME WE HAVE THE SAME FEELINGS FOR EACH OTHER...

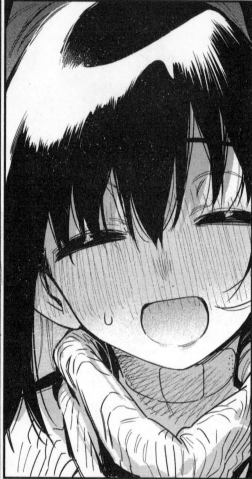

IF THAT'S THE CASE, THEN...

THAT'S GOOD ENOUGH FOR ME.

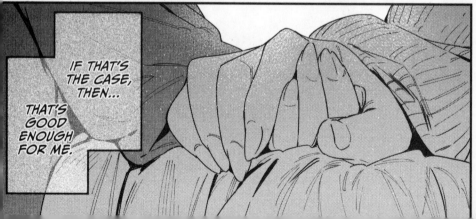

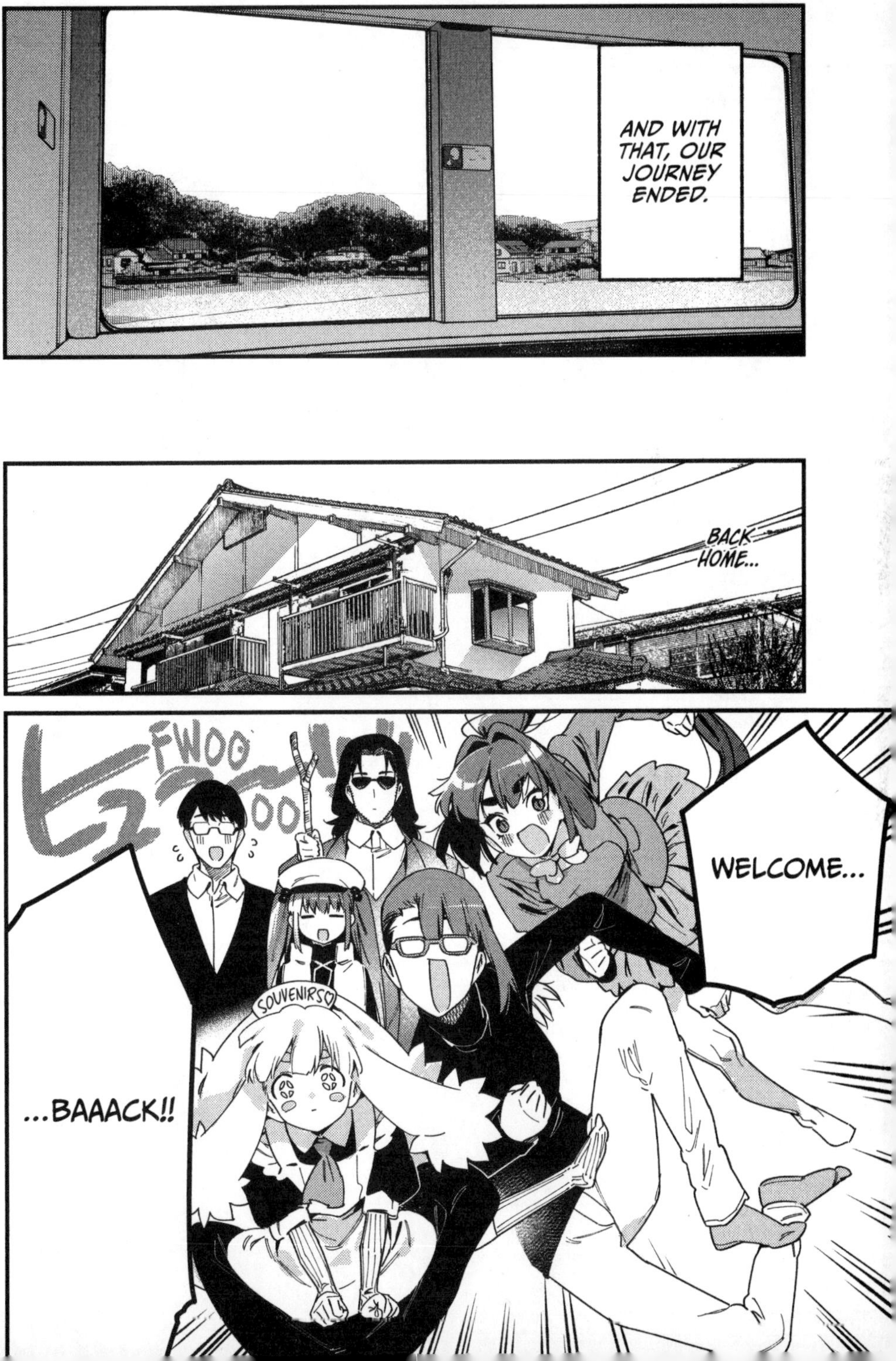
AND WITH THAT, OUR JOURNEY ENDED.
BACK HOME...
WELCOME...
FWOO
OO
SOUVENIRS♡
...BAAACK!!

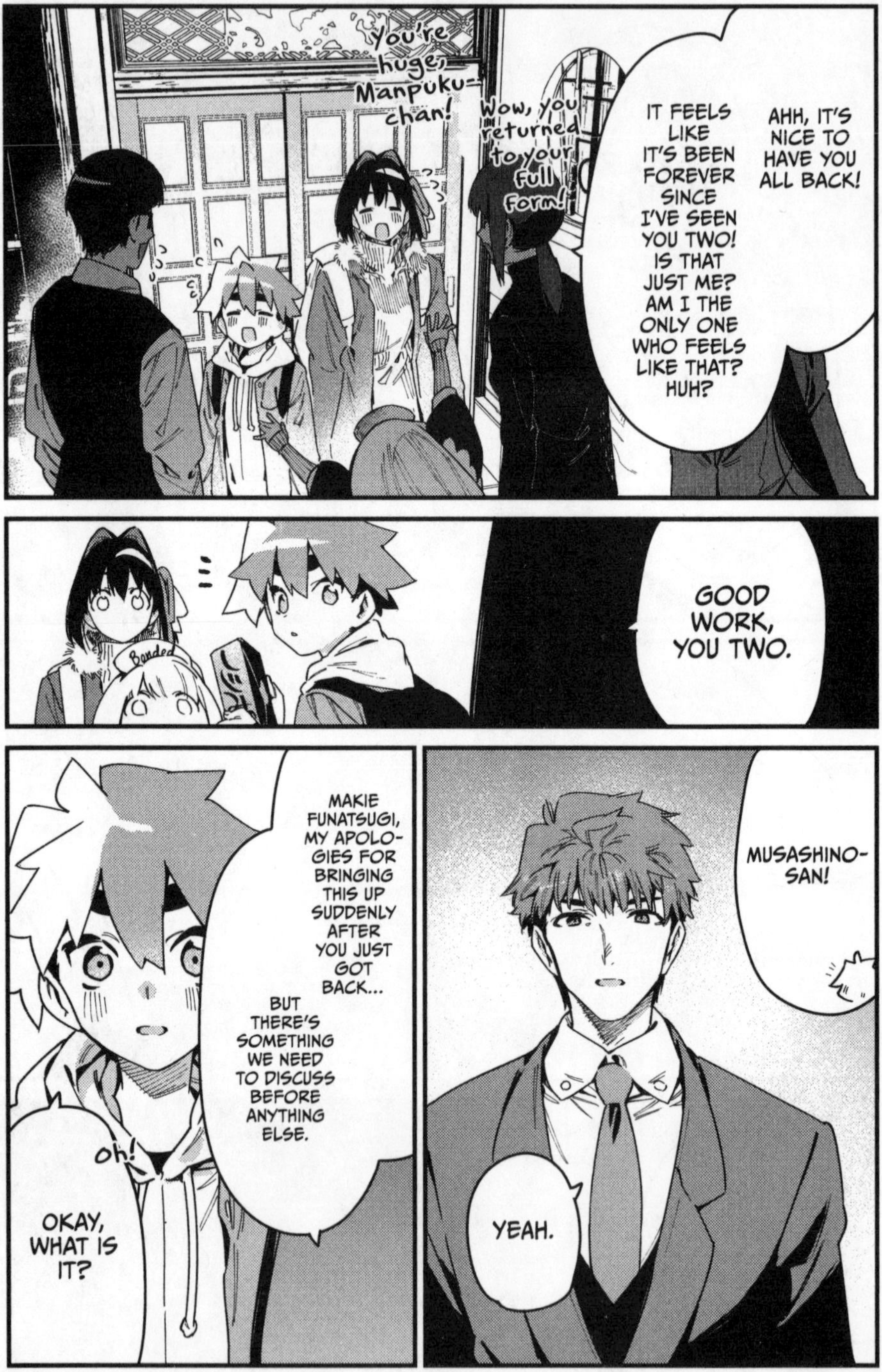
AHH, IT'S NICE TO HAVE YOU ALL BACK!
IT FEELS LIKE IT'S BEEN FOREVER SINCE I'VE SEEN YOU TWO! IS THAT JUST ME? AM I THE ONLY ONE WHO FEELS LIKE THAT? HUH?
Wow, you returned to your full form!
You're huge, Manpuku-chan!
GOOD WORK, YOU TWO.
Bonded
MUSASHINO-SAN!
YEAH.
MAKIE FUNATSUGI, MY APOLOGIES FOR BRINGING THIS UP SUDDENLY AFTER YOU JUST GOT BACK...
BUT THERE'S SOMETHING WE NEED TO DISCUSS BEFORE ANYTHING ELSE.
oh!
OKAY, WHAT IS IT?

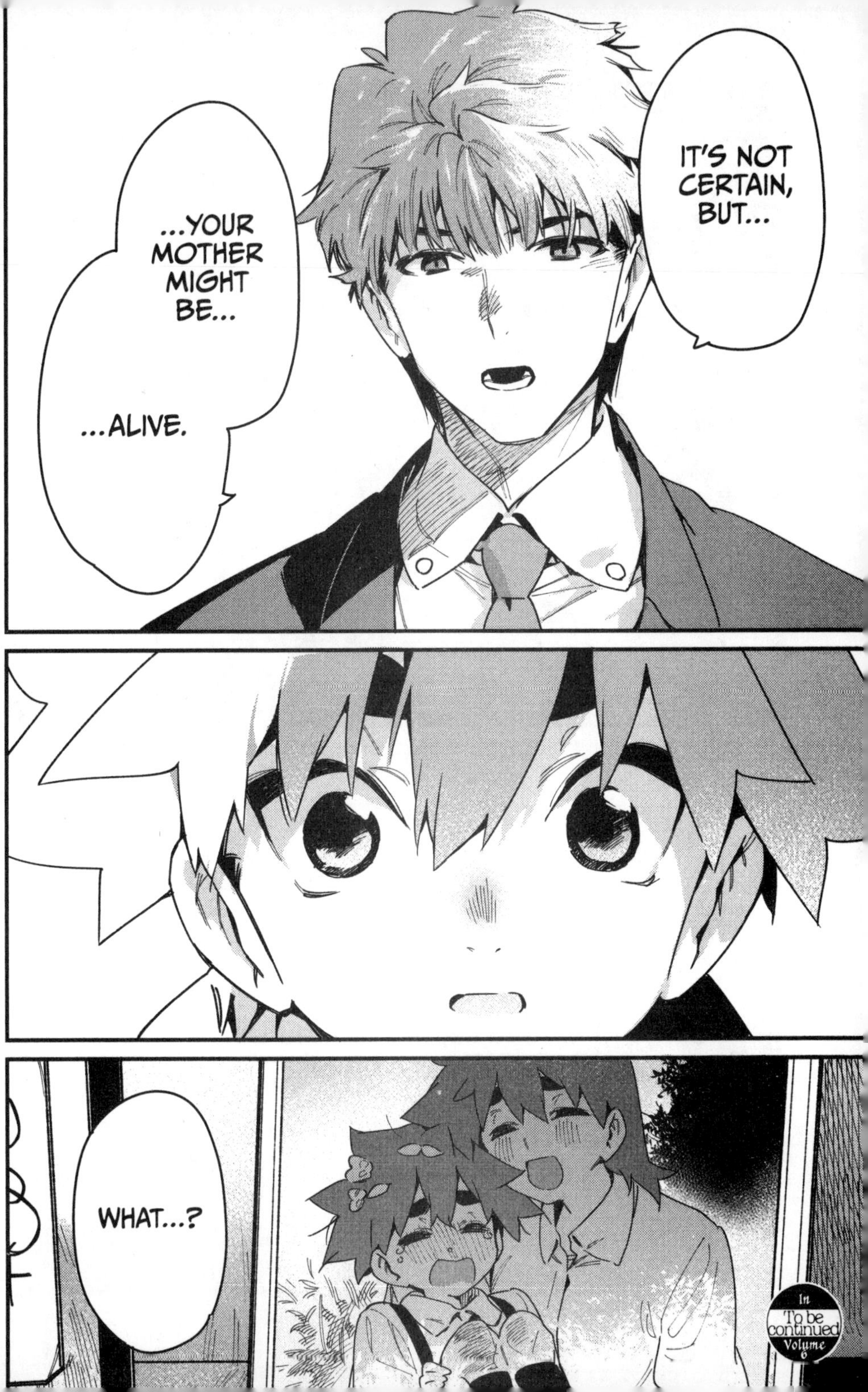
IT'S NOT CERTAIN, BUT...
...YOUR MOTHER MIGHT BE...
...ALIVE.
WHAT...?
In To be continued Volume 6

Sachi's MONSTROUS Appetite

Continued in Volume 6

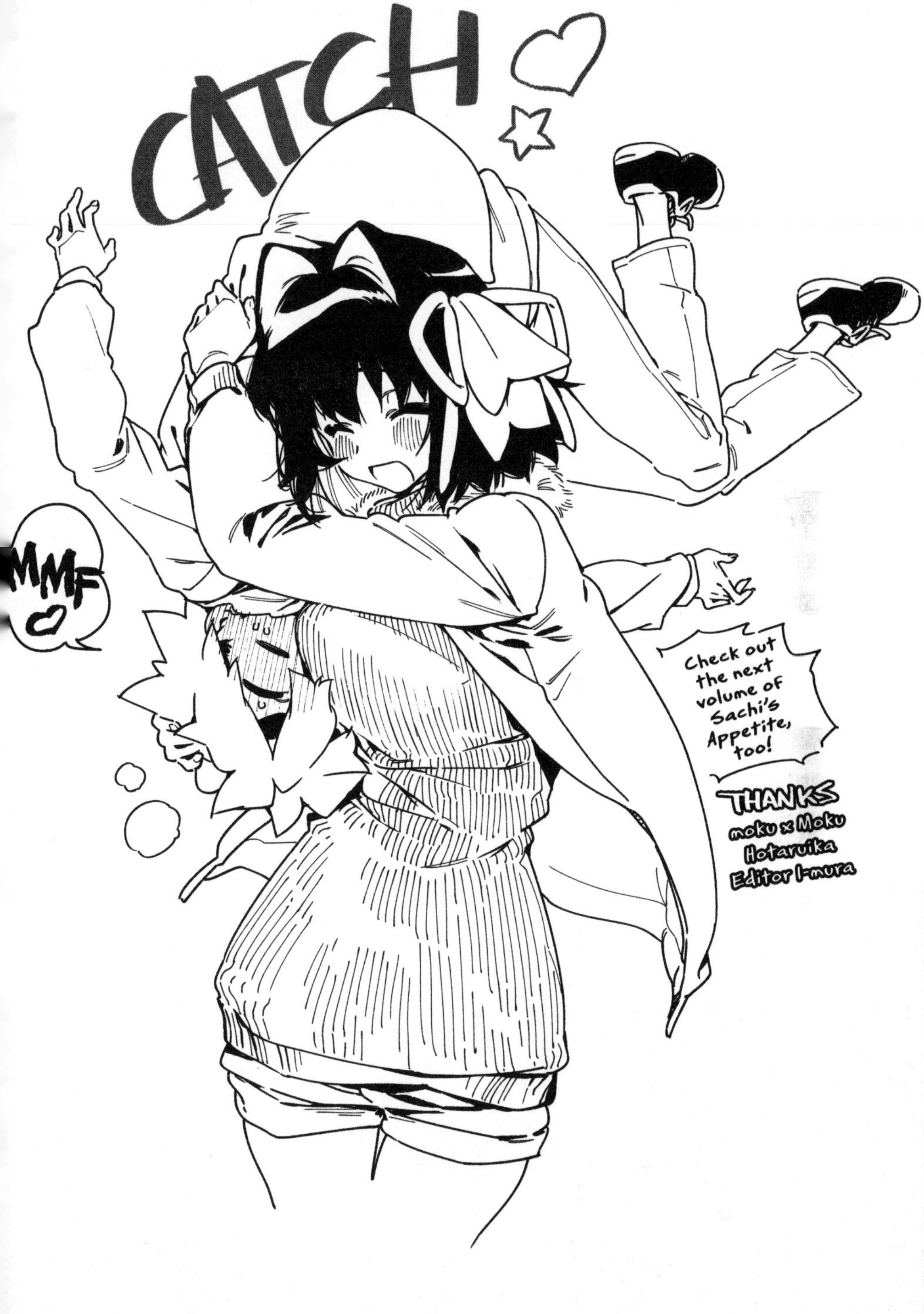
CATCH
MMF
Check out the next volume of Sachi's Appetite, too!
THANKS
moku x Moku
Hotaruika
Editor I-mura

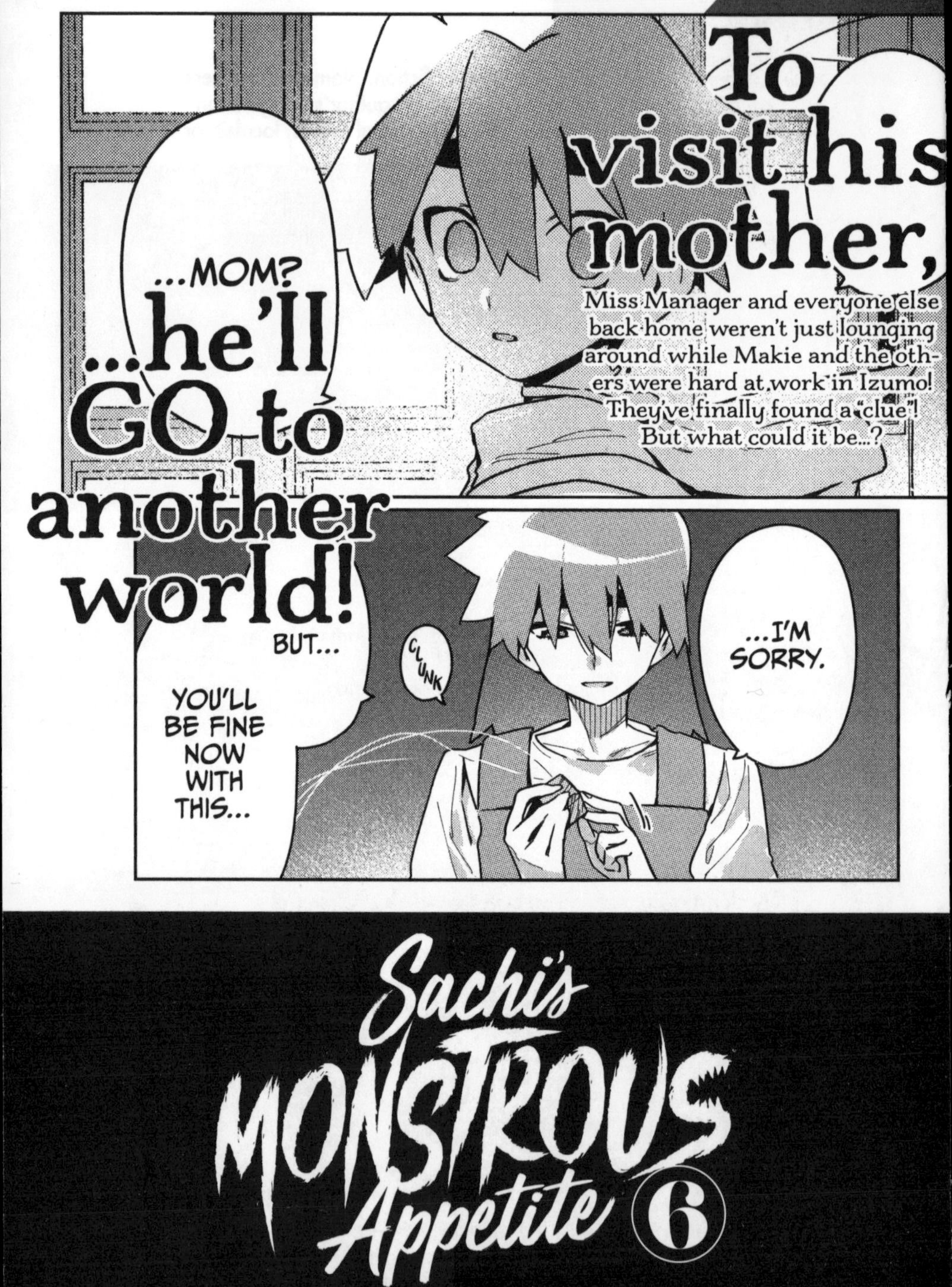
To visit his mother, ...he'll GO to another world!
Miss Manager and everyone else back home weren't just lounging around while Makie and the others were hard at work in Izumo! They've finally found a "clue"! But what could it be...?
...MOM?
...I'M SORRY.
CLUNK
BUT...
YOU'LL BE FINE NOW WITH THIS...

Sachi's MONSTROUS Appetite 6

A Kodansha Comics Trade Paperback Original
Sachi's Monstrous Appetite 5 copyright © 2020 Chomoran
English translation copyright © 2021 Chomoran

Published in the United States by Kodansha Comics, an imprint of
Kodansha USA Publishing, LLC, New York.

Publication rights for this English edition arranged through
Kodansha Ltd., Tokyo.

First published in Japan in 2020 by Kodansha Ltd., Tokyo.

ISBN 978-1-64651-229-4

Original cover design by imagejack danyumi

Printed in the United States of America.

www.kodansha.us

1st Printing
Translation: Ajani Oloye
Lettering: Brandon Bovia
Editing: David Yoo
Kodansha Comics edition cover design by Adam Del Re

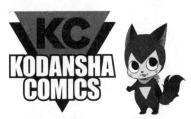

Publisher: Kiichiro Sugawara

Director of publishing services: Ben Applegate
Associate director of operations: Stephen Pakula
Publishing services managing editors: Madison Salters, Alanna Ruse
Production managers: Emi Lotto, Angela Zurlo
Logo and character art ©Kodansha USA Publishing, LLC